# The Complete CAHSEE
# Mathematics Study Guide

*Simplified Solutions*

**For Math Inc.**

# Contact Information

| | |
|---|---|
| **On the Web at** | **ssformath.com** |
| **Phone** | **(916) 204 - 4227** |
| **Email** | **info@ssformath.com** |
| **Workbook Reorder at** | **(916) 204 - 4227** |
| | **or www.lulu.com/jimgcc** |

ISBN 978-0-578-01365-7

## Simplified Solutions
### For Math Inc.

# The Complete
# CAHSEE Mathematics
# Study Guide

To Our Customers,

- Simplified Solutions' Complete CAHSEE Mathematics Study Guide is designed to assist people like you with your **students' success**.

- This study guide is designed to **provide students with the necessary knowledge to pass the CAHSEE exam**.

- This study guide is **standards-based** and **is based exclusively on the California Department of Education's tested mathematics strands**.

- *Simplified Solutions for Math, Inc.* hopes you enjoy using our **"Teacher-made, teacher-tested"** study guide.

# ABOUT THE AUTHORS

**Teresa Cummings** earned her bachelor's degree and Master's degree at California State University, Chico and received her PhD in Education: Curriculum and Instruction, from the University of Illinois, Chicago. Ms. Cummings has been in education for 15 years and has taught at the secondary, community college and university levels.

———————————//———————————

**Pat Haddeman** earned his bachelor's degree at California State University, Sacramento. He earned his teaching credential and master's degree at National University. Throughout his 13 years of teaching, Mr. Haddeman has instructed mathematics at the secondary and college levels.

———————————//———————————

**Jim Gallagher** earned his bachelor's degree and teaching credential at California State University, Sacramento. Mr. Gallagher has been teaching mathematics and computer science for 28 years.

———————————//———————————

**Tim Carter** earned his bachelor's degree at the University of San Diego and he earned his teaching credential at Chapman University. Mr. Carter has been teaching mathematics for 11 years and has been Math Department Chair for 6 years.

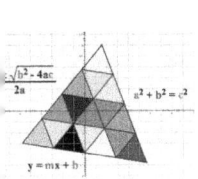

# CAHSEE Math Study Guide
## Table of Contents

*Simplified Solutions For Math Inc.*

### Number Sense

**Unit 1**
| BM 1 | Convert between scientific and standard notation | 1 |
| BM 2 | Use arithmetic operations on integers | 4 |
| BM 3 | Convert between fractions, decimals and percents | 7 |
| BM 4 | Calculate percents of increase and decrease | 10 |
| BM 5 | Calculate discounts, profits, commissions and interest | 13 |
| | *Unit 1 Exam* | **16** |

**Unit 2**
| BM 6 | Multiply and divide terms with negative exponents | 17 |
| BM 7 | Use arithmetic operations on fractions | 20 |
| BM 8 | Use the rules of exponents | 23 |
| BM 9 | Estimate square roots | 26 |
| BM 10 | Find the absolute value of a number | 29 |
| | *Unit 2 Exam* | **32** |

### Statistics, Data Analysis, and Probability

**Unit 3**
| BM 11 | Find the mean, median or mode for a set of data | 33 |
| BM 12 | Judge the validity of claims given information graphically | 36 |
| BM 13 | Compute theoretical probability | 41 |
| BM 14 | Represent probabilities as ratios | 45 |
| BM 15 | Understand independent and dependent events | 49 |
| BM 16 | Know various displays for data | 54 |
| BM 17 | Represent numerical values on a scatter plot | 59 |
| | *Unit 3 Exam* | **64** |

### Measurement and Geometry

**Unit 4**
| BM 18 | Compare measurement systems | 66 |
| BM 19 | Use scale drawings | 69 |
| BM 20 | Solve problems involving rates | 72 |
| BM 21 | Use formulas | 75 |
| BM 22 | Estimate the area of irregular shapes | 79 |
| | *Unit 4 Exam* | **83** |

**Unit 5**
| BM 23 | Compute perimeter, surface area and volume | 86 |
| BM 24 | Relate changes in measurement with a change of scale | 89 |
| BM 25 | Translate and reflect on the coordinate plane | 92 |
| BM 26 | Use the Pythagorean theorem | 97 |
| BM 27 | Use congruent figures | 100 |
| | *Unit 5 Exam* | **103** |

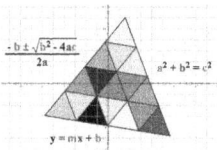

# CAHSEE Math Study Guide
## Table of Contents

### *Algebra and Functions*

| | | | | |
|---|---|---|---|---|
| **Unit 6** | **BM 28** | | Write linear expressions | 107 |
| | **BM 29** | | Evaluate expressions using the order of operations | 110 |
| | **BM 30** | | Represent quantitative relationships graphically | 113 |
| | **BM 31** | | Use the rules of exponents | 119 |
| | **BM 32** | | Extend the process of taking powers and extracting roots | 122 |
| | | | *Unit 6 Exam* | *125* |
| **Unit 7** | **BM 33** | | Graph non-linear functions | 130 |
| | **BM 34** | | Use graphs of linear functions | 134 |
| | **BM 35** | | Read the quantity values from graphs | 138 |
| | **BM 36** | | Solve two-step equations and inequalities | 142 |
| | **BM 37** | | Solve multi-step problems | 145 |
| | | | *Unit 7 Exam* | *148* |

### *Mathematical Reasoning*

| | | | | |
|---|---|---|---|---|
| **Unit 8** | **BM 38** | | Analyze word problems | 153 |
| | **BM 39** | | Formulate conjectures | 156 |
| | **BM 40** | | Estimate to verify the reasonableness of calculations | 160 |
| | **BM 41** | | Estimate unknown quantities graphically | 163 |
| | **BM 42** | | Use inductive and deductive reasoning | 167 |
| | **BM 43** | | Develop generalizations based on mathematical results | 170 |
| | | | *Unit 8 Exam* | *173* |

### *Algebra I*

| | | | | |
|---|---|---|---|---|
| **Unit 9** | **BM 44** | | Understand and use reciprocals, roots, and rules of exponents | 179 |
| | **BM 45** | | Solve equations and inequalities involving the absolute value | 182 |
| | **BM 46** | | Simplify equations and inequalities | 185 |
| | **BM 47** | | Solve multi-step equations and inequalities | 188 |
| | **BM 48** | | Graph a linear equation | 191 |
| | | | *Unit 9 Exam* | *196* |
| **Unit 10** | **BM 49** | | Verify if a point lies on a line and calculate intercepts | 203 |
| | **BM 50** | | Understand parallel and perpendicular lines | 206 |
| | **BM 51** | | Solve a system of linear equations in two variables | 209 |
| | **BM 52** | | Add, subtract, multiply and divide polynomials | 213 |
| | **BM 53** | | Solve rate, work, and mixture problems | 216 |
| | | | *Unit 10 Exams (BM 1-53, versions A, B, and C)* | *220* |
| | | | *Answer Keys* | *244* |

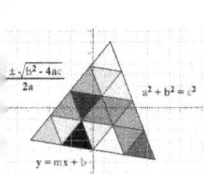

# CAHSEE Bench Mark 1

*Simplified Solutions For Math Inc.*

**Students will successfully convert between scientific and standard notation.**

**CA Standard:** Grade 7, Number Sense 1.1
**CAHSEE Strand:** Number Sense

On the CAHSEE, students will have to convert between the two notations.

**Scientific notation** lists a number as the product of a power of 10 and a number equal to or greater than 1 and less than 10. For example, 1,230,000 would be listed as $1.23 \times 10^6$ or 0.00000987 would be listed as $9.87 \times 10^{-6}$.

**To convert from standard notation to scientific notation**, we need to move the decimal point so that the number is equal to or greater than 1 and less than 10. The number of moves the decimal point makes will determine the value of the exponent . If we move the decimal to the left, the exponent will be positive, and if we move to the right, the exponent will be negative.

---

**EXAMPLE:** Write 5,670,000,000 in scientific notation.

    **a.** $56.7 \times 10^7$    **b.** $5.67 \times 10^8$  **c.** $5.67 \times 10^9$    **d.** $5.67 \times 10^{-9}$

*Choice **a** has a number larger than 10, (56.7), so it is incorrect.*

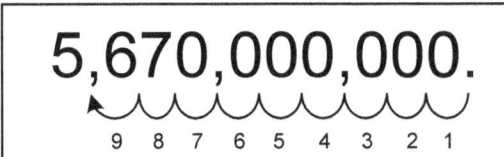

---

5,670,000,000.

9 8 7 6 5 4 3 2 1

The decimal point moved 9 places to the left, so the answer will be the choice with $10^9$.

In our example, choice **c** is correct.

**To convert from scientific notation to standard notation** we need to move the decimal point a number of spaces and in the same direction as the sign of the exponent on the 10. If the exponent is negative, the decimal moves to the left, and if the exponent is positive, it moves to the right.

---

**EXAMPLE:** Write $3.21 \times 10^{-5}$ in standard notation.

    **a.** 0.00000321    **b.** 0.0000321    **c.** 0.00321    **d.** 321,000

*3.21 has a decimal point after the 3 and it needs to be moved 5 places to the left.*

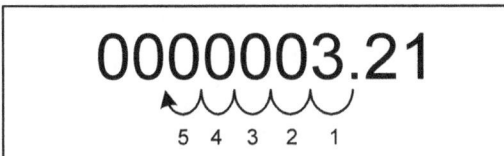

---

0000003.21

5 4 3 2 1

When the decimal point is moved 5 places to the left, the correct answer will be the choice with four zeros between the decimal and the three.

In our example, choice **b** has the decimal in the correct position and is therefore the correct answer.

---

**EXAMPLE:**

The Gross Domestic Product of the United States is $11,750,000,000,000. What is this number in scientific notation?

    **a.** $11.75 \times 10^{12}$    **b.** $1.175 \times 10^{13}$

    **c.** $11.75 \times 10^{13}$    **d.** $1.175 \times 10^{12}$

By definition, scientific notation lists a number as the product of a power of 10 and a number equal to or greater than 1 and less than 10. Choices **a** and **c** have a number larger than 10, (*11.75*), so they are incorrect.

The decimal point moved 13 places to the left, so the answer will be the choice with $10^{13}$.

In this example, choice **b** is correct.

---

# CAHSEE Bench Mark Practice 1

1. The Gross Domestic Product of the United States is $11,750,000,000,000. What is this number in scientific notation?

   a. $11.75 \times 10^{12}$  b. $1.175 \times 10^{13}$

   c. $11.75 \times 10^{13}$  d. $1.175 \times 10^{12}$

2. The largest salt water lake in the world is the Caspian Sea. It has an area of $1.432 \times 10^5$ square miles. What is this number in standard notation?

   a. 143,200  b. 1,430,000

   c. 14,320  d. 14,300,000

3. The diameter of a carbon atom is $2.2 \times 10^{-8}$ cm. What is this number in standard notation?

   a. 0.0000000022  b. 0.00000022

   c. 0.0000022  d. 0.000000022

4. The estimated population of the United States is 298,500,000. What is this number in scientific notation?

   a. $29.85 \times 10^7$  b. $29.85 \times 10^8$

   c. $2.985 \times 10^8$  d. $2.985 \times 10^7$

5. The diameter of a common dust particle is $5.0 \times 10^{-4}$ mm. What is this number in standard notation?

   a. 0.05  b. 0.00005

   c. 0.005  d. 0.0005

6. Jupiter is $4.8388 \times 10^8$ miles from the sun. What is this number in standard notation?

   a. 483,880,000  b. 48,388,000

   c. 4,838,800,000  d. 4,838,800

7. In 2002, the United States had a trade deficit of $418,000,000,000. What is this number in scientific notation?

   a. $41.8 \times 10^{12}$  b. $4.18 \times 10^{11}$

   c. $4.1 \times 10^{11}$  d. $4.18 \times 10^{12}$

8. Venus is $6.724 \times 10^7$ miles from the sun. What is this number in standard notation?

   a. 67,240,000  b. 6,724,000

   c. 672,400,000  d. 6,724,000,000

9. The tallest mountain in the world is Mount Everest in Nepal. It is 29,035 feet tall. What is this number in scientific notation?

   a. $2.9035 \times 10^5$  b. $29.035 \times 10^8$

   c. $2.9035 \times 10^3$  d. $2.9035 \times 10^4$

10. The longest bridge in the world is the 2nd Pontchartrain Causeway in Louisiana. It is 126,054 feet long. What is this number in scientific notation?

    a. $12.6054 \times 10^5$  b. $1.26054 \times 10^6$

    c. $1.26054 \times 10^5$  d. $1.26054 \times 10^4$

2

11. The Gross Domestic Product of Great Britain is $2,016,400,000,000. What is this number in scientific notation?

   **a.** $2.0164 \times 10^{11}$     **b.** $2.0164 \times 10^{12}$

   **c.** $2.0164 \times 10^{10}$     **d.** $2.164 \times 10^{12}$

12. The largest fresh water lake in the world is Lake Superior. It has an area of $3.17 \times 10^4$ square miles. What is this number in standard notation?

   **a.** 317,000     **b.** 31,700,000

   **c.** 3,170,000     **d.** 31,700

13. The diameter of a hydrogen atom is $5.0 \times 10^{-8}$ cm. What is this number in standard notation?

   **a.** 0.000000005     **b.** 0.0000005

   **c.** 0.00000005     **d.** 0.000005

14. The estimated population of China is 1,370,000,000. What is this number in scientific notation?

   **a.** $1.37 \times 10^7$     **b.** $1.4 \times 10^9$

   **c.** $1.37 \times 10^8$     **d.** $1.37 \times 10^9$

15. The diameter of an oxygen atom is $1.0 \times 10^{-8}$ mm. What is this number in standard notation?

   **a.** 0.00000001     **b.** 0.0000001

   **c.** 0.000001     **d.** 0.00000000001

16. Mars is $1.4171 \times 10^8$ miles from the sun. What is this number in standard notation?

   **a.** 1,417,100,000     **b.** 141,710,000

   **c.** 14,171,000     **d.** 14,171,000,000

17. Earth is 93,000,000 miles from the sun. What is this number in scientific notation?

   **a.** $9.3 \times 10^7$     **b.** $9.3 \times 10^8$

   **c.** $9.3 \times 10^9$     **d.** $9.3 \times 10^{10}$

18. Mercury is $3.6 \times 10^7$ miles from the sun. What is this number in standard notation?

   **a.** 360,000,000     **b.** 3,600,000

   **c.** 36,000,000     **d.** 360,000

19. The tallest building in the world is Taipei 101 in Taiwan. It is 1,670 feet tall. What is this number in scientific notation?

   **a.** $1.67 \times 10^5$     **b.** $1.67 \times 10^3$

   **c.** $16.7 \times 10^8$     **d.** $1.67 \times 10^4$

20. There are 604,800 seconds in a week. What is this number in scientific notation?

   **a.** $6.048 \times 10^5$     **b.** $60.48 \times 10^4$

   **c.** $6.048 \times 10^6$     **d.** $6.084 \times 10^5$

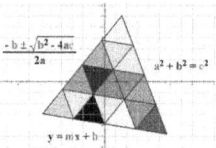

Students will successfully use arithmetic
operations on integers.

**CA Standard:** Grade 7, Number Sense 1.2
**CAHSEE Strand:** Number Sense

| Vocabulary: | | |
|---|---|---|
| | **integer** | positive and negative whole numbers |
| | **positive numbers** | numbers to the right of 0 on the number line |
| | **negative numbers** | numbers to the left of 0 on the number line |

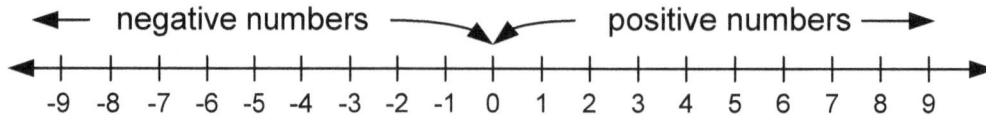

← negative numbers ——— positive numbers →

-9 -8 -7 -6 -5 -4 -3 -2 -1 0 1 2 3 4 5 6 7 8 9

Negative numbers, or negative integers, mirror the positive
integers on the number line. -1 and 1 are next to zero.

Adding and subtracting integers is simply a matter of
moving up or down the number line from a given point.

**adding a positive** means more positive or move up the number line

**subtracting a positive** means less positive or move down the number line

**adding a negative** means more negative or move down the number line

**subtracting a negative** means less negative or move up the number line

---

**EXAMPLE:** Which of the following expressions results in a positive number?

    **a.** $-2 + (-6)$     **b.** $-6 + 2$     **c.** $-2 - (-6)$     **d.** $2 - 6$

---

    **a.** $-2 + (-6)$; begin at -2 and go **down** the number line 6 = - 8

    **b.** $-6 + 2$; begin at - 6 and go **up** the number line 2 = - 4

    **c.** $-2 - (-6)$; begin at - 2 and go **up** the number line 6 = 4

    **d.** $2 - 6$; begin at 2 and go **down** the number line 6 = - 4

Choice **c** has the only positive answer and is therefore correct.

---

**EXAMPLE:**    $-3 - (-6) =$     **a.** 3     **b.** -3     **c.** 9     **d.** -9

We begin at -3 on the number line. Subtracting a
negative means we will be going up the number
line a total of six spaces. We end at 3, therefore,
**-3 - (-6) = 3**

    1   2   3   4   5   6

-5 -4 -3 -2 -1 0 1 2 3 4 5

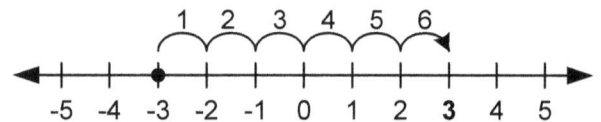

The correct answer is **a.**

# CAHSEE Bench Mark Practice 2

1.  -3 - (-6) =

    a. 3                b. -3

    c. 9                d. -9

2.  Which of the following expressions has a zero value?

    a. -2 - 2 + (-4)        b. -2 + 2 + 4

    c. 2 - 2 + 4           d. -2 – 2 + 4

3.  9 + 4 + (-8) - 7 =

    a. 14               b. -2

    c. -1               d. 15

4.  Which of the following expressions results in a negative number?

    a. 10 - (-9)          b. -10 + 9

    c. 10 - 9            d. 9 - (-10)

5.  3 + (-10) =

    a. 13               b. -7

    c. 7                d. -13

6.  Which of the following expressions has a zero value?

    a. 1- 1 + 1 + 1        b. 1 + 1 + 1 + 1

    c. 1 - 1 - 1 + (-1)      d. 1 - 1 + 1 - 1

7.  9 + (-1) =

    a. -8               b. 10

    c. 8                d. -10

8.  4 - 3 - (-5) + (-6) =

    a. 1                b. 0

    c. 2                d. 3

9.  Which of the following expressions results in a positive number?

    a. 1 + (-2)           b. -1 + 2

    c. -1 - 2            d. -2 - 1

10. Which of the following expressions results in a negative number?

    a. 5 - 4 + 3          b. -5 - (-4) + 3

    c. 3 - 4 + 5          d. 5 - 4 - 3

**11.** Which of the following expressions has a zero value?

   **a.** 2 - 3 + 1        **b.** 1 + 2 + 3

   **c.** 3 - 2 + 1        **d.** 1 - 3 - 2

**12.** -3 - (-2) =

   **a.** -5           **b.** 5

   **c.** 1            **d.** -1

**13.** 102 - (-103) =

   **a.** 1            **b.** -1

   **c.** -205       **d.** 205

**14.** Which of the following expressions results in a positive number?

   **a.** 205 - 206      **b.** -206 + 205

   **c.** 206 - 205      **d.** -206 - 205

**15.** Which of the following expressions results in a negative number?

   **a.** 15 - 14 + 13     **b.** -15 - (-14) + 13

   **c.** 14 - 15 - 13     **d.** 15 + 14 + 13

**16.** 15 - 16 =

   **a.** 1           **b.** 31

   **c.** -31        **d.** -1

**17.** Which of the following expressions has a zero value?

   **a.** -8 + 9 + 1     **b.** 8 - 9 - 1

   **c.** -8 - 9 - 1     **d.** 8 - 9 + 1

**18.** 22 + (-23) =

   **a.** -55         **b.** 1

   **c.** -1          **d.** 55

**19.** Which of the following expressions results in a negative number?

   **a.** 78 - 87       **b.** -78 - (-87)

   **c.** - 78 + 87     **d.** 87 + 78

**20.** 5 + (-11) =

   **a.** -6          **b.** -16

   **c.** 16          **d.** 6

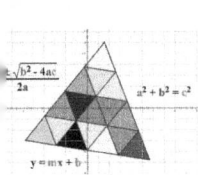

$\mathcal{S}$*implified*
$\mathcal{S}$*olutions*
**For Math Inc.**

---

**Vocabulary:**

| | |
|---|---|
| **percent** | per hundred; fraction with 100 in the denominator |
| **fraction** | breaking a specific amount into portions; any quantity expressed in terms of a numerator and denominator |
| **decimal** | a fraction with an unwritten denominator of 10 or a power of 10 |
| **denominator** | the number below the line in a fraction; stating the size of the parts in relation to the whole |
| **numerator** | the number above the line in a fraction which shows how many parts are taken |
| **decimal point** | period that separates whole numbers from partial numbers |
| **decimal place** | place values to the right of the decimal point |

Converting between fractions, decimals and percents is fairly straightforward.

| **percent to decimal** | **fraction to decimal** | **decimal to fraction** |
|---|---|---|
| move the decimal point twice to the left | divide the numerator by the denominator | convert decimal to percent, then percent to fraction |
| $85\% = 85.0\% = 0.85$ | $\dfrac{3}{10} = 10\overline{)3.0} \; 0.3 = 0.3$ | |

| **percent to fraction** | **fraction to percent** | **decimal to percent** |
|---|---|---|
| percent means per hundred | convert fraction to decimal, then decimal to percent | move the decimal point twice to the right |
| $85\% = \dfrac{85}{100} = \dfrac{17(5)}{20(5)} = \dfrac{17}{20}$ | | $0.92 = 92.0\%$ |

---

**EXAMPLE:** If the Warriors win 9 out of 20 games, what is their winning percentage?

    **a.** 40%    **b.** 30%    **c.** 50%    **d.** 45%

Use the given information to make a fraction. First, convert the fraction to a decimal.

$$\frac{9}{20} = 20\overline{)9.00} = 0.45$$
$$\begin{array}{r} 0.45 \\ \underline{-8.00} \\ 1.00 \\ \underline{-1.00} \\ 0 \end{array}$$

Then convert the decimal to a percent.

$$0.45 = 45.0\%$$

The correct answer is **d.**

# CAHSEE Bench Mark Practice 3

1. If the Warriors win 9 out of 20 games, what is their winning percentage?

   a. 40%          b. 30%

   c. 50%          d. 45%

2. Senator Haddeman won 6 out of his 8 districts in the last election. What percentage of districts did he win?

   a. 75%          b. 90%

   c. 50%          d. 85%

3. If Jim shoots 17 out of 20 targets, what is the percentage of targets he hits?

   a. 85%          b. 80%

   c. 50%          d. 67%

4. Amber balanced her checkbook 4 out of the last 5 months. What percentage of months did she balance her checkbook?

   a. 50%          b. 70%

   c. 80%          d. 75%

5. Mike called in sick to work 4 days out of the last 200. What percentage of days was Mike at work?

   a. 2%           b. 75%

   c. 95%          d. 98%

6. If the Sacramento Kings win 16 out of 20 games, what is their winning percentage?

   a. 80%          b. 90%

   c. 50%          d. 75%

7. If Lauren's dog Ginger has a cast on one of her four legs, what is the percentage of legs on which Ginger has a cast?

   a. 90%          b. 25%

   c. 75%          d. 65%

8. If Tim earns an A on 8 out of 10 tests, what is the percentage of tests on which he received an A?

   a. 85%          b. 67%

   c. 50%          d. 80%

9. Teressa has worked on her degree 7 out of the last 10 years. What is the percentage of years she has worked on her degree?

   a. 80%          b. 75%

   c. 70%          d. 50%

10. If Charlie has missed 9 out of 50 days of school, what is the percentage of school days he has missed?

   a. 27%          b. 30%

   c. 10%          d. 18%

8

# CAHSEE Bench Mark Practice 3

**11.** If Jerry makes 9 out of 10 free throws in a basketball game, what is his free throw shooting percentage?

a. 90%  b. 80%

c. 70%  d. 35%

**12.** If Karla wins six out of ten diving competitions, what is her winning percentage?

a. 75%  b. 60%

c. 50%  d. 55%

**13.** If 15 out of 25 families on the block own cats, what is the percentage of families that own cats?

a. 85%  b. 80%

c. 50%  d. 60%

**14.** 24 out of 40 windows are broken on an abandoned warehouse. What percentage of the windows are broken?

a. 60%  b. 70%

c. 50%  d. 75%

**15.** 3 of the 6 quarters in Pat's pocket are dated 1999. What percentage of quarters are dated 1999?

a. 65%  b. 30%

c. 50%  d. 60%

**16.** If one of the twenty rose bushes in Wanda's garden produce white flowers, what percentage of rose bushes produce flowers that are not white?

a. 95%  b. 5%

c. 85%  d. 15%

**17.** If three of the four horses in Barbara's stable are brown, what percentage of the horses are brown?

a. 90%  b. 25%

c. 75%  d. 65%

**18.** If 8 of the 20 trees along Main Street are maples, what percentage of the trees are maples?

a. 80%  b. 40%

c. 20%  d. 60%

**19.** 3 of the last 25 customers of an ice-cream shop have ordered chocolate sundaes, what percentage of customers did **not** order chocolate sundaes?

a. 88%  b. 30%

c. 12%  d. 77%

**20.** If Tovah has missed 7 out of 50 days of work, what is the percentage of work she has missed?

a. 14%  b. 7%

c. 10%  d. 18%

© 2007 Simplified Solutions for Math, Inc.

9

Students will successfully calculate
percents of increase and decrease.

**CA Standard:** Grade 7, Number Sense 1.6
**CAHSEE Strand:** Number Sense

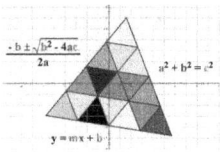

---

**Vocabulary:**

**percent of change**    the percent a quantity increases or decreases
from its original amount

---

To calculate the percent of increase or
decrease, simply use the following formula

**percent of change =** $\dfrac{\textbf{amount of change}}{\textbf{original amount}}$

---

**EXAMPLE:** The price of a toy train has increased from $10.00 to $13.00.
What is the percent of increase?

   **a.** 20%    **b.** 25%    **c.** 30%    **d.** 15%

We insert the given information into the formula then convert the fraction into a percentage.

percent of change = $\dfrac{3}{10}$ = $10\overline{)3.0}$ 0.3    0.30 = 0.30 = 30%

$$-3.0$$
$$0$$

The correct answer is **c.**

---

**EXAMPLE:** The price of a cup of coffee has decreased from $2.50 to $2.00.
What is the percent of decrease?

   **a.** 20%    **b.** 25%    **c.** 30%    **d.** 15%

We insert the given information into the formula then convert the fraction into a percentage.

percent of change = $\dfrac{0.50}{2.50}$ = $2.50\overline{)0.50}$ 0.20    0.20 = 0.20 = 20%

$$-0.50$$
$$0$$

The correct answer is **a.**

---

**EXAMPLE:** The price of a bus ticket has increased from $4.00 to $5.00.
What is the percent of increase?

   **a.** 10%    **b.** 25%    **c.** 50%    **d.** 35%

percent of change = $\dfrac{1.00}{4.00}$ = $\dfrac{1}{4}$ = $4\overline{)1.00}$ 0.25    0.25 = 0.25 = 25%

$$-0.80$$
$$0.20$$
$$-0.20$$
$$0$$

The correct answer is **b.**

# CAHSEE Bench Mark Practice 4

1. The price of a bus ticket has increased from $4.00 to $5.00. What is the percent of increase?

   a. 10%          b. 25%

   c. 50%          d. 35%

2. The price of a computer has decreased from $800.00 to $600.00. What is the percent of decrease?

   a. 10%          b. 50%

   c. 20%          d. 25%

3. The price of a toy train has increased from $10.00 to $12.00. What is the percent of increase?

   a. 20%          b. 25%

   c. 50%          d. 35%

4. The price of a pair of shoes has decreased from $100.00 to $80.00. What is the percent of decrease?

   a. 25%          b. 50%

   c. 20%          d. 10%

5. The price of daycare has decreased from $20.00 a day to $18.00 a day. What is the percent of decrease?

   a. 25%          b. 50%

   c. 20%          d. 10%

6. The price of blocks has decreased from $4.00 to $2.00. What is the percent of decrease?

   a. 25%          b. 50%

   c. 20%          d. 10%

7. The price of a plane ticket has increased from $50.00 to $57.50. What is the percent of increase?

   a. 15%          b. 25%

   c. 7.5%         d. 35%

8. The price of a pair of pants has decreased from $80.00 to $56.00. What is the percent of decrease?

   a. 25%          b. 50%

   c. 30%          d. 10%

9. The price of a toy truck has increased from $12.00 to $16.20. What is the percent of increase?

   a. 20%          b. 25%

   c. 50%          d. 35%

10. The price of a toy train has increased from $10.00 to $14.00. What is the percent of increase?

    a. 40%          b. 25%

    c. 4%           d. 15%

11. The price of a bottle of water has increased from $3.00 to $4.50. What is the percent of increase?

    a. 10%          b. 25%

    c. 50%          d. 35%

12. The price of a cup of coffee has decreased from $4.00 to $2.20. What is the percent of decrease?

    a. 55%          b. 50%

    c. 45%          d. 25%

13. The price of a book has increased from $10.00 to $12.50. What is the percent of increase?

    a. 20%          b. 25%

    c. 50%          d. 35%

14. The price of a box of pencils has decreased from $2.00 to $1.50. What is the percent of decrease?

    a. 25%          b. 50%

    c. 20%          d. 10%

15. The price of a hamburger has decreased from $1.00 to $0.50 . What is the percent of decrease?

    a. 10%          b. 50%

    c. 30%          d. 25%

16. The price of a printer has decreased from $80.00 to $66.00. What is the percent of decrease?

    a. 82.5%        b. 80%

    c. 17.5%        d. 20%

17. The price of trash collection has increased from $8.00 a month to $11.00 a month. What is the percent of increase?

    a. 62.5%        b. 37.5%

    c. 87.5%        d. 12.5%

18. The price of a watch has decreased from $100.00 to $79.00. What is the percent of decrease?

    a. 21%          b. 79%

    c. 20%          d. 12%

19. The price of lawn care has increased from $11.00 a month to $16.50 a month. What is the percent of increase?

    a. 50%          b. 25%

    c. 55%          d. 35%

20. The price of a bed has increased from $120.00 to $138.00. What is the percent of increase?

    a. 85%          b. 20%

    c. 15%          d. 38%

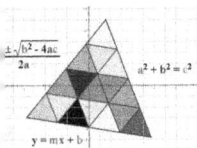

# CAHSEE Bench Mark 5

Students will successfully calculate discounts,
profits, commissions, and interest.

**CA Standard:** Grade 7, Number Sense 1.6
**CAHSEE Strand:** Number Sense

$\mathcal{S}$implified
$\mathcal{S}$olutions
For Math Inc.

| Vocabulary: | | |
|---|---|---|
| | **simple interest** | money paid for the use of money |
| | **discount** | percent or amount of decrease |
| | **markup** | percent or amount of increase |
| | **sale price** | original cost subtract discount |
| | **profit** | selling price subtract original cost |
| | **selling price** | the price an item is sold for; original cost plus profit |
| | **commission** | pay based on the amount of business done |

## SIMPLE INTEREST

### interest = deposit · rate · time

*the rate is in decimal form and the time is in years*

**EXAMPLE:** Jana puts $500.00 in a bank account. Each year her money earns 4% simple interest. How much interest will be earned in 2 years?

**a.** $40.00    **b.** $90.00    **c.** $56.00    **d.** $78.00

interest = 500 · 0.04 · 2

interest = **$40.00**                The correct answer is **a.**

## COMMISSION

### commission = rate · total sale

*the rate is in decimal form*

**EXAMPLE:** A sales person at a used car lot earns a 6% commission on all sales. How much commission does the sales person earn on a $3000.00 sale?

**a.** $120.00    **b.** $175.00    **c.** $180.00    **d.** $17.50

commission = 0.06 · 3000
commission = **$180.00**                The correct answer is **c.**

## SALE PRICE
### original cost subtract discount

**EXAMPLE:** A calculator regularly sells for $90.00. It is on sale for 20% off. What is the sale price of the calculator?

**a.** $63.00    **b.** $72.00    **c.** $18.00    **d.** $108.00

sale price = 90 - (90 · 0.2) = 90 - 18

sale price = **$72.00**
                The correct answer is **b.**

## SELLING PRICE
### the price an item is sold for; original cost plus profit

**EXAMPLE:** Mai Lia bought a truck for $5000.00 and later sold it for a 30% profit. How much did Mai Lia sell the truck for?

**a.** $7500.00    **b.** $6500.00

**c.** $7000.00    **d.** $8000.00

selling price = 5000 + (5000 · 0.3) = 5000 + 1500

selling price = **$6500.00**                The correct answer is **b.**

**EXAMPLE:** Charlie puts $300.00 in a bank account. Each year his money earns 6% simple interest. How much interest will be earned in 5 years?

  **a.** $45.00       **b.** $90.00       **c.** $180.00       **d.** $18.00

  interest = 300 · 0.06 · 5

  interest = **$90.00**

                The correct answer is **b.**

# CAHSEE Bench Mark Practice 5

1. Charlie puts $300.00 in a bank account. Each year his money earns 6% simple interest. How much interest will be earned in 5 years?

   a. $45.00          b. $90.00

   c. $180.00         d. $18.00

2. A watch regularly sells for $80.00. It is on sale for 25% off. What is the sale price of the watch?

   a. $60.00          b. $55.00

   c. $70.00          d. $40.00

3. Lauren bought a bicycle for $50.00 and later sold it for a 20% profit. How much did Lauren sell the bicycle for?

   a. $40.00          b. $55.00

   c. $70.00          d. $60.00

4. A sales person at a music store earns a 3% commission on all sales. How much commission does the sales person earn on a $400.00 sale?

   a. $10.00          b. $12.00

   c. $18.50          d. $17.50

5. A DVD player regularly sells for $100.00. It is on sale for 30% off. What is the sale price of the DVD player?

   a. $60.00          b. $55.00

   c. $70.00          d. $80.00

6. A sales person at a clothing store earns a 5% commission on all sales. How much commission does the sales person earn on a $200.00 sale?

   a. $12.00          b. $10.00

   c. $18.50          d. $17.50

7. Jamika puts $500.00 in a bank account. Each year her money earns 8% simple interest. How much interest will be earned in 7 years?

   a. $40.00          b. $360.00

   c. $280.00         d. $156.00

8. A book regularly sells for $12.00. It is on sale for 30% off. What is the sale price of the book?

   a. $3.60           b. $8.40

   c. $15.60          d. $10.00

9. Bao bought a car for $5000.00 and later sold it for a 10% profit. How much did Bao sell the car for?

   a. $5500.00        b. $6500.00

   c. $7000.00        d. $4000.00

10. A sales person at a sporting goods store earns a 6% commission on all sales. How much commission does the sales person earn on a $900.00 sale?

    a. $72.00          b. $46.00

    c. $90.00          d. $54.00

11. Jose puts $700.00 in a bank account. Each year his money earns 4% simple interest. How much interest will be earned in 2 years?

   a. $56.00          b. $90.00

   c. $45.00          d. $78.00

12. A jar of pickles regularly sells for $3.00. It is on sale for 25% off. What is the sale price of the jar of pickles?

   a. $4.50           b. $1.50

   c. $2.00           d. $2.25

13. Joe bought a tractor for $380.00 and later sold it for a 20% profit. How much did Joe sell the tractor for?

   a. $660.00         b. $456.00

   c. $470.00         d. $387.60

14. A sales person at a home improvement store earns a 5% commission on all sales. How much commission does the sales person earn on a $1200.00 sale?

   a. $52.00          b. $60.00

   c. $48.50          d. $87.50

15. A calculator regularly sells for $90.00. It is on sale for 30% off. What is the sale price of the calculator?

   a. $60.00          b. $27.00

   c. $63.00          d. $80.00

16. A sales person at a used car lot earns a 7% commission on all sales. How much commission does the sales person earn on a $2500.00 sale?

   a. $120.00         b. $175.00

   c. $180.50         d. $17.50

17. Tequilla puts $900.00 in a bank account. Each year her money earns 4% simple interest. How much interest will be earned in 3 years?

   a. $96.00          b. $160.00

   c. $108.00         d. $40.00

18. A CD regularly sells for $22.00. It is on sale for 25% off. What is the sale price of the CD?

   a. $11.00          b. $15.60

   c. $17.00          d. $16.50

19. Mai Lia bought a truck for $6000.00 and later sold it for a 25% profit. How much did Mai Lia sell the truck for?

   a. $7500.00        b. $6500.00

   c. $7000.00        d. $8000.00

20. A sales person at a store earns a 15% commission on all sales. How much commission does the sales person earn on a $500.00 sale?

   a. $72.00          b. $46.00

   c. $50.00          d. $75.00

# CAHSEE Unit 1 Exam
## Bench Marks 1 - 5

**BM 1.** The star, Wolf 359, is 94,000,000,000,000,000 miles from the sun. What is this number in scientific notation?

**a.** $9.4 \times 10^{16}$          **b.** $9.4 \times 10^{17}$

**c.** $94 \times 10^{15}$          **d.** $9.4 \times 10^{15}$

**BM 2.** Which of the following expressions has a zero value?

**a.** 2 + 2 + (-2) - (-2)          **b.** -2 - 2 + (-2) + 2

**c.** 2 - 2 + 2 - 2          **d.** -2 + 2 + 2 - (-2)

**BM 3.** If the Sacramento Kings win 32 out of 40 games, what is their winning percentage?

**a.** 90%          **b.** 80%

**c.** 50%          **d.** 75%

**BM 4.** The price of a plane ticket has increased from $120.00 to $150.00. What is the percent of increase?

**a.** 10%          **b.** 25%

**c.** 20%          **d.** 35%

**BM 5.** Eric puts $900.00 in a bank account. Each year his money earns 5% simple interest. How much interest will be earned in 6 years?

**a.** $135.00          **b.** $160.00

**c.** $540.00          **d.** $270.00

16

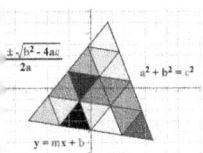

Students will successfully multiply and
divide terms with negative exponents.

**CA Standard:** Grade 7, Number Sense 2.1
**CAHSEE Strand:** Number Sense

$S$implified $S$olutions
For Math Inc.

| Vocabulary: | **exponent** | number used to show repeated multiplication |
|---|---|---|
| | **base** | number repeatedly multiplied |
| | **power** | a base and an exponent |

$$\text{power} \left\{ \underset{\text{base}}{\overset{\text{exponent}}{2^3}} = 2 \cdot 2 \cdot 2 \right.$$

**Rules of exponents:**

| Rule | Examples | |
|---|---|---|
| 1. $a^m \cdot a^n = a^{m+n}$ | $3^2 \cdot 3^5 = 3^{2+5} = 3^7$ | $4^{-5} \cdot 4^{-3} = 4^{-5+(-3)} = 4^{-8}$ |
| 2. $\dfrac{a^m}{a^n} = a^{m-n}$ | $\dfrac{5^6}{5^4} = 5^{6-4} = 5^2$ | $\dfrac{2^{-6}}{2^{-4}} = 2^{-6-(-4)} = 2^{-2}$ or $\dfrac{1}{2^2}$ |
| 3. $a^{-m} = \dfrac{1}{a^m}$ | $5^{-2} = \dfrac{1}{5^2} = \dfrac{1}{25}$ | $\dfrac{1}{2^{-2}} = 2^2 = 4$ |

We can use the meaning of exponents to examine the above rules.

$3^2 \cdot 3^5 = 3 \cdot 3 \cdot 3 \cdot 3 \cdot 3 \cdot 3 \cdot 3 = 3^7$

When we multiply with the same base, we add the exponents.

$\dfrac{5^6}{5^4} = \dfrac{\cancel{5} \cdot \cancel{5} \cdot \cancel{5} \cdot \cancel{5} \cdot 5 \cdot 5}{\cancel{5} \cdot \cancel{5} \cdot \cancel{5} \cdot \cancel{5}} = 5^2$

When we divide with the same base, we subtract the exponents.

$5^{-2} = \dfrac{1}{5^2} = \dfrac{1}{5 \cdot 5} = \dfrac{1}{25}$

Negative exponents tell us to move the base and make the exponent positive.

---

**EXAMPLE:**

Multiply. $3^{-2} \cdot 3^{-3}$

**a.** $6^6$     **b.** $9^{-5}$     **c.** $3^{-5}$     **d.** $3^6$

By rule, when we multiply with the same base, we add the exponents.

Therefore, $3^{-2} \cdot 3^{-3} = 3^{-2+(-3)} = 3^{-5}$

The correct answer is **c.**

# CAHSEE Bench Mark Practice 6

1. Multiply. $3^{-2} \cdot 3^{-3}$

   a. $6^6$       b. $9^{-5}$

   c. $3^{-5}$       d. $3^6$

2. Divide. $\dfrac{7^{-3}}{7^{-6}}$

   a. $7^{-3}$       b. $7^3$

   c. $1^3$       d. $\dfrac{1}{7^9}$

3. Multiply. $5^{-8} \cdot 5^3$

   a. $5^{-5}$       b. $5^5$

   c. $25^{11}$       d. $25^{-5}$

4. Divide. $\dfrac{25^{-8}}{25^{-2}}$

   a. $25^{-10}$       b. $25^{10}$

   c. $\dfrac{1}{25^{-6}}$       d. $\dfrac{1}{25^6}$

5. Multiply. $2^{-4} \cdot 2^{-5}$

   a. $2^9$       b. $\dfrac{1}{2^9}$

   c. $\dfrac{1}{2^{-9}}$       d. $2^{20}$

6. Which number equals $3^{-2}$?

   a. $-6$       b. $\dfrac{1}{6}$

   c. $\dfrac{1}{9}$       d. $\dfrac{-1}{6}$

7. Multiply. $13^{-8} \cdot 13^{-5}$

   a. $\dfrac{1}{13^{13}}$       b. $13^{-3}$

   c. $13^3$       d. $13^{40}$

8. Divide. $\dfrac{17^{-6}}{17^{-7}}$

   a. $17$       b. $\dfrac{1}{17}$

   c. $1^3$       d. $17^3$

9. Multiply. $12^{-1} \cdot 12^{-1}$

   a. $12$       b. $12^{-2}$

   c. $\dfrac{1}{12^{-2}}$       d. $\dfrac{1}{12}$

10. Which number equals $2^{-3}$?

    a. $\dfrac{1}{6}$       b. $\dfrac{1}{8}$

    c. $-6$       d. $\dfrac{-1}{8}$

**11.** Multiply. $2^{-3} \cdot 2^{-4}$

    **a.** $2^{-7}$         **b.** $4^{-7}$

    **c.** $8^{-7}$         **d.** $2$

**16.** Which number equals $4^{-2}$?

    **a.** $-8$         **b.** $\dfrac{1}{16}$

    **c.** $\dfrac{1}{8}$         **d.** $\dfrac{-1}{16}$

**12.** Divide. $\dfrac{8^{-5}}{8^{-2}}$

    **a.** $\dfrac{1}{8^{-3}}$         **b.** $8^{3}$

    **c.** $\dfrac{-1}{8^{3}}$         **d.** $\dfrac{1}{8^{3}}$

**17.** Multiply. $11^{-5} \cdot 11^{-5}$

    **a.** $\dfrac{1}{11^{10}}$         **b.** $-11^{10}$

    **c.** $1$         **d.** $121^{5}$

**13.** Multiply. $4^{-6} \cdot 4^{2}$

    **a.** $4^{-8}$         **b.** $16^{-4}$

    **c.** $4^{-4}$         **d.** $16^{8}$

**18.** Divide. $\dfrac{23^{-9}}{23^{-7}}$

    **a.** $23$         **b.** $\dfrac{1}{23^{16}}$

    **c.** $23^{-2}$         **d.** $23^{-16}$

**14.** Divide. $\dfrac{10^{-2}}{10^{-7}}$

    **a.** $10^{-9}$         **b.** $10^{5}$

    **c.** $10^{-5}$         **d.** $\dfrac{1}{10^{5}}$

**19.** Multiply. $5^{-8} \cdot 5^{-7}$

    **a.** $5$         **b.** $5^{-1}$

    **c.** $\dfrac{1}{5^{-1}}$         **d.** $\dfrac{1}{5^{15}}$

**15.** Multiply. $6^{-1} \cdot 6^{-7}$

    **a.** $6^{-8}$         **b.** $\dfrac{1}{6^{6}}$

    **c.** $\dfrac{1}{6^{-8}}$         **d.** $6^{-6}$

**20.** Which number equals $5^{-2}$?

    **a.** $\dfrac{1}{25}$         **b.** $\dfrac{1}{10}$

    **c.** $-10$         **d.** $\dfrac{-1}{25}$

*Simplified Solutions For Math Inc.*

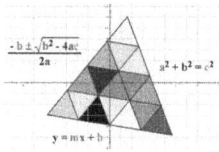

Adding and subtracting fractions is a simple matter of finding the lowest common denominator. Factoring different denominators to **prime** numbers is a straightforward way to accomplish this.

For example, $\dfrac{5}{6} + \dfrac{3}{8}$    Before we can add these two fractions, we must find the lowest common denominator. We begin by factoring the denominators to **prime** numbers.

2, 3, 5, 7, 11, and 13 are common **prime** numbers. As a rule, 2 is the only even **prime** number, so if a number is even and not 2, it is not a **prime** number.

Writing a number as the product of all of its **prime** factors is the **prime** factorization of a number. Factor trees are are a simple way to **prime** factor.

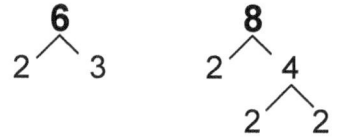

*The prime factors of 6 are 2 & 3, the prime factors of 8 are $2^3$.*

To find the lowest common denominator, list the **prime** factors. If a factor appears more than once, list the factor with the highest exponent. In this example, 2 appears as a **prime** factor of both 6 and 8, so we will list $2^3$ because it has a higher exponent.

The lowest common denominator will be $2^3 \cdot 3$ or 24.

Once we have found the lowest common denominator, we will need to adjust the numerators.

To make the 6 a 24, we multiply by 4. If we multiply the denominator by 4, we must also multiply the numerator by 4.    $\dfrac{5}{6} \cdot \dfrac{4}{4} = \dfrac{20}{24}$

To make the 8 a 24, we multiply by 3. If we multiply the denominator by 3, we must also multiply the numerator by 3.    $\dfrac{3}{8} \cdot \dfrac{3}{3} = \dfrac{9}{24}$

The final step is to add or subtract the numerators. In this example, we will add them.

$$\dfrac{20}{24} + \dfrac{9}{24} = \dfrac{29}{24} \qquad \text{Therefore,} \qquad \dfrac{5}{6} + \dfrac{3}{8} = \dfrac{29}{24}$$

---

**EXAMPLE:**    Which of the following is the **prime** factored form of the lowest common denominator of $\dfrac{2}{5} - \dfrac{3}{8}$

a. $2 \cdot 2 \cdot 2 \cdot 5$     b. $2 \cdot 2 \cdot 3 \cdot 5$     c. $5 \cdot 1$     d. $4 \cdot 2$

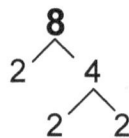

5 is a prime number and the prime factors of 8 are $2^3$.

None of the factors repeat, so we list them all.

$2 \cdot 2 \cdot 2 \cdot 5$

The correct answer is **a.**

# CAHSEE Bench Mark Practice 7

1. Which of the following is the prime factored form of the lowest common denominator of $\frac{2}{5} - \frac{3}{8}$ ?

   a. $2 \cdot 2 \cdot 2 \cdot 5$   b. $2 \cdot 2 \cdot 3 \cdot 5$

   c. $5 \cdot 1$   d. $4 \cdot 2$

2. Which fraction is equivalent to $\frac{2}{4} + \frac{1}{8}$ ?

   a. $\frac{3}{12}$   b. $\frac{4}{8}$

   c. $\frac{3}{8}$   d. $\frac{5}{8}$

3. What is $\frac{3}{8} - \frac{1}{6}$ ?

   a. $\frac{2}{2}$   b. $\frac{4}{14}$

   c. $\frac{5}{24}$   d. $\frac{2}{48}$

4. $\frac{8}{10} - \left( \frac{1}{2} + \frac{1}{5} \right)$

   a. $\frac{3}{10}$   b. $\frac{1}{10}$

   c. $\frac{7}{10}$   d. $\frac{5}{10}$

5. Which of the following is the prime factored form of the lowest common denominator of $\frac{11}{12} - \frac{7}{8}$ ?

   a. $2 \cdot 2 \cdot 2 \cdot 3$   b. $4 \cdot 8 \cdot 3$

   c. $8 \cdot 1$   d. $8 \cdot 12$

6. Which fraction is equivalent to $\frac{3}{7} - \frac{1}{3}$ ?

   a. $\frac{2}{4}$   b. $\frac{4}{10}$

   c. $\frac{2}{10}$   d. $\frac{2}{21}$

7. What is $\frac{3}{4} + \frac{2}{3}$ ?

   a. $\frac{5}{12}$   b. $\frac{17}{12}$

   c. $\frac{17}{7}$   d. $\frac{5}{7}$

8. $\frac{8}{14} + \left( \frac{1}{2} - \frac{1}{7} \right)$

   a. $\frac{10}{14}$   b. $\frac{8}{23}$

   c. $\frac{13}{14}$   d. $\frac{8}{9}$

9. Which of the following is the prime factored form of the lowest common denominator of $\frac{5}{7} + \frac{2}{3}$ ?

   a. $21 \cdot 1$   b. $5 \cdot 2$

   c. $2 \cdot 3 \cdot 7$   d. $3 \cdot 7$

10. Which fraction is equivalent to $\frac{2}{8} + \frac{7}{10}$ ?

    a. $\frac{9}{80}$   b. $\frac{1}{2}$

    c. $\frac{19}{20}$   d. $\frac{9}{18}$

**11.** Which of the following is the prime factored form of the lowest common denominator of $\frac{2}{5} - \frac{1}{6}$ ?

   **a.** $6 \cdot 5$        **b.** $2 \cdot 3 \cdot 5$

   **c.** $2 \cdot 1$        **d.** $1 \cdot 30$

**12.** Which fraction is equivalent to $\frac{5}{6} - \frac{2}{5}$ ?

   **a.** $\frac{3}{1}$        **b.** $\frac{7}{11}$

   **c.** $\frac{13}{30}$        **d.** $\frac{7}{30}$

**13.** What is $\frac{4}{8} - \frac{1}{5}$ ?

   **a.** $\frac{3}{3}$        **b.** $\frac{5}{13}$

   **c.** $\frac{3}{10}$        **d.** $\frac{5}{10}$

**14.** $\frac{8}{12} - \left( \frac{1}{3} + \frac{1}{4} \right)$

   **a.** $\frac{8}{13}$        **b.** $\frac{1}{12}$

   **c.** $\frac{7}{12}$        **d.** $\frac{5}{12}$

**15.** Which of the following is the prime factored form of the lowest common denominator of $\frac{7}{18} - \frac{11}{12}$ ?

   **a.** $2 \cdot 2 \cdot 2 \cdot 3 \cdot 3$        **b.** $7 \cdot 11$

   **c.** $2 \cdot 2 \cdot 3 \cdot 3$        **d.** $18 \cdot 12$

**16.** Which fraction is equivalent to $\frac{5}{8} - \frac{1}{10}$ ?

   **a.** $\frac{21}{40}$        **b.** $\frac{4}{-2}$

   **c.** $\frac{4}{40}$        **d.** $\frac{4}{18}$

**17.** What is $\frac{8}{10} + \frac{3}{8}$ ?

   **a.** $\frac{11}{18}$        **b.** $\frac{47}{18}$

   **c.** $\frac{11}{40}$        **d.** $\frac{47}{40}$

**18.** $\frac{13}{16} + \left( \frac{1}{2} - \frac{1}{8} \right)$

   **a.** $\frac{13}{10}$        **b.** $\frac{19}{16}$

   **c.** $\frac{23}{16}$        **d.** $\frac{23}{10}$

**19.** Which of the following is the prime factored form of the lowest common denominator of $\frac{1}{2} + \frac{2}{3}$ ?

   **a.** $2 \cdot 3$        **b.** $6 \cdot 1$

   **c.** $2 \cdot 3 \cdot 3$        **d.** $3 \cdot 3$

**20.** Which fraction is equivalent to $\frac{1}{7} + \frac{7}{9}$ ?

   **a.** $\frac{8}{63}$        **b.** $\frac{1}{2}$

   **c.** $\frac{58}{63}$        **d.** $\frac{8}{16}$

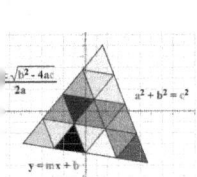

Students will successfully use the rules of exponents.

**CA Standard:** Grade 7, Number Sense 2.3
**CAHSEE Strand:** Number Sense

Many Algebra 1 techniques will become increasingly important in advanced math classes like Algebra 2 and Trigonometry. The following rules of exponents are fundamental to an understanding of exponential and logarithmic functions.

| Rule | Examples | |
|---|---|---|
| 1. $a^m \cdot a^n = a^{m+n}$ | $3^2 \cdot 3^5 = 3^{2+5} = 3^7$ | $2^{\frac{1}{2}} \cdot 2^{\frac{1}{3}} = 2^{\frac{1}{2}+\frac{1}{3}} = 2^{\frac{5}{6}}$ |
| 2. $\dfrac{a^m}{a^n} = a^{m-n}$ | $\dfrac{5^6}{5^4} = 5^{6-4} = 5^2$ | $\dfrac{3^{\frac{2}{3}}}{3^{\frac{1}{5}}} = 3^{\frac{2}{3}-\frac{1}{5}} = 3^{\frac{7}{15}}$ |
| 3. $a^{-m} = \dfrac{1}{a^m}$ | $5^{-2} = \dfrac{1}{5^2} = \dfrac{1}{25}$ | $\dfrac{1}{2^{-2}} = 2^2 = 4$ |
| 4. $a^0 = 1, a \neq 0$ | $309^0 = 1$ | $\left(\dfrac{3}{4}\right)^0 = 1$ |
| 5. $(a^m)^n = a^{mn}$ | $(8^2)^5 = 8^{2(5)} = 8^{10}$ | $(16.5^8)^3 = 16.5^{8(3)} = 16.5^{24}$ |
| 6. $(ab)^n = a^n b^n$ | $(2x)^3 = 2^3 x^3 = 8x^3$ | $(3a^2 b^5)^4 = 3^4 a^{2(4)} b^{5(4)} = 81 a^8 b^{20}$ |
| 7. $\left(\dfrac{a}{b}\right)^n = \dfrac{a^n}{b^n}$ | $\left(\dfrac{2}{3}\right)^2 = \dfrac{2^2}{3^2} = \dfrac{4}{9}$ | $\left(\dfrac{x^2}{5}\right)^3 = \dfrac{x^{2(3)}}{5^3} = \dfrac{x^6}{125}$ |

**EXAMPLE:** $\left(\dfrac{7^2}{2^5}\right)^2$

a. $\dfrac{7^4}{2^{10}}$   b. $\left(\dfrac{14}{10}\right)^2$   c. $\dfrac{7^4}{2^7}$   d. $14^{-6}$

We will be using rule 7 from the list above and raise both the numerator and denominator to the second power.

$$\dfrac{(7^2)^2}{(2^5)^2}$$

We will next use rule 5 from the list above, the power rule, and simplify the numerator and the denominator.

$$\dfrac{(7^2)^2}{(2^5)^2} = \dfrac{7^4}{2^{10}}$$

The correct answer is **a.**

**EXAMPLE:** $(4^2)^3$

a. $4^5$   b. $16^6$   c. $8^3$   d. $4^6$

This is a simple power rule problem. When we raise a power to a power, we multiply the exponents.

$(4^2)^3 = 4^{2(3)} = 4^6$

The correct answer is **d.**

**1.** $(4^2)^3$

    **a.** $4^5$        **b.** $16^6$

    **c.** $8^3$        **d.** $4^6$

**2.** $\dfrac{8^5}{8^2}$

    **a.** $8^7$        **b.** $8^{-3}$

    **c.** $8^3$        **d.** $24$

**3.** $2^7 \cdot 2^3$

    **a.** $2^4$        **b.** $2^{10}$

    **c.** $2^{21}$        **d.** $4^{10}$

**4.** $(5^4)^6$

    **a.** $5^{24}$        **b.** $5^{10}$

    **c.** $20^6$        **d.** $25^6$

**5.** $\dfrac{9^{10}}{9}$

    **a.** $1$        **b.** $9^{11}$

    **c.** $9^9$        **d.** $90$

**6.** $6 \cdot 6^5$

    **a.** $36^5$        **b.** $6^6$

    **c.** $6^5$        **d.** $6^4$

**7.** $(4 \cdot 7)^3$

    **a.** $11^3$        **b.** $28$

    **c.** $4 \cdot 7^3$        **d.** $4^3 \cdot 7^3$

**8.** $\left(\dfrac{3}{5}\right)^6$

    **a.** $\dfrac{18}{30}$        **b.** $\dfrac{3^6}{5^6}$

    **c.** $\dfrac{3^6}{5}$        **d.** $\dfrac{18}{5}$

**9.** $(8^2)^0$

    **a.** $1$        **b.** $64$

    **c.** $8^2$        **d.** $8$

**10.** $4^3 \cdot 4^9$

    **a.** $16^{12}$        **b.** $4^6$

    **c.** $4^{27}$        **d.** $4^{12}$

**11.** $\dfrac{7^4}{7^4}$

   **a.** $7^0$         **b.** $7^8$

   **c.** $7^{-8}$        **d.** $49$

**12.** $\left(\dfrac{8}{9}\right)^5$

   **a.** $\dfrac{40}{9}$        **b.** $\dfrac{8^5}{9^5}$

   **c.** $\dfrac{8}{45}$       **d.** $\dfrac{40}{45}$

**13.** $\left(\dfrac{3^4}{5^6}\right)^2$

   **a.** $\dfrac{3^6}{5^8}$       **b.** $\left(\dfrac{12}{30}\right)^2$

   **c.** $\dfrac{3^8}{5^{12}}$     **d.** $5^2$

**14.** $(7^2 \cdot 9^8)^3$

   **a.** $7^6 \cdot 9^{24}$     **b.** $7^5 \cdot 9^{11}$

   **c.** $7^6 \cdot 9^{11}$     **d.** $7^5 \cdot 9^{24}$

**15.** $(6^2)^4 \cdot (4^3)^0$

   **a.** $6^6 \cdot 4^3$      **b.** $6^8 \cdot 1$

   **c.** $24^9$        **d.** $6^8 \cdot 4^3$

**16.** $8^4 \cdot 8^4$

   **a.** $64^8$       **b.** $8^{16}$

   **c.** $32^2$       **d.** $8^8$

**17.** $\dfrac{6^{12}}{6^4}$

   **a.** $6^8$        **b.** $1$

   **c.** $6^3$        **d.** $6^{16}$

**18.** $(15^0)^2$

   **a.** $15^2$       **b.** $15$

   **c.** $1$         **d.** $30$

**19.** $(7^2)^4 \cdot (7^3)$

   **a.** $49^9$       **b.** $7^{11}$

   **c.** $7^9$        **d.** $7^{14}$

**20.** $\left(\dfrac{9^0}{9^3}\right)^2$

   **a.** $\dfrac{1}{9^6}$       **b.** $\dfrac{1}{29^{14}}$

   **c.** $\dfrac{1}{29^{-14}}$    **d.** $29^{14}$

Students will successfully estimate square roots.

**CA Standard:** Grade 7, Number Sense 2.4
**CAHSEE Strand:** Number Sense

---

**The following table has the squares of the numbers from 1 to 30.**

| 1 | 2 | 3 | 4 | 5 | 6 | 7 | 8 | 9 | 10 | 11 | 12 | 13 | 14 | 15 |
|---|---|---|---|---|---|---|---|---|----|----|----|----|----|----|
| 1 | 4 | 9 | 16 | 25 | 36 | 49 | 64 | 81 | 100 | 121 | 144 | 169 | 196 | 225 |

| 16 | 17 | 18 | 19 | 20 | 21 | 22 | 23 | 24 | 25 | 26 | 27 | 28 | 29 | 30 |
|----|----|----|----|----|----|----|----|----|----|----|----|----|----|----|
| 256 | 289 | 324 | 361 | 400 | 441 | 484 | 529 | 576 | 625 | 676 | 729 | 784 | 841 | 900 |

Finding the square root of a perfect square is a simple matter of memorization. When we want to find the square root of a number that is not a perfect square, we can estimate its value.

**EXAMPLE:** The square root of 32 is between

   **a.** 5 and 6     **b.** 6 and 7     **c.** 7 and 8     **d.** 8 and 9

32 falls between 25 and 36. From this information we can estimate that the square root of 32 is between 5 and 6.

The correct answer is **a.**

**EXAMPLE:** The square of a <u>whole</u> number is between 900 and 1,000. The number must be between

   **a.** 25 and 30     **b.** 30 and 35     **c.** 35 and 40     **d.** 40 and 45

The most straightforward way to answer this question is to square the answers and select the correct one.

$25(25) = 625$

*A square between 900 and 1,000 will be between 30 and 35.* $\longrightarrow$ $30(30) = 900$

$35(35) = 1225$

The correct answer is **b.**

**EXAMPLE:**

The square of a <u>whole</u> number is between 1,400 and 1,500. The number must be between

   **a.** 25 and 30     **b.** 30 and 35     **c.** 35 and 40     **d.** 40 and 45

The most straightforward way to answer this question is to square the answers and select the correct one.

$25(25) = 625$

$30(30) = 900$

$35(35) = 1225$

*A square between 1,400 and 1,500 will be between 35 and 40.* $\longrightarrow$

$40(40) = 1600$

The correct answer is **c.**

# CAHSEE Bench Mark Practice 9

1. The square of a <u>whole</u> number is between 1,400 and 1,500. The number must be between

   a. 25 and 30        b. 30 and 35

   c. 35 and 40        d. 40 and 45

2. The square root of 57 is between

   a. 6 and 7          b. 7 and 8

   c. 8 and 9          d. 9 and 10

3. The square of a <u>whole</u> number is between 1,600 and 1,700. The number must be between

   a. 25 and 30        b. 30 and 35

   c. 35 and 40        d. 40 and 45

4. The square root of 21 is between

   a. 4 and 5          b. 5 and 6

   c. 6 and 7          d. 7 and 8

5. The square of a <u>whole</u> number is between 2,100 and 2,200. The number must be between

   a. 30 and 35        b. 35 and 40

   c. 40 and 45        d. 45 and 50

6. The square of a <u>whole</u> number is between 700 and 800. The number must be between

   a. 25 and 30        b. 30 and 35

   c. 35 and 40        d. 40 and 45

7. The square root of 72 is between

   a. 5 and 6          b. 6 and 7

   c. 7 and 8          d. 8 and 9

8. The square of a <u>whole</u> number is between 1,300 and 1,400. The number must be between

   a. 25 and 30        b. 30 and 35

   c. 35 and 40        d. 40 and 45

9. The square root of 365 is between

   a. 16 and 17        b. 17 and 18

   c. 18 and 19        d. 19 and 20

10. The square of a <u>whole</u> number is between 2,700 and 2,800. The number must be between

   a. 40 and 45        b. 45 and 50

   c. 50 and 55        d. 55 and 60

**11.** The square of a <u>whole</u> number is between 3,400 and 3,500. The number must be between

   **a.** 55 and 60     **b.** 60 and 65

   **c.** 65 and 70     **d.** 70 and 75

**12.** The square root of 15 is between

   **a.** 1 and 2     **b.** 2 and 3

   **c.** 3 and 4     **d.** 4 and 5

**13.** The square of a <u>whole</u> number is between 100 and 200. The number must be between

   **a.** 5 and 10     **b.** 10 and 15

   **c.** 15 and 20     **d.** 20 and 25

**14.** The square root of 154 is between

   **a.** 11 and 12     **b.** 12 and 13

   **c.** 13 and 14     **d.** 14 and 15

**15.** The square of a <u>whole</u> number is between 4,500 and 4,600. The number must be between

   **a.** 60 and 65     **b.** 65 and 70

   **c.** 70 and 75     **d.** 75 and 80

**16.** The square of a <u>whole</u> number is between 300 and 400. The number must be between

   **a.** 15 and 20     **b.** 20 and 25

   **c.** 25 and 30     **d.** 30 and 35

**17.** The square root of 40 is between

   **a.** 6 and 7     **b.** 7 and 8

   **c.** 8 and 9     **d.** 9 and 10

**18.** The square of a <u>whole</u> number is between 1,900 and 2,000. The number must be between

   **a.** 25 and 30     **b.** 30 and 35

   **c.** 35 and 40     **d.** 40 and 45

**19.** The square root of 246 is between

   **a.** 14 and 15     **b.** 15 and 16

   **c.** 16 and 17     **d.** 17 and 18

**20.** The square of a <u>whole</u> number is between 5,700 and 5,800. The number must be between

   **a.** 65 and 70     **b.** 70 and 75

   **c.** 75 and 80     **d.** 80 and 85

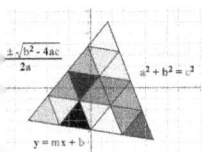

Students will successfully find the absolute
value of a number.

**CA Standard:** Grade 7, Number Sense 2.5
**CAHSEE Strand:** Number Sense

---

Absolute value ( the symbol | | ) is asking the question,
*"how far is a number from zero on the number line?"*

---

**EXAMPLE:**  What is the absolute value of -9?

**a.** 0            **b.** -9            **c.** 9            **d.** 1

---

On the number line, -9 is 9 away from zero. All distances are positive
numbers; therefore, there are no negative distances.

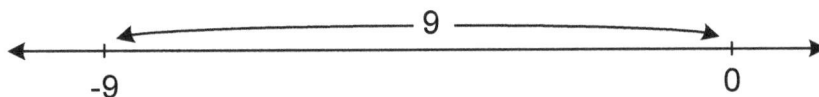

The correct answer is **c.**

---

**EXAMPLE:**  If |x| = 7 then what is the value of x?

**a.** 7            **b.** -7 or 7            **c.** 1            **d.** -7

---

If |7| = 7 and |-7| = 7, then |x| = 7  means x equals both 7 and -7. The question is asking you
*"what numbers are seven away from zero on the number line?"*
We know that both 7 and -7 are seven away from zero on the number line.

The correct answer is **b.**

---

**EXAMPLE:**  If |x| = 5, what is the value of x?

**a.** -5 or 5        **b.** -5 or 0        **c.** 0 or 5        **d.** -25 or 25

---

If |5| = 5 and |-5| = 5, then |x| = 5  means x equals both 5 and -5. The question is asking you
*"what numbers are five away from zero on the number line?"*
We know that both 5 and -5 are five away from zero on the number line.

The correct answer is **a.**

# CAHSEE Bench Mark Practice 10

1. If $|x| = 5$, what is the value of x?

   a. -5 or 5          b. -5 or 0

   c. 0 or 5           d. -25 or 25


2. What is the absolute value of -7?

   a. $\frac{1}{7}$           b. $\frac{-1}{7}$

   c. -7              d. 7


3. If $|x| = 12$, what is the value of x?

   a. 0 or 12          b. -12 or 0

   c. -12 or 12        d. -24 or 24


4. What is the absolute value of 8?

   a. -8             b. $\frac{-1}{8}$

   c. $\frac{1}{8}$           d. 8


5. If $|x| = 1$, what is the value of x?

   a. 0 or -1          b. -1 or 1

   c. 0 or 1           d. 0


6. What is the absolute value of -12?

   a. $\frac{-1}{12}$          b. 12

   c. -12             d. $\frac{1}{12}$


7. If $|x| = 17$, what is the value of x?

   a. -17 or 17        b. -17 or 0

   c. 17 or 0          d. -17 or 1


8. What is the absolute value of 23?

   a. $\frac{1}{23}$          b. $\frac{-1}{23}$

   c. 23             d. -23


9. If $|x| = 20$, what is the value of x?

   a. 20 or 1          b. -20 or 0

   c. -20 or 20        d. -20 or 1


10. What is the absolute value of -52?

    a. -52            b. 52

    c. $\frac{1}{52}$          d. $\frac{-1}{52}$

**11.** If $|x| = 11$, what is the value of x?

    **a.** -11 or 1      **b.** -11 or 11

    **c.** 0 or -11      **d.** 0 or 11

**12.** What is the absolute value of 6?

    **a.** -6      **b.** $\frac{-1}{6}$

    **c.** $\frac{1}{6}$      **d.** 6

**13.** If $|x| = 9$, what is the value of x?

    **a.** -9 or 9      **b.** -9 or 0

    **c.** -9 or 1      **d.** -81 or 81

**14.** What is the absolute value of -18?

    **a.** -18      **b.** 18

    **c.** $\frac{1}{18}$      **d.** $\frac{-1}{18}$

**15.** If $|x| = 16$, what is the value of x?

    **a.** 0      **b.** -1 or 16

    **c.** -16 or 1      **d.** -16 or 16

**16.** What is the absolute value of -144?

    **a.** $\frac{-1}{144}$      **b.** 12

    **c.** -144      **d.** 144

**17.** If $|x| = 13$, what is the value of x?

    **a.** 6 or 7      **b.** -13 or 13

    **c.** 13 or 0      **d.** -13 or 1

**18.** What is the absolute value of 2?

    **a.** $\frac{1}{2}$      **b.** $\frac{-1}{2}$

    **c.** -2      **d.** 2

**19.** If $|x| = 18$, what is the value of x?

    **a.** -18 or 0      **b.** -18 or 1

    **c.** 1 or 18      **d.** -18 or 18

**20.** What is the absolute value of 100?

    **a.** 10      **b.** -100

    **c.** 100      **d.** $\frac{-1}{10}$

# CAHSEE Unit 2 Exam
## Bench Marks 1 - 10

**BM 1.** The largest fresh water lake in the world is Lake Superior. It has an area of $3.17 \times 10^4$ square miles. What is this number in standard notation?

a. 317,000

b. 31,700,000

c. 3,170,000

d. 31,700

**BM 2.** $9 + (-1) =$

a. -8

b. 10

c. 8

d. -10

**BM 3.** 24 out of 40 windows are broken on an abandoned warehouse. What percentage of the windows are broken?

a. 60%

b. 70%

c. 50%

d. 75%

**BM 4.** The price of a toy truck has increased from $12.00 to $18.00. What is the percent of increase?

a. 20%

b. 25%

c. 50%

d. 35%

**BM 5.** A sales person at a used car lot earns a 7% commission on all sales. How much commission does the sales person earn on a $2500.00 sale?

a. $120.00

b. $175.00

c. $180.50

d. $17.50

**BM 6.** Divide. $\dfrac{10^{-2}}{10^{-7}}$

a. $10^{-9}$

b. $10^5$

c. $10^{-5}$

d. $\dfrac{1}{10^5}$

**BM 7.** Which of the following is the prime factored form of the lowest common denominator of $\dfrac{11}{12} - \dfrac{7}{8}$

a. $2 \cdot 2 \cdot 2 \cdot 3$

b. $4 \cdot 8 \cdot 3$

c. $8 \cdot 1$

d. $8 \cdot 12$

**BM 8.** $(15^0)^2$

a. $15^2$

b. 15

c. 1

d. 30

**BM 9.** The square root of 365 is between

a. 16 and 17

b. 17 and 18

c. 18 and 19

d. 19 and 20

**BM 10.** If $|x| = 18$, what is the value of x?

a. -18 or 0

b. -18 or 1

c. 1 or 18

d. -18 or 18

32

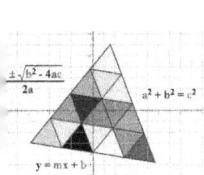

# CAHSEE Bench Mark 11

Students will successfully find the mean,
median, or mode of a set of data.

**CA Standard:** Grade 6, Statistics, Data analysis, and Probability 1.1
**CAHSEE Strand:** Statistics, Data analysis, and Probability

| Vocabulary: | data | facts or figures to be processed; information |
|---|---|---|
| | **mean** | the sum of the data items divided by the number of data items |
| | **median** | the middle number when the data items are written in order |
| | **mode** | the data item that occurs most often |

Mean, median and mode are measures of central tendency of a set of data.

For example, consider the data set, 6, 8, 5, 9, 6, 6, 2, which has an odd number of data pieces.

When computing measures of central tendency, it is beneficial to *list the numbers from greatest to least.*

9
8
6
⑥
6
5
2

6 is the middle number and is therefore the **median**.

The number 6 occurs most often and is therefore the **mode**.

To find the **mean**, we need to add the numbers together and divide the sum by 7 because there are seven pieces of data

$9 + 8 + 6 + 6 + 6 + 5 + 2 = 42$

$42 \div 7 = 6$   Therefore the **mean** is 6.

For another example, consider the data set, 5, 8, 14, 6, 8, 4, which has an even number of data pieces.

*list the numbers from greatest to least*

14
8
8
6
5
4

The middle of this set of data is between 8 and 6. The **median** is the **mean** of 8 and 6.
$8 + 6 = 14$ and $14 \div 2 = 7$
Therefore the **median** is 7.

The number 8 occurs most often and is therefore the **mode**.

To find the **mean**, we need to add the numbers together and divide the sum by 6 because there are six pieces of data

$14 + 8 + 8 + 6 + 5 + 4 = 45$

$45 \div 6 = 7.5$

Therefore the **mean** is 7.5.

---

**EXAMPLE:**   Find the mean of the following four numbers: 3, 4, 5, and 8.

**a.** 4        **b.** 4.5        **c.** 20        **d.** 5

*list the numbers from greatest to least*

8
5
4
3

To find the mean, we need to add the numbers together and divide the sum by 4 because there are four pieces of data

$8 + 5 + 4 + 3 = 20$

$20 \div 4 = 5$

The correct answer is **d.**

# CAHSEE Bench Mark Practice 11

1. Find the mean of the following four numbers: 3, 4, 5, and 8.

   a. 4           b. 4.5

   c. 20         d. 5

2. Find the median of the following four numbers: 3, 4, 5, and 8.

   a. 3           b. 4

   c. 4.5        d. 5

3. Find the mode of the following six numbers: 2, 5, 7, 7, 9, 12.

   a. 7           b. 5

   c. 9           d. 10

4. Find the median of the following numbers: 4, 7, 8, 11, 13.

   a. 7           b. 8

   c. 11         d. 9

5. Find the mean of the following numbers: 7, 9, 10, 11, 13.

   a. 9           b. 10.5

   c. 10         d. 6

6. Find the mode of the following numbers: 2, 3, 7, 2, 4, 3, 1, 2.

   a. 2           b. 3

   c. 5           d. 7

7. Find the median of the following numbers: 2, 3, 7, 2, 4, 3, 1, 2.

   a. 3           b. 6

   c. 5           d. 2.5

8. The box below shows Elijah's last five quiz scores.

   > 12, 15, 13, 12, 17

   Find the mode of Elijah's scores.

   a. 13         b. 12

   c. 17         d. 5

9. The chart below shows the homework scores for three students.

   | | Homework | | | | |
   |---|---|---|---|---|---|
   | | 1 | 2 | 3 | 4 | 5 |
   | Myles | 13 | 10 | 14 | 12 | 16 |
   | Julia | 12 | 15 | 7 | 14 | 17 |
   | Andrew | 11 | 14 | 9 | 13 | 15 |

   What is Julia's mean score?

   a. 7           b. 15

   c. 14         d. 13

10. Davion compared the prices for a certain birthday gift. See the box below.

    > $11.00, $8.00, $10.00, $13.00, $15.00, $10.00

    What is the mode of the data?

    a. $10.00       b. $7.00

    c. $10.50       d. $11.00

11. Christopher's scores for the first five paragraphs on an English paper are 13, 9, 16, 11, and 14. Find the median score.

    a. 16         b. 7

    c. 13         d. 13.5

34

# CAHSEE Bench Mark Practice 11

**12.** The box below shows Cameron's first six quiz scores.

| |
|---|
| 9, 14, 11, 9, 16, 13 |

What is Cameron's mean score?

**a.** 12 **b.** 9

**c.** 7 **d.** 11

**13.** The chart below shows the exam scores for three students.

| | Exam | | | | |
|---|---|---|---|---|---|
| | 1 | 2 | 3 | 4 | 5 |
| Amy | 78 | 85 | 84 | 80 | 92 |
| Manuel | 82 | 84 | 79 | 85 | 83 |
| Kurone | 80 | 90 | 82 | 84 | 88 |

What is the mode of this data?

**a.** 80 **b.** 82

**c.** 85 **d.** 84

**14.** At Jaimes's fund raiser, he collected checks for \$12.00, \$9.00, \$13.00, \$10.00, \$8.00, and \$12.00. What is the median value of the checks collected?

**a.** \$12.00 **b.** \$11.00

**c.** \$5.00 **d.** \$23.50

**15.** The football team auctioned off nine pies. Use the data in the box below to find the mode.

| |
|---|
| \$27.00, \$33.00, \$30.00, \$34.00, \$33.00, \$32.00, \$29.00,\$33.00, \$27.00 |

**a.** \$27.00 **b.** \$32.00

**c.** \$33.00 **d.** \$34.00

**16.** Brittney received the following scores on her senior project: 27, 33, 30, 34, and 33. Find her median score.

**a.** 33 **b.** 30

**c.** 7 **d.** 157

**17.** What is the mean of the data in the box below?

| |
|---|
| 27, 36, 24, 33 |

**a.** 60 **b.** 30

**c.** 9 **d.** 120

**18.** Amondo's first seven homework scores are 3, 5, 4, 5, 3, 4, and 5. What is the mode of Amondo's scores?

**a.** 4 **b.** 3

**c.** 9 **d.** 5

**19.** Amondo's first seven homework scores are 3, 5, 4, 5, 3, 4, and 5. What is the median of Amondo's scores?

**a.** 4 **b.** 3

**c.** 9 **d.** 5

**20.** The chart below shows the quiz scores for two students.

| | Quiz | | | | |
|---|---|---|---|---|---|
| | 1 | 2 | 3 | 4 | 5 |
| David | 3 | 10 | 5 | 4 | 8 |
| Maria | 5 | 9 | 5 | 4 | 7 |

What is David's mean score?

**a.** 5 **b.** 7

**c.** 6 **d.** 30

## Students will successfully judge the validity of claims given information graphically.

**CA Standard:** Grade 6, Statistics, Data analysis, and Probability 2.5
**CAHSEE Strand:** Statistics, Data analysis, and Probability

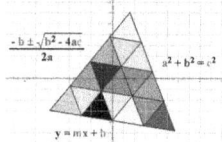

| Vocabulary: | judge | to form an idea, opinion, or estimate about |
|---|---|---|
| | logic | the science of correct reasoning |
| | valid | correctly derived or inferred according to logic |
| | claim | to state as a fact |
| | observation | the practice of noticing facts and events |

Judging the validity of claims is generally observing the answer choices and eliminating those choices that are incorrect.

For example, a family wanted to look at their expenses for a year.
**According to the circle graph shown, which of the following is true?**

*(The numbers represent percentages)*

a. Insurance and Car expenses combined are the greatest expenses.
b. Health and Car expenses combined are less than Food and Other combined.
c. More than one-half of the expenses are Entertainment, Other, and Housing combined.
d. Housing is approximately one-third of the total budget.

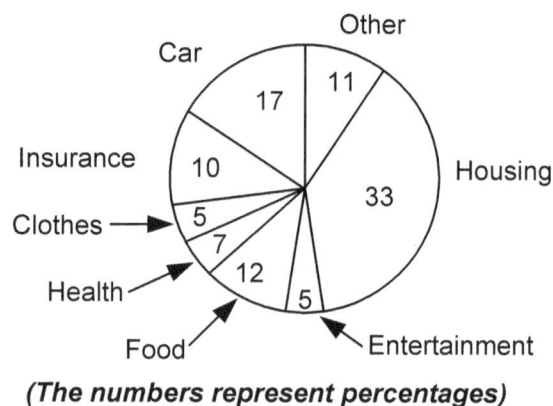

**Judge the validity of each claim presented in the answer choices. We are looking for a true statement.**

a. Insurance and Car expenses combined are the greatest expenses.
  10% + 17% = 27%, which is less than housing at 33%. **a** is a **false** statement.

b. Health and Car expenses combined are less than Food and Other combined.
  7% + 17% = 24%, 12% + 11% = 23%. 24% is not less than 23%. **b** is a **false** statement.

c. More than one-half of the expenses are Entertainment, Other, and Housing combined.
  5% + 11% + 33% = 49%, which is less than 50%. **c** is a **false** statement.

d. Housing is approximately one-third of the total budget.
  $\frac{1}{3} \approx 33\%$   **d** is a **true** statement.

The correct answer is **d**.

**EXAMPLE:** The following table represents a certain major at the local university.

| | Number of Applicants | Percent Admitted |
|---|---|---|
| Women | 341 | 7 |
| Men | 373 | 6 |

Which of the following statements is false?
a. More men apply for the major.
b. Fewer women are admitted into the major.
c. A greater percentage of women are admitted.
d. Fewer men are admitted into the major.

By observation, we will judge the validity of each answer, eliminate incorrect choices and select the correct one.

We are looking for a false statement so we will eliminate true statements.

a. More men apply for the major.

  M: 373 is greater than W: 341.
  **a** is a true statement

b. Fewer women are admitted into the major.
  W: 341(0.07) = 23.87   M: 373(0.06) = 22.38
  W: 23.87 is not less than  M: 22.38
  **b** is a false statement

The correct answer is **b**.

**1.** The following table represents a certain major at the local university.

|  | Number of Applicants | Percent Admitted |
|---|---|---|
| Women | 341 | 7 |
| Men | 373 | 6 |

Which of the following statements is false?

a.  More men apply for the major.

b.  Fewer women are admitted into the major.

c.  A greater percentage of women are admitted.

d.  Fewer men are admitted into the major.

**2.** The following two pie charts represent the same set of data.

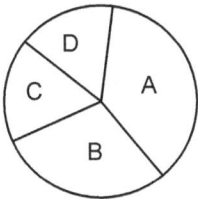

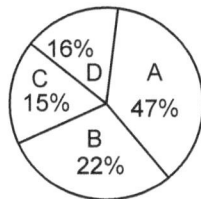

Figure 1                     Figure 2

If Figure 1 was the only circle graph given, why would it be misleading?

a.  Group B appears much bigger than it should.

b.  The pie chart in figure 1 is divided into four equal parts.

c.  Group C appears to be smaller than Group D.

d.  Group C appears to be bigger than Group A.

The bar chart below represents the grades for one class. Answer questions 3 and 4.

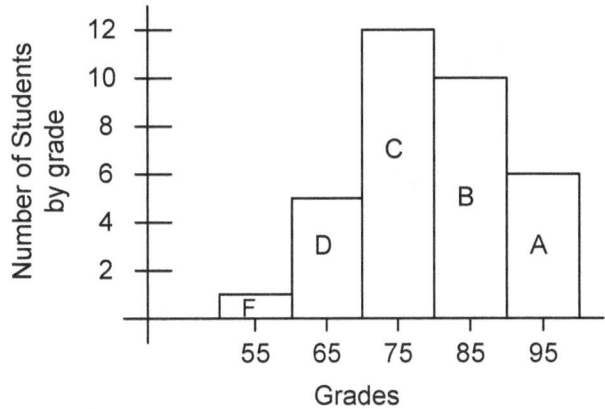

**3.** How many students are in the class?

a. 375          b. 78

c. 18           d. 34

**4.** Which of the following statements is true?

a.  Eighteen students had a grade below C.

b.  Ten students scored between 60 and 70.

c.  Only one student failed the class.

d.  Twice the number of students received an A as compared to the number of students who received a D.

**5.** Two-thirds of 24 students attended the field trip. Two of those who did not go on the field trip were female. Which of the following statements can be answered with the given information?

    **a.** How many males went on the field trip?

    **b.** How many males did not go on the field trip?

    **c.** How many females went on the field trip?

    **d.** How many females were suppose to go on the field trip?

**6.** The following two graphs represent the test scores of the same three students.

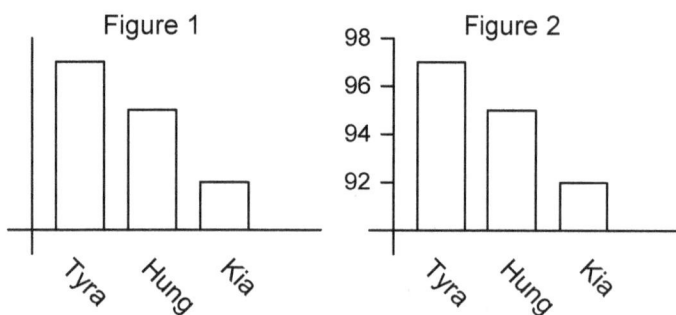

Figure 1

Figure 2

If figure 1 was the only bar graph given, which statement would appear to be true?

    **a.** Hung would appear to have the high score.

    **b.** Tyra would appear to have the low score.

    **c.** Tyra would appear to have the high score.

    **d.** Kia would appear to have the high score.

**7.** A teacher drew the following circle graph to represent the number of siblings of his students.

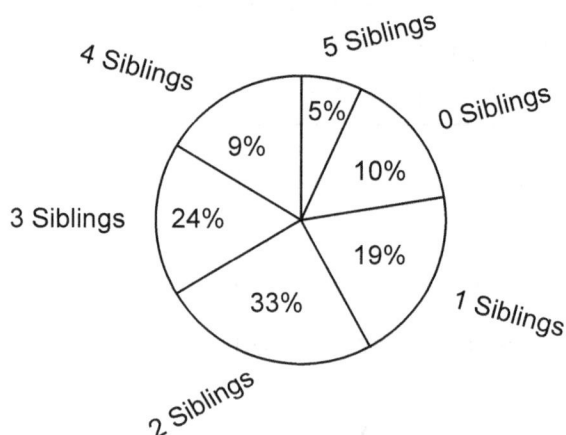

According to the pie chart shown, which statement is true?

    **a.** The number of students with zero, four, and five siblings combined is more than those students with one sibling.

    **b.** Students with two and three siblings combined is less than half of all the students.

    **c.** Two of the students have six siblings.

    **d.** Ninety-five percent of all students have at least one sibling.

**8.** Five-sevenths of 42 members of the band arrived early for the game. Eighteen of the members who arrived early are males. Which can be answered with the given information?

  **a.** How many males did not arrive early?

  **b.** How many females did not arrive early?

  **c.** How many males are in the band?

  **d.** How many females arrived early?

**9.** The following table represents the number of students who take geometry.

|          | Pass | Fail |
|----------|------|------|
| Period 1 | 14   | 12   |
| Period 3 | 11   | 9    |

Which of the following statements is false?

  **a.** The percentage of students who passed period 1 is greater than the percentage of students who passed period 3.

  **b.** Period 1 had six more students than period 3.

  **c.** The ratio of pass to fail in period 1 is seven to six.

  **d.** The percentage of students who passed period 1 is less than period 3.

**10.** A family wanted to look at their expenses for a year.

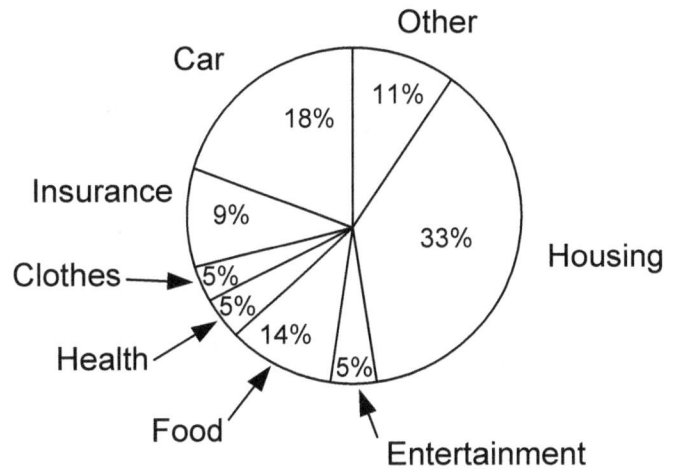

According to the circle graph shown, which statement is true?

  **a.** Food and Car expenses combined are the greatest expenses.

  **b.** Housing is approximately one-third of the total budget.

  **c.** More than one-half of the expenses are Insurance, Other, Entertainment, Health, and Car combined.

  **d.** Health and Car expenses combined are more than Food and Other combined.

**11.** A certain drug company wants to market a new anti-depression drug. The bar graph below shows the results of testing.

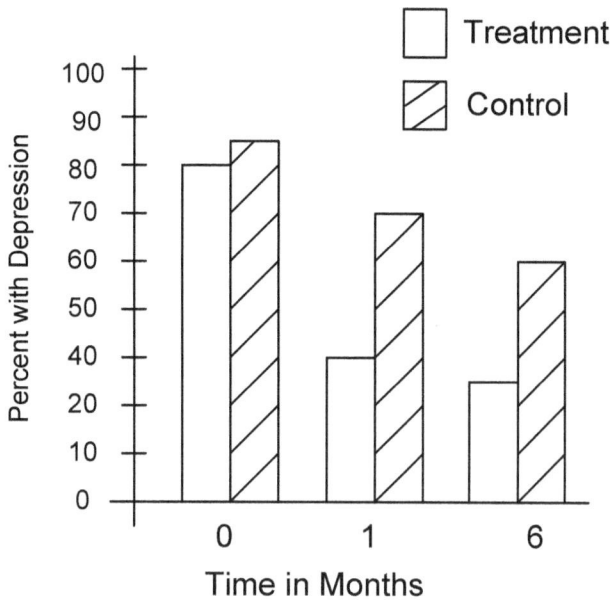

The treatment group is the only group receiving the drug. Using the information displayed in the bar graph, determine which statement is true?

a. The drug did not decrease depression in the treatment group over the six month study.

b. The control group had an increase in depression over the six month study.

c. From time 0 to time six months, the treatment group had a 25% decrease in depression.

d. From time 0 to time six months, over 50% of the treatment group had a decrease in depression.

**12.** The table below shows the quiz scores for four students. Which student had the third lowest quiz score?

| | Q1 | Q2 | Q3 | Q4 | Q5 | Q6 |
|---|---|---|---|---|---|---|
| Hien | 7 | 6 | 5 | 5 | 6 | 1 |
| Myles | 8 | 9 | 0 | 6 | 8 | 9 |
| Ida | 9 | 5 | 7 | 8 | 4 | 8 |
| Jaime | 8 | 10 | 9 | 7 | 10 | 9 |

a. Hien

b. Myles

c. Ida

d. Jaime

**13.** Teacher B uses the data in the table below to support his claim, "I have one-fourth the number of student complaints when compared to Teacher A." Why is this claim misleading?

| Teacher | Student Complaints | Years Teaching |
|---|---|---|
| A | 120 | 20 |
| B | 30 | 2 |

a. Teacher B should claim, "one-tenth the number of student complaints."

b. On average Teacher B has more student complaints per year.

c. On average Teacher A has more student complaints per year.

d. Teacher B should claim, "one-sixth the number of student complaints."

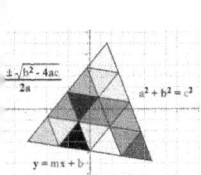

Students will successfully compute theoretical probability.

**CA Standard:** Grade 6, Statistics, Data analysis, and Probability 3.1
**CAHSEE Strand:** Statistics, Data analysis, and Probability

| **Vocabulary:** | **outcome** | result or consequence |
|---|---|---|
| | **theoretical** | hypothetical; not practiced or applied |
| | **probability** | the likelihood of an event |
| | **favorable** | advantageous or desirable |

$$\text{Theoretical probability} = \frac{\text{Favorable outcomes}}{\text{Total outcomes}}$$

For example, if you were to roll a fair number cube, what is the probability that you will roll a five?

### TOTAL OUTCOMES

Total outcomes will be all of the possibilities of outcomes when you roll a number cube.
*i.e. 1, 2, 3, 4, 5, 6*

### FAVORABLE OUTCOMES

Favorable outcomes are those specific outcomes that are 5.

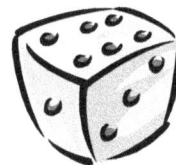

$$\text{Theoretical probability} = \frac{\text{Favorable outcomes}}{\text{Total outcomes}} = \frac{1}{6}$$

**EXAMPLE:** What is the probability of flipping a quarter and it lands 'heads up'?

a. $\frac{1}{2}$  b. $\frac{1}{4}$  c. $\frac{1}{3}$  d. $\frac{2}{3}$

A quarter has only two sides; heads and tails. Therefore, the number of possible outcomes is 2.

Only one side of a quarter is heads. Therefore, the number of favorable outcomes is 1.

$$\text{Theoretical probability} = \frac{\text{Favorable outcomes}}{\text{Total outcomes}} = \frac{1}{2}$$

The correct answer is **a.**

1. What is the probability of flipping a quarter and it lands heads up?

    a. $\dfrac{1}{2}$      b. $\dfrac{1}{4}$

    c. $\dfrac{1}{3}$      d. $\dfrac{2}{3}$

2. Manuel has three different choices for pants and 4 different choices for shirts. Use the diagram below to determine the probability that Manuel wears FUBU pants and a Green shirt.

Shirts

| Pants | Yellow | White | Green | Purple |
|---|---|---|---|---|
| Levi | LY | LW | LG | LP |
| FUBU | FY | FW | FG | FP |
| Paco | PY | PW | PG | PP |

    a. $\dfrac{1}{6}$      b. $\dfrac{1}{12}$

    c. $\dfrac{1}{3}$      d. $\dfrac{2}{3}$

3. If a fair number cube is rolled once, what is the probability of getting a two?

    a. $\dfrac{1}{2}$      b. $\dfrac{1}{12}$

    c. $\dfrac{1}{6}$      d. $\dfrac{1}{3}$

A deck of cards contains a total of 52 cards divided into the black cards (spades and clubs) and the red cards (diamonds and hearts). Note that the spades, clubs, diamonds and hearts are also called the four suits. Use this information to answer Questions 4 through 6.

4. If you pick a card at random from a complete deck of cards, what is the probability that it will be a diamond?

    a. $\dfrac{1}{4}$      b. $\dfrac{1}{3}$

    c. $\dfrac{1}{3}$      d. $\dfrac{2}{3}$

5. If you pick a card at random from a complete suit of clubs, what is the probability that it will be an eight?

    a. $\dfrac{1}{2}$      b. $\dfrac{8}{13}$

    c. $\dfrac{1}{12}$      d. $\dfrac{1}{13}$

6. If you pick a card at random from a complete deck of cards, what is the probability that it will be black?

    a. $\dfrac{1}{4}$      b. $\dfrac{1}{2}$

    c. $\dfrac{1}{12}$      d. $\dfrac{2}{13}$

# CAHSEE Bench Mark Practice 13

If two fair number cubes are rolled at the same time, then the theoretical probability of their sums are listed in the table below. Use this table to help answer Questions 7 through 11.

Number cube 1

| Sum | 1 | 2 | 3 | 4 | 5 | 6 |
|-----|---|---|---|---|---|---|
| 1 | 2 | 3 | 4 | 5 | 6 | 7 |
| 2 | 3 | 4 | 5 | 6 | 7 | 8 |
| 3 | 4 | 5 | 6 | 7 | 8 | 9 |
| 4 | 5 | 6 | 7 | 8 | 9 | 10 |
| 5 | 6 | 7 | 8 | 9 | 10 | 11 |
| 6 | 7 | 8 | 9 | 10 | 11 | 12 |

Number cube 2

7. The probability of rolling a sum of three is one-eighteenth. What other sum has the same probability?

   a. 4     b. 5     c. 11     d. 12

8. What is the probability of rolling a sum of six?

   a. $\frac{5}{36}$     b. $\frac{1}{4}$

   c. $\frac{1}{6}$     d. $\frac{5}{18}$

9. Which sum has the probability of one-sixth?

   a. 4     b. 7     c. 6     d. 8

10. Which sum has the probability of one-ninth?

   a. 12     b. 11     c. 10     d. 9

11. What is the probability of rolling a sum of four?

   a. $\frac{1}{36}$     b. $\frac{1}{12}$

   c. $\frac{1}{9}$     d. $\frac{1}{6}$

12. A bag contains 3 green marbles, 4 orange marbles, and 2 yellow marbles. If you cannot see the marbles and they are all the same size, what is the probability that you will be able to reach into the bag and pick out one green marble?

   a. $\frac{1}{9}$     b. $\frac{4}{9}$

   c. $\frac{2}{3}$     d. $\frac{1}{3}$

13. A bag contains 6 green marbles, 10 orange marbles, and 14 yellow marbles. If you cannot see the marbles and they are all the same size, what is the probability that you will be able to reach into the bag and pick an orange marble?

   a. $\frac{1}{12}$     b. $\frac{1}{4}$

   c. $\frac{1}{3}$     d. $\frac{2}{3}$

14. Each letter of the word ALGEBRA is on its own note card, lying face down on a desk. If you pick up one note card, what is the probability it will be the letter A?

   a. $\frac{1}{2}$     b. $\frac{3}{4}$

   c. $\frac{2}{7}$     d. $\frac{1}{3}$

# CAHSEE Bench Mark Practice 13

The possible outcomes of flipping a fair quarter three times is contained in the tree diagram below. Use this information to answer Questions 15 through 18.

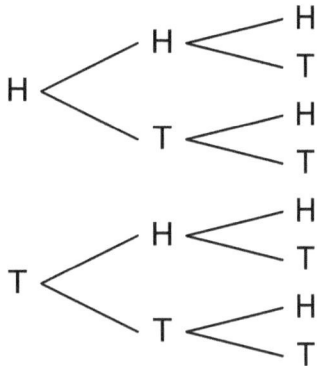

**15.** What is the total of possible outcomes?

    **a.** 2        **b.** 3

    **c.** 4        **d.** 8

**16.** What is the probability of getting three heads?

    **a.** $\dfrac{1}{8}$        **b.** $\dfrac{1}{4}$

    **c.** $\dfrac{1}{3}$        **d.** $\dfrac{1}{2}$

**17.** What is the probability of getting two heads and one tail?

    **a.** $\dfrac{1}{4}$        **b.** $\dfrac{3}{8}$

    **c.** $\dfrac{1}{2}$        **d.** $\dfrac{3}{4}$

**18.** What is the probability of getting exactly one head?

    **a.** $\dfrac{3}{4}$        **b.** $\dfrac{1}{2}$

    **c.** $\dfrac{1}{3}$        **d.** $\dfrac{3}{8}$

**19.** A bag contains 5 green marbles, 4 orange marbles, and 3 yellow marbles. If you cannot see the marbles and they are all the same size, what is the probability that you will be able to reach into the bag and pick an orange marble?

    **a.** $\dfrac{1}{12}$        **b.** $\dfrac{1}{4}$

    **c.** $\dfrac{1}{3}$        **d.** $\dfrac{2}{3}$

**20.** Each letter of the word MATH is on its own note card, lying face down on a desk. If you pick up one note card, what is the probability it will be the letter A?

    **a.** $\dfrac{1}{2}$        **b.** $\dfrac{3}{4}$

    **c.** $\dfrac{1}{4}$        **d.** $\dfrac{1}{3}$

**21.** A classroom raffle contains the names of 20 students. If there are 12 females and 8 males in the class, what is the probability that the name selected will be a male?

    **a.** $\dfrac{1}{2}$        **b.** $\dfrac{3}{5}$

    **c.** $\dfrac{2}{3}$        **d.** $\dfrac{2}{5}$

# CAHSEE Bench Mark 14
### Students will successfully represent probabilities as ratios.

**CA Standard:** Grade 6, Statistics, Data analysis, and Probability 3.3
**CAHSEE Strand:** Statistics, Data analysis, and Probability

| Vocabulary: | | |
|---|---|---|
| | **ratio** | a comparison of two quantities using division |
| | **probability** | the likelihood of an event |

## PROBABILITY
**"the likelihood of an event"**

← *less likely* | *more likely* →

**0**      **0.5**      **1**

not likely at all    as likely as not    very likely

***"never happens"***    ***"might happen, might not"***    ***"is going to happen"***

For example, if you were to roll a fair number cube, what is the probability that you will **not** roll a two?

There are six numbers on a number cube;
1, 2, 3, 4, 5 and 6.

Five of these numbers are **not** 2;
1, 3, 4, 5 and 6.

Theoretical probability = $\dfrac{\text{Favorable outcomes}}{\text{Total outcomes}} = \dfrac{5}{6}$

---

**EXAMPLE:**

What is the probability that the spinner will not stop on c?

a. $\dfrac{1}{2}$    b. $\dfrac{1}{4}$    c. $\dfrac{3}{4}$    d. $\dfrac{2}{3}$

The spinner has only four areas; a, b, c and d. Therefore, the number of possible outcomes is 4.

3 of the areas are **not** c. Therefore, the number of favorable outcomes is 3.

Theoretical probability = $\dfrac{\text{Favorable outcomes}}{\text{Total outcomes}} = \dfrac{3}{4}$

The correct answer is **c.**

45

© 2007 Simplified Solutions for Math, Inc.

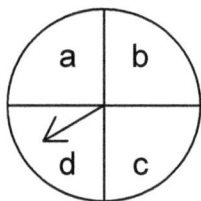

1. What is the probability that the spinner will not stop on c?

   a. $\dfrac{1}{2}$    b. $\dfrac{1}{4}$

   c. $\dfrac{3}{4}$    d. $\dfrac{2}{3}$

2. If a fair quarter is flipped. What is the probability that it will not land heads up?

   a. $\dfrac{1}{4}$    b. $\dfrac{1}{25}$

   c. $\dfrac{1}{3}$    d. $\dfrac{1}{2}$

3. If a fair number cube is rolled once, what is the probability of not getting a two?

   a. $\dfrac{1}{6}$    b. $\dfrac{1}{2}$

   c. $\dfrac{5}{6}$    d. $\dfrac{1}{3}$

A deck of cards contains a total of 52 cards divided into the black cards (spades and clubs) and the red cards (diamonds and hearts). Note that the spades, clubs, diamonds and hearts are also called the four suits. Use this information to answer Questions 4 through 6.

4. If you pick a card at random from a complete deck of cards, what is the probability that it will not be a diamond?

   a. $\dfrac{1}{4}$    b. $\dfrac{3}{13}$

   c. $\dfrac{1}{2}$    d. $\dfrac{3}{4}$

5. If you pick a card at random from a complete suit of clubs, what is the probability that it will not be an eight?

   a. $\dfrac{12}{13}$    b. $\dfrac{8}{13}$

   c. $\dfrac{1}{12}$    d. $\dfrac{1}{13}$

6. If you pick a card at random from a complete deck of cards, what is the probability that it will not be an ace?

   a. $\dfrac{1}{4}$    b. $\dfrac{1}{13}$

   c. $\dfrac{1}{12}$    d. $\dfrac{12}{13}$

If two fair number cubes are rolled at the same time, then the theoretical probability of their sums are listed in the table below. Use this table to help answer Questions 7 through 9.

Number cube 1

| Sum | 1 | 2 | 3 | 4 | 5 | 6 |
|---|---|---|---|---|---|---|
| 1 | 2 | 3 | 4 | 5 | 6 | 7 |
| 2 | 3 | 4 | 5 | 6 | 7 | 8 |
| 3 | 4 | 5 | 6 | 7 | 8 | 9 |
| 4 | 5 | 6 | 7 | 8 | 9 | 10 |
| 5 | 6 | 7 | 8 | 9 | 10 | 11 |
| 6 | 7 | 8 | 9 | 10 | 11 | 12 |

Number cube 2

7. The probability of rolling a sum of three is two out of thirty-six. What is the probability of not rolling a three?

    a. $\frac{1}{18}$    b. $\frac{17}{18}$

    c. $\frac{1}{9}$    d. $\frac{1}{6}$

8. What is the probability of not rolling a sum of six?

    a. $\frac{5}{36}$    b. $\frac{1}{4}$

    c. $\frac{31}{36}$    d. $\frac{5}{18}$

9. If the probability of rolling a sum of nine is one-ninth and the probability of rolling a sum of ten one-twelfth, what is the probability of not having a sum of nine or ten?

    a. $\frac{11}{12}$    b. $\frac{5}{6}$

    c. $\frac{29}{36}$    d. $\frac{1}{6}$

10. A bag contains 3 green marbles, 4 orange marbles, and 2 yellow marbles. If you cannot see the marbles and they are all the same size, what is the probability that you will be able to reach into the bag and not pick out one green marble?

    a. $\frac{2}{3}$    b. $\frac{1}{3}$

    c. $\frac{1}{9}$    d. $\frac{1}{6}$

11. A bag contains 5 green marbles, 4 orange marbles, and 3 yellow marbles. If you cannot see the marbles and they are all the same size, what is the probability that you will be able to reach into the bag and not pick an orange marble?

    a. $\frac{1}{12}$    b. $\frac{5}{12}$

    c. $\frac{3}{4}$    d. $\frac{2}{3}$

# CAHSEE Bench Mark Practice 14

The possible outcomes of flipping a fair quarter three times is contained in the table below. Use this information to answer Questions 12 through 14.

Flip Number

| 1 | 2 | 3 |
|---|---|---|
| H | H | H |
| H | H | T |
| H | T | H |
| H | T | T |
| T | H | H |
| T | H | T |
| T | T | H |
| T | T | T |

**12.** What is the total of possible outcomes?

a. 24   b. 8

c. 12   d. 4

**13.** What is the probability of not getting three heads?

a. $\frac{7}{8}$   b. $\frac{1}{8}$

c. $\frac{3}{8}$   d. $\frac{1}{2}$

**14.** What is the probability of not getting two heads and one tail?

a. $\frac{1}{2}$   b. $\frac{3}{8}$

c. $\frac{5}{8}$   d. $\frac{3}{4}$

**15.** Each letter of the word MATH is on its own note card, lying face down on a desk. If you pick up one note card, what is the probability it will not be the letter A?

a. $\frac{1}{2}$   b. $\frac{3}{4}$

c. $\frac{1}{4}$   d. $\frac{1}{3}$

**16.** A classroom raffle contains the names of 20 students. If there are 12 females and 8 males in the class, what is the probability that the name selected will not be a male?

a. $\frac{1}{2}$   b. $\frac{2}{5}$

c. $\frac{2}{3}$   d. $\frac{3}{5}$

**17.** If the probability of an event happening is 37%, then what is the probability that the event will not happen?

a. 0.63   b. 37%

c. $\frac{2}{3}$   d. $\frac{3}{5}$

**18.** If the probability of an event happening is 65%, then what is the probability that the event will not happen?

a. 0.65   b. $\frac{7}{20}$

c. $\frac{2}{3}$   d. $\frac{3}{5}$

48

© 2007 Simplified Solutions for Math, Inc.

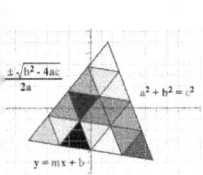

Students will successfully understand the difference
between independent and dependent events.

**CA Standard:** Grade 6, Statistics, Data analysis, and Probability 3.5
**CAHSEE Strand:** Statistics, Data analysis, and Probability

| **Vocabulary:** | **independent** | free from the determination of another |
|---|---|---|
| | **dependent** | influenced by something else |

**Independent** events are events where the outcome of the first event does not affect the outcome of the second event.

*To compute the probability of two independent events, you multiply the probability of the first event by the probability of the second event.*

For example, what is the probability of flipping a fair coin and getting heads, then rolling a number cube and getting a six?

The probability of getting heads is $\frac{1}{2}$. The probability of rolling a 6 is $\frac{1}{6}$.

Therefore, $\frac{1}{2} \cdot \frac{1}{6} = \frac{1}{12}$

**Dependent** events are events where the outcome of the first event affects the outcome of the second event.

*To compute the probability of two dependent events, you multiply the probability of the first event by the probability of the second event, after the first event has occurred.*

For example, what is the probability of selecting the 5 of diamonds from a fair deck of cards, and without replacement, then selecting a 10?

The probability of selecting the 5 of diamonds is $\frac{1}{52}$ ← one 5 of diamonds / ← 52 cards in the deck

The probability of next selecting a 10 is $\frac{4}{51}$ ← four 10s in a deck / ← 51 cards left in the deck

Therefore, $\frac{1}{52} \cdot \frac{4}{51} = \frac{4}{2652} = \frac{1}{663}$

| **EXAMPLE:** | Veronica's **event** will list the **outcomes** of flipping a fair coin five times. Which of the following best describes Veronica's event? |
|---|---|

    **a.** Independent         **b.** Dependent

    **c.** Need more information to determine independence or dependence.     **d.** If Veronica's coin lands tails up twice in a row, she should get a different coin.

Any flip of a coin will not affect the next flip. This is an **independent** event.

The correct answer is **a.**

1. Veronica's **event** will list the **outcomes** of flipping a fair coin five times. Which of the following best describes Veronica's event?

   a.  Independent.

   b.  Dependent.

   c.  Need more information to determine independence or dependence.

   d.  If Veronica's coin lands tails up twice in a row, she should get a different coin.

2. Brianna's **event** will list the **outcomes** of drawing two cards from a complete deck of 52 cards. Which of the following best describes Brianna's event?

   a.  Independent.

   b.  Dependent.

   c.  Need more information to determine independence or dependence.

   d.  If Briana draws two Clubs in a row, she should get a different deck of cards.

3. Philip's **event** will list the **outcomes** of drawing two cards from a complete deck of 52 cards. Philip will draw the first card and then, without putting the first card back in the deck, he will draw the second card. Which of the following best describes Philip's event?

   a.  Independent.

   b.  Dependent.

   c.  Need more information to determine independence or dependence.

   d.  If Philip draws two Hearts in a row, he should get a different deck of cards.

4. Elisa's **event** will list the **outcomes** of flipping a fair coin three times and rolling a die three times. For each outcome, she will flip the coin and wait until the coin has landed before she rolls the die. Which of the following best describes Elisa's event?

   a.  Independent.

   b.  Dependent.

   c.  Need more information to determine independence or dependence.

   d.  If Elisa's rolls a five twice in a row, she should get a different die.

5. Edgar's **event** will list the **outcomes** of drawing two marbles from a bag containing seven green, four yellow, and nine tan marbles. In each outcome, he will draw the first marble with his left hand and keep it in his left hand, and then he will draw the second marble with his right hand. Which of the following best describes Edgar's event?

   a.  Independent.

   b.  Dependent.

   c.  Need more information to determine independence or dependence.

   d.  Edgar's event would have better results if he used gold, brown and orange marbles.

6. Ashlyn's **event** will list the **outcomes** of drawing two marbles from a bag containing eight gold, five brown, and ten orange marbles. In each outcome, she will draw the first marble with her left hand and she will draw the second marble with her right hand. Which of the following best describes Ashlyn's event?

   a. Independent.

   b. Dependent.

   c. Need more information to determine independence or dependence.

   d. Ashlyn's event would have better results if she used green, yellow, and tan marbles.

7. Jessica's **event** will list the **outcomes** of flipping a fair coin six times. If she records a head for the first five outcomes, what is the probability that the coin will land heads up on the final flip?

   a. Since this is a dependent event, the probability remains 50% that the coin will land heads up.

   b. Since this is a dependent event, the probability is 1 out of 64.

   c. Since this is an independent event, the probability is 1 out of 64.

   d. Since this is an independent event, the probability remains 50% that the coin will land heads up.

8. Keyonna's **event** will list the **outcomes** of drawing two cards from a complete deck of 52 cards. Keyonna will draw the first card and then, without putting the first card back in the deck, she will draw the second card. If she draws a jack on the first draw, what is the probability that she will draw a jack on the second draw?

   a. Since the event is dependent, she will have a 1 out of 17 chance to draw the second jack.

   b. Since the event is dependent, she will have a 1 out of 13 chance to draw the second jack.

   c. Need more information to make a determination.

   d. Since the event is independent, she will have a 1 out of 17 chance to draw the second jack.

9. A bag contains 5 green marbles, 4 orange marbles, and 2 yellow marbles. If an orange marble is drawn and not replaced, what is the theoretical probability that a second orange marble will be drawn next?

   a. $\frac{1}{5}$      b. $\frac{5}{11}$

   c. $\frac{4}{11}$      d. $\frac{3}{10}$

10. A bag contains 5 green marbles, 4 orange marbles, and 2 yellow marbles. What is the theoretical probability that two orange marbles will be drawn at the same time?

   a. $\frac{1}{5}$      b. $\frac{6}{55}$

   c. $\frac{4}{11}$      d. $\frac{3}{10}$

11. Natasha wants to draw two cards from a set of face cards (jack, queen, king, and ace). All four suits are in the set of face cards. Natasha will draw the the two cards without replacement. What is the probability that she will draw two kings?

   a. $\frac{1}{4}$      b. $\frac{1}{5}$

   c. $\frac{1}{20}$      d. $\frac{1}{2}$

12. Jacky wants to draw two cards from a set of face cards (jack, queen, king, and ace). All four suits are in the set of face cards. Jacky will draw the the two cards without replacement. If Jacky draws a king on the first draw, then what is the probability that he will draw a king on the second draw?

   a. $\frac{1}{4}$      b. $\frac{1}{5}$

   c. $\frac{1}{20}$      d. $\frac{1}{2}$

13. Fam wants to draw two cards from a set of face cards (jack, queen, king, and ace). All four suits are in the set of face cards. Fam will draw the the two cards with replacement. If Fam draws a king on the first draw, then what is the probability that she will draw a king on the second draw?

   a. $\frac{1}{4}$      b. $\frac{1}{5}$

   c. $\frac{1}{20}$      d. $\frac{1}{2}$

14. Each letter of the word MATH is on its own note card, lying face down on a desk. Jacob will pick up two note cards without replacement. On the first card, Jacob picks up the M, what is the probability that the next card will be the letter A?

   a. $\frac{1}{4}$      b. $\frac{1}{12}$

   c. $\frac{1}{3}$      d. $\frac{1}{2}$

15. Each letter of the word MATH is on its own note card, lying face down on a desk. Beatrice will pick up two note cards without replacement. What is the probability that Beatrice will pick up the M and the A?

   a. $\frac{1}{4}$      b. $\frac{1}{12}$

   c. $\frac{1}{3}$      d. $\frac{1}{2}$

**16.** Each letter of MATH IS FUN is on its own note card, lying face down on a desk. Sou wants to pick a card and then roll a six sided number cube. If Sou picks the letter I, what is the probability that he will roll a five?

    **a.**   $\dfrac{1}{9}$      **b.**   $\dfrac{5}{54}$

    **c.**   $\dfrac{1}{54}$      **d.**   $\dfrac{1}{6}$

**17.** Each letter of MATH IS FUN is on its own note card, lying face down on a desk. Sandy wants to pick a card and then roll a six sided number cube. What is the probability that she will pick the I and roll a five?

    **a.**   $\dfrac{1}{9}$      **b.**   $\dfrac{5}{54}$

    **c.**   $\dfrac{1}{54}$      **d.**   $\dfrac{1}{6}$

**18.** Each letter of MATH IS FUN is on its own note card, lying face down on a desk. Lucky wants to pick two cards without replacement. What is the probability that he will pick the I and the N?

    **a.**   $\dfrac{1}{72}$      **b.**   $\dfrac{1}{8}$

    **c.**   $\dfrac{1}{9}$      **d.**   $\dfrac{2}{9}$

**19.** Each letter of MATH IS FUN is on its own note card, lying face down on a desk. Lucy wants to pick two cards without replacement. If Lucy draws the F, what is the probability that she will pick the T?

    **a.**   $\dfrac{1}{72}$      **b.**   $\dfrac{1}{8}$

    **c.**   $\dfrac{1}{9}$      **d.**   $\dfrac{2}{9}$

**20.** Saul has a standard deck of cards and two fair number cubes. Which statement below best describes the theoretical probability for Saul if he wants to randomly pick a black seven and roll the two number cubes for a sum of seven.

*Hint: Draw a table for the sum of rolling two number cubes.*

    **a.**   Since this is a dependent event, the probability for drawing a black seven is 2 out of 52.

    **b.**   Since this is a dependent event, the probability is 1 out of 156.

    **c.**   Since this is an independent event, the probability is 1 out of 26.

    **d.**   Since this is an independent event, the probability is 1 out of 156.

### Students will successfully know various displays of data.

**CA Standard:** Grade 7, Statistics, Data analysis, and Probability 1.1
**CAHSEE Strand:** Statistics, Data analysis, and Probability

*Simplified Solutions*
*For Math Inc.*

---

**Vocabulary:**

| | |
|---|---|
| **frequency table** | table which lists each data item with the number of times it occurs |
| **pie chart (circle graph)** | graph which displays data as sections of a circle |
| **bar graph** | graph which compares amounts |
| **histogram** | a bar graph where the height of the bar is the frequency of the data; there are no spaces between the bars |
| **line graph** | graph which shows changes over time |

The following are examples of different graphic (pictorial) ways of displaying data.

**Frequency table**

| Grade | 6 | 7 | 8 |
|---|---|---|---|
| # of students | 21 | 32 | 27 |

**Pie chart (circle graph)**

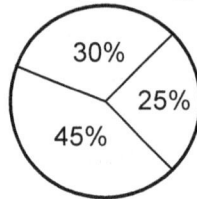

30%
25%
45%

**Bar graph**

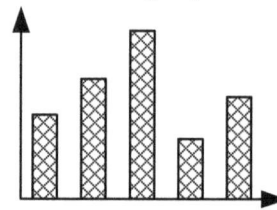

**Histogram**

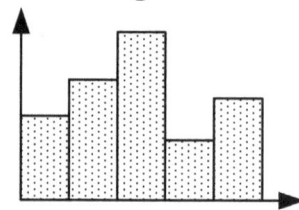

**Line graph**

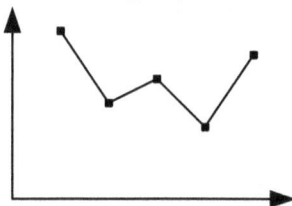

We will be examining different graphical displays and make observations and judge the validity of certain claims.

---

**EXAMPLE:** The following frequency table represents the grades of a certain high school math class.

| Grade | A | B | C | D | F |
|---|---|---|---|---|---|
| # of Students | 4 | 8 | 18 | 8 | 2 |

**Which of the following statements is false?**

a. Twice as many students received an A as received an F.

b. Students who received a B and a D combined are more than those who received a C.

c. Twenty percent of the students received a B.

d. Five percent of the students received an F.

By observation, we will judge the validity of each answer, eliminate incorrect choices and select the correct one.

*We are looking for a false statement so we will eliminate true statements.*

a. Twice as many students received an A as received an F.
A = 4 and F = 2; 2(2) = 4, **a** is a **true** statement.

b. Students who received a B and a D combined are more than those who received a C.
B = 8 and D = 8; 8 + 8 = 16; C = 18; 16 is not more than 18, **b** is a **false** statement.

The correct answer is **b.**

1. The following frequency table represents the grades of a certain high school math class.

| Grade | A | B | C | D | F |
|-------|---|---|----|---|---|
| # of Students | 4 | 8 | 18 | 8 | 2 |

Which of the following statements is false?

a. Twice as many students received an A as received an F.

b. Students who received a B and a D combined are more than those who received a C.

c. Twenty percent of the students received a B.

d. Five percent of the students received an F.

2. The following pie chart represents the grades of fifty students in two math classes.

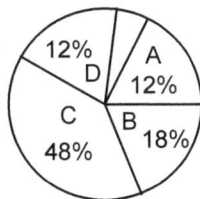

The information for the grade of F is missing. Determine which statement best describes the missing data.

a. Five students, which is ten percent of all the students, received a grade of F.

b. Five students, which is twelve percent of all the students, received a grade of F.

c. Six students, which is ten percent of all the students, received a grade of F.

d. Six students, which is twelve percent of all the students, received a grade of F.

3. The histogram below represents the grades for one class.

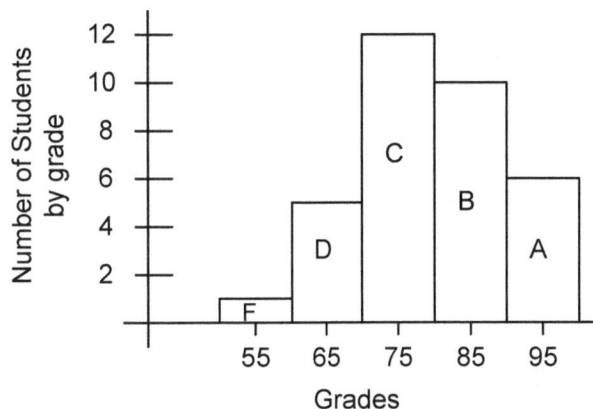

Which of the following statements best describes the data?

a. About 32% of the students had a grade of C.

b. About 5% of the students had a grade of F.

c. About 29% of the students had a grade of B.

d. About 21% of the students had a grade of A.

4. The table below represents the enrollment cost and monthly cost of a cell phone for four companies. If the number of minutes is the same for each plan, which company would cost the least for one year?

| Company | Enrollment Cost | Monthly Cost |
|---------|-----------------|--------------|
| 1 | 110 | 65 |
| 2 | 140 | 60 |
| 3 | 130 | 55 |
| 4 | 150 | 50 |

a. 1     b. 2

c. 3     d. 4

**5.** The line graph below represents the change of the daily cost of fresh lobster during five days in December.

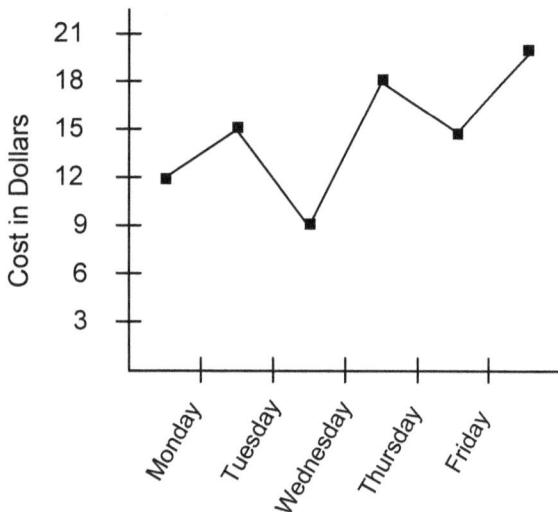

The cost of a Lobster increased by a certain amount on Monday. Determine which statement below is false.

**a.** Friday's ending price is the same as Monday's starting price.

**b.** Tuesday's starting price is the same as Thursday's ending price.

**c.** Lobsters were the cheapest on Tuesday night and Wednesday morning.

**d.** Lobsters were most expensive on Friday.

**6.** A teacher drew the following circle graph to represent the number of siblings of his thirty-four students.

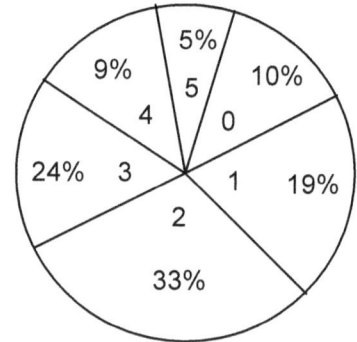

Use the pie chart above to determine which statement is true.

**a.** About five students have five siblings.

**b.** About eleven students have two siblings.

**c.** About ten students have three siblings.

**d.** About five students are only children.

**7.** The line graph below represents the change of the daily cost of fresh lobster during five days in December.

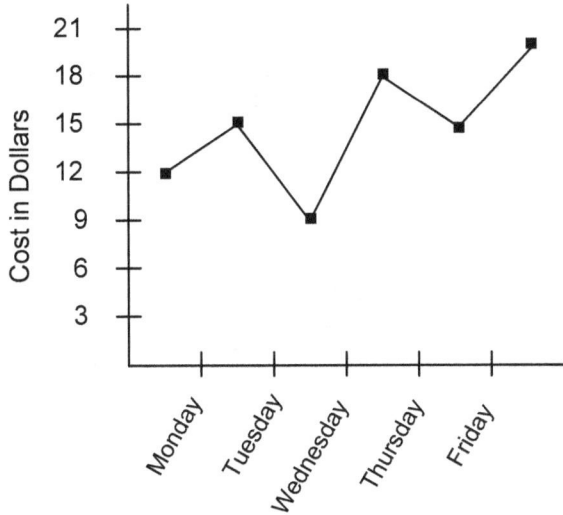

Determine which day experienced the greatest change in Lobster daily cost.

a. Monday

b. Tuesday

c. Wednesday

d. Friday

**8.** The table below represents the enrollment cost and monthly cost for comparable health insurance policies for four companies. Which company would cost the least for one year?

| Company | Enrollment Cost | Monthly Cost |
|---------|-----------------|--------------|
| 1 | 750 | 70 |
| 2 | 770 | 60 |
| 3 | 760 | 75 |
| 4 | 780 | 65 |

a. 1  b. 2

c. 3  d. 4

**9.** A family wanted to look at their annual distribution of net income for the year.

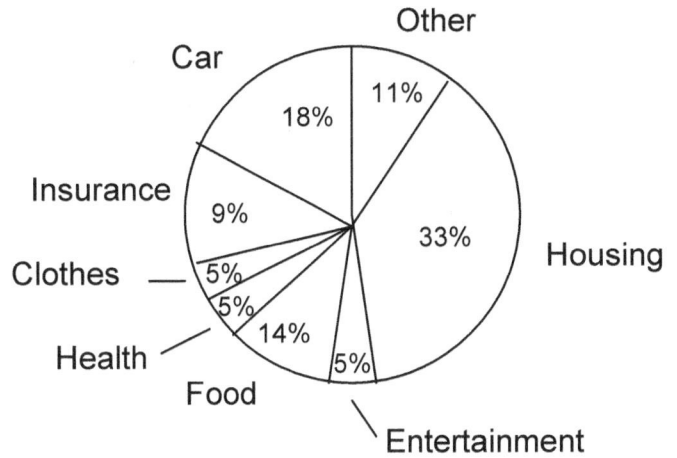

The family forecasts that they will have an annual net income of $42000.00. Use this information and the pie chart to determine which of the below statements is false.

a. Food expense will be $588.00 per month.

b. Annual Clothing, Health, and Entertainment will cost $6300.00

c. Housing will cost $1155.00 per month.

d. Annual Car expenses will be $7560.00.

**10.** A certain drug company wants to market a new anti-depression drug. The bar graph below shows the results of testing.

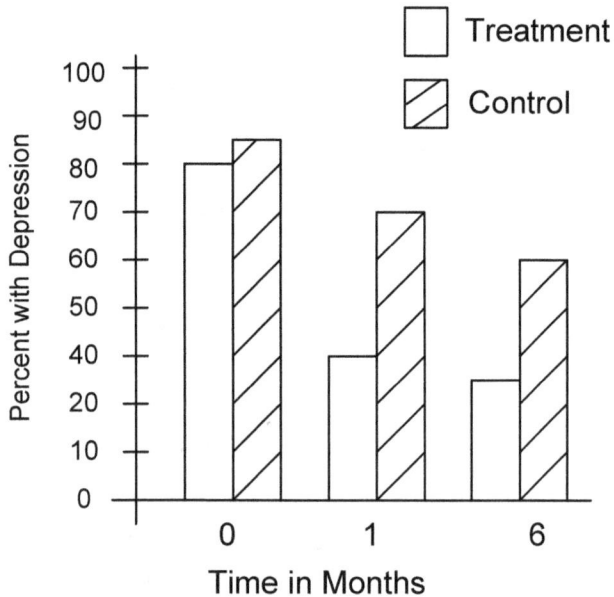

The Treatment group is the only group receiving the drug. Using the information displayed in the bar graph, determine which statement is true.

a. At a certain point in time, all the participants had an 85% depression rate.

b. The treatment group had an increase in depression over the six month study.

c. At a certain point in time, the participants experienced similar rates of depression.

d. Based upon the results of the six month study, the company should conclude that the drug is not working.

**11.** The table below shows the quiz scores for four students.

|       | Q1 | Q2 | Q3 | Q4 | Q5 | Q6 |
|-------|----|----|----|----|----|----|
| Hien  | 7  | 6  | 2  | 5  | 6  | 1  |
| Myles | 8  | 9  | 0  | 6  | 8  | 9  |
| Ida   | 9  | 5  | 3  | 8  | 5  | 8  |
| Jaime | 9  | 10 | 6  | 9  | 10 | 9  |

Each quiz has a total point value of ten. Use the information in the table to draw the best conclusion for the data.

a. Based upon Hien's quiz scores, we may conclude that Hien needs more practice with her math. That is, she needs to get some help with her studies.

b. Based upon Myles' other quiz scores, we may conclude that Myles was absent for Quiz 3.

c. Based upon Ida's quiz scores, she can expect a grade of C.

d. Based upon Jaime's quiz scores, we may conclude that Jaime does not understand the material.

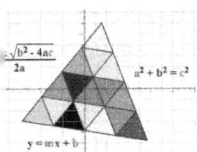

Students will successfully represent
numerical values on a scatter plot.

**CA Standard:** Grade 7, Statistics, Data analysis, and Probability 1.2
**CAHSEE Strand:** Statistics, Data analysis, and Probability

*S*implified
*S*olutions
For Math Inc.

---

**Vocabulary:**     **scatter plot**     a graph that displays the relationship between two sets of data

---

Scatter plots can be used to determine certain trends and the degree of these trends.
Following are examples of different correlations.

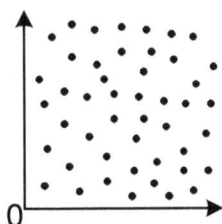

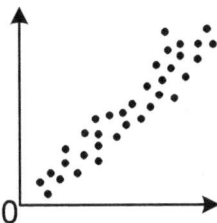

**Zero Correlation**          **Strong Positive Correlation**          **Weak Positive Correlation**

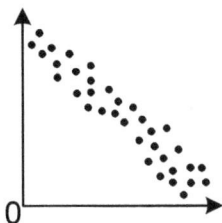

**Strong Negative Correlation**          **Weak Negative Correlation**

---

**EXAMPLE:**     The below scatter plot appears to be what type of correlation?

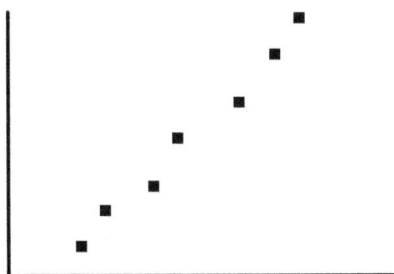

a.   Strong Positive Correlation

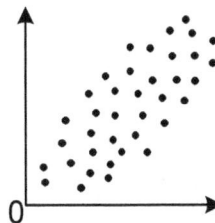

b.   Strong Negative Correlation

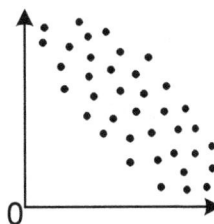

c.   Weak Positive Correlation

d.   Weak Negative Correlation

The data displayed on this scatter plot appears to have a positive trend. The data is
grouped in an almost linear array. We can determine that the trend displayed has a
**strong positive correlation**.

The correct answer is **a.**

**1.** The below scatter plot appears to be what type of correlation?

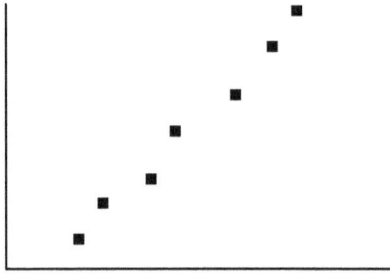

a. Strong Positive Correlation

b. Strong Negative Correlation

c. Weak Positive Correlation

d. Weak Negative Correlation

**2.** The below scatter plot appears to be what type of correlation?

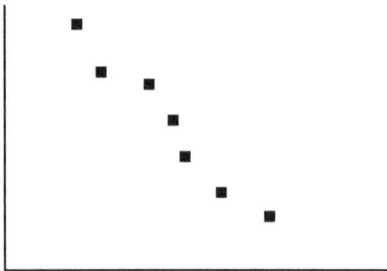

a. Strong Positive Correlation

b. Strong Negative Correlation

c. Zero Correlation

d. Weak Negative Correlation

**3.** The below scatter plot appears to be what type of correlation?

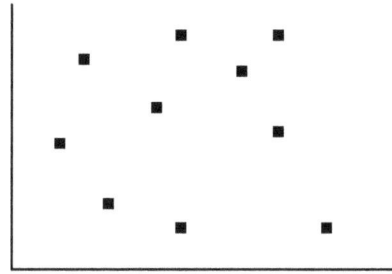

a. Strong Positive Correlation

b. Strong Negative Correlation

c. Weak Positive Correlation

d. Zero Correlation

**4.** The below scatter plot appears to be what type of correlation?

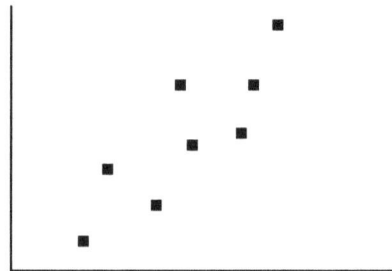

a. Strong Positive Correlation

b. Zero Correlation

c. Weak Positive Correlation

d. Weak Negative Correlation

**5.** The below scatter plot appears to be what type of correlation?

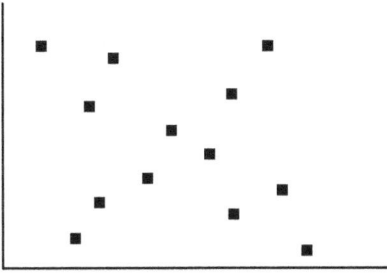

a. Strong Positive Correlation

b. Strong Negative Correlation

c. Zero Correlation

d. Weak Negative Correlation

**6.** The below scatter plot appears to be what type of correlation?

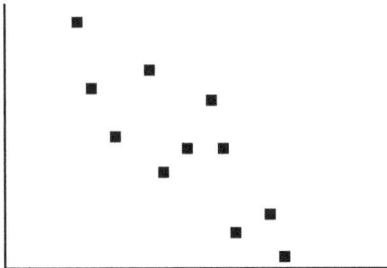

a. Zero Correlation

b. Strong Negative Correlation

c. Weak Positive Correlation

d. Weak Negative Correlation

**7.** A chemist is using the Henderson-Hasselbalch equation to measure the the pH balance of the acid alanine as a base is slowly added. The scatter plot below is the result of the data collected.

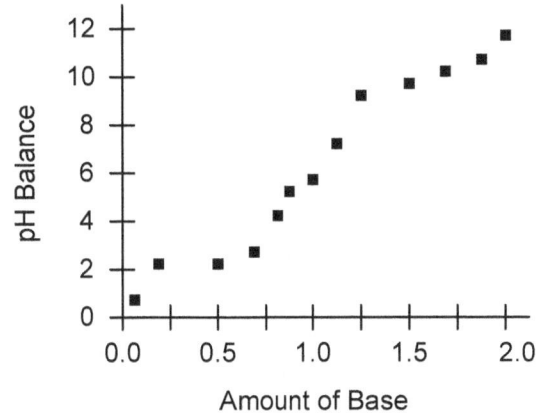

Which statement best supports the data graphed on the scatter plot?

a. Appears to be a positive correlation where the pH increases as the amount of Base increases.

b. Appears to be a negative correlation where the pH increases and the amount of base decreases.

c. Appears to be a positive correlation where the pH increases as the amount of Base decreases.

d. Appears to be a negative correlation where the pH decreases as the amount of Base increases.

**8.** A doctor has ordered a glucose tolerance test to check the patient for diabetes. After an initial blood test, the patient drinks 75 grams of a glucose solution and the blood is drawn at regular intervals. The scatter plot below is the result of the data collected.

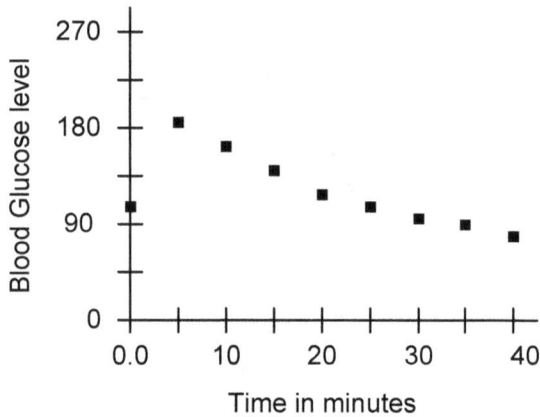

Which statement best supports the data graphed on the scatter plot?

a. Not counting the initial test, as the time increases, the blood glucose increases.

b. Not counting the initial test, as the time increases, the blood glucose decreases.

c. Not counting the initial test, there does not appear to be any correlation between the data.

d. Not counting the initial test, the blood glucose remains constant as the time increases.

**9.** A microbiologist is measuring the amount of heat produced during a chemical reaction over a period of time. The scatter plot below is the result of the data collected.

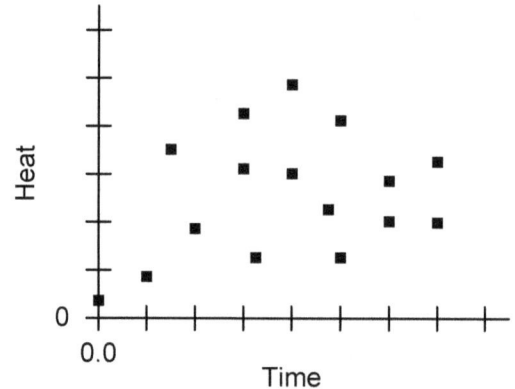

Which statement best supports the data graphed on the scatter plot?

a. As the time increases, the heat increases.

b. As the time increases, the heat decreases.

c. As the time increases, the heat remains constant.

d. There does not appear to be any correlation between the data.

**10.** A certain college has produced a scatter plot of their students income at age 25 as compared to the number of years that the student attended the college.

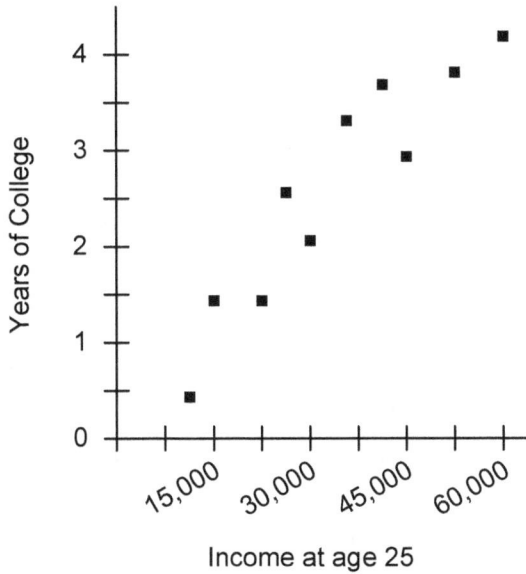

Income at age 25

Which statement best supports the data graphed on the scatter plot?

a. No correlation exists between years in college and income earned.

b. As the time in college increases, the future income earned decreases.

c. As the time in college decreases, the future income earned decreases.

d. As the time in college decreases, the future income earned increases.

**11.** A nutritionist has produced a scatter plot of the number of calories as carbohydrates in foods.

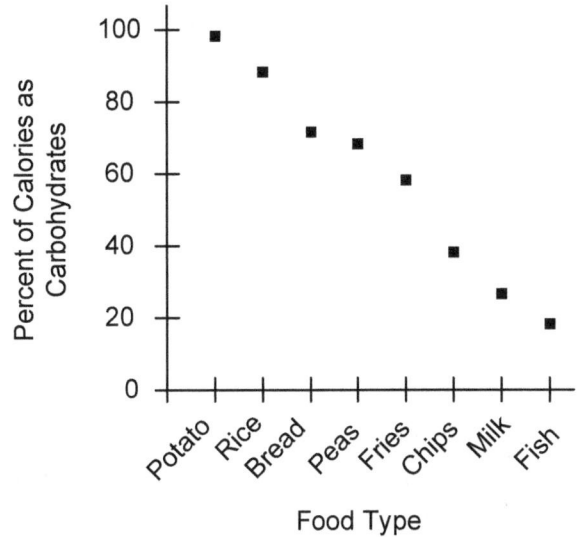

Food Type

Which statement best supports the data graphed on the scatter plot?

a. The negative correlation indicates that Milk and Fish provide an excellent source of carbohydrates.

b. The negative correlation indicates that the best sources of carbohydrates are Potatoes and Rice.

c. The negative correlation indicates that Milk is a better source of carbohydrates than Peas.

d. The positive correlation indicates that the best sources of carbohydrates are Potatoes and Rice.

# CAHSEE Unit 3 Exam
## Bench Marks 1 - 17

**BM 1.** The diameter of a hydrogen atom is $5.0 \times 10^{-8}$ cm. What is this number in standard notation?

    **a.** 0.000000005     **b.** 0.0000005

    **c.** 0.00000005     **d.** 0.000005

**BM 2.** Which of the following expressions results in a positive number?

    **a.** 1 + (-2)     **b.** -1 + 2

    **c.** -1 - 2     **d.** -2 - 1

**BM 3.** If 15 out of 25 families on the block own cats, what is the percentage of families that own cats?

    **a.** 85%     **b.** 80%

    **c.** 50%     **d.** 60%

**BM 4.** The price of a box of pencils has decreased from $2.00 to $1.50. What is the percent of decrease?

    **a.** 25%     **b.** 50%

    **c.** 20%     **d.** 10%

**BM 5.** A CD regularly sells for $22.00. It is on sale for 25% off. What is the sale price of the CD?

    **a.** $11.00     **b.** $15.60

    **c.** $17.00     **d.** $16.50

**BM 6.** Multiply. $4^{-6} \cdot 4^2$

    **a.** $4^{-8}$     **b.** $16^{-4}$

    **c.** $4^{-4}$     **d.** $16^8$

**BM 7.** What is $\frac{3}{8} - \frac{1}{6}$ ?

    **a.** $\frac{2}{2}$     **b.** $\frac{4}{14}$

    **c.** $\frac{5}{24}$     **d.** $\frac{2}{48}$

**BM 8.** $(5^4)^6$

    **a.** $5^{24}$     **b.** $5^{10}$

    **c.** $20^6$     **d.** $25^6$

**BM 9.** The square of a <u>whole</u> number is between 100 and 200. The number must be between

    **a.** 5 and 10     **b.** 10 and 15

    **c.** 15 and 20     **d.** 20 and 25

**BM 10.** What is the absolute value of 2?

    **a.** $\frac{1}{2}$     **b.** $\frac{-1}{2}$

    **c.** -2     **d.** 2

**BM 11.** The box below shows Elijah's last five quiz scores.

    | 12, 15, 13, 12, 17 |

    Find the mode of Elijah's scores.

    **a.** 13     **b.** 12

    **c.** 17     **d.** 5

**BM 12.** The table below shows the quiz scores for four students. Which student had the third lowest quiz score?

|       | Q1 | Q2 | Q3 | Q4 | Q5 | Q6 |
|-------|----|----|----|----|----|----|
| Hien  | 7  | 6  | 5  | 5  | 6  | 1  |
| Myles | 8  | 9  | 0  | 6  | 8  | 9  |
| Ida   | 9  | 5  | 7  | 8  | 4  | 8  |
| Jaime | 8  | 10 | 9  | 7  | 10 | 9  |

**a.** Hien      **b.** Myles

**c.** Ida      **d.** Jaime

**BM 13.** A bag contains 6 green marbles, 10 orange marbles, and 14 yellow marbles. If you cannot see the marbles and they are all the same size, what is the probability that you will be able to reach into the bag and pick an orange marble?

**a.** $\dfrac{1}{12}$      **b.** $\dfrac{1}{4}$

**c.** $\dfrac{1}{3}$      **d.** $\dfrac{2}{3}$

**BM 14.** A classroom raffle contains the names of 20 students. If there are 12 females and 8 males in the class, what is the probability that the name selected will not be a male?

**a.** $\dfrac{1}{2}$      **b.** $\dfrac{2}{5}$

**c.** $\dfrac{2}{3}$      **d.** $\dfrac{3}{5}$

**BM 15.** Each letter of the word MATH is on its own note card, lying face down on a desk. Beatrice will pick up two note cards without replacement. What is the probability that Beatrice will pick up the M and the A?

**a.** $\dfrac{1}{4}$      **b.** $\dfrac{1}{12}$

**c.** $\dfrac{1}{3}$      **d.** $\dfrac{1}{2}$

**BM 16.** The table below represents the enrollment cost and monthly cost of a cell phone for four companies. If the number of minutes is the same for each plan, which company would cost the least for one year?

| Company | Enrollment cost | Monthly Cost |
|---------|-----------------|--------------|
| 1       | 110             | 65           |
| 2       | 140             | 60           |
| 3       | 130             | 55           |
| 4       | 150             | 50           |

**a.** 1      **b.** 2

**c.** 3      **d.** 4

**BM 17.** The below scatter plot appears to be what type of correlation?

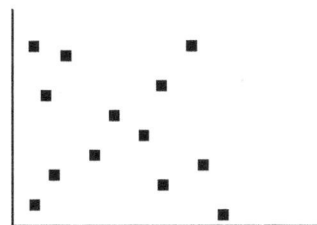

**a.** Strong Positive Correlation

**b.** Strong Negative Correlation

**c.** Zero Correlation

**d.** Weak Negative Correlation

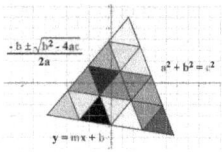

*Simplified Solutions*
*For Math Inc.*

---

| **Vocabulary:** | | |
|---|---|---|
| **milli** | prefix meaning one thousandth part of, or | $\frac{1}{1000}$ |
| **centi** | prefix meaning one hundredth part of, or | $\frac{1}{100}$ |
| **kilo** | prefix meaning 1,000 | |

---

Comparing and converting measurement systems is a simple process of multiplication and division. The skill lies in knowing how and when to do so.

We will be dealing primarily with customary and metric systems of length.

The **meter** is the standard metric unit of measurement.
The **foot** is the standard customary unit of measurement.

1 **meter** = 100 **centimeters** = 1,000 **millimeters**          1 **foot** = 12 **inches**

1 **kilometer** = 1,000 **meters**          1 **yard** = 3 **feet**

1 **mile** = 5,280 **feet** = 1,760 **yards**

Following are some simple approximations;

For estimating,     a **millimeter** is about the thickness of a dime

a **centimeter** is about a half of an inch

a **meter** is about a yard

a **kilometer** is a little over a half of a mile.

We will also be dealing with units of time.          1 **hour** = 60 **minutes** = 3,600 **seconds**
The **hour** is the standard unit of measurement.          1 **minute** = 60 **seconds**

---

**EXAMPLE:**

One centimeter is-

    **a.** 10 meters     **b.** $\frac{1}{100}$ of a meter     **c.** $\frac{1}{10}$ of a meter     **d.** 100 meters

A centimeter is a fraction of a meter, so we can eliminate choices **a** and **d**.

The prefix centi means one hundredth part of, or $\frac{1}{100}$

The correct answer is **b.**

---

# CAHSEE Bench Mark Practice 18

**1.** One centimeter is-

   **a.** 10 meters      **b.** $\frac{1}{100}$ of a meter

   **c.** $\frac{1}{10}$ of a meter      **d.** 100 meters

**2.** A bookshelf is 3 meters tall. About how tall is the bookshelf in feet (ft) and inches (in.)? (1 meter ≈ 39 inches)

   **a.** 9 ft 3 in.      **b.** 10 ft 9 in.

   **c.** 10 ft 3 in.      **d.** 9 ft 9 in.

**3.** Chandra ran for one hour and 30 minutes. How many <u>seconds</u> did Chandra run?

   **a.** 4,500      **b.** 5,400

   **c.** 6,300      **d.** 7,200

**4.** Jim is driving at 45 miles per hour, what is his approximate speed in kilometers per hour? (1 mile ≈ 1.6 kilometers)

   **a.** 72      **b.** 81

   **c.** 90      **d.** 99

**5.** One meter is-

   **a.** 10 centimeters      **b.** 1,000 millimeters

   **c.** $\frac{1}{10}$ of a kilometer      **d.** 1,000 centimeters

**6.** A young man is 2 meters tall. About how tall is he in feet (ft) and inches (in.)? (1 meter ≈ 39 inches)

   **a.** 5 ft 6 in.      **b.** 6 ft 0 in.

   **c.** 6 ft 6 in.      **d.** 7 ft 0 in.

**7.** One millimeter is-

   **a.** $\frac{1}{1000}$ of a meter      **b.** $\frac{1}{100}$ of a meter

   **c.** $\frac{1}{10}$ of a meter      **d.** 1000 meters

**8.** Jamile read for two hours. How many <u>seconds</u> did Jamile read?

   **a.** 4,500      **b.** 5,400

   **c.** 6,300      **d.** 7,200

**9.** One kilometer is-

   **a.** 1,000 meters      **b.** $\frac{1}{10}$ of a millimeter

   **c.** $\frac{1}{1000}$ of a meter      **d.** 1,000 centimeters

**10.** Tomarah is driving at 35 miles per hour, what is her approximate speed in kilometers per hour? (1 mile ≈ 1.6 kilometers)

   **a.** 48      **b.** 56

   **c.** 64      **d.** 72

# CAHSEE Bench Mark Practice 18

**11.** One centimeter is-

    **a.** 10 millimeters     **b.** $\frac{1}{1000}$ of a meter

    **c.** $\frac{1}{10}$ of a millimeter     **d.** 100 meters

**12.** A ladder is 4 meters tall. About how tall is the ladder in feet (ft) and inches (in.)? (1 meter ≈ 39 inches)

    **a.** 13 ft 0 in.     **b.** 13 ft 6 in.

    **c.** 14 ft 0 in.     **d.** 14 ft 6 in.

**13.** Nicholas rode his bicycle for 9,000 seconds. How many <u>hours</u> did Nicholas ride his bicycle?

    **a.** 1.5     **b.** 2.0

    **c.** 2.5     **d.** 3.0

**14.** Juan is driving at 60 miles per hour, what is his approximate speed in kilometers per hour? (1 mile ≈ 1.6 kilometers)

    **a.** 64     **b.** 72

    **c.** 84     **d.** 96

**15.** One meter is-

    **a.** 100 centimeters     **b.** 100 millimeters

    **c.** $\frac{1}{10}$ of a kilometer     **d.** 1,000 centimeters

**16.** A building is 22 meters tall. About how tall is it in feet (ft) and inches (in.)? (1 meter ≈ 39 inches)

    **a.** 70 ft 6 in.     **b.** 71 ft 0 in.

    **c.** 71 ft 6 in.     **d.** 72 ft 0 in.

**17.** One millimeter is-

    **a.** $\frac{1}{1000}$ of a kilometer     **b.** $\frac{1}{100}$ of a kilometer

    **c.** $\frac{1}{10}$ of a centimeter     **d.** 100 centimeters

**18.** Rosa slept for 10,800 seconds. How many <u>hours</u> did Rosa sleep?

    **a.** 2.5     **b.** 3.0

    **c.** 3.5     **d.** 4.0

**19.** One kilometer is-

    **a.** 1,000 centimeters     **b.** 10,000 centimeters

    **c.** 100,000 centimeters     **d.** 10 meters

**20.** Anthony is flying his plane at 110 miles per hour, what is his approximate speed in kilometers per hour? (1 mile ≈ 1.6 kilometers)

    **a.** 176     **b.** 192

    **c.** 204     **d.** 216

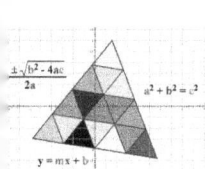

Students will successfully use scale drawings.

**CA Standard:** Grade 7, Measurement and Geometry 1.2
**CAHSEE Strand:** Measurement and Geometry

*Simplified Solutions*
**For Math Inc.**

| Vocabulary: | | |
|---|---|---|
| | ratio | a comparison of two quantities using division |
| | **proportion** | an equality of two ratios |
| | scale drawing | an enlarged or reduced drawing that is similar to the actual object |
| | scale | the ratio of the distance in the drawing to the actual distance |

Scale drawings are very common items. You may very often see them as roadmaps or building blueprints as well as many other things.

Scale drawings must have a key which will describe the ratio of the distance in the drawing to the actual distance, or scale.

For example: The scale drawing of the football field shown below is drawn using a scale of 1 inch (in.) = 30 feet (ft).

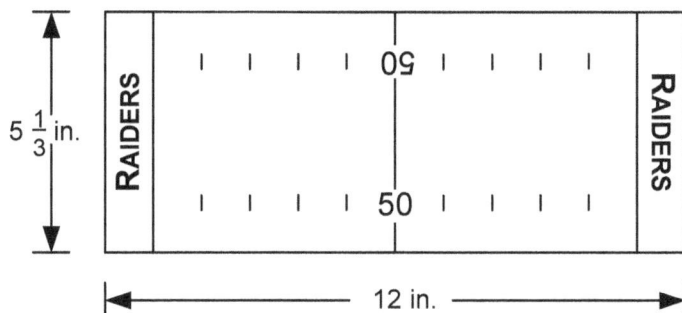

What is the width of the field in feet?

a. 144 ft     b. 132 ft

c. 160 ft     d. 152 ft

**Set up a proportion.**      **Solve for x.**

$$\frac{1 \text{ in.}}{30 \text{ ft}} = \frac{\frac{16}{3} \text{ in.}}{x \text{ ft}} \qquad 5\frac{1}{3} \text{ in.} = \frac{16}{3} \text{ in.} \qquad x = \frac{480}{3} \qquad x = 160$$

The correct answer is **c.**

---

**EXAMPLE:** The actual width (*w*) of a rectangle is 20 inches (in.). Use the scale drawing of the rectangle to find the actual length (*l*).

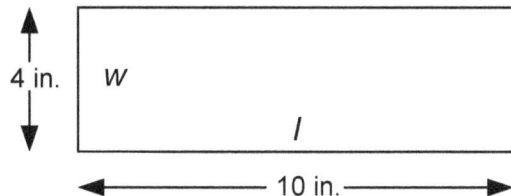

a. 30 in.     b. 40 in.

c. 50 in.     d. 60 in.

Set up a proportion.      Solve for x.

$$\frac{4 \text{ in.}}{20 \text{ in.}} = \frac{10 \text{ in.}}{x \text{ in.}} \qquad \begin{array}{l} 4x = 200 \\ x = 50 \end{array}$$

The correct answer is **c.**

**1.** The actual width (*w*) of a rectangle is 20 inches (in.). Use the scale drawing of the rectangle to find the actual length (*l*).

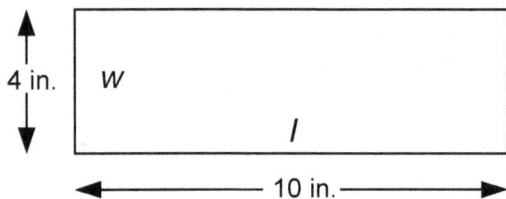

4 in. | *w*
*l*
10 in.

**a.** 30 in.          **b.** 40 in.

**c.** 50 in.          **d.** 60 in.

**2.** The scale drawing of the football field shown below is drawn using a scale of 1 inch (in.) = 80 feet (ft).

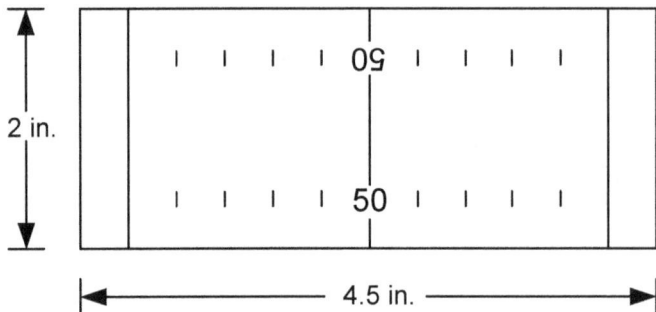

2 in.

50

50

4.5 in.

What is the width of the field in feet?

**a.** 132 ft          **b.** 144 ft

**c.** 152 ft          **d.** 160 ft

**3.** The actual width (*w*) of a rectangle is 12 inches (in.). Use the scale drawing of the rectangle to find the actual length (*l*).

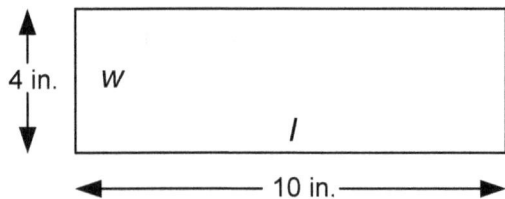

4 in. | *w*
*l*
10 in.

**a.** 30 in.          **b.** 40 in.

**c.** 50 in.          **d.** 60 in.

**4.** The scale drawing of the hockey rink shown below is drawn using a scale of 1 inch (in.) = 50 feet (ft).

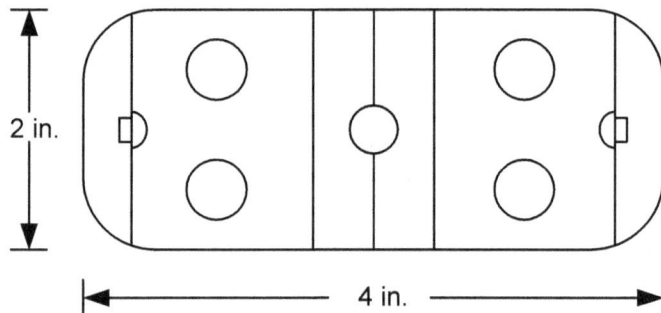

2 in.

4 in.

What is the length of the rink in feet?

**a.** 200 ft          **b.** 180 ft

**c.** 160 ft          **d.** 140 ft

**5.** The actual width (*w*) of a rectangle is 16 inches (in.). Use the scale drawing of the rectangle to find the actual length (*l*).

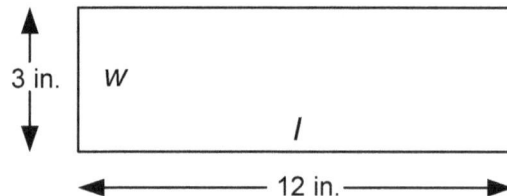

3 in. | *w*
*l*
12 in.

**a.** 48 in.          **b.** 56 in.

**c.** 64 in.          **d.** 72 in.

**6.** The actual width (*w*) of a rectangle is 12 inches (in.). Use the scale drawing of the rectangle to find the actual length (*l*).

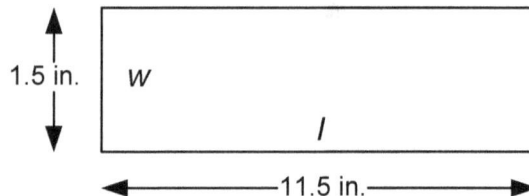

1.5 in. | *w*
*l*
11.5 in.

**a.** 84 in.          **b.** 92 in.

**c.** 104 in.          **d.** 112 in.

**7.** The actual width ($w$) of a rectangle is 12 inches (in.). Use the scale drawing of the rectangle to find the actual length ($l$).

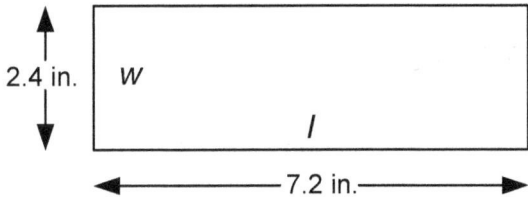

2.4 in.    $w$

$l$

7.2 in.

**a.** 30 in.            **b.** 34 in.

**c.** 36 in.            **d.** 40 in.

**8.** The scale drawing of the soccer field shown below is drawn using a scale of 1 inch (in.) = 30 yards (yd).

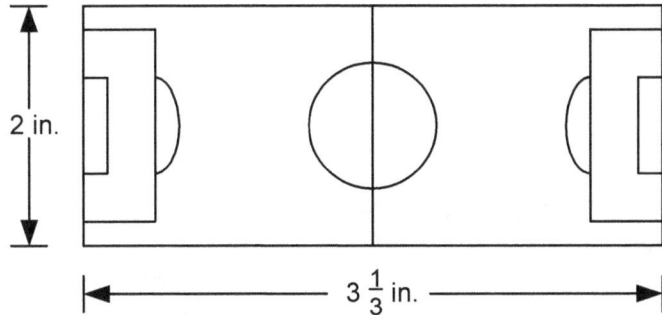

2 in.

$3\frac{1}{3}$ in.

What is the length of the field in yards?

**a.** 100 yd            **b.** 120 yd

**c.** 140 yd            **d.** 160 yd

**9.** The actual width ($w$) of a rectangle is 21 inches (in.). Use the scale drawing of the rectangle to find the actual length ($l$).

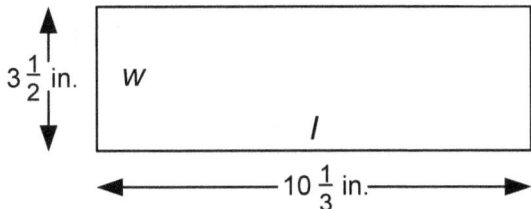

$3\frac{1}{2}$ in.    $w$

$l$

$10\frac{1}{3}$ in.

**a.** 54 in.            **b.** 62 in.

**c.** 76 in.            **d.** 84 in.

**10.** The scale drawing of the tennis court shown below is drawn using a scale of 1 inch (in.) = 18 feet (ft).

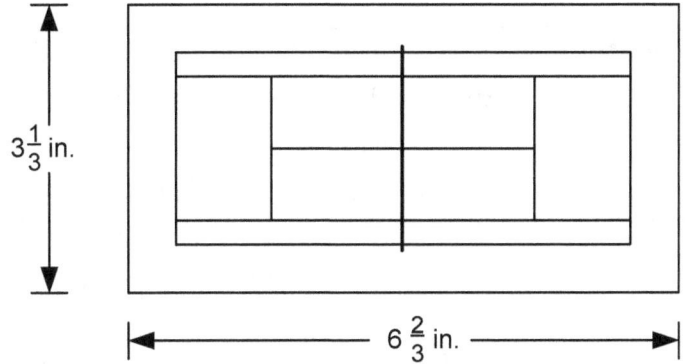

$3\frac{1}{3}$ in.

$6\frac{2}{3}$ in.

What is the length of the court in feet?

**a.** 105 ft            **b.** 110 ft

**c.** 115 ft            **d.** 120 ft

**11.** The actual width ($w$) of a rectangle is 36 inches (in.). Use the scale drawing of the rectangle to find the actual length ($l$).

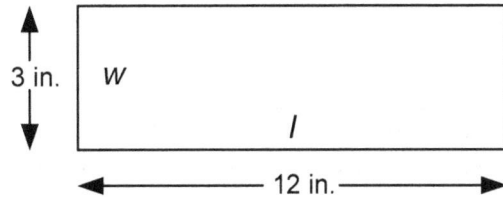

3 in.    $w$

$l$

12 in.

**a.** 100 in.            **b.** 121 in.

**c.** 144 in.            **d.** 169 in.

**12.** The actual width ($w$) of a rectangle is 22 inches (in.). Use the scale drawing of the rectangle to find the actual length ($l$).

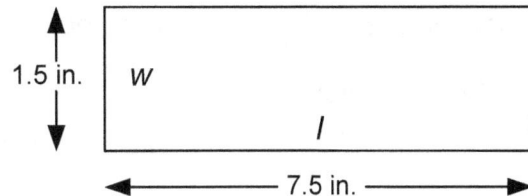

1.5 in.    $w$

$l$

7.5 in.

**a.** 84 in.            **b.** 92 in.

**c.** 104 in.            **d.** 110 in.

# CAHSEE Bench Mark 20

### Students will successfully solve problems involving rates.

**CA Standard:** Grade 7, Measurement and Geometry 1.3
**CAHSEE Strand:** Measurement and Geometry

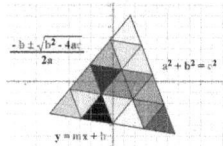

| Vocabulary: | ratio | a comparison of two quantities using division |
|---|---|---|
| | proportion | an equality of two ratios |
| | rate | a ratio that compares two quantities in different units |
| | unit rate | a rate with a denominator of 1 |

Some common rates that you may already be familiar with are;
miles per hour, words per minute, feet per second, etc.

When working with rates, we need to pay close attention to the units of
measurement and understand what the question is asking.

---

**EXAMPLE:** Lamont ran 8 miles at the speed of three miles per hour. How long did it take him to run that distance?

**a.** $2\frac{1}{2}$ hrs     **b.** $2\frac{2}{3}$ hrs     **c.** $3\frac{1}{3}$ hrs     **d.** $3\frac{2}{3}$ hrs

---

We begin with the unit rate $\dfrac{3 \text{ miles}}{1 \text{ hour}}$ and understand that the question is asking: If he can run 3 miles in 1 hour, how long will it take him to run 8 miles?

We will set up and solve a proportion.     $\dfrac{3 \text{ miles}}{1 \text{ hour}} = \dfrac{8 \text{ miles}}{x \text{ hours}}$     $3x = 8$     $x = \dfrac{8}{3} = 2\frac{2}{3}$ hrs

The correct answer is **b.**

---

**EXAMPLE:** A contractor estimates that a new job will take one person 72 hours to complete. If three people work on the job and they each work 8-hour days, how many days are needed to complete the job?

**a.** 5     **b.** 4     **c.** 3     **d.** 2

---

If three people work 8-hour days, then 24 hours worth of work will be completed each day. The question then becomes, 72 ÷ 24.

$$72 \div 24 = 3$$

The correct answer is **c.**

---

**EXAMPLE:** One hundred and twenty miles per hour is the same as which of the following?

**a.** 1 mile per minute     **b.** 2 miles per second     **c.** 12 miles per minute     **d.** 2 miles per minute

The nature of the answer choices suggests that we should first convert to miles per minute. Then, if needed, we can convert to miles per second.

***Remember to watch your units of measurement.***

$$\dfrac{120 \text{ miles}}{1 \text{ hour}} \cdot \dfrac{1 \text{ hour}}{60 \text{ minutes}}$$

$$= \dfrac{12\cancel{0} \text{ miles}}{1 \cancel{\text{hour}}} \cdot \dfrac{1 \cancel{\text{hour}}}{6\cancel{0} \text{ minutes}}$$

$$= \dfrac{12 \text{ miles}}{6 \text{ minutes}} = \dfrac{2 \text{ miles}}{1 \text{ minute}}$$

The correct answer is **d.**

1. One hundred and twenty miles per hour is the same as which of the following?

    **a.** 1 mile per minute

    **b.** 2 miles per second

    **c.** 12 miles per minute

    **d.** 2 miles per minute

2. Amber ran 8 miles at the speed of five miles per hour. How long did it take her to run that distance?

    **a.** $\frac{4}{5}$ hr

    **b.** $1\frac{1}{5}$ hrs

    **c.** $1\frac{3}{5}$ hrs

    **d.** 2 hrs

3. Maurice can read about 35 words per minute. If he reads at this rate for 40 minutes without stopping, about how many words will he read?

    **a.** 1,400

    **b.** 1,200

    **c.** 2,100

    **d.** 1,700

4. A plumber estimates that a new job will take one person 96 hours to complete. If four people work on the job and they each work 8-hour days, how many days are needed to complete the job?

    **a.** 3

    **b.** 4

    **c.** 5

    **d.** 6

5. Edith drove 150 miles at the speed of 45 miles per hour. How long did it take her to drive that distance?

    **a.** $\frac{2}{3}$ hr

    **b.** $2\frac{3}{5}$ hrs

    **c.** $3\frac{1}{3}$ hrs

    **d.** $3\frac{2}{3}$ hrs

6. An electrician estimates that a new job will take one person 60 hours to complete. If two people work on the job and they each work 6-hour days, how many days are needed to complete the job?

    **a.** 2

    **b.** 3

    **c.** 4

    **d.** 5

7. Thirty miles per hour is the same as which of the following?

    **a.** 0.3 mile per minute

    **b.** 0.3 miles per second

    **c.** 0.5 miles per minute

    **d.** 2 miles per minute

8. Lamont rode his bicycle 12 miles at the speed of eight miles per hour. How long did it take him to ride that distance?

    **a.** $\frac{4}{5}$ hr

    **b.** $1\frac{1}{3}$ hrs

    **c.** $1\frac{1}{2}$ hrs

    **d.** 2 hrs

9. Edwin can type about 45 words per minute. If he types at this rate for 25 minutes without stopping, about how many words will he type?

    **a.** 1,450

    **b.** 1,125

    **c.** 1,175

    **d.** 1,225

10. A carpenter estimates that a new job will take one person 144 hours to complete. If four people work on the job and they each work 6-hour days, how many days are needed to complete the job?

    **a.** 4

    **b.** 5

    **c.** 6

    **d.** 7

11. One hundred and eighty miles per hour is the same as which of the following?

    a. 3 miles per minute

    b. 2 miles per minute

    c. 6 miles per minute

    d. 18 miles per minute

12. Lisa ran twelve miles at the speed of four miles per hour. How long did it take her to run that distance?

    a. $\frac{11}{12}$ hr

    b. $1\frac{4}{5}$ hrs

    c. $2\frac{2}{5}$ hrs

    d. 3 hrs

13. Matt can read about 25 words per minute. If he reads at this rate for 35 minutes without stopping, about how many words will he read?

    a. 825

    b. 850

    c. 875

    d. 900

14. A plumber estimates that a new job will take one person 36 hours to complete. If three people work on the job and they each work 4-hour days, how many days are needed to complete the job?

    a. 2

    b. 3

    c. 4

    d. 5

15. Pahoa drove 225 miles at the speed of 50 miles per hour. How long did it take her to drive that distance?

    a. $3\frac{1}{3}$ hr

    b. $3\frac{1}{2}$ hrs

    c. 4 hrs

    d. $4\frac{1}{2}$ hrs

16. An electrician estimates that a new job will take one person 126 hours to complete. If three people work on the job and they each work 6-hour days, how many days are needed to complete the job?

    a. 4

    b. 5

    c. 6

    d. 7

17. Forty five miles per hour is the same as which of the following?

    a. 0.75 miles per minute

    b. 2 miles per minute

    c. 4.5 miles per minute

    d. 6 miles per minute

18. Larry rode his bicycle 24 miles at the speed of ten miles per hour. How long did it take him to ride that distance?

    a. $1\frac{3}{5}$ hrs

    b. $2\frac{2}{5}$ hrs

    c. $3\frac{1}{5}$ hrs

    d. 4 hrs

19. Kennedy can type about 65 words per minute. If she types at this rate for 20 minutes without stopping, about how many words will she type?

    a. 1,300

    b. 1,450

    c. 1,550

    d. 1,700

20. A carpenter estimates that a new job will take one person 240 hours to complete. If six people work on the job and they each work 8-hour days, how many days are needed to complete the job?

    a. 4

    b. 5

    c. 6

    d. 7

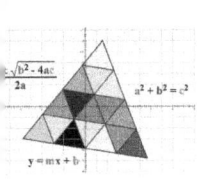

Students will successfully use formulas.

**CA Standard:** Grade 7, Measurement and Geometry 2.1
**CAHSEE Strand:** Measurement and Geometry

**Vocabulary:**

| | |
|---|---|
| **area** | the measure of a bounded region on a flat surface |
| **volume** | the amount of space an object occupies in three dimensions |
| **perimeter** | the sum of the lengths of the sides of an object |
| **circumference** | the distance around the outside of a circle |
| **radius** | the distance from the center of a circle to any point on the circle |
| **diameter** | any straight line segment that passes through the center of a circle and whose endpoints are on the circle; equal to twice the radius |

**PERIMETER**

square: $P = 4s$

rectangle: $P = 2w + 2\ell$

**CIRCUMFERENCE**

circle: $C = 2\pi r$

**VOLUME**

$V = \ell w h$

**AREA**

square: $A = s^2$

rectangle: $A = \ell w$

triangle: $A = \frac{1}{2}bh$

circle: $A = \pi r^2$

**RADIUS**

circle

**DIAMETER**

circle: $d = 2r$

**EXAMPLE:**

In the figure above, the radius of the inscribed circle is 12 inches (in.). What is the perimeter of the square ABCD?

a. 48 π in.
b. 96 in.
c. 72 π in.
d. 48 in.

The radius is given as 12 inches, which means that the diameter is 24 inches.

In this configuration, the diameter will be equal to the length of the side of the square.

The formula for the perimeter of a square is 4s. Therefore, 4(24) = 96

The correct answer is **b.**

**1.**

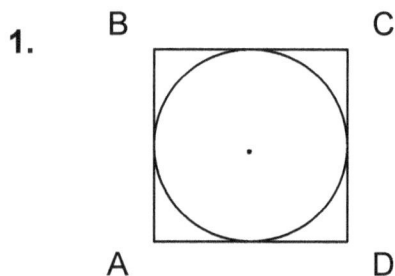

B      C

A      D

In the figure above, the radius of the inscribed circle is 12 inches (in.). What is the perimeter of the square ABCD?

**a.** $48\pi$ in.      **b.** 96 in.

**c.** $72\pi$ in.      **d.** 48 in.

**2.**

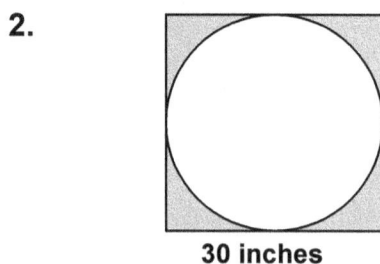

**30 inches**

The largest possible circle is to be cut from a 30-inch square board. What will be the approximate area, in square inches, of the remaining board (shaded region)?

$(A = \pi r^2$ and $\pi \approx 3.14)$

**a.** 190      **b.** 210

**c.** 230      **d.** 250

**3.**

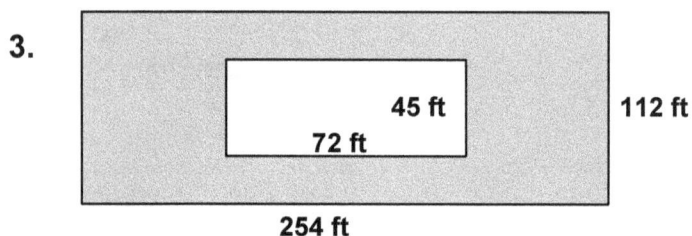

45 ft      112 ft
72 ft

**254 ft**

A rectangular pool 72 feet by 45 feet is on a rectangular lot 254 feet by 112 feet. The rest of the lot is grass. Approximately how many square feet is grass?

**a.** 2,300      **b.** 25,200

**c.** 2,500      **d.** 27,900

**4.**

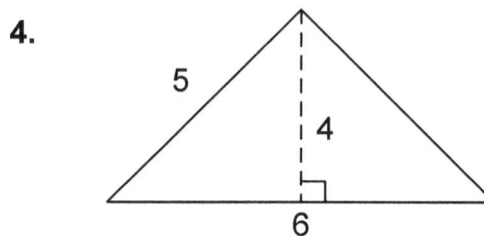

5      4

6

What is the area of the triangle shown above?

**a.** 10 square units      **b.** 12 square units

**c.** 8 square units      **d.** 6 square units

**5.**

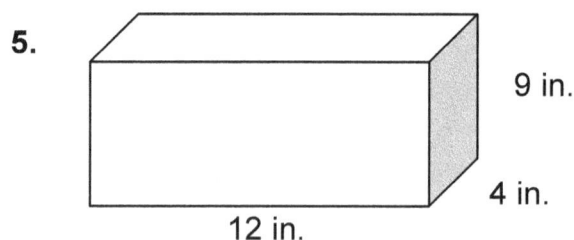

9 in.

4 in.

12 in.

What is the volume of the box shown above in cubic inches (in.³)?

**a.** 25      **b.** 48

**c.** 346      **d.** 432

**6.**

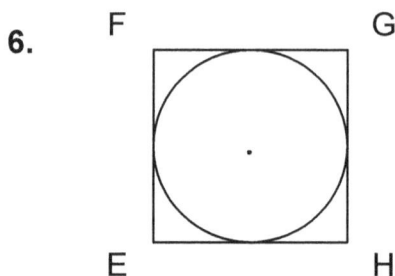

F      G

E      H

In the figure above, the radius of the inscribed circle is 18 inches (in.). What is the perimeter of the square EFGH?

**a.** 144 in.      **b.** 72 in.

**c.** $108\pi$ in.      **d.** $72\pi$ in.

**7.**

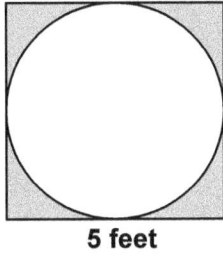

**5 feet**

The largest possible circle is to be cut from a 5-foot square board. What will be the approximate area, in square feet, of the remaining board (shaded region)?

($A = \pi r^2$ and $\pi \approx 3.14$)

**a.** 3          **b.** 4

**c.** 5          **d.** 6

**8.**

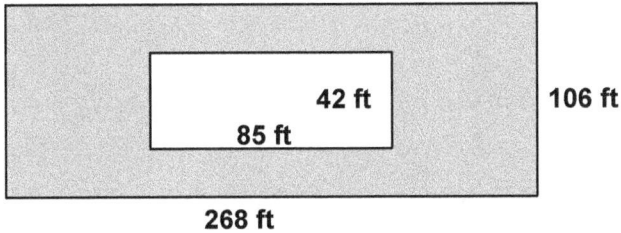

A rectangular pool 85 feet by 42 feet is on a rectangular lot 268 feet by 106 feet. The rest of the lot is grass. Approximately how many square feet is grass?

**a.** 24,800          **b.** 25,900

**c.** 2,500          **d.** 2,900

**9.**

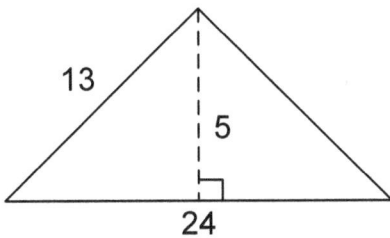

What is the area of the triangle shown above?

**a.** 42 square units          **b.** 60 square units

**c.** 312 square units          **d.** 120 square units

**10.**

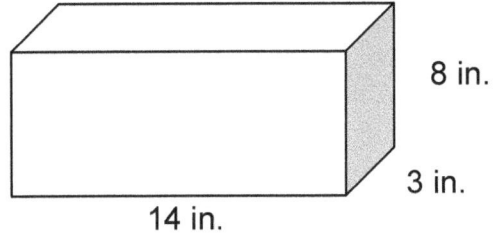

8 in.

3 in.

14 in.

What is the volume of the box shown above in cubic inches (in.³)?

**a.** 25          **b.** 126

**c.** 123          **d.** 336

**11.**

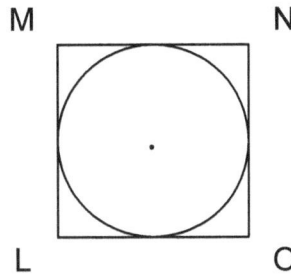

M          N

L          O

In the figure above, the radius of the inscribed circle is 10 inches (in.). What is the perimeter of the square LMNO?

**a.** 100π in.          **b.** 80π in.

**c.** 100 in.          **d.** 80 in.

**12.**

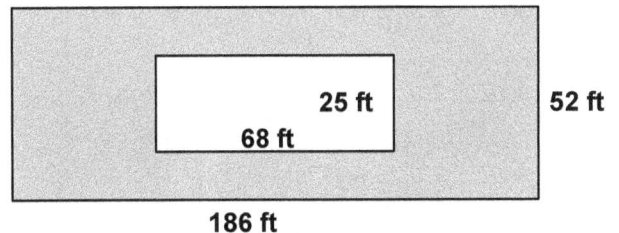

25 ft          52 ft

68 ft

186 ft

A rectangular pool 68 feet by 25 feet is on a rectangular lot 186 feet by 52 feet. The rest of the lot is grass. Approximately how many square feet is grass?

**a.** 8,000          **b.** 26,000

**c.** 6,500          **d.** 12,400

**13.**

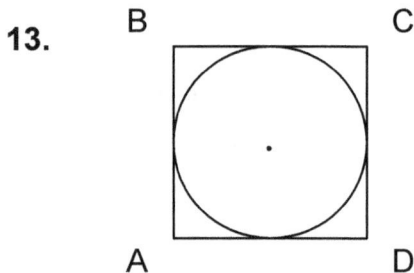

In the figure above, the radius of the inscribed circle is 6 inches (in.). What is the perimeter of the square ABCD?

a. 48π in.

b. 96 in.

c. 72π in.

d. 48 in.

**14.**

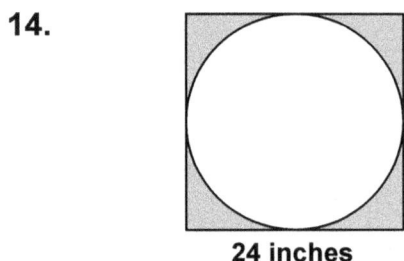

**24 inches**

The largest possible circle is to be cut from a 24-inch square board. What will be the approximate area, in square inches, of the remaining board (shaded region)?

(A = π r² and π ≈ 3.14)

a. 124

b. 168

c. 96

d. 110

**15.**

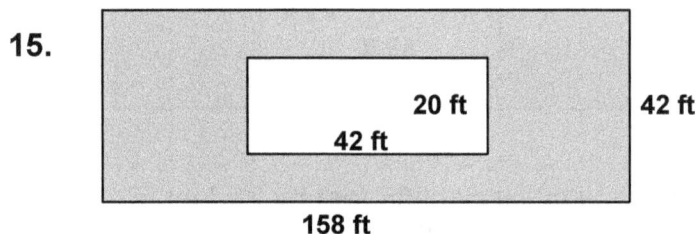

**158 ft**

A rectangular pool 42 feet by 20 feet is on a rectangular lot 158 feet by 42 feet. The rest of the lot is grass. Approximately how many square feet is grass?

a. 6,300

b. 10,200

c. 5,800

d. 7,900

**16.**

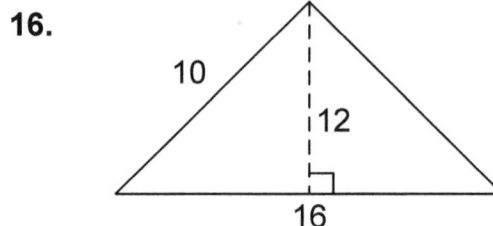

What is the area of the triangle shown above?

a. 96 square units

b. 192 square units

c. 160 square units

d. 80 square units

**17.**

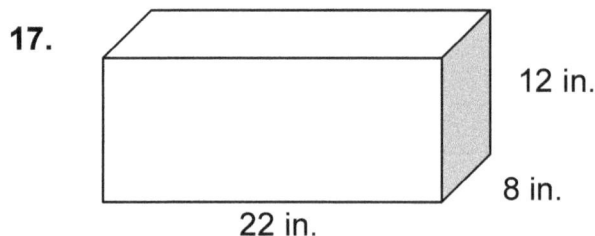

What is the volume of the box shown above in cubic inches (in.³)?

a. 25

b. 2,112

c. 564

d. 1,056

**18.**

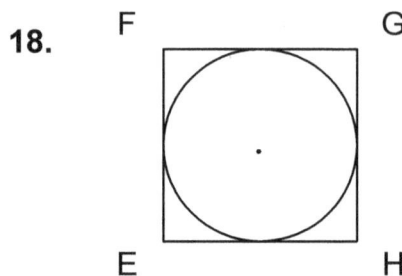

In the figure above, the radius of the inscribed circle is 36 inches (in.). What is the perimeter of the square EFGH?

a. 288 in.

b. 316 in.

c. 176π in.

d. 144π in.

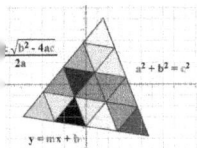

### Students will successfully estimate the area of irregular shapes.

**CA Standard:** Grade 7, Measurement and Geometry 2.2
**CAHSEE Strand:** Measurement and Geometry

---

| | | |
|---|---|---|
| **Vocabulary:** | **area** | the measure of a bounded region on a flat surface |
| | **surface area** | the sum of the areas of the bases and sides of a three dimensional shape |

To find the area of an irregular shape, it will be beneficial to try to create shapes
which have areas that are easy to find, then add or subtract the extras.
For example, find the area, in square units, of the shape below. *All corners are right angles.*

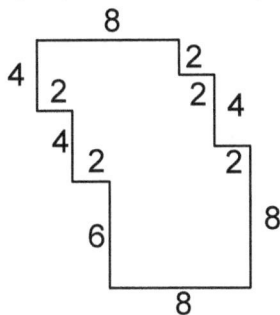

First, add in the missing areas at the corners to make a rectangle. Then find the area of the rectangle.

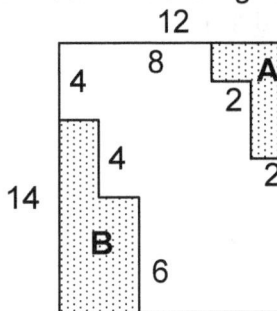

12(14) = 168

We will next need to find the area of the added pieces and subtract them from 168.

We can make **A** and **B** into regular shapes by 'breaking' them into 2 pieces.

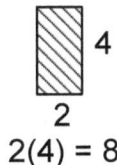

2(4) = 8

2(4) = 8

**8 + 8 = 16**
This is the first area we need to subtract from 168.

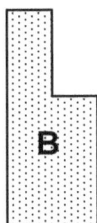

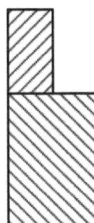

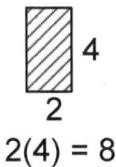

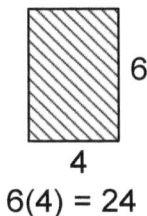

2(4) = 8

6(4) = 24

**8 + 24 = 32**
This is the second area we need to subtract from 168.

**Area = 168 - (16 + 32)**
**= 168 - 48**
**= 120**

---

**EXAMPLE:** One-inch square cubes are stacked as shown in the drawing.

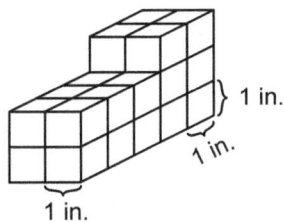

1 in.
1 in.
1 in.

What is the <u>total</u> surface area?

**a.** 56 in.$^2$          **b.** 64 in.$^2$

**c.** 72 in.$^2$          **d.** 80 in.$^2$

We will first take apart the shape by areas, then we will add each individual area together to get the surface area.

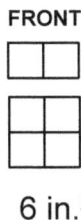

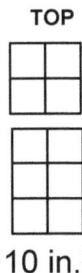

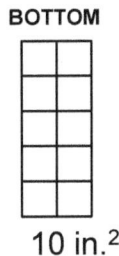

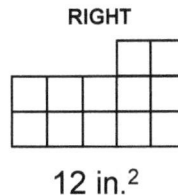

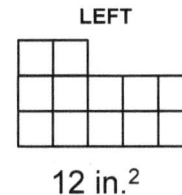

| FRONT | BACK | TOP | BOTTOM | RIGHT | LEFT |
|---|---|---|---|---|---|

6 in.$^2$          6 in.$^2$          10 in.$^2$          10 in.$^2$          12 in.$^2$          12 in.$^2$

**6 + 6 + 10 + 10 + 12 + 12 = 56**          The correct answer is **a.**

**1.** One-inch square cubes are stacked as shown in the drawing below.

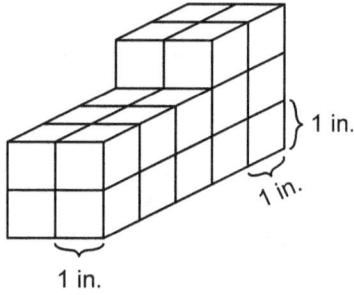

1 in.

1 in.

1 in.

What is the <u>total</u> surface area?

**a.** 56 in.²          **b.** 64 in.²

**c.** 72 in.²          **d.** 80 in.²

**2.**

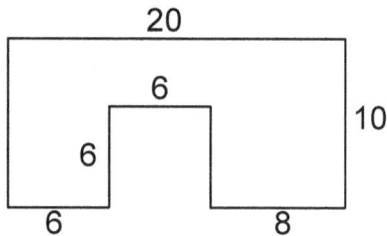

20

6

6

10

6

6          8

In the figure shown above, all the corners form right angles. What is the area of the figure in square units?

**a.** 106          **b.** 124

**c.** 148          **d.** 164

**3.** What is the area of the shaded region in the figure shown below?

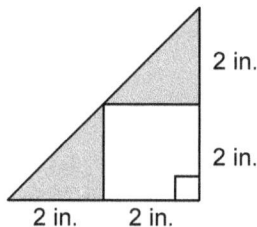

2 in.

2 in.

2 in.     2 in.

**a.** 16 in.²          **b.** 8 in.²

**c.** 6 in.²          **d.** 4 in.²

**4.** A right triangle is removed from a rectangle as shown in the figure below. Find the area of the remaining part of the rectangle.

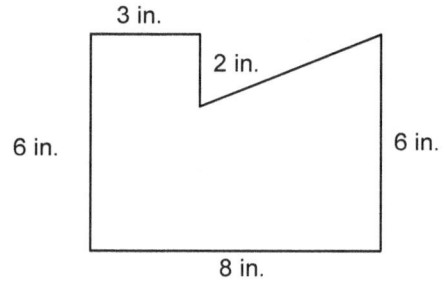

3 in.

2 in.

6 in.                    6 in.

8 in.

**a.** 61 in.²          **b.** 52 in.²

**c.** 47 in.²          **d.** 43 in.²

**5.** In the figure shown below, all the corners form right angles.

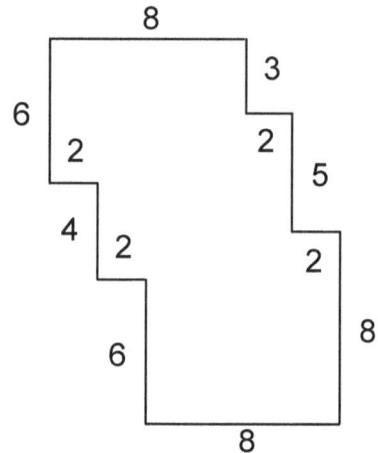

8

3

6

2          2

5

4

2          2

8

6

8

What is the area of the figure in square units?

**a.** 114          **b.** 138

**c.** 156          **d.** 164

**6.** One-inch square cubes are stacked as shown in the drawing below.

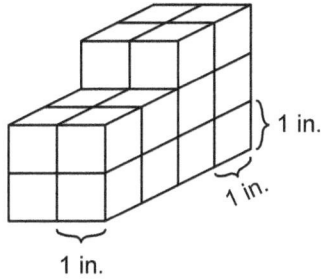

What is the <u>total</u> surface area?

**a.** 56 in.²          **b.** 48 in.²

**c.** 42 in.²          **d.** 36 in.²

**7.**

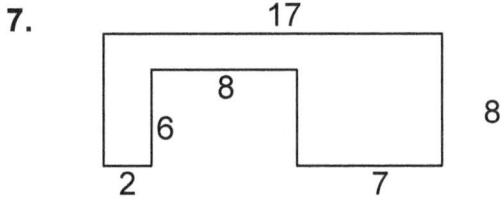

In the figure shown above, all the corners form right angles. What is the area of the figure in square units?

**a.** 80          **b.** 88

**c.** 96          **d.** 108

**8.** What is the area of the shaded region in the figure shown below?

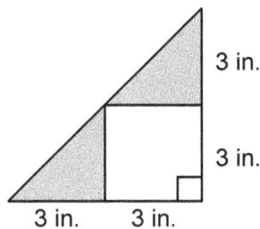

**a.** 9 in.²          **b.** 8 in.²

**c.** 6 in.²          **d.** 10 in.²

**9.** A right triangle is removed from a rectangle as shown in the figure below. Find the area of the remaining part of the rectangle.

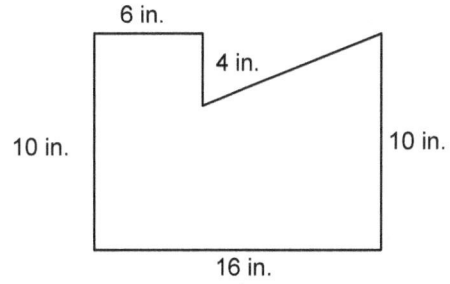

**a.** 100 in.²          **b.** 120 in.²

**c.** 140 in.²          **d.** 160 in.²

**10.** In the figure shown below, all the corners form right angles.

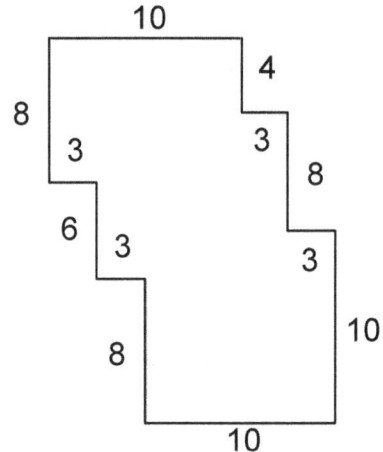

What is the area of the figure in square units?

**a.** 224          **b.** 238

**c.** 188          **d.** 164

**11.** One-inch square cubes are stacked as shown in the drawing below.

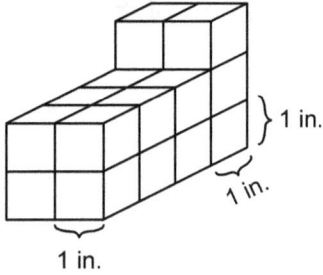

What is the <u>total</u> surface area?

a. 46 in.$^2$          b. 52 in.$^2$

c. 64 in.$^2$          d. 78 in.$^2$

**12.**

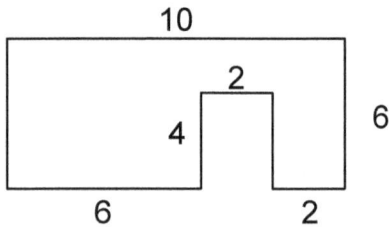

In the figure shown above, all the corners form right angles. What is the area of the figure in square units?

a. 78          b. 64

c. 52          d. 44

**13.** What is the area of the shaded region in the figure shown below?

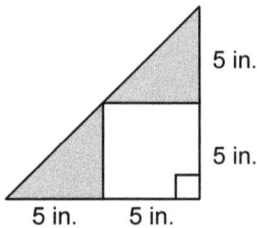

a. 10 in.$^2$          b. 25 in.$^2$

c. 50 in.$^2$          d. 40 in.$^2$

**14.** A right triangle is removed from a rectangle as shown in the figure below. Find the area of the remaining part of the rectangle.

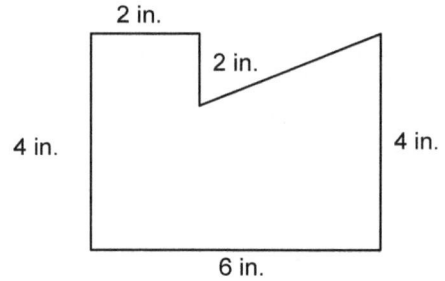

a. 16 in.$^2$          b. 34 in.$^2$

c. 28 in.$^2$          d. 20 in.$^2$

**15.** In the figure shown below, all the corners form right angles.

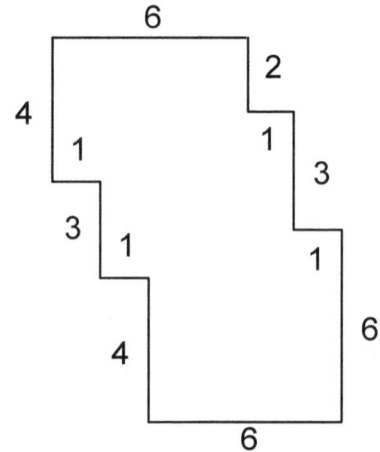

What is the area of the figure in square units?

a. 64          b. 52

c. 70          d. 40

**BM 1.** The estimated population of China is 1,370,000,000. What is this number in scientific notation?

  **a.** $1.37 \times 10^7$  **b.** $1.4 \times 10^9$

  **c.** $1.37 \times 10^8$  **d.** $1.37 \times 10^9$

**BM 2.** $3 + (-10) =$

  **a.** 13  **b.** -7

  **c.** 7  **d.** -13

**BM 3.** 3 of the last 25 customers of an ice-cream shop have ordered chocolate sundaes, what percentage of customers did **not** order chocolate sundaes?

  **a.** 88%  **b.** 30%

  **c.** 12%  **d.** 77%

**BM 4.** The price of a bed has increased from $120.00 to $138.00. What is the percent of increase?

  **a.** 85%  **b.** 20%

  **c.** 15%  **d.** 38%

**BM 5.** Mai Lia bought a truck for $6000.00 and later sold it for a 25% profit. How much did Mai Lia sell the truck for?

  **a.** $7500.00  **b.** $6500.00

  **c.** $7000.00  **d.** $8000.00

**BM 6.** Divide. $\dfrac{8^{-5}}{8^{-2}}$

  **a.** $\dfrac{1}{8^{-3}}$  **b.** $8^3$

  **c.** $\dfrac{-1}{8^3}$  **d.** $\dfrac{1}{8^3}$

**BM 7.** $\dfrac{8}{14} + \left( \dfrac{1}{2} - \dfrac{1}{7} \right)$

  **a.** $\dfrac{10}{14}$  **b.** $\dfrac{8}{23}$

  **c.** $\dfrac{13}{14}$  **d.** $\dfrac{8}{9}$

**BM 8.** $(8^2)^0$

  **a.** 1  **b.** 64

  **c.** $8^2$  **d.** 8

**BM 9.** The square root of 246 is between

  **a.** 14 and 15  **b.** 15 and 16

  **c.** 16 and 17  **d.** 17 and 18

**BM 10.** If $|x| = 1$, what is the value of x?

  **a.** 0 or -1  **b.** -1 or 1

  **c.** 0 or 1  **d.** 0

**BM 11.** Christopher's scores for the first five paragraphs on an English paper are 13, 9, 16, 11, and 14. Find the median score.

  **a.** 16  **b.** 7

  **c.** 13  **d.** 13.5

**BM 12.** Two-thirds of 24 students attended the field trip. Two of those who did not go on the field trip were female. Which of the following statements can be answered with the given information?

   **a.** How many males went on the field trip?

   **b.** How many males did not go on the field trip?

   **c.** How many females went on the field trip?

   **d.** How many females were suppose to go on the field trip?

**BM 13.** Each letter of the word ALGEBRA is on its own note card, lying face down on a desk. If you pick up one note card, what is the probability it will be the letter A?

   **a.** $\dfrac{1}{2}$     **b.** $\dfrac{3}{4}$

   **c.** $\dfrac{2}{7}$     **d.** $\dfrac{1}{3}$

**BM 14.** If the probability of an event happening is 37%, then what is the probability that the event will not happen?

   **a.** 0.63     **b.** 37%

   **c.** $\dfrac{2}{3}$     **d.** $\dfrac{3}{5}$

**BM 15.** Natasha wants to draw two cards from a set of face cards (jack, queen, king, and ace). All four suits are in the set of face cards. Natasha will draw the the two cards without replacement. What is the probability that she will draw two kings?

   **a.** $\dfrac{1}{4}$     **b.** $\dfrac{1}{5}$

   **c.** $\dfrac{1}{20}$     **d.** $\dfrac{1}{2}$

**BM 16.** The following pie chart represents the grades of fifty students in two math classes.

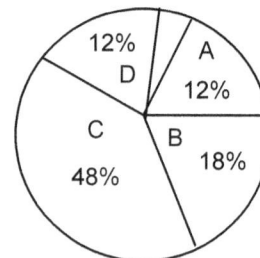

The information for the grade of F is missing. Determine which statement best describes the missing data.

   **a.** Five students, which is ten percent of all the students, received a grade of F.

   **b.** Five students, which is twelve percent of all the students, received a grade of F.

   **c.** Six students, which is ten percent of all the students, received a grade of F.

   **d.** Six students, which is twelve percent of all the students, received a grade of F.

**BM 17.** The below scatter plot appears to be what type of correlation?

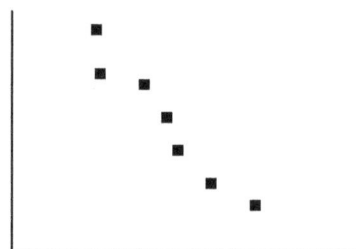

   **a.** Strong Positive Correlation

   **b.** Strong Negative Correlation

   **c.** Zero Correlation

   **d.** Weak Negative Correlation

**BM 18.** Jim is driving at 45 miles per hour, what is his approximate speed in kilometers per hour? (1 mile ≈ 1.6 kilometers)

    **a.** 72　　　　**b.** 81

    **c.** 90　　　　**d.** 99

**BM 19.** The actual width (*w*) of a rectangle is 22 inches (in.). Use the scale drawing of the rectangle to find the actual length (*l*).

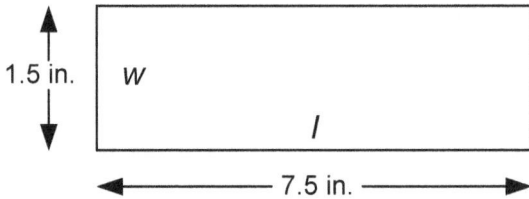

    **a.** 84 in.　　　**b.** 92 in.

    **c.** 104 in.　　**d.** 110 in.

**BM 20.** A carpenter estimates that a new job will take one person 240 hours to complete. If six people work on the job and they each work 8-hour days, how many days are needed to complete the job?

    **a.** 4　　　　**b.** 5

    **c.** 6　　　　**d.** 7

**BM 21.**

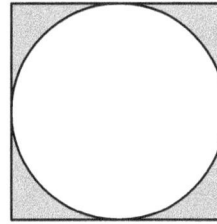

**24 inches**

The largest possible circle is to be cut from a 24-inch square board. What will be the approximate area, in square inches, of the remaining board (shaded region)?

($A = \pi r^2$ and $\pi \approx 3.14$)

    **a.** 124　　　**b.** 168

    **c.** 96　　　　**d.** 110

**BM 22.** In the figure shown below, all the corners form right angles.

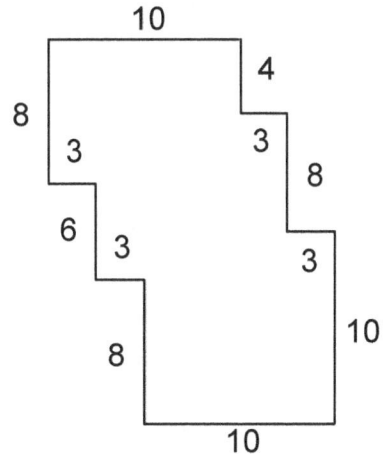

What is the area of the figure in square units?

    **a.** 224　　　**b.** 238

    **c.** 188　　　**d.** 164

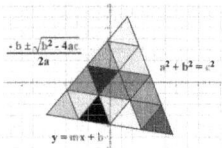

Students will successfully compute
perimeter, surface area, and volume.

**CA Standard:** Grade 7, Measurement and Geometry 2.3
**CAHSEE Strand:** Measurement and Geometry

| Vocabulary: | | |
|---|---|---|
| | **area** | the measure of a bounded region on a flat surface |
| | **radius** | the distance from the center of a circle to any point on the circle |
| | **surface area** | the sum of the areas of the bases and sides of a three dimensional shape |
| | **volume** | the amount of space an object occupies in three dimensions |
| | **circumference** | the distance around the outside of a circle |
| | **diameter** | any straight line segment that passes through the center of a circle and whose endpoints are on the circle; equal to twice the radius |
| | **corresponding** | same relative position |
| | **scale factor** | the ratio of two corresponding parts of similar figures |
| | **perimeter** | the sum of the lengths of the sides of an object |

To find the **volume** of a three dimensional shape, multiply the area of the base by the height of the object.

To find the **volume** of an irregular shape, it will be beneficial to try to create shapes which have volumes that are easy to find, then add the volumes of these shapes together.

For example, find the volume of the shape below.

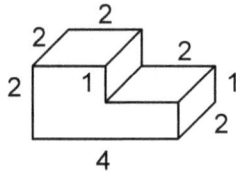

This is an irregular shape.     Create two shapes.    Find the volumes then add them together.

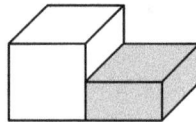

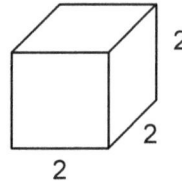

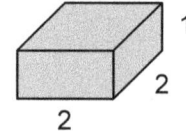

$$2(2)(2) = 8, \ 2(2)(1) = 4$$
$$8 + 4 = 12 \text{ cubic units}$$

---

**Scale factors** are ratios and can be written in several ways. For example, "a is to b," "a to b," a:b, or $\frac{a}{b}$

**Theorem:** If the scale factor of two similar figures is a:b, then (1) the ratio of areas is $a^2:b^2$ and
(2) the ratio of volumes is $a^3:b^3$.

If the scale factor of two similar figures is 3:4, then the ratio of the areas is $3^2:4^2$ or 9:16 and the ratio of the volumes is $3^3:4^3$ or 27:64.

**EXAMPLE:** Thao has computed the scale factor between two similar figures to be two-thirds. She wants to convert the scale factor to find Surface Area and Volume respectively. Which of the following are the correct conversions for the scale factor?

**a.** $\frac{2}{3}$ and $\frac{4}{9}$     **b.** $\frac{4}{9}$ and $\frac{8}{27}$     **c.** $\frac{2}{3}$ and $\frac{8}{27}$     **d.** $\frac{2}{9}$ and $\frac{8}{9}$

If the scale factor of two similar figures is 2:3, then the ratio of the areas is $2^2:3^2$ or 4:9 and the ratio of the volumes is $2^3:3^3$ or 8:27.

The correct answer is **b.**

1. Thao has computed the scale factor between two similar figures to be two-thirds. She wants to convert the scale factor to find Surface Area and Volume respectively. Which of the following are the correct conversions for the scale factor?

   a. $\frac{2}{3}$ and $\frac{4}{9}$   b. $\frac{4}{9}$ and $\frac{8}{27}$

   c. $\frac{2}{3}$ and $\frac{8}{27}$   d. $\frac{2}{9}$ and $\frac{8}{9}$

2. Lor found the circumference of circle A to be $8\pi$ and the circumference of circle B to be $6\pi$. Which of the following is the scale factor of circle A to circle B?

   a. $\frac{4}{3}$   b. $\frac{3}{4}$

   c. $\frac{16}{9}$   d. $\frac{9}{16}$

3. The two circles below have a radius as indicated. Find the scale factor of circle 2 to circle 1.

   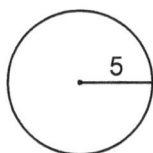   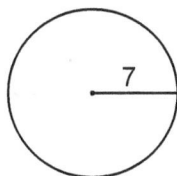

   Circle 1          Circle 2

   a. $\frac{5}{7}$   b. $\frac{2}{1}$

   c. $\frac{7}{5}$   d. $\frac{1}{2}$

4. Emily has a rectangular box with square ends. If the square ends have a side length of 7 inches and the box is 15 inches long, then what is the surface area of the box?

   a. 735 in²   b. 468 in²

   c. 336 in²   d. 518 in²

Use the Diagram of the steps into Fou's home to answer questions 5, 6, and 7. Note: all units are in feet.

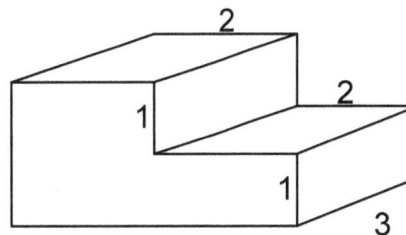

5. The steps into Fou's house are solid. Find the Volume in cubic feet.

   a. 22 ft³   b. 18 ft³

   c. 24 ft³   d. 6 ft³

6. Find the surface area in square feet.

   a. 52 ft²   b. 39 ft²

   c. 24 ft²   d. 48 ft²

7. Every summer, Fou must paint the steps. Since he can only paint the top, both sides and the front, what is the surface area of those faces?

   a. 30 ft²   b. 18 ft²

   c. 24 ft²   d. 36 ft²

8. Alexander has two similar rectangular boxes. The dimensions of box A are three times bigger then box B. How many times greater is the surface area of box A?

   a. 1   b. 3

   c. 6   d. 9

**9.** The two circles below have a diameter as indicated. Find the scale factor of circle 1 to circle 2.

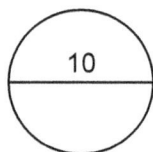 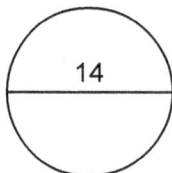

Circle 1          Circle 2

**a.** $\frac{5}{7}$          **b.** $\frac{2}{1}$

**c.** $\frac{7}{5}$          **d.** $\frac{1}{2}$

**10.** Cindy has two similar rectangular boxes. She found that the scale factor of the dimensions is four-thirds. If the surface area of the small box is 27 square units, find the surface area of the big box.

**a.** 36 units$^2$          **b.** 64 units$^2$

**c.** 48 units$^2$          **d.** 144 units$^2$

**11.** Naton has two similar rectangular boxes. He found the scale factor to be three-halves. If the volume of the little box is 24 cubic units, find the volume of the large box.

**a.** 36 units$^3$          **b.** 81 units$^3$

**c.** 72 units$^3$          **d.** 96 units$^3$

**12.** Yasman has a rectangular box with square ends. If the square ends have a side length of 6 inches and the box is 13 inches long, then what is the volume of the box?

**a.** 78 in$^3$          **b.** 384 in$^3$

**c.** 348 in$^3$          **d.** 468 in$^3$

**13.** Mui wants to paint the outside of a toy box that she made for the childrens hospital. Use the diagram below to find the surface area.

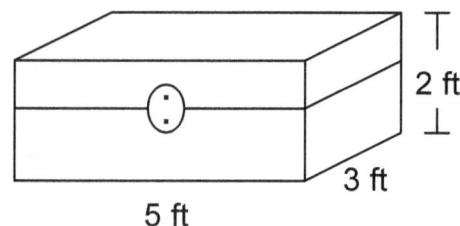

**a.** 30 ft$^2$          **b.** 60 ft$^2$

**c.** 62 ft$^2$          **d.** 64 ft$^2$

**14.** Karina has two similar rectangular boxes. The dimensions of box A are four times bigger then box B. How many times greater is the volume of box A?

**a.** 4          **b.** 8

**c.** 16          **d.** 64

The diagram below is the podium for the awards ceremony at a track and field meet. Answer questions 15 and 16. Note: the units are in feet and it is 3 feet wide.

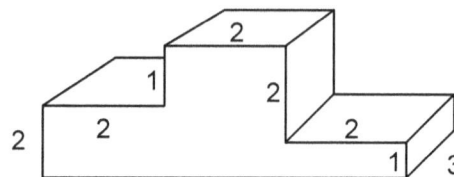

**15.** Find the surface area.

**a.** 78 ft$^2$          **b.** 54 ft$^2$

**c.** 45 ft$^2$          **d.** 36 ft$^2$

**16.** Find the Volume.

**a.** 54 ft$^3$          **b.** 36 ft$^3$

**c.** 30 ft$^3$          **d.** 18 ft$^3$

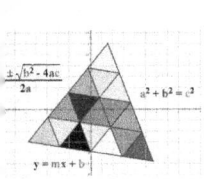

# CAHSEE Bench Mark 24
Students will successfully relate changes in measurement
with changes in scale.
**CA Standard:** Grade 7, Measurement and Geometry 2.4
**CAHSEE Strand:** Measurement and Geometry

| **Vocabulary:** | **ratio** | a comparison of two quantities using division |
| | **proportion** | an equality of two ratios |

In order to relate changes in measurements with changes in scale, we will use ratios and proportions. It is very important to pay close attention to the different units.

---

**EXAMPLE:** One cubic foot is equal to approximately 7.5 gallons. How many gallons of water are needed to fill a small rectangular pond that is 4 feet wide by 6 feet long by 2 feet deep?

   **a.** 330 gallons    **b.** 48 gallons    **c.** 360 gallons    **d.** 220 gallons

---

To solve this problem, we need to set up a proportion. We must first find the volume of the pond.
**Remember**, *pay close attention to the units.*

Volume equals length multiplied by width multiplied by height.    4(6)(2) = 48 cubic feet

Set up a proportion, then solve for x.

$$\frac{48 \text{ cubic feet}}{x \text{ gallons}} = \frac{1 \text{ cubic foot}}{7.5 \text{ gallons}}$$

cross multiply

(48 cubic feet)(7.5 gallons) = (x gallons)(1 cubic foot)

*the cubic foot measurements will cancel out*

(48)(7.5 gallons) = x gallons
360 gallons = x gallons

           The correct answer is **c.**

---

**EXAMPLE:** Tanisha knows that the area of her patio is 28 square yards. She needs to convert the area into square feet. If there are 9 square feet in one square yard, find the area of the patio in square feet.

   **a.** 27 ft$^2$    **b.** 81 ft$^2$    **c.** 252 ft$^2$    **d.** 9 ft$^2$

Set up a proportion, then solve for x.

$$\frac{28 \text{ square yards}}{x \text{ square feet}} = \frac{1 \text{ square yard}}{9 \text{ square feet}}$$

x = 252 square feet

           The correct answer is **c.**

---

1. Tanisha knows that the area of her patio is 28 square yards. She needs to convert the area into square feet. If there are 9 square feet in one square yard, find the area of the patio in square feet.

   a. 27 ft²
   b. 81 ft²
   c. 252 ft²
   d. 9 ft²

2. Larissa is surveying some property that she would like to buy. The county map indicates that the property is 10 rods wide by 18 rods long. If there are 16.5 feet in one rod, what are the dimensions of the property in feet?

   a. 165 ft x 29.7 ft
   b. 165 ft x 297 ft
   c. 10 ft x 18 ft
   d. 16.5 ft x 297 ft

3. The circle below has a radius as indicated. Find the circumference in inches.

   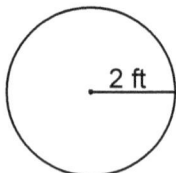

   2 ft

   a. 48$\pi$ in
   b. 4$\pi$ in
   c. 8$\pi$ in
   d. 16$\pi$ in

4. Shawn has a rectangular box with square ends. If the square ends have a side length of 7 inches and the box is 12 inches long, then what is the approximate surface area of the box in square feet? {1 square foot = 144 square inches}

   a. 434 in²
   b. 2 ft²
   c. 3 ft²
   d. 4 ft²

5. Find the area of the rectangle below in square feet. {1 yard = 3 feet}

   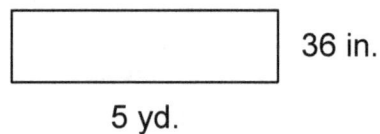

   36 in.

   5 yd.

   a. 180 ft²
   b. 15 ft²
   c. 36 ft²
   d. 45 ft²

6. Find the Perimeter (in centimeters) of the triangle below. {1 inch = 2.54 cm}

   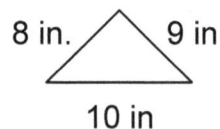

   8 in.    9 in

   10 in

   a. 27 in.
   b. 68.6 cm
   c. 54 cm
   d. 68.6 in.

7. The height of a horse is measured in hands. If one hand equals 4 inches, find the height of a horse (in feet) that is 18 hands tall.

   a. 72 in.
   b. 5.5 ft
   c. 6 ft
   d. 6.5 ft

8. Gasoline is made from oil which is sold in barrels. If one barrel of oil is equal to 42 gallons, then how many barrels would be needed to hold 882 gallons of oil?

   a. 21 barrels
   b. 37002 barrels
   c. 882 barrels
   d. 42 barrels

9. One cubic foot is equal to approximately 7.5 gallons. How many gallons of milk can "the farmer in the dell" put in a tank that is 3 ft x 5 ft x 6 ft?

   a. 90 gallons
   b. 180 gallons
   c. 12 gallons
   d. 675 gallons

**10.** At sea level the the weight of the air measured in Atmospheres is defined to be One atmosphere which is approximately 14.7 pounds per square inch. Convert one atmosphere into pounds per square foot. {1 ft$^2$ = 144 in$^2$}

   **a.** 147 lbs/ft$^2$    **b.** 2116.8 lbs/ft$^2$

   **c.** 2000 lbs/ft$^2$    **d.** 9.7 lbs/ft$^2$

**11.** A certain motorcycle engine is rated at 1340 cc. If you know that one cubic inch is approximately 16.4 cubic centimeters, about how many cubic inches does the engine have?

   **a.** 88 in$^3$    **b.** 73 in$^3$

   **c.** 80 in$^3$    **d.** 54 in$^3$

**12.** A certain car advertises a 5.0 liter engine. If a liter is 1000 cubic centimeters (cc) and one cubic inch is approximately 16.4 cc, then about how big is the engine in cubic inches?

   **a.** 305 in$^3$    **b.** 61 in$^3$

   **c.** 289 in$^3$    **d.** 440 in$^3$

**13.** A cook needs to add 4 tablespoons (tbs.) of an ingredient to a recipe. If the only measuring device available is a teaspoon (tsp.), then how many teaspoons must be added to the recipe? {1 tbs. = 3 tsp.}

   **a.** 1.3 tsp.    **b.** 7 tsp.

   **c.** 9 tsp.    **d.** 12 tsp.

**14.** Latroya wants to paint the outside of a toy box that she made for the children's hospital. Use the diagram below to find the surface area in square centimeters. {1 ft$^2$ is approximately 929 cm$^2$}

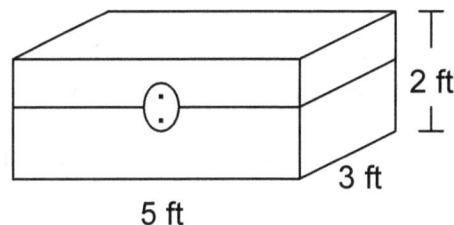

   **a.** 14.9 cm$^2$    **b.** 57598 cm$^2$

   **c.** 62 ft$^2$    **d.** 60000 cm$^2$

**15.** If one mile per hour is equal to 88 feet per minute, then how many miles per hour is a car traveling when it is going 5984 feet per minute?

   **a.** 65 mph    **b.** 70 mph

   **c.** 68 mph    **d.** 680 mph

**16.** If one mile per hour is approximately 1.5 feet per second, then how many feet per second is a car traveling when it is traveling at 70 miles per hour?

   **a.** 105 fps    **b.** 47 fps

   **c.** 140 fps    **d.** 210 fps

**17.** A plot of land is 330 ft by 660 ft. If an one acre is equal to 43560 square feet, then how many acres does the plot of land contain?

   **a.** 2 acres    **b.** 3 acres

   **c.** 4 acres    **d.** 5 acres

Students will successfully translate and reflect on
the coordinate plane.

**CA Standard:** Grade 7, Measurement and Geometry 3.2
**CAHSEE Strand:** Measurement and Geometry

*Simplified Solutions*
For Math Inc.

---

**Vocabulary:** **transformation** a change of position or size of a figure

**translation** a transformation that moves points the same distance in the same direction

**reflection** a transformation that results in a mirror image

**image** the figure resulting from a transformation

---

Before beginning transformations, we need a bank of figures and some of their characteristics.

| NAME | SHAPE | NUMBER OF SIDES | NUMBER OF VERTICES |
|------|-------|-----------------|--------------------|
| Triangle | | 3 | 3 |
| Parallelogram | | 4 | 4 |
| Rectangle | | 4 | 4 |
| Square | | 4 | 4 |
| Trapezoid | | 4 | 4 |
| Pentagon | | 5 | 5 |
| Hexagon | | 6 | 6 |

A **translation** is a transformation that moves points the same distance in the same direction.

The following is an example of triangle ABC translated 5 units left and 3 units up.

To name a point of an image we use prime notation. If the original point was A, then the point after transformation is A'.

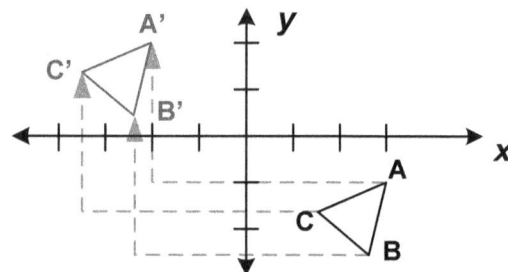

---

**EXAMPLE:** Suppose that point G(2, -3) will be moved right three units and up two units. Which of the following are the coordinates of G'?

    **a.** G'(-1, -5)     **b.** G'(5, -5)     **c.** G'(5, -1)     **d.** G'(-1, -1)

Moving the point right three units will add three to the x-coordinate. 2 + 3 = 5

Moving the point up two units will add two to the y-coordinate. -3 + 2 = -1

The correct answer is **c.**

92

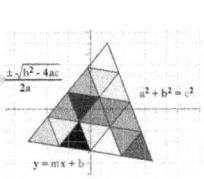

A **reflection** is a transformation that results in a mirror image.

The following is an example of triangle ABC reflected over both the x-axis and y-axis.

Notice the coordinates of point A.
When the shape is reflected over the x-axis, the y-coordinate changes signs and the x-coordinate stays the same.
When the shape is reflected over the y-axis, the x-coordinate changes signs and the y-coordinate stays the same.

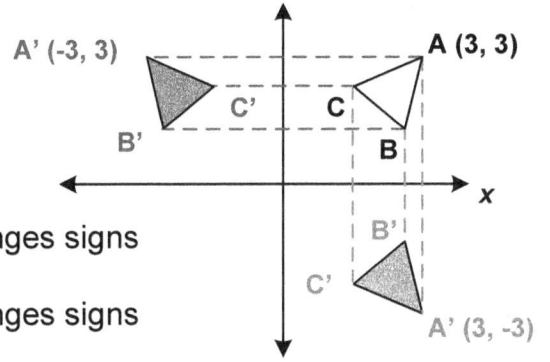

A' (-3, 3)          A (3, 3)

A' (3, -3)

---

EXAMPLE:

Which of the following triangles A'B'C' is the image of triangle ABC that results from reflecting triangle ABC across the x-axis?

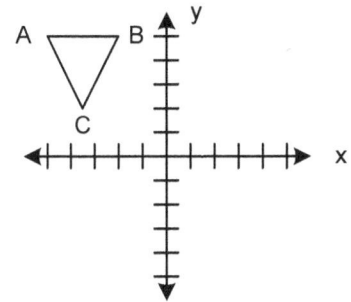

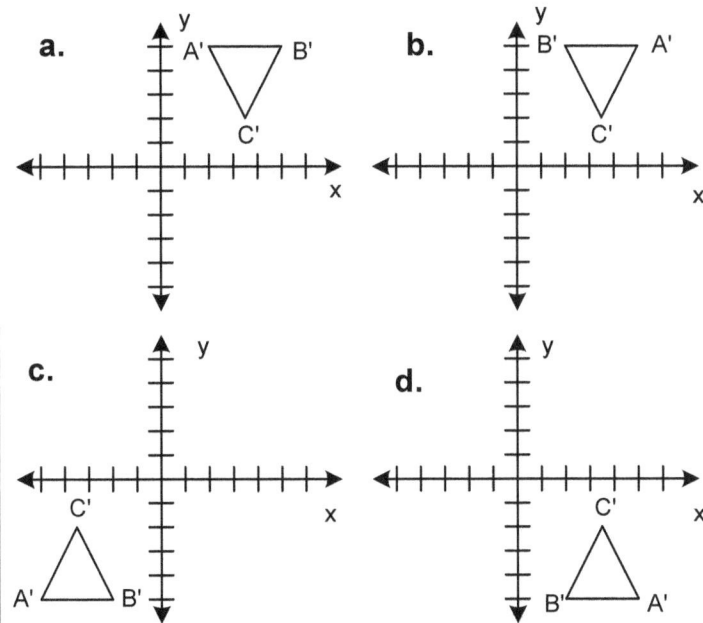

**a.**

**b.**

We know that when the shape is reflected over the x-axis, the y-coordinate changes signs and the x-coordinate stays the same.

**c.**

**d.**

The only choice that meets this criteria is choice **c**.

The correct answer is **c.**

---

There are several miscellaneous problems included in this section that are comparatively simple.

---

EXAMPLE:

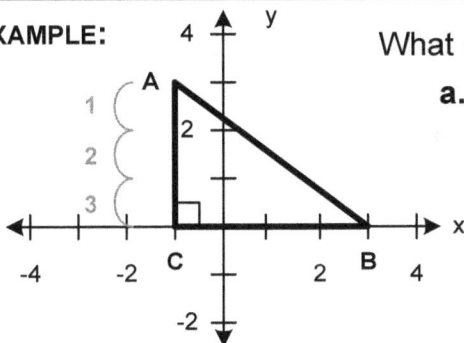

What is the length, in units, of $\overline{AC}$?

**a.** 3    **b.** 4    **c.** 5    **d.** 7

We simply count vertically from point A to point C.

We can see that $\overline{AC}$ is 3 units long.

The correct answer is **a.**

Use the graph of triangle ABC below for questions 1 and 2.

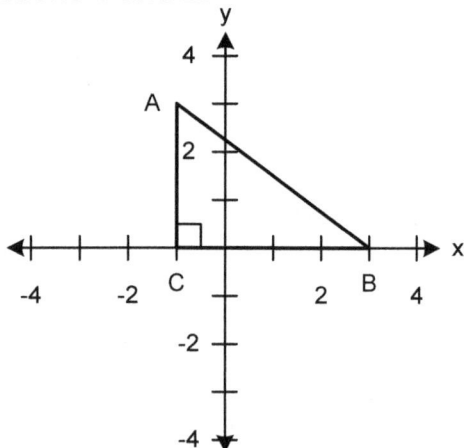

**1.** What is the length, in units, of $\overline{AC}$?

    **a.** 3         **b.** 4

    **c.** 5         **d.** 7

**2.** What is the area, in square units, of triangle ABC?

    **a.** 12       **b.** 8

    **c.** 6        **d.** 4

**3.** The points (-1,-1), (0, 1), (2, 1), and (3,-1) are vertices of a polygon. What type of polygon is formed by these points?

    **a.** Hexagon     **b.** Pentagon

    **c.** Triangle      **d.** Trapezoid

**4.** The points (-2,-2), (-1, 1), (2, 1), and (1,-2) are vertices of a polygon. What type of polygon is formed by these points?

    **a.** Rectangle     **b.** Parallelogram

    **c.** Square       **d.** Pentagon

Use the graph of triangle ABC below for questions 5 and 6.

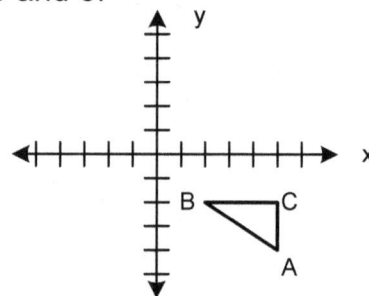

**5.** What is the length, in units, of $\overline{CA}$?

    **a.** -2        **b.** 3

    **c.** 2         **d.** - 4

**6.** Which of the following triangles A'B'C' is the image of triangle ABC that results from reflecting triangle ABC across the x-axis?

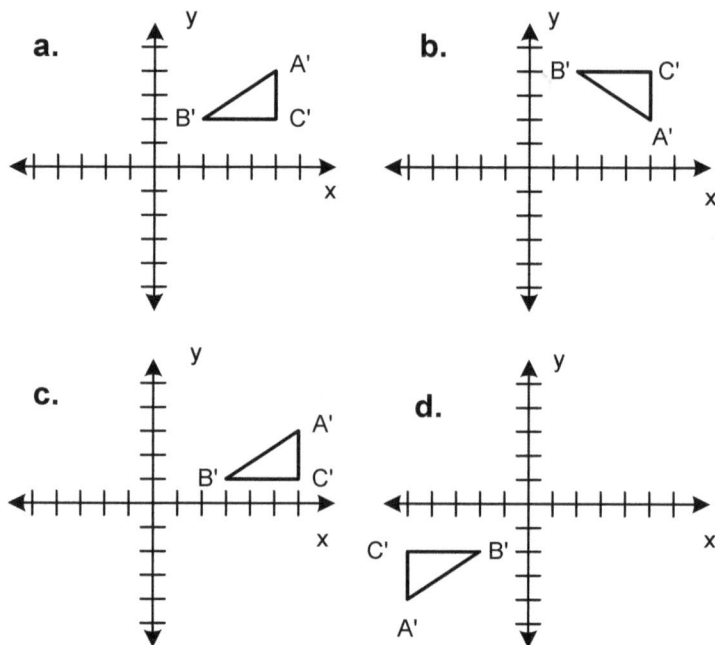

**7.** The points (-2, -1), (-2, 3), and (1, -1) are vertices of a polygon. What type of polygon is formed by these points?

    **a.** Rectangle     **b.** Triangle

    **c.** Square       **d.** Pentagon

# CAHSEE Bench Mark Practice 25

Use the graph of polygon PQRS shown below for questions 8 and 9.

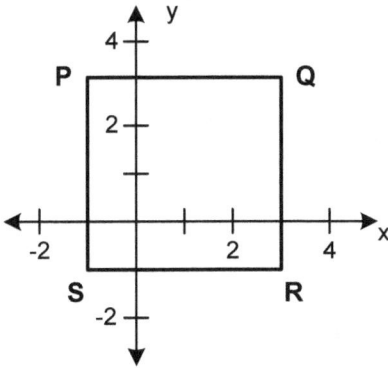

**8.** Polygon PQRS is what type of polygon?

   **a.** Trapezoid     **b.** Square

   **c.** Pentagon     **d.** Triangle

**9.** What is the area, in square units, of polygon PQRS?

   **a.** 9     **b.** 4

   **c.** 8     **d.** 16

**10.** Suppose that point A(1, -1) will be moved right two units and up three units. Which of the following are the coordinates of A'?

   **a.** A'(3, 2)     **b.** A'(2, 3)

   **c.** A'(-3, 2)     **d.** A'(3, 3)

**11.** Point B has translated to point B'. Use the graph below to describe the translation.

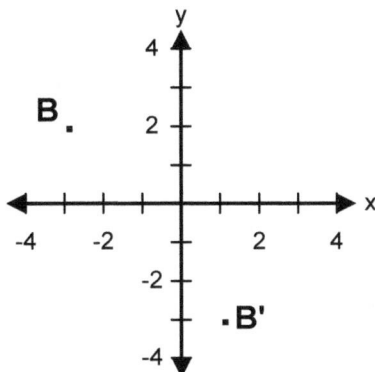

   a. left 4, down 3     b. right 4, down 3

   c. right 4, up 5     d. right 4, down 5

**12.** The points (-2,-2), (-2, 1), (0, 3), (2, 1) and (2,-2) are vertices of a polygon. What type of polygon is formed by these points?

   **a.** Rectangle     **b.** Parallelogram

   **c.** Square     **d.** Pentagon

Use the graph of rectangle ABCD below for questions 13 and 14.

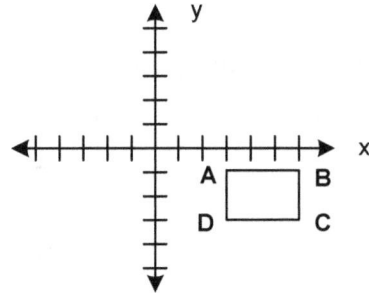

**13.** What is the length, in units, of $\overline{CD}$?

   **a.** 4     **b.** -3

   **c.** 3     **d.** -4

**14.** Which of the following rectangles A'B'C'D' is the image of rectangle ABCD that results from reflecting rectangle ABCD across the x-axis?

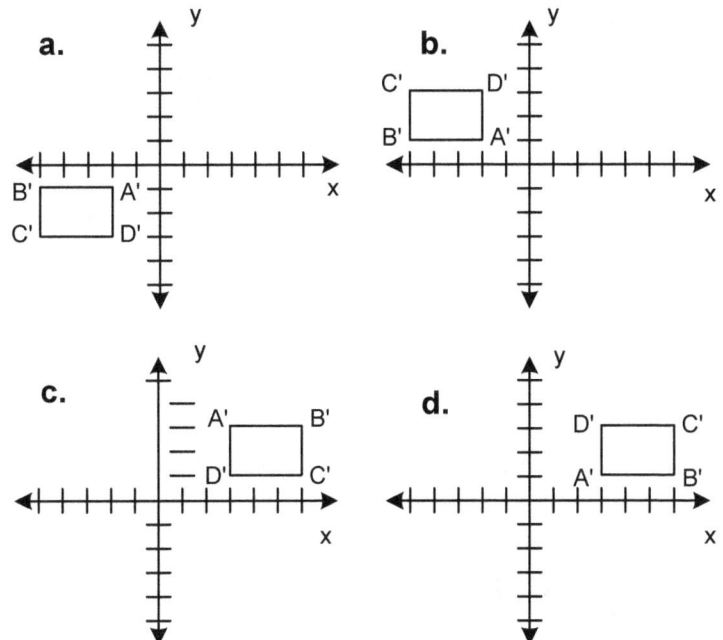

   **a.**

   **b.**

   **c.**

   **d.**

Use the graph of triangle ABC for questions 15 and 16.

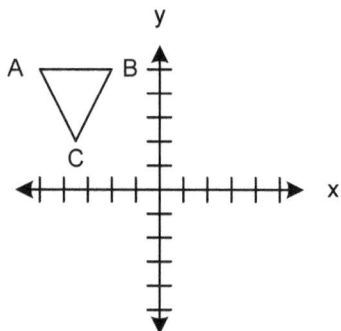

**15.** What is the length, in units, of $\overline{AB}$?

    **a.** 5          **b.** 4

    **c.** 3          **d.** 7

**16.** Which of the following triangles A'B'C' is the image of triangle ABC that results from reflecting triangle ABC across the y-axis?

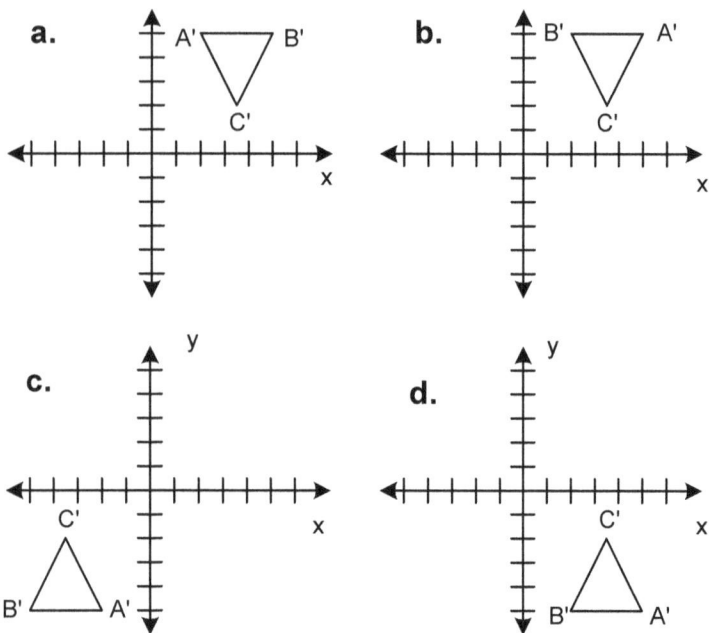

  **a.**                  **b.**

  **c.**                  **d.**

**17.** Suppose that point C(3, 2) will reflect about the y-axis. Which of the following are the coordinates of C'?

    **a.** C'(6, 4)          **b.** C'(0, 0)

    **c.** C'(-3, 2)         **d.** C'(-3, -2)

**18.** Which of the following figures represents the translation of square ABCD right 3 and down 2?

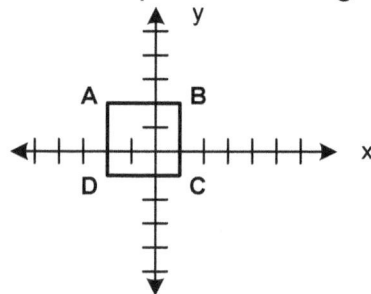

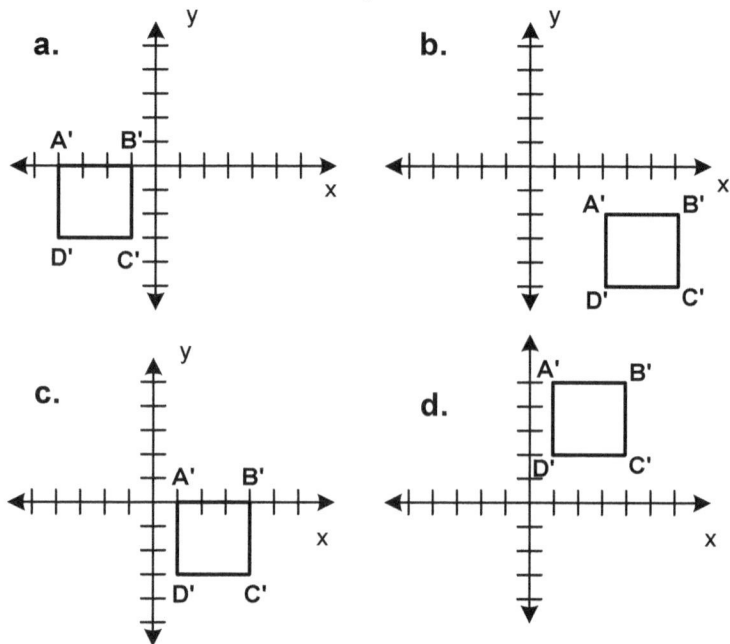

  **a.**                  **b.**

  **c.**                  **d.**

**19.** The points (-2,-2), (-2, 2), (4, -2), and (4, 2) are vertices of a polygon. What type of polygon is formed by these points?

    **a.** Rectangle        **b.** Parallelogram

    **c.** Square           **d.** Pentagon

**20.** Suppose that point R(-2, 0) will reflect about the x-axis. Which of the following are the coordinates of R'?

    **a.** R'(0, 0)          **b.** R'(2, 0)

    **c.** R'(-2, 0)         **d.** R'(0, -2)

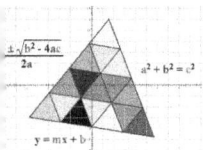

Students will successfully use the Pythagorean theorem.

**CA Standard:** Grade 7, Measurement and Geometry 3.3
**CAHSEE Strand:** Measurement and Geometry

---

| **Vocabulary:** | **right triangle** | a triangle with one angle that measures 90° |
| | **hypotenuse** | the longest side in a right triangle; the side opposite the right angle |
| | **legs** | the sides of a right triangle; not the hypotenuse |

The **Pythagorean theorem** states that "in a right triangle, the square of the hypotenuse is equal to the sum of the squares of the other two sides."

This theorem is also commonly referenced by $a^2 + b^2 = c^2$ ,where c is the length of the hypotenuse and a and b are the lengths of the other two sides called legs.

The theorem can be used to solve right triangles. This means that given the lengths of any two sides of a right triangle, we can calculate the length of the third side.

**For example, find the length of the missing side in the right triangle below.**

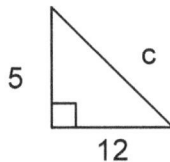

$5^2 + 12^2 = c^2$   Simplify.

$25 + 144 = c^2$   Simplify.

$169 = c^2$         Take the square root of both sides.

$\sqrt{169} = \sqrt{c^2}$   Simplify. *Note: the square root of c squared is c.*

$13 = c$            Therefore, the length of the missing side is 13.

---

The theorem can be also be used to find the length of a line segment given the endpoints.

**For example, find the length of the segment joining points A and B.**

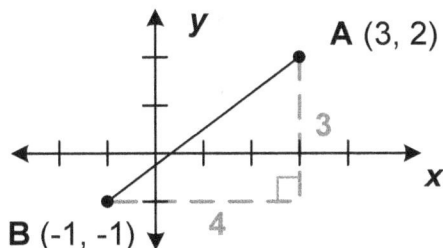

The segment joining points A and B is actually the hypotenuse of a right triangle and its length can be found using the Pythagorean theorem.

$3^2 + 4^2 = c^2$   Therefore the length of
$9 + 16 = c^2$       the segment joining
$25 = c^2$           points A and B is 5
$5 = c$              units long.

---

| **EXAMPLE:** | In a right triangle, if a = 3 and b = 4, then c = ? |

**a.** 3   **b.** 4   **c.** 6   **d.** 5

We can answer this problem by substituting the given values into $a^2 + b^2 = c^2$.

$$3^2 + 4^2 = c^2$$
$$9 + 16 = c^2$$
$$25 = c^2$$
$$5 = c$$

The correct answer is **d.**

---

The **converse** of the theorem is "if the square of the hypotenuse is equal to the sum of the squares of the other two sides, then it is a right triangle."
This can be used to determine if a triangle is a right triangle.

1. In a right triangle, if a = 3 and b = 4, then c = ?

   **a.** 3      **b.** 4

   **c.** 6      **d.** 5

2. In a right triangle, if a = 5 and b = 12, then c = ?

   **a.** 11      **b.** 13

   **c.** 15      **d.** 17

3. In a right triangle, if a = 7 and b = 24, then c = ?

   **a.** 25      **b.** 26

   **c.** 28      **d.** 30

4. In a right triangle, if the length of one leg equals 8 and and the length of the other leg equals 15, what is the length of the hypotenuse?

   **a.** 15      **b.** 16

   **c.** 17      **d.** 18

5. In a right triangle, if a = 3 and c = 5, then b = ?

   **a.** 12      **b.** 4

   **c.** 13      **d.** 5

6. In a right triangle, if the length of one leg equals 12 and the length of the hypotenuse equals 13, what is the length of the other leg?

   **a.** 12      **b.** 4

   **c.** 13      **d.** 5

7. In a right triangle, if a = 7 and c = 25, then b = ?

   **a.** 24      **b.** 12

   **c.** 13      **d.** 5

8. Which of the following are not the sides of a right triangle?

   **a.** 3, 4, 5      **b.** 5, 12, 13

   **c.** 2, 3, 4      **d.** 8, 15, 17

9. Find the length of the segment joining points A and B.

   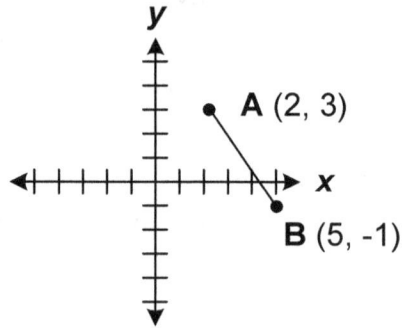

   **a.** 4

   **b.** 5

   **c.** 6

   **d.** 7

10. In a right triangle, if a = 9 and b = 12, then c = ?

    **a.** 12      **b.** 13

    **c.** 14      **d.** 15

11. In a right triangle, if the length of one leg equals 30 and the length of the hypotenuse equals 34, what is the length of the other leg?

    **a.** 16      **b.** 8

    **c.** 17      **d.** 10

12. Find the value of x in the right triangle below.

    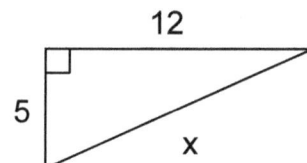

    **a.** 24      **b.** 13

    **c.** 17      **d.** 25

**13.** A group of campers left point A and rode their bicycles 3 miles to point B for lunch. After lunch, they rode 4 miles to point C. They left point C and rode back to point A. How far is it from point C to point A?

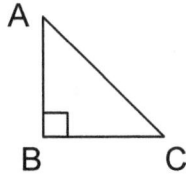

 **a.** 3 miles    **b.** 4 miles

 **c.** 5 miles    **d.** 6 miles

**14.** Find the value of x in the right triangle below.

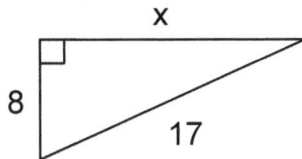

 **a.** 6     **b.** 15

 **c.** 24    **d.** 25

**15.** Find the value of x in the right triangle below.

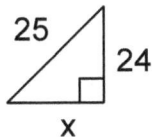

 **a.** 7     **b.** 8

 **c.** 18    **d.** 15

**16.** Which of the following does not satisfy the Pythagorean Theorem?

 **a.** Let a = 16, b = 30, and c = 34

 **b.** Let a = 24, b = 7, and c = 25

 **c.** Let a = $\sqrt{6}$ , b = $\sqrt{5}$ , and c = $\sqrt{11}$

 **d.** Let a = $\frac{1}{2}$ , b = $\frac{1}{6}$ , and c = $\frac{2}{3}$

**17.** Which of the following does not satisfy the Pythagorean Theorem?

 **a.** Let a = 16, b = 12, and c = 20

 **b.** Let a = 4, b = 9, and c = 10

 **c.** Let a = $\sqrt{3}$ , b = $\sqrt{5}$ , and c = $\sqrt{8}$

 **d.** Let a = $\frac{3}{4}$, b = 1, and c = $\frac{5}{4}$

**18.** Does the following diagram represent a right triangle?

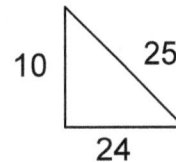

 **a.** Yes, this is a right triangle.

 **b.** No, this is not a right triangle. However, it would be a right triangle if you changed the 24 to a 12.

 **c.** No, this is not a right triangle. However, it would be a right triangle if you changed the 25 to a 26.

 **d.** No, this is not a right triangle. However, it would be a right triangle if you changed the 10 to 8.

**19.** Find the length of the segment joining points A and B.

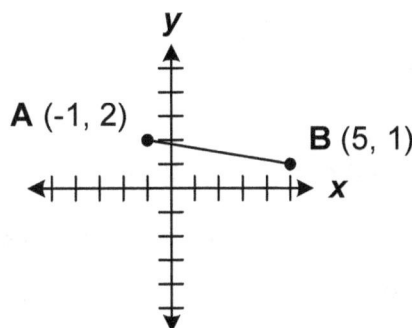

 **a.** 7

 **b.** $\sqrt{56}$

 **c.** $\sqrt{37}$

 **d.** 6

**20.** In a right triangle, if a = 12 and b = 16, then c = ?

 **a.** 12    **b.** 13

 **c.** 20    **d.** 15

**CA Standard:** Grade 7, Measurement and Geometry 3.4
**CAHSEE Strand:** Measurement and Geometry

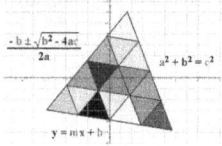

| **Vocabulary:** | **congruent** figures having identical shape and size; the symbol for congruent is $\cong$ |
| | **corresponding** same relative position |

Two shapes are congruent if and only if the vertices can be matched in such a way that the measures of the the angles and sides are equal.

Triangles ABC and JKL are identical figures and are therefore congruent shapes.

Trapezoids ABCD and WXYZ are <u>not</u> identical figures and are therefore <u>not</u> congruent shapes.

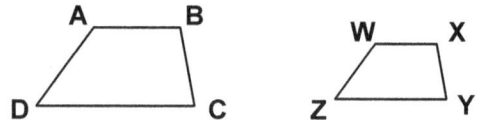

If two shapes are congruent, then the corresponding parts (sides and angles) are congruent.

Triangles ABC and JKL are congruent shapes. Therefore corresponding parts are congruent.

**The 'tick' marks indicate equal measurements.**

In our example;

| angle A $\cong$ angle J | side $\overline{AB} \cong$ side $\overline{JK}$ |
| angle B $\cong$ angle K | side $\overline{BC} \cong$ side $\overline{KL}$ |
| angle C $\cong$ angle L | side $\overline{CA} \cong$ side $\overline{LJ}$ |

Corresponding parts can also be determined by the order in which they are listed. If triangle DEF is congruent to triangle RST then;

| angle D $\cong$ angle R | side $\overline{DE} \cong$ side $\overline{RS}$ |
| angle E $\cong$ angle S | side $\overline{EF} \cong$ side $\overline{ST}$ |
| angle F $\cong$ angle T | side $\overline{FD} \cong$ side $\overline{TR}$ |

**EXAMPLE:** If triangle ABC is congruent to triangle PQR, then which of the following is false?

**a.** Angle B is congruent to angle Q.   **b.** Side $\overline{AB}$ is congruent to side $\overline{PQ}$.

**c.** Angle C is congruent to angle P.   **d.** Side $\overline{PR}$ is congruent to side $\overline{AC}$.

It will be helpful to draw a picture.

We know that corresponding parts of congruent figures are congruent, so by observation, we can see that answer choices **a**, **b**, and **d** are true.

The correct answer is **c.**

1. If triangle ABC is congruent to triangle PQR, then which of the following is false?

   a. Angle B is congruent to angle Q.

   b. Side $\overline{AB}$ is congruent to side $\overline{PQ}$.

   c. Angle C is congruent to angle P.

   d. Side $\overline{PR}$ is congruent to side $\overline{AC}$.

2. If quadrilateral ABCD is congruent to quadrilateral PQRS, then which of the following is false?

   a. Angle C is congruent to angle R.

   b. Side $\overline{AB}$ is congruent to side $\overline{PQ}$.

   c. Angle D is congruent to angle S.

   d. Side $\overline{PR}$ is congruent to side $\overline{AC}$.

3. If trapezoid ABCD is congruent to trapezoid PQRS, then which of the following is false?

   a. Angle A is congruent to angle P.

   b. If the length of side $\overline{CD}$ is 3 units, then the length of side $\overline{RS}$ is 4 units.

   c. If the measure of angle B is 105 degrees, then the measure of angle Q is 105 degrees.

   d. If the length of side $\overline{AB}$ is 4 units, then the length of side $\overline{PQ}$ is 4 units.

4. If two figures are congruent, then which of the following is false?

   a. The figures can have different shapes.

   b. Corresponding angles are congruent.

   c. Corresponding sides are congruent.

   d. The figures must have the same shape.

5.

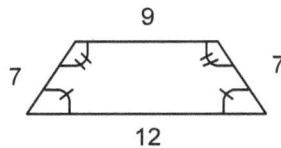

Which figure is congruent to the figure shown above?

   a. 

   b. 

   c. 

   d. 

6. The two triangles are congruent. Find the value of x.

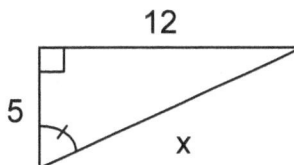

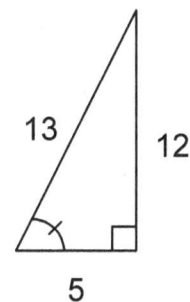

   a. 24          b. 13

   c. 17          d. 25

**7.** The pentagon JACKS is congruent to pentagon NOVEL. Which side of pentagon NOVEL is the same length as $\overline{CK}$?

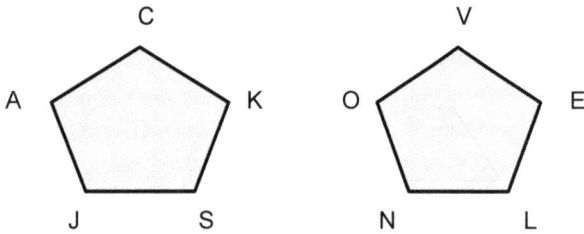

**a.** $\overline{OV}$

**b.** $\overline{AJ}$

**c.** $\overline{KS}$

**d.** $\overline{VE}$

**8.** The pentagon JUDYS is congruent to pentagon TEXAN. Which angle of pentagon JUDYS has the same measure as angle X?

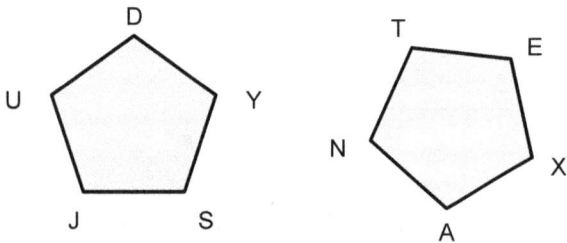

**a.** Angle D

**b.** Angle S

**c.** Angle Y

**d.** Angle U

**9.** Triangle ABC is congruent to triangle DEF. If the measure of angle A = 52$^0$, the measure of angle B = 57$^0$ and the measure of angle C = 71$^0$, then what is the measure of angle E?

**a.** 52$^0$

**b.** 48$^0$

**c.** 71$^0$

**d.** 57$^0$

**10.** Figure ABCD is a parallelogram.

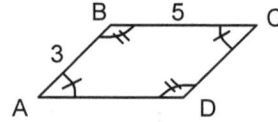

Which figure is congruent to the figure shown above?

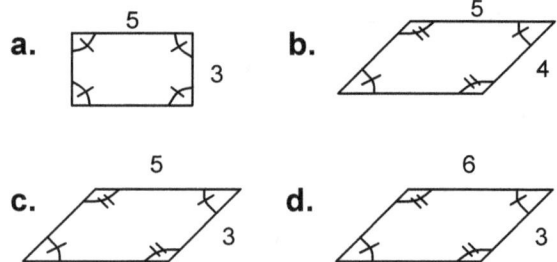

**a.** 

**b.** 

**c.** 

**d.** 

**11.** Triangle LMN is congruent to triangle STU. If the measure of angle S = 36$^0$, the measure of angle T = 70$^0$ and the measure of angle U = 74$^0$, then what is the measure of angle L?

**a.** 36$^0$

**b.** 70$^0$

**c.** 74$^0$

**d.** 54$^0$

**12.** Right triangle ABC is congruent to right triangle PQR. If the length of the sides, in units, are p = 7, q = 24, and r = 25, then which statement below is false?

**a.** Side a = 7.

**b.** Side b = 25

**c.** The measure of angle R is equal to the measure of angle C.

**d.** The perimeter of triangle ABC is equal to the perimeter of triangle PQR.

# CAHSEE Unit 5 Exam
## Bench Marks 1 - 27

**BM 1.** The tallest building in the world is Taipei 101 in Taiwan. It is 1,670 feet tall. What is this number in scientific notation?

   **a.** $1.67 \times 10^5$        **b.** $1.67 \times 10^3$

   **c.** $16.7 \times 10^8$        **d.** $1.67 \times 10^4$

**BM 2.** Which of the following expressions results in a negative number?

   **a.** 5 - 4 + 3        **b.** -5 - (-4) + 3

   **c.** 3 - 4 + 5        **d.** 5 - 4 - 3

**BM 3.** 3 of the 6 quarters in Pat's pocket are dated 1999. What percentage of quarters are dated 1999?

   **a.** 65%        **b.** 30%

   **c.** 50%        **d.** 60%

**BM 4.** The price of a watch has decreased from $100.00 to $79.00. What is the percent of decrease?

   **a.** 21%        **b.** 79%

   **c.** 20%        **d.** 12%

**BM 5.** A sales person at a sporting goods store earns a 6% commission on all sales. How much commission does the sales person earn on a $900.00 sale?

   **a.** $72.00        **b.** $46.00

   **c.** $90.00        **d.** $54.00

**BM 6.** Multiply. $12^{-1} \cdot 12^{-1}$

   **a.** 12        **b.** $12^{-2}$

   **c.** $\dfrac{1}{12^{-2}}$        **d.** $\dfrac{1}{12}$

**BM 7.** Which fraction is equivalent to $\dfrac{3}{7} - \dfrac{1}{3}$ ?

   **a.** $\dfrac{2}{4}$        **b.** $\dfrac{4}{10}$

   **c.** $\dfrac{2}{10}$        **d.** $\dfrac{2}{21}$

**BM 8.** $(7^2 \cdot 9^8)^3$

   **a.** $7^6 \cdot 9^{24}$        **b.** $7^5 \cdot 9^{11}$

   **c.** $7^6 \cdot 9^{11}$        **d.** $7^5 \cdot 9^{24}$

**BM 9.** The square of a <u>whole</u> number is between 100 and 200. The number must be between

   **a.** 5 and 10        **b.** 10 and 15

   **c.** 15 and 20        **d.** 20 and 25

**BM 10.** What is the absolute value of -18?

   **a.** -18        **b.** 18

   **c.** $\dfrac{1}{18}$        **d.** $\dfrac{-1}{18}$

**BM 11.** The box below shows Cameron's first six quiz scores.

> 9, 14, 11, 9, 16, 13

What is Cameron's mean score?

   **a.** 12        **b.** 9

   **c.** 7        **d.** 11

**BM 12.** The following table represents the number of students who take geometry.

|          | Pass | Fail |
|----------|------|------|
| Period 1 | 14   | 12   |
| Period 3 | 11   | 9    |

Which of the following statements is false?

a. The percentage of students who passed period 1 is greater than the percentage of students who passed period 3.

b. Period 1 had six more students then period 3.

c. The ratio of pass to fail in period 1 is seven to six.

d. The percentage of students who passed period 1 is less than period 3.

**BM 13.** If you pick a card at random from a complete deck of cards, what is the probability that it will be black?

a. $\dfrac{1}{4}$     b. $\dfrac{1}{2}$

c. $\dfrac{1}{12}$     d. $\dfrac{2}{13}$

**BM 14.** If a fair quarter is flipped. What is the probability that it will not land heads up?

a. $\dfrac{1}{4}$     b. $\dfrac{1}{25}$

c. $\dfrac{1}{3}$     d. $\dfrac{1}{2}$

**BM 15.** Brianna's **event** will list the **outcomes** of drawing two cards from a complete deck of 52 cards. Which of the following best describes Brianna's event?

a. Independent.

b. Dependent.

c. Need more information to determine independence or dependence.

d. If Briana draws two Clubs in a row, she should get a different deck of cards.

**BM 16.** The table below represents the enrollment cost and monthly cost of a cell phone for four companies. If the number of minutes is the same for each plan, which company would cost the least for one year?

| Company | Enrollment Cost | Monthly Cost |
|---------|-----------------|--------------|
| 1       | 110             | 65           |
| 2       | 140             | 60           |
| 3       | 130             | 55           |
| 4       | 150             | 50           |

a. 1     b. 2     c. 3     d. 4

**BM 17.** The below scatter plot appears to be what type of correlation?

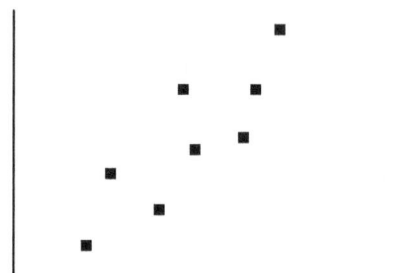

a. Strong Positive Correlation

b. Zero Correlation

c. Weak Positive Correlation

d. Weak Negative Correlation

**BM 18.** A building is 22 meters tall. About how tall is it in feet (ft) and inches (in.)? (1 meter ≈ 39 inches)

a. 70 ft 6 in.　　b. 71 ft 0 in.

c. 71 ft 6 in.　　d. 72 ft 0 in.

**BM 19.** The scale drawing of the tennis court shown below is drawn using a scale of 1 inch (in.) = 18 feet (ft).

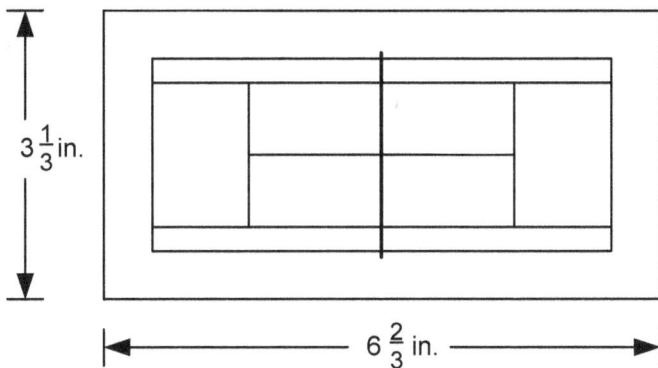

$3\frac{1}{3}$ in.

$6\frac{2}{3}$ in.

What is the length of the court in feet?

a. 105 ft　　b. 110 ft

c. 115 ft　　d. 120 ft

**BM 20.** Kennedy can type about 65 words per minute. If she types at this rate for 20 minutes without stopping, about how many words will she type?

a. 1,300　　b. 1,450

c. 1,550　　d. 1,700

**BM 21.**

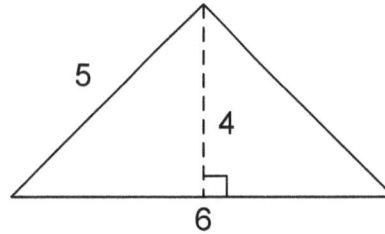

5　4　6

What is the area of the triangle shown above?

a. 10 square units　　b. 12 square units

c. 8 square units　　d. 6 square units

**BM 22.**

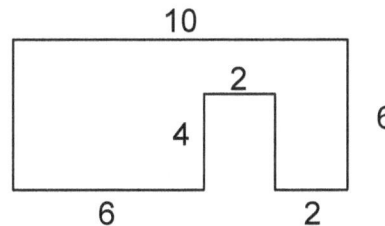

10　2　6　4　6　2

In the figure shown above, all the corners form right angles. What is the area of the figure in square units?

a. 78　　b. 64

c. 52　　d. 44

**BM 23.** Yasman has a rectangular box with square ends. If the square ends have a side length of 6 inches and the box is 13 inches long, then what is the volume of the box?

a. 78 in$^3$　　b. 384 in$^3$

c. 348 in$^3$　　d. 468 in$^3$

**BM 24.** Latroya wants to paint the outside of a toy box that she made for the children's hospital. Use the diagram below to find the surface area in square centimeters. {1 ft² is approximately 929 cm²}

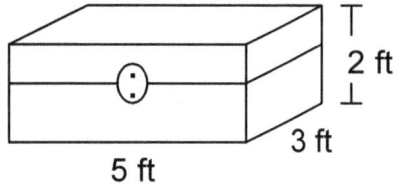

2 ft

3 ft

5 ft

**a.** 14.9 cm²  **b.** 57598 cm²

**c.** 62 ft²  **d.** 60000 cm²

**BM 25.**

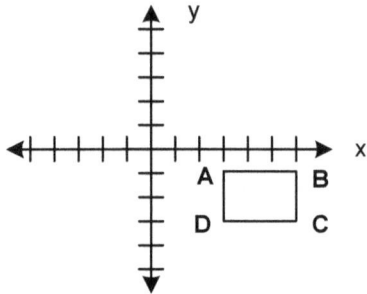

Which of the following rectangles A'B'C'D' is the image of rectangle ABCD that results from reflecting rectangle ABCD across the x-axis?

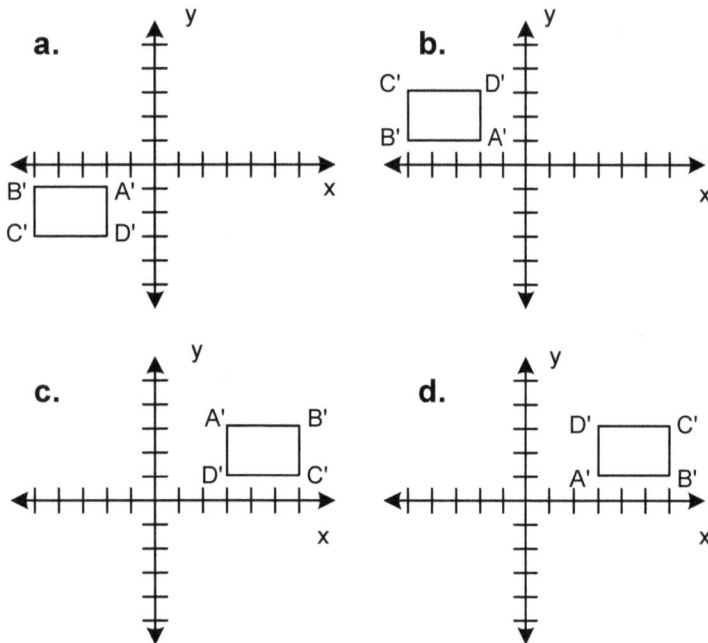

**a.** 

**b.** 

**c.** 

**d.** 

**BM 26.** In a right triangle, if the length of one leg equals 12 and the length of the hypotenuse equals 13, what is the length of the other leg?

**a.** 12  **b.** 4

**c.** 13  **d.** 5

**BM 27.**

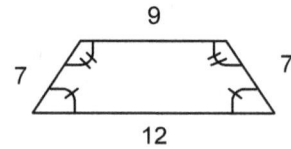

Which figure is congruent to the figure shown above?

**a.** 

**b.** 

**c.** 

**d.**

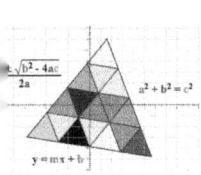

**Students will successfully write linear expressions.**

**CA Standard:** Grade 7, Algebra and Functions 1.1
**CAHSEE Strand:** Algebra and Functions

A difficult task in algebra is to translate between English and mathematics.
The following are some common translations.

+     add, addition, increase, more, plus, sum

−     subtract, subtraction, decrease, less, minus, difference

•     multiply, multiplication, times, product

÷     divide, division, quotient

=     equal, equals, the same as, is

<     is less than

≤     is less than or equal to

>     is greater than

≥     is greater than or equal to

---

**EXAMPLE:** Multiply a number by 2 and add 5. The answer is 10. Which equation matches the information.

**a.** $2x - 10 = 5$     **b.** $2x + 10 = 5$     **c.** $2x + 5 = 10$     **d.** $2x - 5 = 10$

---

"A number" in algebra translates into the variable for the expression or equation. The most common letter to use is x.

"multiply a number by 2" will be $2x$

"and add 5" will be $2x + 5$

"the answer is 10" will be $2x + 5 = 10$

The correct answer is **c.**

---

**EXAMPLE:** Which of the following inequalities represents the statement, "A number, x, decreased by 6 is less than or equal to 5?"

       **a.** $6 - x > 5$        **b.** $x - 6 \leq 5$

       **c.** $x - 6 \geq 5$        **d.** $6 - x \leq 5$

       "a number, x, decreased by 6" will be $x - 6$

       "is less than or equal to 5" will be $x - 6 \leq 5$

The correct answer is **b.**

# CAHSEE Bench Mark Practice 28

1. Which of the following inequalities represents the statement, "A number, x, decreased by 6 is less than or equal to 5?"

   **a.** $6 - x > 5$        **b.** $x - 6 \leq 5$

   **c.** $x - 6 \geq 5$      **d.** $6 - x \leq 5$

2. A store owner has x pounds of coffee in stock. She sells 12 pounds and then receives a new shipment of 15 pounds. Which expression represents the weight of the coffee she now has?

   **a.** $x - 12 + 15$      **b.** $x + 12 + 15$

   **c.** $x - 12 - 15$      **d.** $x + 12 - 15$

3. Multiply a number by 3 and add 4 to the result. The answer is 10. Which of the following equations matches these statements?

   **a.** $3(x + 4) = 10$    **b.** $4 = 10 + 3x$

   **c.** $3x + 10 = 4$      **d.** $3x + 4 = 10$

4. In a certain restaurant, the number of forks, f, is equal to 2 times the number of spoons, s. Which equation matches the information?

   **a.** $2s = f$           **b.** $2f = s$

   **c.** $fs = 2$           **d.** $2f = 2s$

5. Divide a number by 5 and add 8 to the result. The answer is 32. Which of the following equations matches these statements?

   **a.** $\dfrac{x + 8}{5} = 32$     **b.** $\dfrac{x + 5}{8} = 32$

   **c.** $\dfrac{x}{5} + 8 = 32$     **d.** $\dfrac{x}{5} - 8 = 32$

6. A man weighs x pounds before his diet. He loses 19 pounds and then regains 6 pounds. Which expression represents the weight of the man now ?

   **a.** $x - 19 - 6$       **b.** $19 - x + 6$

   **c.** $x - 19 + 6$       **d.** $x - 6 + 15$

7. Multiply a number by 7 and subtract 6 from the result. The answer is 16. Which of the following equations matches these statements?

   **a.** $7x - 6 = 16$      **b.** $16 = 6 + 7x$

   **c.** $7x + 16 = 6$      **d.** $7x + 6 = 16$

8. In a certain classroom, the number of desks, d, is equal to 4 times the number of tables, t. Which equation matches the information?

   **a.** $4d = t$           **b.** $4d = 4t$

   **c.** $4t = d$           **d.** $d = t$

9. Which of the following inequalities represents the statement, "A number, x, increased by 11 is less than 21?"

   **a.** $11 + x > 21$      **b.** $x + 21 \leq 11$

   **c.** $x + 11 < 21$      **d.** $21 + x < 11$

10. Multiply a number by 2 and subtract 12 from the result. The answer is 36. Which of the following equations matches these statements?

    **a.** $2x - 12 = 36$    **b.** $36 = 12 - 2x$

    **c.** $2x + 12 = 36$    **d.** $2x + 36 = 12$

**11.** Which of the following inequalities represents the statement, "A number, x, decreased by 4 is less than or equal to 7?"

**a.** $x - 4 \leq 7$          **b.** $x - 7 < 4$

**c.** $x - 4 > 7$          **d.** $4 - x \leq 7$

**12.** A store owner has x pounds of flour in stock. She receives 25 pounds and then sells a new shipment of 50 pounds. Which expression represents the weight of the flour she now has?

**a.** $x - 25 - 50$          **b.** $x - 25 + 50$

**c.** $x - 50 - 25$          **d.** $x + 25 - 50$

**13.** Multiply a number by 7 and add 2 to the result. The answer is 21. Which of the following equations matches these statements?

**a.** $7(x + 2) = 21$          **b.** $2 = 21 + 7x$

**c.** $7x + 21 = 2$          **d.** $7x + 2 = 21$

**14.** At a certain car lot, the number of cars, c, is equal to 3 times the number of trucks, t. Which equation matches the information?

**a.** $c = 3t$          **b.** $3c = t$

**c.** $ct = 3$          **d.** $3c = 3t$

**15.** Divide a number by 6 and add 7 to the result. The answer is 54. Which of the following equations matches these statements?

**a.** $\frac{x}{6} + 7 = 54$          **b.** $\frac{x}{6} - 7 = 54$

**c.** $\frac{x + 6}{7} = 54$          **d.** $\frac{x + 7}{6} = 54$

**16.** A gold miner finds gold that weighs x ounces. He sells 10 ounces and then sells another 12 ounces. Which expression represents the amount of gold the miner has now ?

**a.** $x - 10 - 12$          **b.** $12 - x + 10$

**c.** $x - 10 + 12$          **d.** $x - 12 + 10$

**17.** Multiply a number by 2 and subtract 10 from the result. The answer is 24. Which of the following equations matches these statements?

**a.** $24 - 2x = 10$          **b.** $2x - 10 = 24$

**c.** $2x + 10 = 24$          **d.** $2x + 24 = 10$

**18.** In a certain toy store, the number of trains, t, is equal to 10 times the number of blocks, b. Which equation matches the information?

**a.** $10t = b$          **b.** $10b = 10t$

**c.** $10b = t$          **d.** $b = t$

**19.** Which of the following inequalities represents the statement, "A number, x, increased by 2 is less than 4?"

**a.** $4 + x > 2$          **b.** $x + 2 \leq 4$

**c.** $x + 4 < 2$          **d.** $x + 2 < 4$

**20.** Multiply a number by 11 and subtract 5 from the result. The answer is 9. Which of the following equations matches these statements?

**a.** $11x - 5 = 9$          **b.** $5 = 9 - 11x$

**c.** $11x + 5 = 9$          **d.** $9 - 11x = 5$

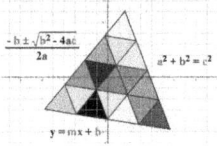

# CAHSEE Bench Mark 29

Students will successfully evaluate expressions using the
order of operations.

**CA Standard:** Grade 7, Algebra and Functions 1.2
**CAHSEE Strand:** Algebra and Functions

*Simplified Solutions*
For Math Inc.

| Vocabulary: | | |
|---|---|---|
| | **order of operations** | an agreed upon order to perform arithmetic operations |
| | **simplify** | make plainer or easier |
| | **expression** | symbol or group of symbols expressing some mathematical process or quantity |
| | **evaluate** | to find the numerical value |
| | **substitute** | to replace one thing with another, commonly used in algebra, a number will replace a variable |

In mathematics, there can only be one correct answer.
To avoid confusion, mathematicians have agreed on an **order of operations**.

When confronted with a calculation involving more than one arithmetic
operation, follow this standard order:

**P**arenthesis    simplify anything inside of parenthesis, brackets, or braces
**E**xponents    simplify anything with exponents
**M**ultiply/**D**ivide    multiply and divide left to right (whichever you see first, you do first)
**A**dd/**S**ubtract    add and subtract left to right (whichever you see first, you do first)

When **substituting and evaluating**, replace the indicated variable with the given number, then
perform the order of operations.

---

**EXAMPLE:** If x = 3 and y = 2, then x(y + 1)=

   **a.** 7      **b.** 9      **c.** 11      **d.** 13

---

Begin by replacing x with 3 and y with 2.      3(2 + 1)

Simplify inside the parenthesis.      3(3)

Multiply.      9      The correct answer is **b.**

---

**EXAMPLE:**      If w = 2 and r = 3, then r(w + 5)=

     **a.** 16      **b.** 9      **c.** 21      **d.** 27

Begin by replacing w with 2 and r with 3.      3(2 + 5)

Simplify inside the parenthesis.      3(7)

Multiply.      21

The correct answer is **c.**

---

# CAHSEE Bench Mark Practice 29

1. If w = 2 and r = 3, then r(w + 5)=

   a. 16  b. 9

   c. 21  d. 27

2. If u = 4 and v = 6, then $\frac{uv - 2}{2}$ + 3 =

   a. 22  b. 17

   c. 10  d. 14

3. If h = 4 and k = $\frac{1}{2}$, then h(k + 2)=

   a. 10  b. 3

   c. 16  d. 8

4. If m = 5 and n = 3, then $\frac{2mn}{3}$ + 1 =

   a. 24  b. 11

   c. 10  d. 32

5. If p = 7 and q = 9, then q(p - 6)=

   a. 16  b. 9

   c. 21  d. 27

6. If a = 3 and b = 5, then $\frac{ab + 5}{4}$ - 2 =

   a. 12  b. 1

   c. 3  d. 20

7. If c = 3 and d = $\frac{2}{3}$, then c(d + 3)=

   a. 14  b. 11

   c. 4  d. 9

8. If w = 10 and x = 4, then $\frac{4wx}{80}$ - 1 =

   a. 8  b. 5

   c. 21  d. 1

9. If f = 12 and g = 8, then g(f - 2)=

   a. 72  b. 96

   c. 108  d. 80

10. If s = 11 and t = 5, then 2s(t - 4)=

    a. 19  b. 18

    c. 22  d. 26

**11.** If w = 5 and r = 2, then r(w + 3)=

    **a.** 15          **b.** 9

    **c.** 20         **d.** 16

**12.** If u = 3 and v = 8, then $\dfrac{uv - 2}{2} + 3 =$

    **a.** 22         **b.** 17

    **c.** 10         **d.** 14

**13.** If h = 10 and k = $\dfrac{1}{2}$, then h(k + 1)=

    **a.** 10         **b.** 3

    **c.** 15         **d.** 8

**14.** If m = 9 and n = 3, then $\dfrac{2mn}{3} + 5 =$

    **a.** 24         **b.** 23

    **c.** 10         **d.** 32

**15.** If p = 4 and q = 2, then q(p - 1)=

    **a.** 16         **b.** 9

    **c.** 6          **d.** 3

**16.** If a = 10 and b = 2, then $\dfrac{ab + 4}{4} - 2 =$

    **a.** 12         **b.** 1

    **c.** 4          **d.** 8

**17.** If c = 6 and d = $\dfrac{1}{3}$, then c(d + 2)=

    **a.** 14         **b.** 11

    **c.** 4          **d.** 9

**18.** If w = 15 and x = 3, then $\dfrac{2wx}{9} - 8 =$

    **a.** 1          **b.** 4

    **c.** 2          **d.** 16

**19.** If f = 14 and g = 3, then g(f - 10)=

    **a.** 12         **b.** 8

    **c.** 22         **d.** 16

**20.** If s = 20 and t = 4, then 2t(s - 10)=

    **a.** 120       **b.** 80

    **c.** 50        **d.** 240

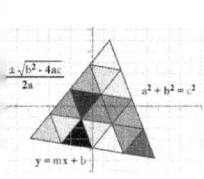

Students will successfully represent quantitative relationships graphically.

**CA Standard:** Grade 7, Algebra and Functions 1.5
**CAHSEE Strand:** Algebra and Functions

Reading data from a graph is a fairly simple process of understanding what is being asked and being able to pull the information needed from the graph.

---

**EXAMPLE:** The cost of two internet providers, company A and company B, is shown on the graph below.

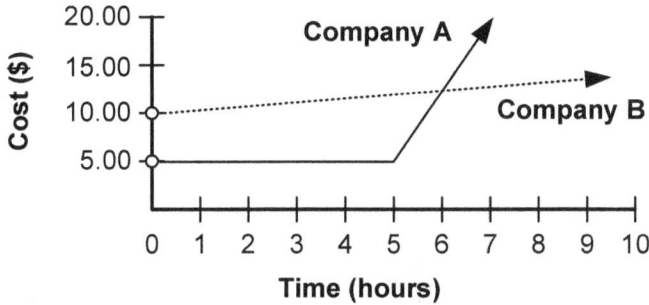

Company A is cheaper than company B for

**a.** more than 6 hours    **b.** any amount of time

**c.** less than 6 hours    **d.** 6 hours only

---

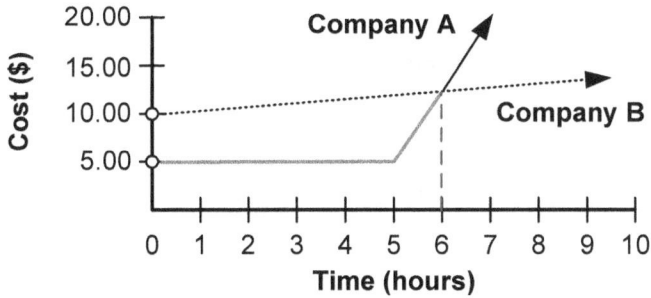

From the graph, we must first understand that prices are on the cost axis, therefore the lower line is the cheaper deal.

We must also observe that hours are represented on the time axis.

Company A's line is below Company B's line for times less than 6 hours of service.

The correct answer is **c.**

---

**EXAMPLE:**

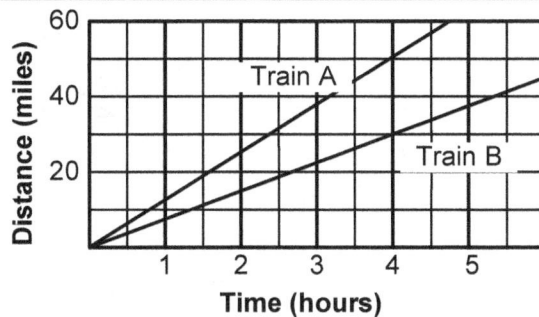

After four hours of travel, Train A is about how many miles ahead of Train B?

**a.** 2    **b.** 15    **c.** 20    **d.** 25

Reading the graph at four hours, Train A has traveled 50 miles and Train B has traveled 30 miles. 50 - 30 = 20 miles.

The correct answer is **c.**

**1.**

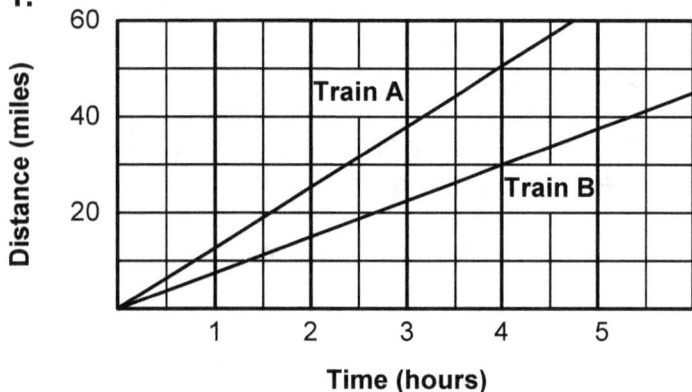

After four hours of travel, Train A is about how many miles ahead of Train B?

**a.** 2

**b.** 15

**c.** 20

**d.** 25

**2.** The cost of operating a gas clothes dryer and an electric clothes dryer is shown on the graph below.

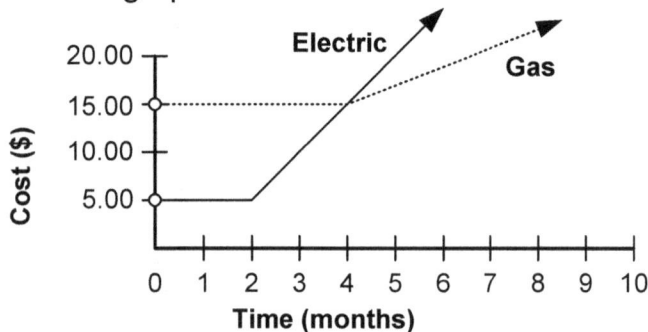

The electric dryer is less expensive than the gas dryer for

**a.** more than 3 months

**b.** less than 4 months

**c.** 4 months only

**d.** any month

**3.** The graph below shows the relationship between the temperature outside and the number of popsicles sold at a certain ice cream stand.

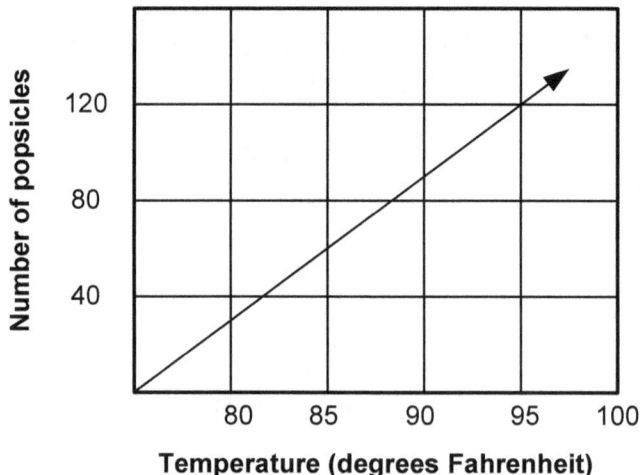

What is the approximate number of popsicles sold on a 95° day?

**a.** 40

**b.** 90

**c.** 120

**d.** 140

**4.**

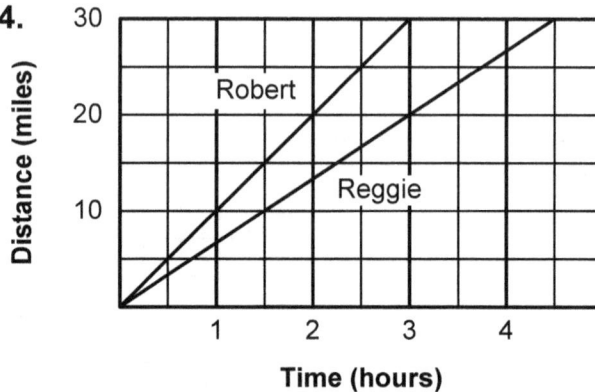

After three hours of a cross country race, Robert is about how many miles ahead of Reggie?

**a.** 2

**b.** 10

**c.** 20

**d.** 25

**5.** The graph below shows the relationship between the wind speed and the height of a kite flown at the park.

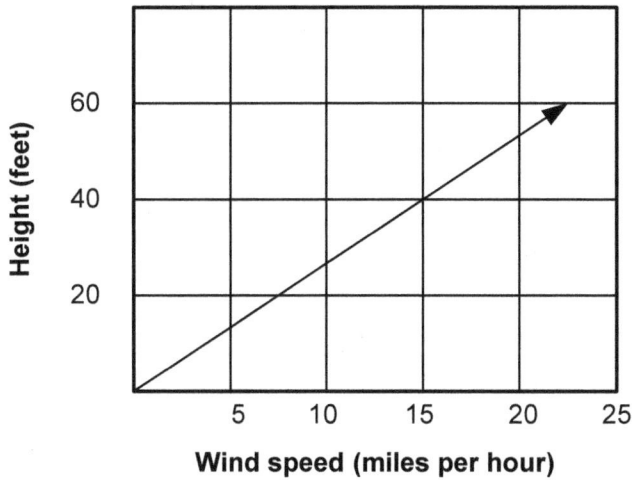

What is the approximate height of the kite when the wind blows at 15 miles per hour?

**a.** 40          **b.** 90

**c.** 120          **d.** 140

**6.** The cost of two internet providers, company A and company B, is shown on the graph below.

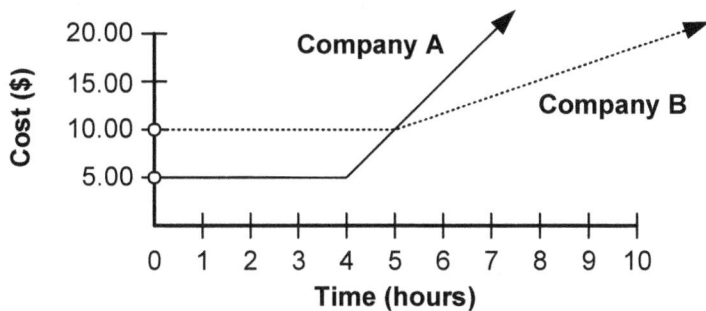

Company A is cheaper than company B for

**a.** less than 5 hours

**b.** more than 5 hours

**c.** 5 hours only

**d.** any amount of time

**7.**

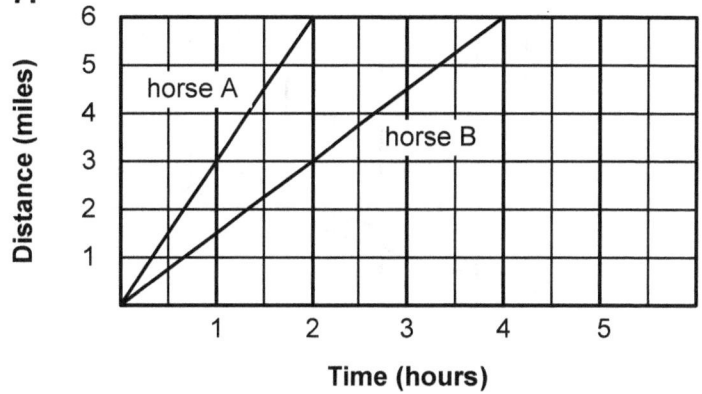

After two hours of racing, horse A is about how many miles ahead of horse B?

**a.** 2          **b.** 4

**c.** 3          **d.** 6

**8.** The graph below shows the relationship between the time spent fishing and the number of fish caught at a certain pond.

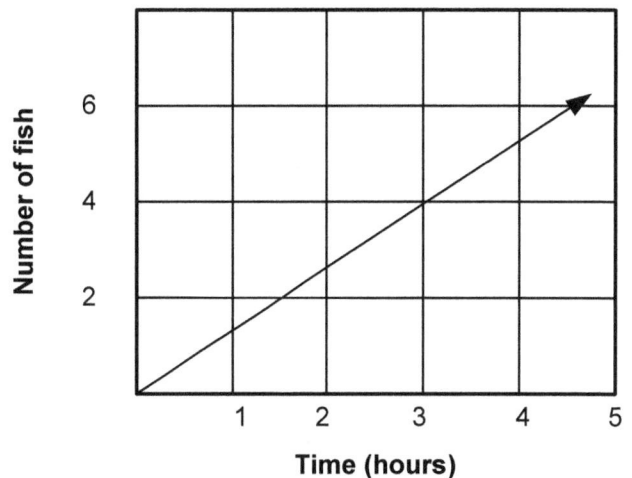

What is the approximate number of fish caught at 3 hours?

**a.** 5          **b.** 4

**c.** 2          **d.** 3

115

**9.**

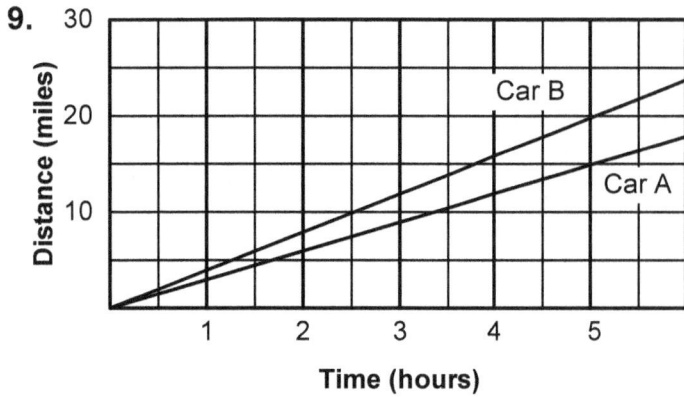

**Time (hours)**

After five hours of travel, Car B is about how many miles ahead of Car A?

**a.** 2

**b.** 10

**c.** 5

**d.** 15

**10.** The cost of renting movies from two different movie rental companies is shown on the graph below.

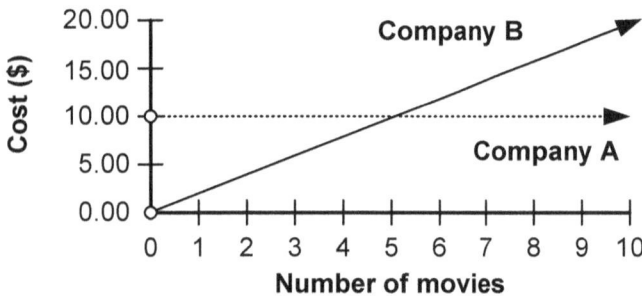

**Number of movies**

Company A is less expensive than Company B for:

**a.** any amount of movies

**b.** less than 5 movies

**c.** 5 movies only

**d.** more than 5 movies

**11.** The graph below shows the relationship between the number of people at the park with the number of hot dogs sold at a certain stand.

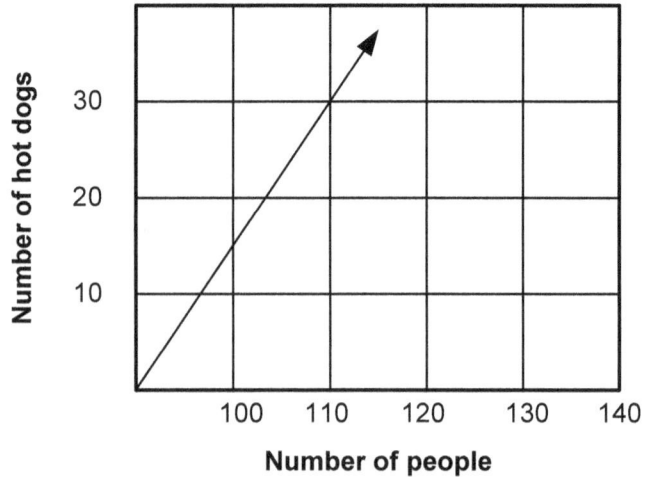

**Number of people**

What is the approximate number of hot dogs sold when 110 people are at the park?

**a.** 50

**b.** 20

**c.** 40

**d.** 30

**12.**

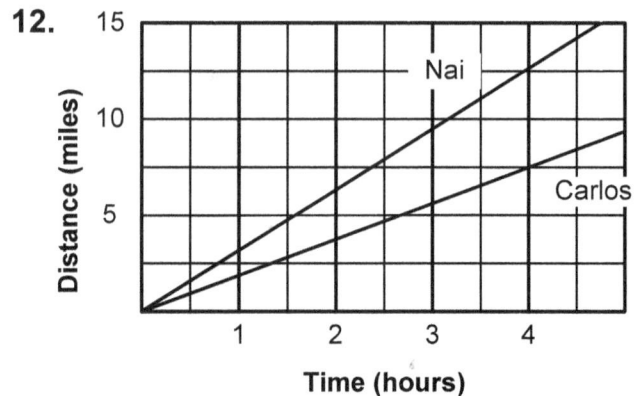

**Time (hours)**

After four hours of a cross country race, Nai is about how many miles ahead of Carlos?

**a.** 10

**b.** 5

**c.** 20

**d.** 15

**13.** The graph below shows the relationship between the temperature outside and the number of popsicles sold at a certain ice cream stand.

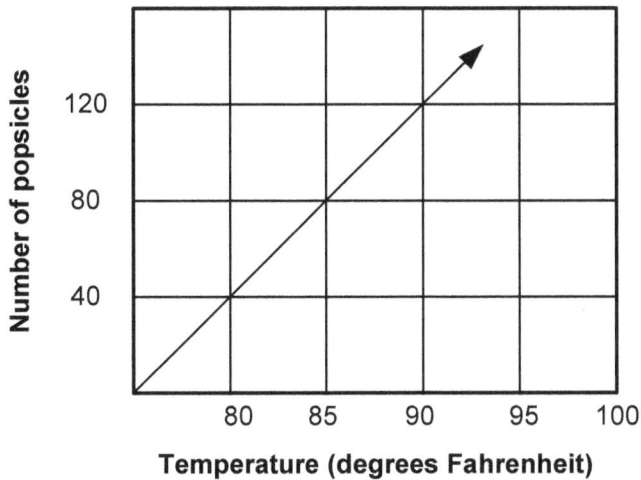

Temperature (degrees Fahrenheit)

What is the approximate number of popsicles sold on a 85° day?

a. 40          b. 90

c. 80          d. 120

**14.** The cost of operating a gas clothes dryer and an electric clothes dryer is shown on the graph below.

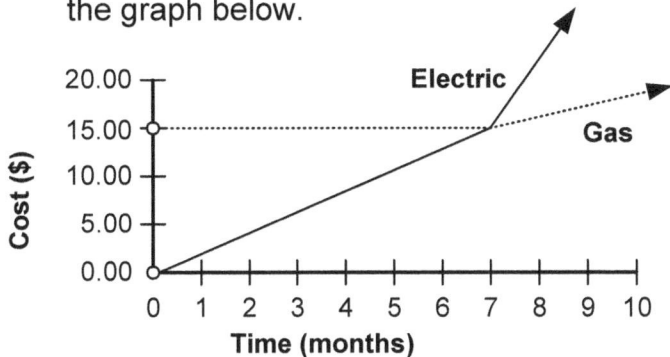

The electric dryer is less expensive than the gas dryer for:

a. more than 7 months

b. any month

c. less than 7 months

d. 7 months only

**15.**

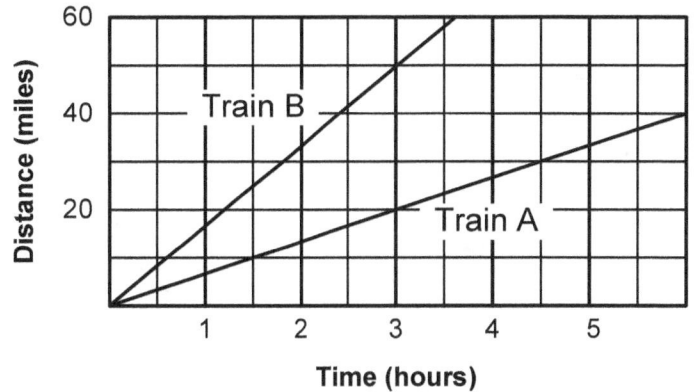

After three hours of travel, Train B is about how many miles ahead of Train A?

a. 35          b. 30

c. 20          d. 25

**16.** The graph below shows the relationship between the temperature outside and the number of ice cream cones sold at a certain ice cream stand.

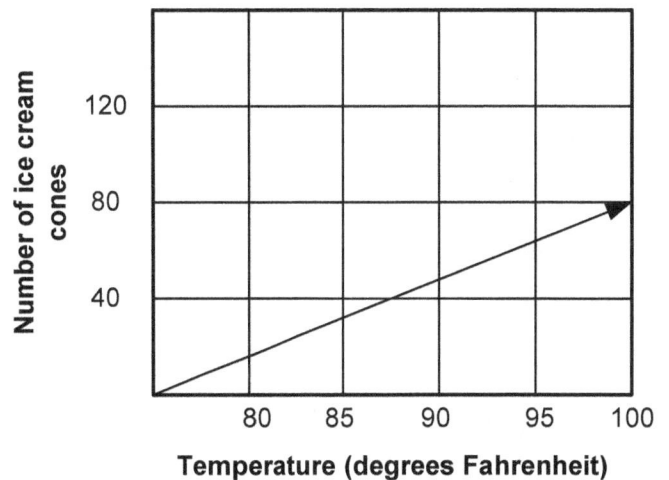

Temperature (degrees Fahrenheit)

What is the approximate number of ice cream cones sold on a 100° day?

a. 40          b. 90

c. 120         d. 80

**17.**

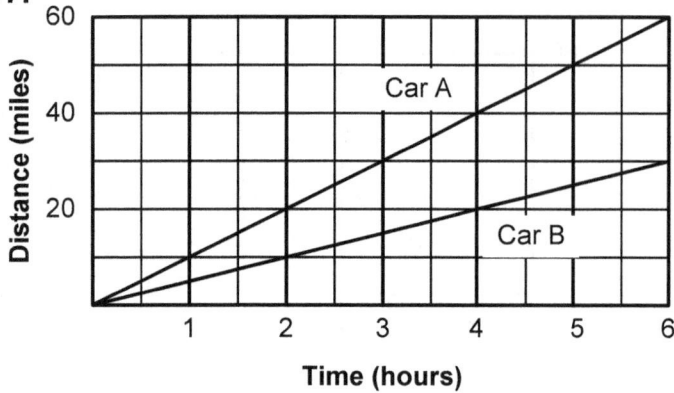

After six hours of travel, Car A is about how many miles ahead of Car B?

**a.** 30

**b.** 35

**c.** 20

**d.** 25

**18.** The cost of two internet providers, company A and company B, is shown on the graph below.

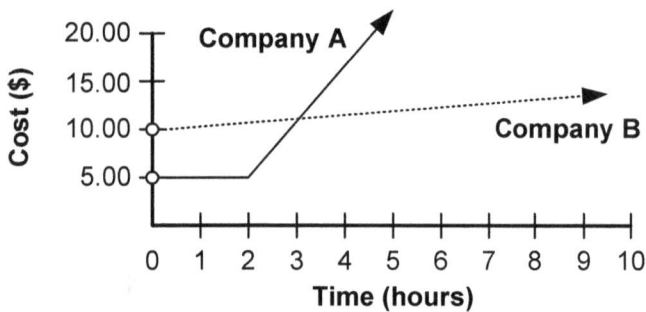

Company A is cheaper than company B for:

**a.** more than 3 hours

**b.** 3 hours only

**c.** any amount of time

**d.** less than 3 hours

**19.** The graph below shows the relationship between the number of people at the park with the number of hot dogs sold at a certain stand.

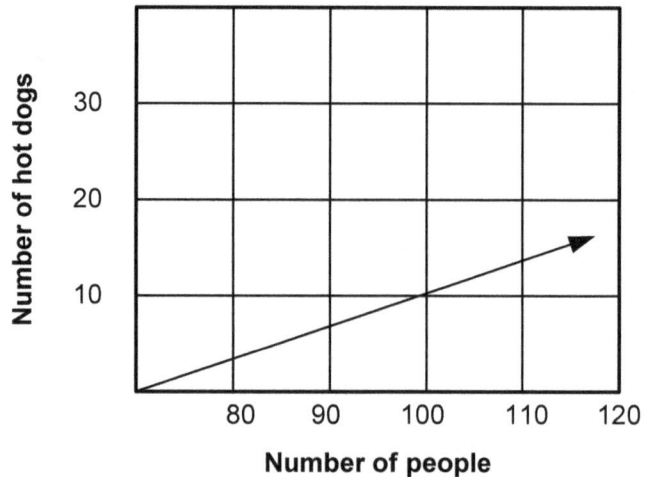

What is the approximate number of hot dogs sold when 100 people are at the park?

**a.** 40

**b.** 10

**c.** 20

**d.** 30

**20.**

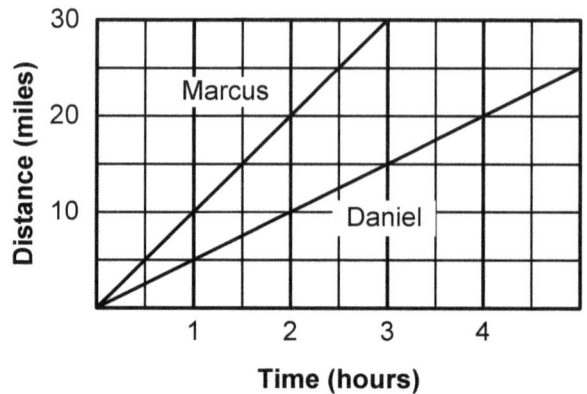

After two hours of a cross country race, Marcus is about how many miles ahead of Daniel?

**a.** 20

**b.** 15

**c.** 10

**d.** 25

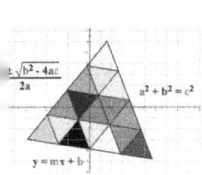

Students will successfully use the rules of exponents.

**CA Standard:** Grade 7, Algebra and Functions 2.1
**CAHSEE Strand:** Algebra and Functions

| Vocabulary: | **exponent** | number used to show repeated multiplication |
|---|---|---|
| | **base** | number repeatedly multiplied |
| | **power** | a base and an exponent |

power $\Big\{$ $2^3 = 2 \cdot 2 \cdot 2$ ← exponent, ← base

**Rule**

$a^m \cdot a^n = a^{m+n}$

**Example**

$3^2 \cdot 3^5 = 3^{2+5} = 3^7$

When confronted with a calculation involving more than one arithmetic operation, follow this standard order:

**P**arenthesis    simplify anything inside of parenthesis, brackets, or braces
**E**xponents    simplify anything with exponents
**M**ultiply/**D**ivide    multiply and divide left to right (whichever you see first, you do first)
**A**dd/**S**ubtract    add and subtract left to right (whichever you see first, you do first)

When **substituting and evaluating**, replace the indicated variable with the given number, then perform the order of operations.

---

**EXAMPLE:** If m = -3 and n = 5, then $mn^2$ =

   **a.** -75     **b.** -225     **c.** 45     **d.** $\dfrac{-1}{225}$

Begin by replacing m with -3 and n with 5.     $-3(5)^2$

Simplify the exponent.     -3(25)

Multiply.     -75     The correct answer is **a.**

---

**EXAMPLE:**    $x^5y^2$ =

   **a.** 7xy     **b.** 10xy     **c.** xxxxxyy     **d.** $(xy)^7$

Based upon the possible solutions, we can conclude that this question is asking for the meaning of an exponent.

$x^5y^2$ means that we are multiplying x by itself 5 times and multiplying y by itself 2 times.

The correct answer is **c.**

# CAHSEE Bench Mark Practice 31

1. $x^5y^2 =$

   a. $7xy$          b. $10xy$

   c. $xxxxxyy$          d. $(xy)^7$

2. What does $g^3$ equal when $g = -3$?

   a. $\dfrac{1}{9}$          b. $-27$

   c. $-9$          d. $\dfrac{1}{27}$

3. Which of the following is equivalent to $(x + 5)(x + 5)(x - 5)$?

   a. $(x - 5)^3$          b. $(x - 5)^2(x + 5)$

   c. $(x + 5)^3$          d. $(x + 5)^2(x - 5)$

4. If $w = 4$ and $x = -2$, then $x^w =$

   a. $\dfrac{1}{16}$          b. $-16$

   c. $16$          d. $\dfrac{-1}{8}$

5. $c^3d^6 =$

   a. $cccddddd$          b. $(cd)^9$

   c. $9cd$          d. $ccccccddd$

6. Simplify the expression shown below.

   $(3x^2y^3)(2x^3y^2)$

   a. $6x^6y^5$          b. $6x^5y^6$

   c. $6x^5y^5$          d. $6x^6y^6$

7. Which expression is equivalent to $4x^5y \cdot 3xz^3$ ?

   a. $12x^6yz^4$          b. $12x^5y^4z$

   c. $12x^6yz^3$          d. $24x^6yz^3$

8. Simplify the expression shown below.
   $(7ab^2c)(2a^3bc)$

   a. $14a^2b^3c^4$          b. $49a^4b^3c^2$

   c. $49a^2b^3c^4$          d. $14a^4b^3c^2$

9. Which of the following is equivalent to $(7x - 3)(7x - 3)(7x + 3)$?

   a. $(7x - 3)^2(7x + 3)$      b. $(7x - 3)^3$

   c. $(7x + 3)^2(7x - 3)$      d. $(7x + 3)^3$

10. If $m = -3$ and $n = 5$, then $mn^2 =$

    a. $-75$          b. $-225$

    c. $45$          d. $\dfrac{-1}{225}$

# CAHSEE Bench Mark Practice 31

**11.** $x^3y^4 =$

**a.** xxxyyyy **b.** xxyyy

**c.** 7xy **d.** $(xy)^7$

**12.** What does $g^3$ equal when $g = -4$?

**a.** $\frac{-1}{64}$ **b.** 64

**c.** -64 **d.** $\frac{1}{64}$

**13.** Which of the following is equivalent to $(4x + 2)(4x + 2)(4x - 2)$?

**a.** $(4x - 2)^3$ **b.** $(4x + 2)^3$

**c.** $(4x - 2)^2(4x + 2)$ **d.** $(4x + 2)^2(4x - 2)$

**14.** If $w = 5$ and $x = -2$, then $2wx^2 =$

**a.** -28 **b.** $\frac{1}{40}$

**c.** 40 **d.** $\frac{-1}{40}$

**15.** $c^2d^7 =$

**a.** $(cd)^9$ **b.** ccddddddd

**c.** ccccccccdd **d.** 9cd

**16.** Simplify the expression shown below.

$(4x^6y^2)(8x^4y^9)$

**a.** $12x^{12}y^{18}$ **b.** $32x^{10}y^{11}$

**c.** $32x^{12}y^{11}$ **d.** $12x^{24}y^{11}$

**17.** Which expression is equivalent to $12x^2y \cdot 4xz^5$ ?

**a.** $48x^3yz^5$ **b.** $16x^3y^5z$

**c.** $16x^3yz^5$ **d.** $48x^5yz^3$

**18.** Simplify the expression shown below.

$(10ab^5c)(3a^4bc)$

**a.** $13a^5b^6c^2$ **b.** $30a^4b^5c$

**c.** $30a^5b^6c^2$ **d.** $13a^2b^3c^6$

**19.** Which of the following is equivalent to $(12x - 5)(12x - 5)(12x + 5)$?

**a.** $(12x - 5)^3$ **b.** $(12x - 5)^2(12x + 5)$

**c.** $(12x + 5)^2(12x - 5)$ **d.** $(12x + 5)^3$

**20.** If $m = -2$ and $n = 4$, then $2mn^2 =$

**a.** 64 **b.** -32

**c.** -64 **d.** $\frac{-1}{32}$

# CAHSEE Bench Mark 32

Students will successfully extend the process of taking
powers and extracting roots.

**CA Standard:** Grade 7, Algebra and Functions 2.2
**CAHSEE Strand:** Algebra and Functions

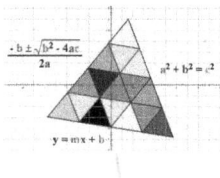

One of the most important concepts dealing with exponents is rational or fractional exponents.

$$\sqrt[n]{a^m} = a^{\frac{m}{n}}$$

The exponent of the base becomes the numerator of the rational exponent and the root index becomes the denominator when we convert from radical form to exponential form.

When there is no visible exponent, we assume that it is one.
When there is no visible root index, we assume that it is two.

The following table has the squares of the numbers from 1 to 15.

| 1 | 2 | 3 | 4 | 5 | 6 | 7 | 8 | 9 | 10 | 11 | 12 | 13 | 14 | 15 |
|---|---|---|---|---|---|---|---|---|----|----|----|----|----|----|
| 1 | 4 | 9 | 16 | 25 | 36 | 49 | 64 | 81 | 100 | 121 | 144 | 169 | 196 | 225 |

**EXAMPLE:** $\sqrt{196h^8}$ =    **a.** $14h$    **b.** $14h^8$    **c.** $14h^2$    **d.** $14h^4$

There is no visible root index, so we will assume that it is two.

The square root of 196 is 14.

The square root of $h^8$ simplifies as follows;

$$\sqrt{h^8} = \sqrt[2]{h^8} = h^{\frac{8}{2}} = h^4$$

Therefore, $\sqrt{196h^8} = 14h^4$    The correct answer is **d.**

**EXAMPLE:** $\sqrt{25x^6}$ =

    **a.** $5x$        **b.** $5x^3$

    **c.** $25x$        **d.** $25x^6$

There is no visible root index, so we will assume that it is two.

The square root of 25 is 5.

The square root of $x^6$ is $x^3$.

$\sqrt{25x^6} = 5x^3$

The correct answer is **b.**

# CAHSEE Bench Mark Practice 32

1. $\sqrt{25x^6}$ =

   **a.** $5x$             **b.** $5x^3$

   **c.** $25x$            **d.** $25x^6$

2. $\sqrt{16x^8}$ =

   **a.** $4x^4$           **b.** $4x$

   **c.** $16x$           **d.** $16x^8$

3. $\sqrt{81x^6 y^2}$ =

   **a.** $9xy$          **b.** $9x^3y^2$

   **c.** $81xy$         **d.** $9x^3y$

4. $\sqrt{36x^2}$ =

   **a.** $6x$            **b.** $36x$

   **c.** $6x^2$           **d.** $36x^2$

5. $\sqrt{64a^4 b^2}$ =

   **a.** $8ab$          **b.** $8a^4b^2$

   **c.** $64ab$         **d.** $8a^2b$

6. $\sqrt{4m^4 n^{10}}$ =

   **a.** $4mn$          **b.** $2mn$

   **c.** $2m^2n^5$        **d.** $2m^2n$

7. $\sqrt{144h^2}$ =

   **a.** $12h$          **b.** $12h^2$

   **c.** $144h$        **d.** $144h^2$

8. $\sqrt{225w^{12}}$ =

   **a.** $225w^6$       **b.** $15w$

   **c.** $15w^{12}$       **d.** $15w^6$

9. $\sqrt{p^4 q^2}$ =

   **a.** $pq$            **b.** $p^4q^2$

   **c.** $p^2q^2$         **d.** $p^2q$

10. $\sqrt{100j^4}$ =

   **a.** $10j$          **b.** $100j$

   **c.** $10j^2$        **d.** $100j^2$

11. $\sqrt{36x^8}$ =

   a. 36x               b. $6x^4$

   c. 6x               d. $36x^8$

12. $\sqrt{49x^2}$ =

   a. $49x^2$          b. 7x

   c. 7                d. $7x^2$

13. $\sqrt{64x^2 y^6}$ =

   a. 8xy            b. $8xy^3$

   c. 64xy          d. $8x^3y$

14. $\sqrt{4x^2}$ =

   a. 2x               b. 4x

   c. $2x^2$          d. $4x^2$

15. $\sqrt{81a^8 b^{12}}$ =

   a. $9a^4b^6$        b. $9a^4b^2$

   c. 9ab           d. $9a^4b$

16. $\sqrt{9m^2 n^{18}}$ =

   a. 3mn          b. 9mn

   c. $3mn^9$       d. $9mn^9$

17. $\sqrt{169h^2}$ =

   a. 14h          b. $13h^2$

   c. 12h          d. 13h

18. $\sqrt{196w^{14}}$ =

   a. $196w^7$       b. 14w

   c. $14w^7$       d. $14w^{14}$

19. $\sqrt{p^{12} q^{26}}$ =

   a. pq            b. $p^6q^{13}$

   c. $p^{12}q^{26}$     d. $p^6q$

20. $\sqrt{400j^6}$ =

   a. 20j          b. 400j

   c. $20j^3$       d. $400j^3$

# CAHSEE Unit 6 Exam
## Bench Marks 1 - 32

**BM 1.** There are 604,800 seconds in a week. What is this number in scientific notation?

    **a.** $6.048 \times 10^5$      **b.** $60.48 \times 10^4$

    **c.** $6.048 \times 10^6$      **d.** $6.084 \times 10^5$

**BM 2.** Which of the following expressions results in a positive number?

    **a.** 205 - 206      **b.** -206 + 205

    **c.** 206 - 205      **d.** -206 - 205

**BM 3.** If 8 of the 20 trees along Main Street are maples, what percentage of the trees are maples?

    **a.** 80%      **b.** 40%

    **c.** 20%      **d.** 60%

**BM 4.** The price of lawn care has increased from $11.00 a month to $16.50 a month. What is the percent of increase?

    **a.** 50%      **b.** 25%

    **c.** 55%      **d.** 35%

**BM 5.** Tequilla puts $900.00 in a bank account. Each year her money earns 4% simple interest. How much interest will be earned in 3 years?

    **a.** $96.00      **b.** $160.00

    **c.** $108.00      **d.** $40.00

**BM 6.** Which number equals $4^{-2}$?

    **a.** -8      **b.** $\frac{1}{16}$

    **c.** $\frac{1}{8}$      **d.** $\frac{-1}{16}$

**BM 7.** Which of the following is the prime factored form of the lowest common denominator of $\frac{5}{7} + \frac{2}{3}$ ?

    **a.** $21 \cdot 1$      **b.** $5 \cdot 2$

    **c.** $2 \cdot 3 \cdot 7$      **d.** $3 \cdot 7$

**BM 8.** $(6^2)^4 \cdot (4^3)^0 =$

    **a.** $6^6 \cdot 4^3$      **b.** $6^8 \cdot 1$

    **c.** $24^9$      **d.** $6^8 \cdot 4^3$

**BM 9.** The square root of 154 is between

    **a.** 11 and 12      **b.** 12 and 13

    **c.** 13 and 14      **d.** 14 and 15

**BM 10.** If $|x| = 17$, what is the value of x?

    **a.** -17 or 17      **b.** -17 or 0

    **c.** 17 or 0      **d.** -17 or 1

**BM 11.** Brittney received the following scores on her senior project: 27, 33, 30, 34, and 33. Find her median score.

    **a.** 33      **b.** 30

    **c.** 7      **d.** 157

**BM 12.** A teacher drew the following circle graph to represent the number of siblings of his students.

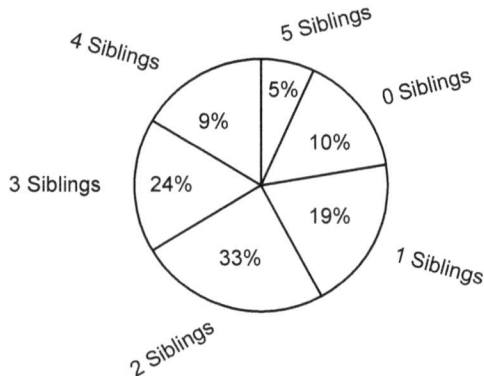

According to the pie chart shown, which statement is true?

a. The number of students with zero, four, and five siblings combined is more than those students with one sibling.

b. Students with two and three siblings combined is less than half of all the students.

c. Two of the students have six siblings.

d. Ninety-five percent of all students have at least one sibling.

**BM 13.** If you pick a card at random from a complete deck of cards, what is the probability that it will be a diamond?

a. $\dfrac{1}{4}$    b. $\dfrac{1}{3}$

c. $\dfrac{1}{3}$    d. $\dfrac{2}{3}$

**BM 14.** If you pick a card at random from a complete deck of cards, what is the probability that it will not be an ace?

a. $\dfrac{1}{4}$    b. $\dfrac{1}{13}$

c. $\dfrac{1}{12}$    d. $\dfrac{12}{13}$

**BM 15.** A bag contains 5 green marbles, 4 orange marbles, and 2 yellow marbles. What is the theoretical probability that two orange marbles will be drawn at the same time?

a. $\dfrac{1}{5}$    b. $\dfrac{6}{55}$

c. $\dfrac{4}{11}$    d. $\dfrac{3}{10}$

**BM 16.** The table below shows the quiz scores for four students.

|       | Q1 | Q2 | Q3 | Q4 | Q5 | Q6 |
|-------|----|----|----|----|----|----|
| Hien  | 7  | 6  | 2  | 5  | 6  | 1  |
| Myles | 8  | 9  | 0  | 6  | 8  | 9  |
| Ida   | 9  | 5  | 3  | 8  | 5  | 8  |
| Jaime | 9  | 10 | 6  | 9  | 10 | 9  |

Each quiz has a total point value of ten. Use the information in the table to draw the best conclusion for the data.

a. Based upon Hien's quiz scores, we may conclude that Hien needs more practice with her math. That is, she needs to get some help with her studies.

b. Based upon Myles' other quiz scores, we may conclude that Myles was absent for Quiz 3.

c. Based upon Ida's quiz scores, she can expect a grade of C.

d. Based upon Jaime's quiz scores, we may conclude that Jaime does not understand the material.

**BM 17.** A certain college has produced a scatter plot of their students income at age 25 as compared to the number of years that the student attended the college.

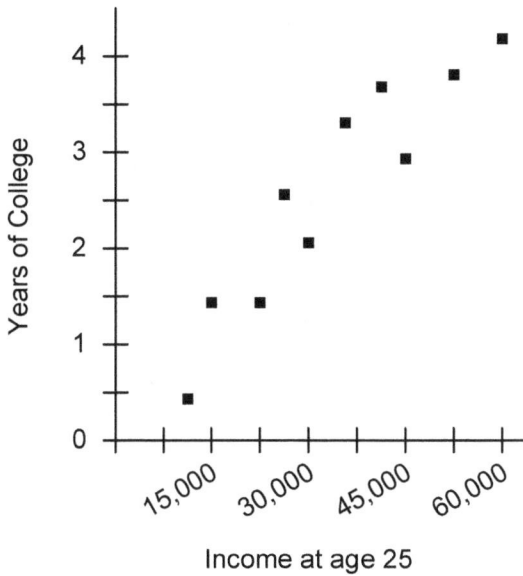

Income at age 25

Which statement best supports the data graphed on the scatter plot?

a. No correlation exists between years in college and income earned.

b. As the time in college increases, the future income earned decreases.

c. As the time in college decreases, the future income earned decreases.

d. As the time in college decreases, the future income earned increases.

**BM 18.** Anthony is flying his plane at 110 miles per hour, what is his approximate speed in kilometers per hour?
(1 mile ≈ 1.6 kilometers)

a. 176          b. 192

c. 204          d. 216

**BM 19.** The scale drawing of the football field shown below is drawn using a scale of 1 inch (in.) = 80 feet (ft).

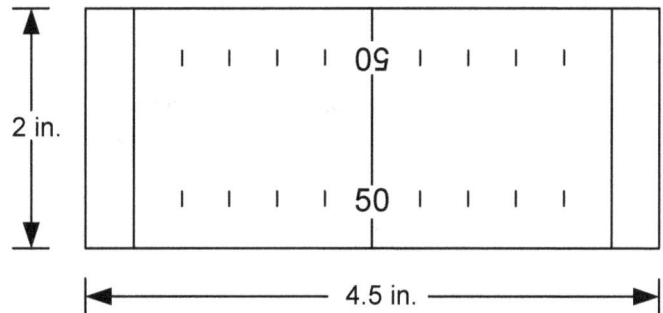

What is the width of the field in feet?

a. 132 ft          b. 144 ft

c. 152 ft          d. 160 ft

**BM 20.** An electrician estimates that a new job will take one person 126 hours to complete. If three people work on the job and they each work 6-hour days, how many days are needed to complete the job?

a. 4          b. 5

c. 6          d. 7

**BM 21.**

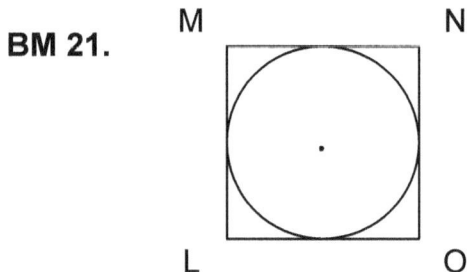

In the figure above, the radius of the inscribed circle is 10 inches (in.). What is the perimeter of the square LMNO?

a. $100\pi$ in.       b. $80\pi$ in.

c. 100 in.       d. 80 in.

**BM 22.** What is the area of the shaded region in the figure shown below?

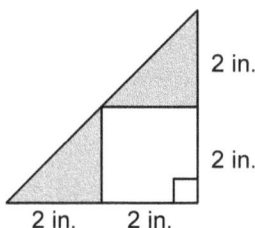

a. 16 in.$^2$       b. 8 in.$^2$

c. 6 in.$^2$       d. 4 in.$^2$

**BM 23.** Lor found the circumference of circle A to be $8\pi$ and the circumference of circle B to be $6\pi$. Which of the following is the scale factor of circle A to circle B?

a. $\dfrac{4}{3}$       b. $\dfrac{3}{4}$

c. $\dfrac{16}{9}$       d. $\dfrac{9}{16}$

**BM 24.** Find the area of the rectangle below in square feet. {1 yard = 3 feet}

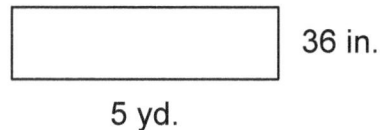

5 yd.

a. 15 ft$^2$       b. 180 ft$^2$

c. 45 ft$^2$       d. 36 ft$^2$

**BM 25.** The points (-2,-2), (-2, 1), (0, 3), (2, 1) and (2,-2) are vertices of a polygon. What type of polygon is formed by these points?

a. Rectangle       b. Parallelogram

c. Square       d. Pentagon

**BM 26.** In a right triangle, if a = 9 and b = 12, then c = ?

a. 14       b. 15

c. 12       d. 13

**BM 27.** Triangle ABC is congruent to triangle DEF. If the measure of angle A = 52°, the measure of angle B = 57° and the measure of angle C = 71°, then what is the measure of angle E?

a. 52°       b. 48°

c. 71°       d. 57°

**BM 28.** Multiply a number by 2 and subtract 10 from the result. The answer is 24. Which of the following equations matches these statements?

    **a.** $24 - 2x = 10$      **b.** $2x - 10 = 24$

    **c.** $2x + 10 = 24$      **d.** $2x + 24 = 10$

**BM 29.** If $c = 3$ and $d = \dfrac{2}{3}$, then $c(d + 3) =$

    **a.** 14      **b.** 11

    **c.** 4      **d.** 9

**BM 30.**

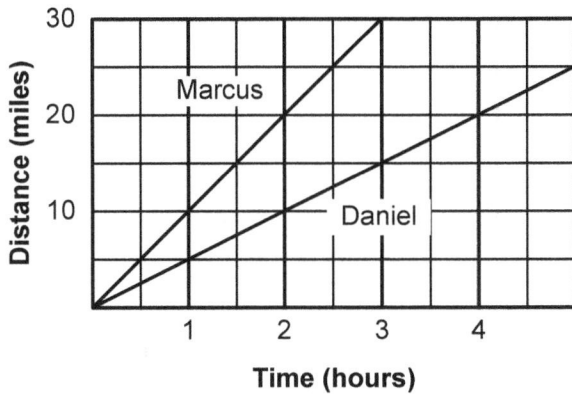

After two hours of a cross country race, Marcus is about how many miles ahead of Daniel?

    **a.** 20      **b.** 15

    **c.** 10      **d.** 25

**BM 31.** Which of the following is equivalent to $(12x - 5)(12x - 5)(12x + 5)$?

    **a.** $(12x - 5)^3$      **b.** $(12x - 5)^2(12x + 5)$

    **c.** $(12x + 5)^2(12x - 5)$      **d.** $(12x + 5)^3$

**BM 32.**    $\sqrt{400j^6} =$

    **a.** $20j$      **b.** $400j$

    **c.** $20j^3$      **d.** $400j^3$

**CA Standard:** Grade 7, Algebra and Functions 3.1
**CAHSEE Strand:** Algebra and Functions

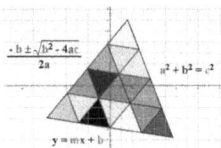

---

**Vocabulary:**

**function**    a relationship in which each input is paired with exactly one output

**non-linear**    **not** a line, (i.e. $x^2$, $x^3$, and $|x|$ )

**graph**    a visual representation of an equation

COORDINATE PLANE

y-axis

Quadrant II    Quadrant I

x-axis

origin

Quadrant III    Quadrant IV

ORDERED PAIR

**(x, y)**

x-coordinate    y-coordinate

position left or right of y-axis    position above or below the x-axis

---

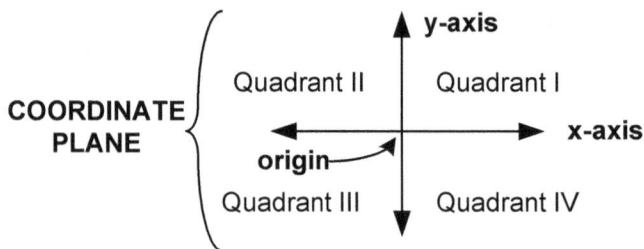

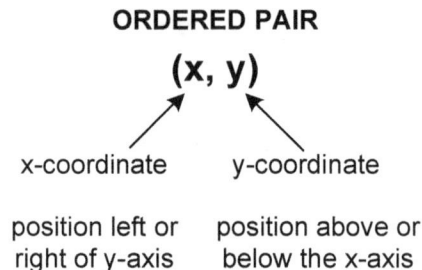

Cataloguing the graphs of certain functions can be very beneficial to one's success in many math classes.

Following are the graphs of 3 common non-linear functions.

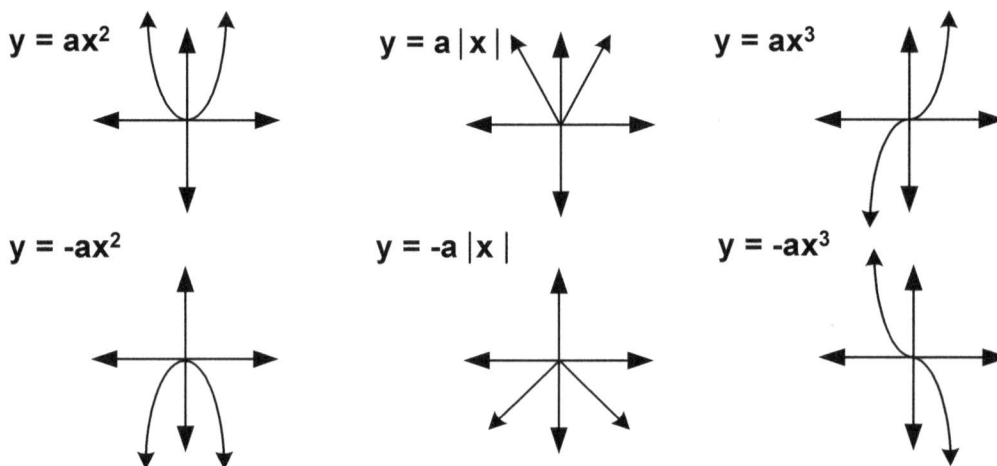

$y = ax^2$

$y = a|x|$

$y = ax^3$

$y = -ax^2$

$y = -a|x|$

$y = -ax^3$

Remembering the general shape of each function is a simple matter of memorization.

---

**EXAMPLE:**    Which of the following is the graph of $y = 2x^3$?

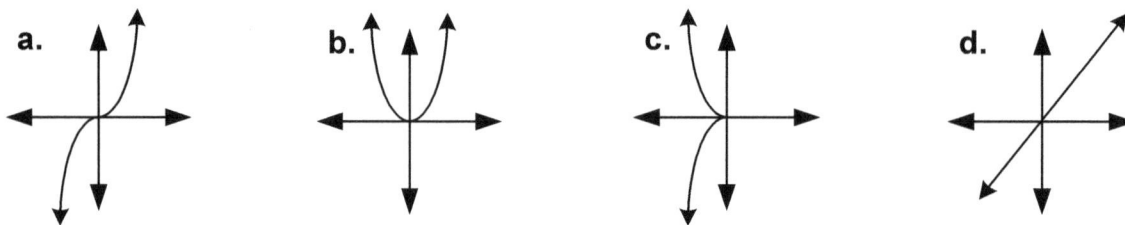

a.

b.

c.

d.

Answer **c** does not look like any of the common functions and answer **d** is linear so these <u>cannot</u> be the correct answers.

Answer **a** has the form of the base function $x^3$ and is therefore the correct answer.

**1.** Which of the following is the graph of $y = 2x^3$?

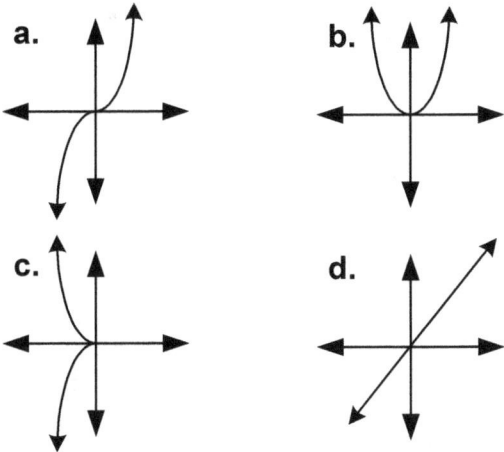

a.

b.

c.

d.

**2.** Which of the following is the graph of $y = 3x^2$?

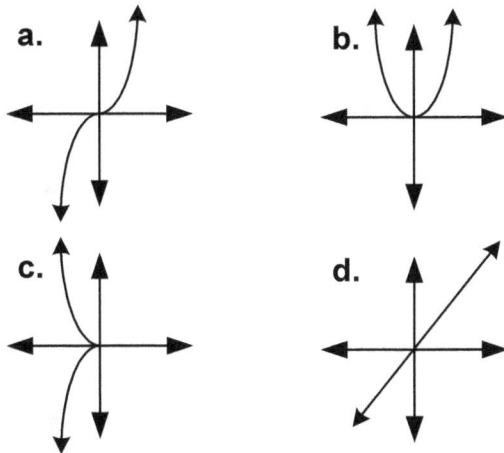

a.

b.

c.

d.

**3.** Which of the following is the graph of $y = 2|x|$?

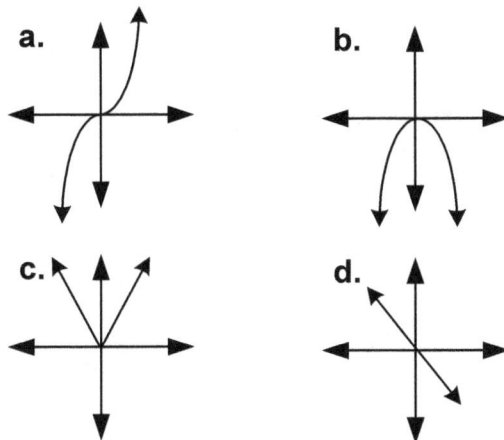

a.

b.

c.

d.

**4.** Which of the following is the graph of $y = -x^2$?

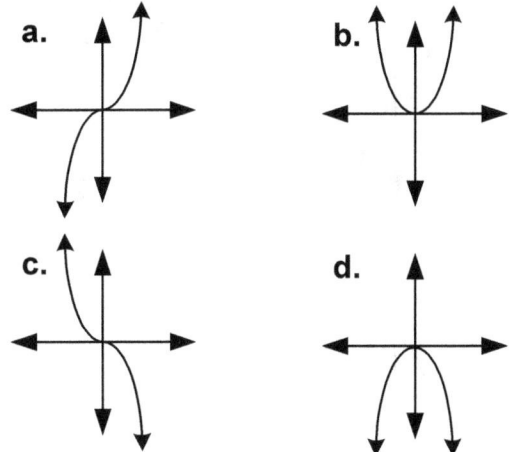

a.

b.

c.

d.

**5.** Which of the following is the graph of $y = -x^3$?

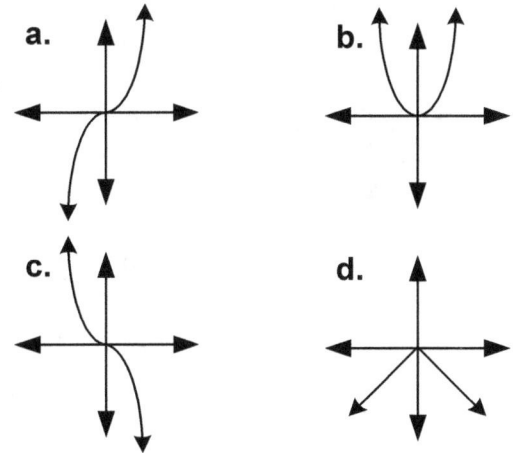

a.

b.

c.

d.

**6.** Which of the following is the graph of $y = -|x|$?

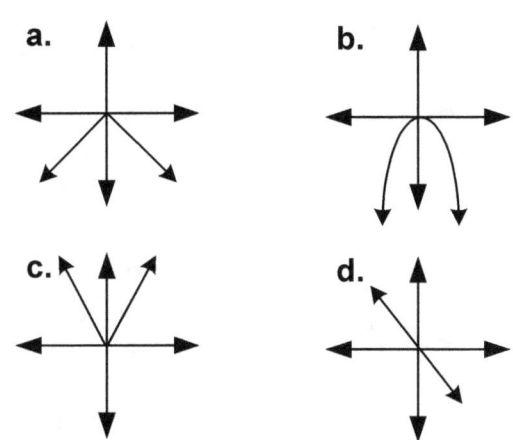

a.

b.

c.

d.

**7.** Which of the following is the graph of $y = -3x^3$?

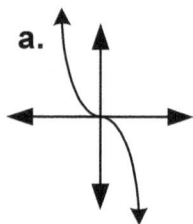

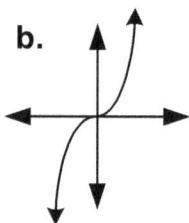

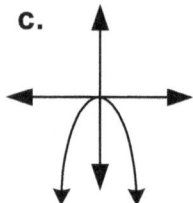

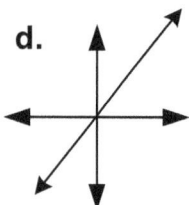

a.

b.

c.

d.

**8.** Which of the following is the graph of $y = 3x^2$?

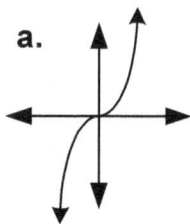

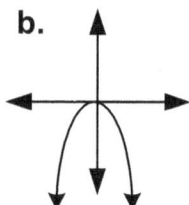

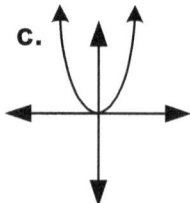

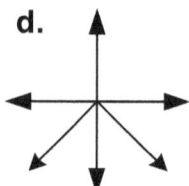

a.

b.

c.

d.

**9.** Which of the following is the graph of $y = -3|x|$?

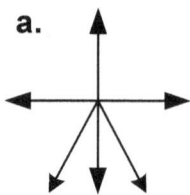

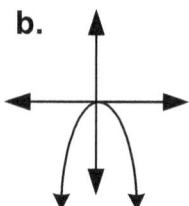

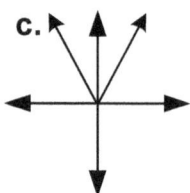

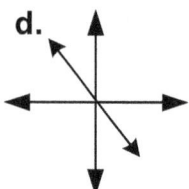

a.

b.

c.

d.

**10.** Which of the following is the graph of $y = -7x^3$?

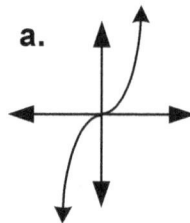

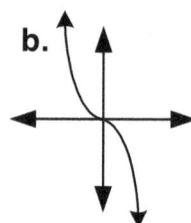

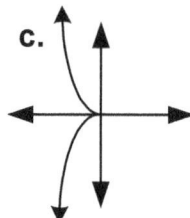

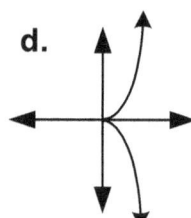

a.

b.

c.

d.

**11.** Which of the following is the graph of $y = 5|x|$?

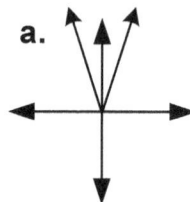

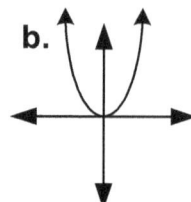

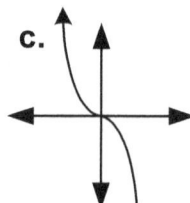

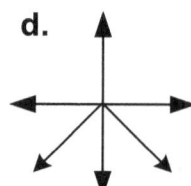

a.

b.

c.

d.

**12.** Which of the following is the graph of $y = \frac{1}{2}|x|$?

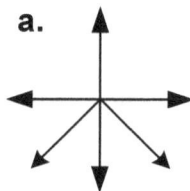

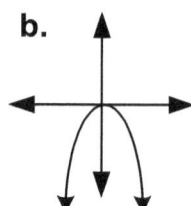

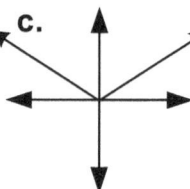

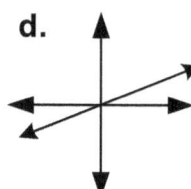

a.

b.

c.

d.

**13.** Which of the following is the graph of $y = 2x^2$?

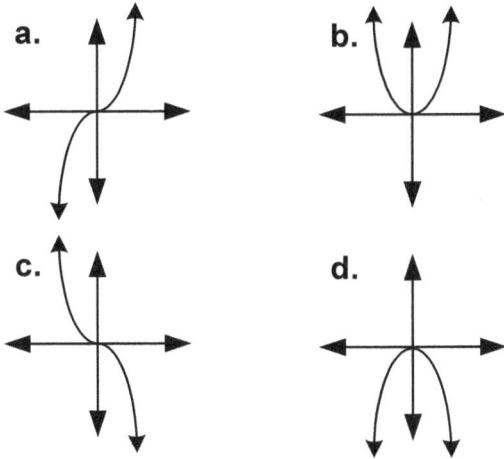

a.

b.

c.

d.

**14.** Which of the following is the graph of $y = -8x^2$?

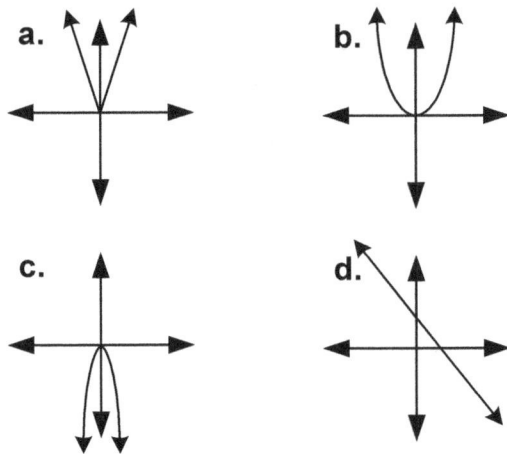

a.

b.

c.

d.

**15.** Which of the following is the graph of $y = -9|x|$ ?

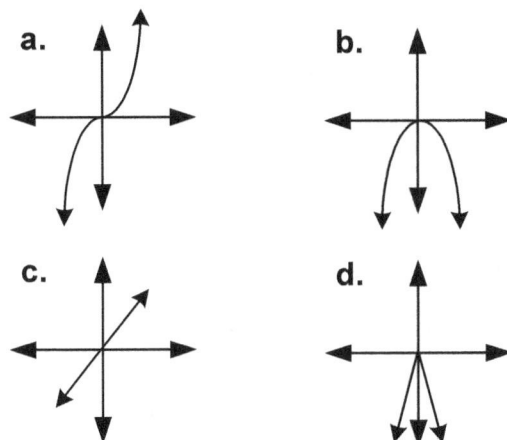

a.

b.

c.

d.

**16.** Which of the following is the graph of $y = -4x^2$?

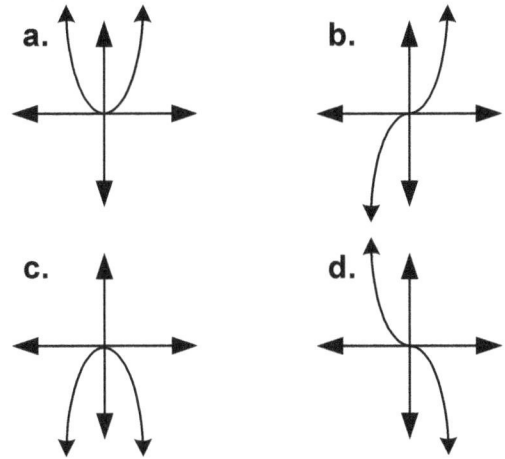

a.

b.

c.

d.

**17.** Which of the following is the graph of $y = -6x^3$?

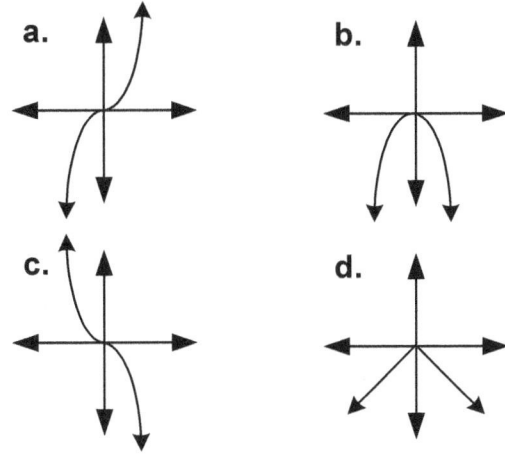

a.

b.

c.

d.

**18.** Which of the following is the graph of $y = 3|x|$ ?

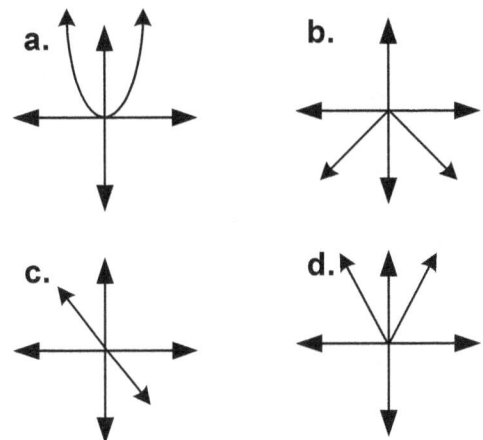

a.

b.

c.

d.

Students will successfully use graphs of linear functions.

**CA Standard:** Grade 7, Algebra and Functions 3.3
**CAHSEE Strand:** Algebra and Functions

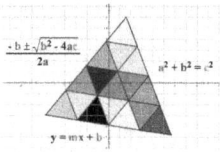

| **Vocabulary:** | **linear** | a straight line |
| | **y-intercept** | point where a graph crosses the y-axis |
| | **slope** | steepness of a line |

**Slope, ($m$)**, the steepness of a line, and the **y-intercept (b)**, the point where the line crosses the y-axis can be determined from the line's equation or a graph.

For this lesson, we will be given the graph of a line and will be asked to find the slope or the equation of the line in the form of $y = mx + b$.

Slope can be determined by a number of ways. For this lesson we will focus on the definition.

$$m = \frac{rise}{run}$$ where **rise** is the vertical change from one point on the line to another and **run** is the horizontal change from one point on the line to another.

For example, the slope of the line on the graph to the right is $\frac{6}{11}$ because the **rise** is **6** and the **run** is **11**.

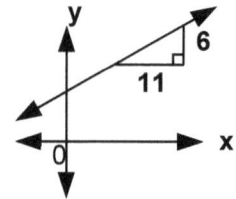

*NOTE: We read from left to right. If the line goes up, it has a positive slope and if it goes down, it has a negative slope.*

For another example, we want to find the equation of the line in the form of $y = mx + b$ on the graph to the right.

We can see that the slope is $\frac{-1}{2}$ and the **y-intercept** is 4.

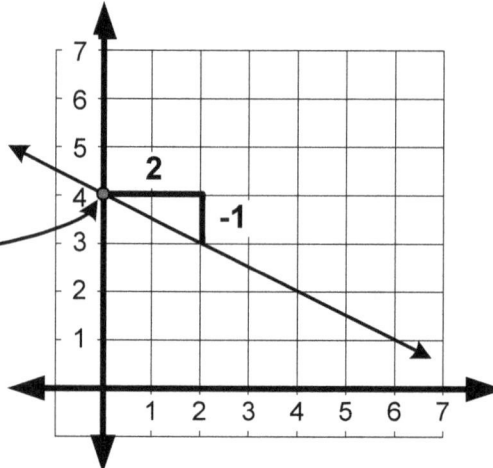

Therefore, the equation of the line is $y = \frac{-1}{2}x + 4$

---

**EXAMPLE:**

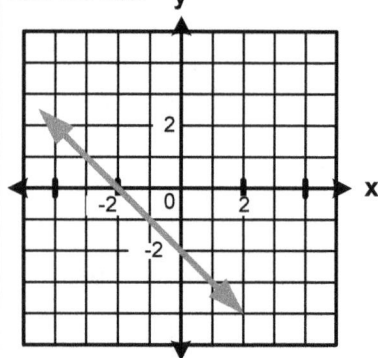

What is the slope of the line shown in the graph to the left?

a. -2    b. -1    c. 1    d. $\frac{-1}{2}$

$$Slope = m = \frac{rise}{run}$$

We first observe that the line goes down, so it will have a negative slope. Therefore, answer **c** is incorrect.

For this example, we can see from the graph that the rise is -1 and the run is 1.

Therefore, the slope of the line is -1.    The correct answer is **b**.

# CAHSEE Bench Mark Practice 34

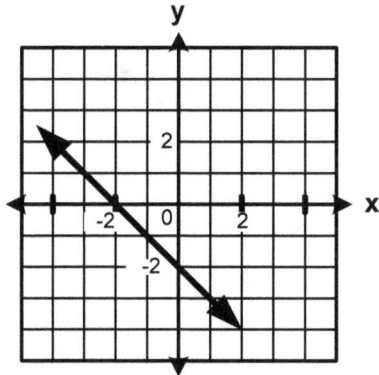

**1.** What is the slope of the line shown in the graph above?

    **a.** -2                **b.** -1

    **c.** 1                **d.** $\frac{-1}{2}$

**2.** The slope of the line shown below is $\frac{1}{2}$.

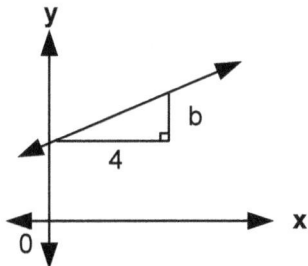

What is the value of b?

    **a.** 1                **b.** 4

    **c.** 2                **d.** 3

**3.** What is the equation of the graph shown below?

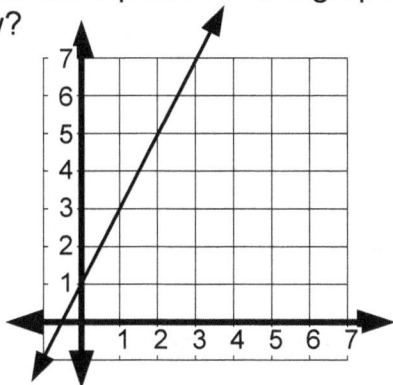

    **a.** y = 2x + 1        **b.** y = 2x - 1

    **c.** y = 2x - 2        **d.** y = 2x + 2

**4.** What is the slope of the line below?

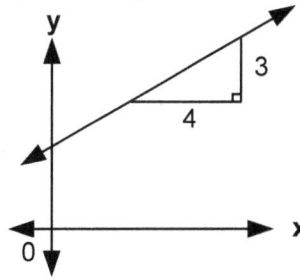

    **a.** $\frac{3}{4}$                **b.** $\frac{-4}{3}$

    **c.** $\frac{4}{3}$                **d.** $\frac{-3}{4}$

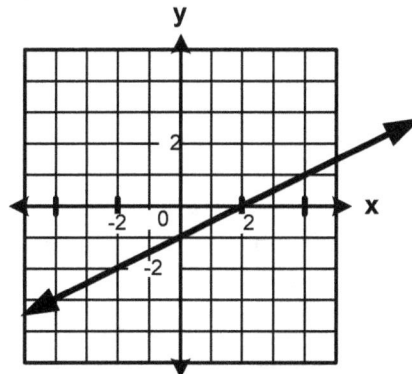

**5.** What is the slope of the line shown in the graph above?

    **a.** $\frac{1}{2}$                **b.** -2

    **c.** 2                **d.** $\frac{-1}{2}$

**6.** The slope of the line shown below is $\frac{-2}{3}$.

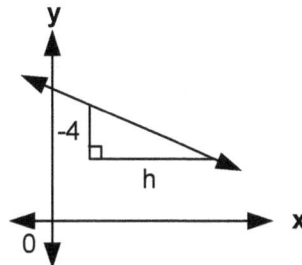

What is the value of h?

    **a.** 5                **b.** 4

    **c.** 6                **d.** 3

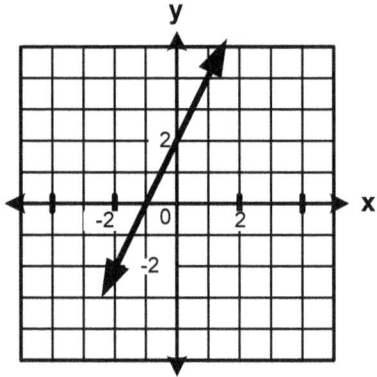

**7.** What is the slope of the line shown in the graph above?

    **a.** 2                **b.** -1

    **c.** $\dfrac{1}{2}$           **d.** 1

**8.** The slope of the line shown below is $\dfrac{3}{4}$.

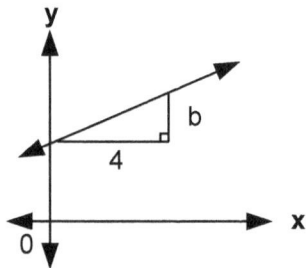

What is the value of b?

    **a.** 1                **b.** 4

    **c.** 2                **d.** 3

**9.** What is the equation of the graph shown below?

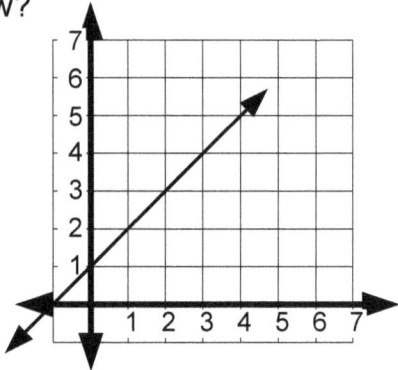

    **a.** y = x + 2       **b.** y = x - 1

    **c.** y = x + 1       **d.** y = x - 2

**10.** What is the slope of the line below?

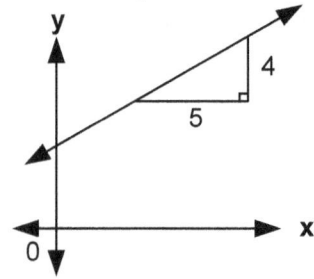

    **a.** $\dfrac{5}{4}$          **b.** $\dfrac{-4}{5}$

    **c.** $\dfrac{4}{5}$          **d.** $\dfrac{-5}{4}$

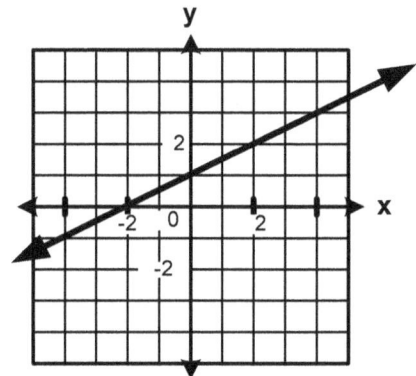

**11.** What is the slope of the line shown in the graph above?

    **a.** $\dfrac{-1}{2}$         **b.** 2

    **c.** -2              **d.** $\dfrac{1}{2}$

**12.** The slope of the line shown below is $\dfrac{-2}{5}$.

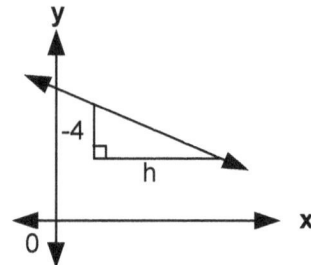

What is the value of h?

    **a.** 5                **b.** 7

    **c.** 10              **d.** 3

# CAHSEE Bench Mark Practice 34

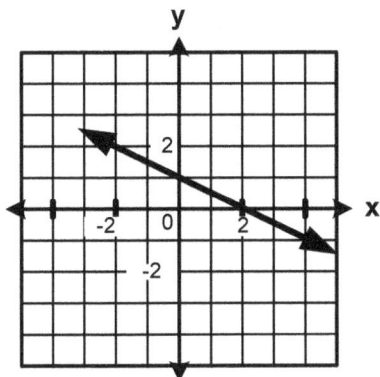

**13.** What is the slope of the line shown in the graph above?

   **a.** 2            **b.** $\frac{-1}{2}$

   **c.** $\frac{1}{2}$          **d.** -1

**14.** The slope of the line shown below is $\frac{3}{5}$.

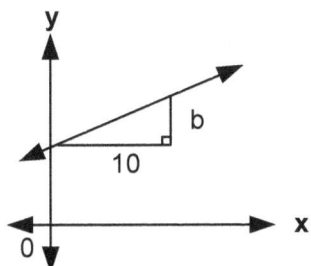

What is the value of b?

   **a.** 6            **b.** 3

   **c.** 8            **d.** 5

**15.** What is the equation of the graph shown below?

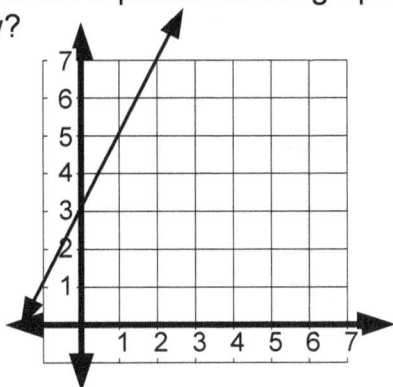

   **a.** y = 2x + 2     **b.** y = 2x + 3

   **c.** y = 2x + 1     **d.** y = 2x - 2

**16.** What is the slope of the line below?

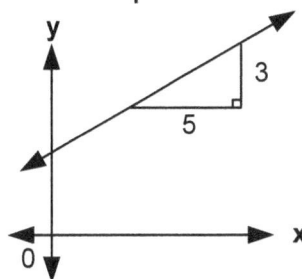

   **a.** $\frac{3}{5}$          **b.** $\frac{-3}{5}$

   **c.** $\frac{-5}{3}$         **d.** $\frac{5}{3}$

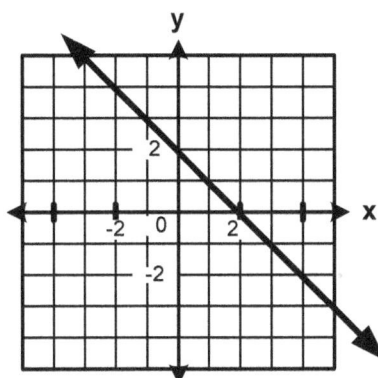

**17.** What is the slope of the line shown in the graph above?

   **a.** $\frac{-1}{2}$         **b.** 1

   **c.** -1           **d.** $\frac{1}{2}$

**18.** The slope of the line shown below is $\frac{-3}{4}$.

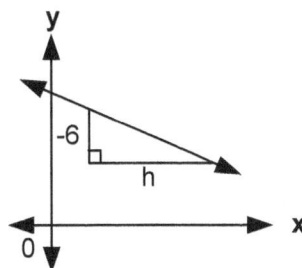

What is the value of h?

   **a.** 3            **b.** 7

   **c.** 4            **d.** 8

**CA Standard:** Grade 7, Algebra and Functions 3.4
**CAHSEE Strand:** Algebra and Functions

| **Vocabulary:** | **quantity** | the amount being discussed |
| | **total cost** | the cost for the quantity in question |
| | **unit cost** | the cost per individual unit |

$$\text{unit cost} = \frac{\text{total cost}}{\text{quantity}}$$

The graph below shows Lauren's gasoline bill for three different months. What is the price per gallon for Lauren's gasoline?

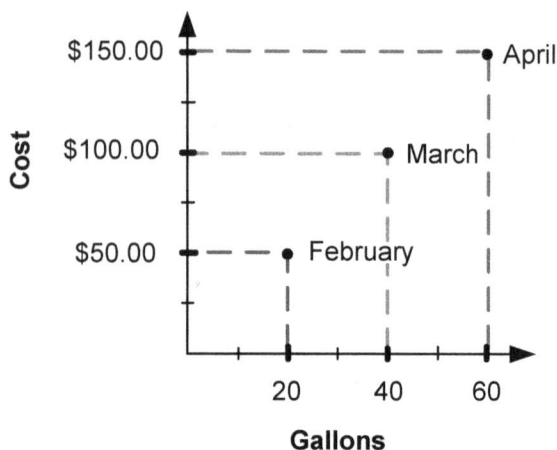

$$\text{unit cost} = \frac{\$50.00}{20 \text{ gallons}} = \$2.50/\text{gallon}$$

$$\frac{\$100.00}{40 \text{ gallons}} = \$2.50/\text{gallon}$$

$$\frac{\$150.00}{60 \text{ gallons}} = \$2.50/\text{gallon}$$

We can see than no matter which month we select, the unit cost is the same. In this example, Lauren's cost is **$2.50 per gallon**.

---

**EXAMPLE:** The graph below shows Manuel's phone bill for three different months. What is the price per minute for Manuel's phone?

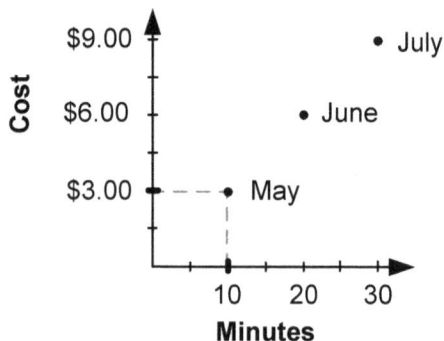

Since we know that the unit cost will be the same for any month, we can select the most convenient. In this case, May has the smallest numbers, so we will work with these.

| a. $0.15 | b. $0.30 |
| c. $1.50 | d. $3.33 |

$$\text{unit cost} = \frac{\$3.00}{10 \text{ minutes}}$$

$$= \$0.30/\text{minute}$$

The correct answer is **b**.

# CAHSEE Bench Mark Practice 35

**1.** The graph below shows Manuel's phone bill for three different months. What is the price per minute for Manuel's phone?

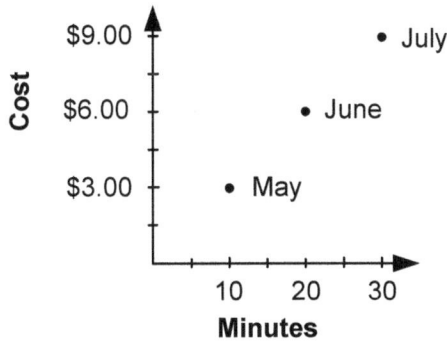

**a.** $0.15

**b.** $0.30

**c.** $1.50

**d.** $3.33

**2.** The graph below shows the cost of three bags of candy. What is the price per pound of the candy?

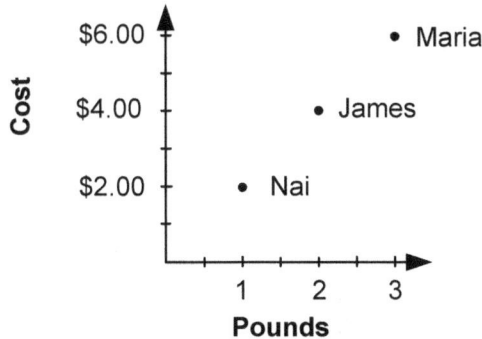

**a.** $0.25

**b.** $0.50

**c.** $2.00

**d.** $3.50

**3.** Three friends go to a carnival. The graph below shows the cost of tickets for the rides. What is the price per ticket?

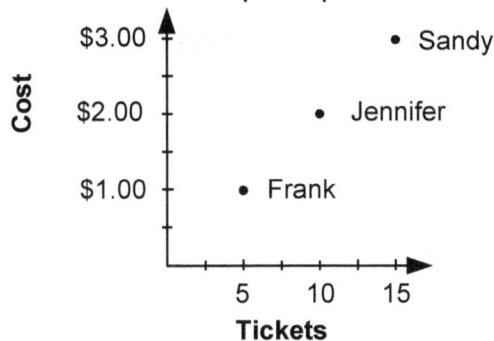

**a.** $0.10

**b.** $0.20

**c.** $2.00

**d.** $5.00

**4.** The graph below shows the cost to rent 3 different limousines for senior ball. What is the price per hour to rent a limousine?

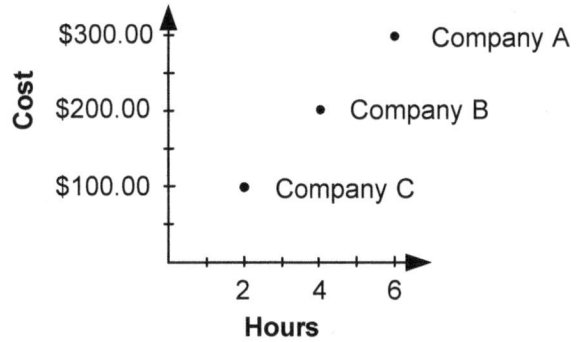

**a.** $0.50

**b.** $25.00

**c.** $50.00

**d.** $100.00

**5.** The graph below shows Marquette's gasoline bill for three different months. What is the price per gallon for gasoline?

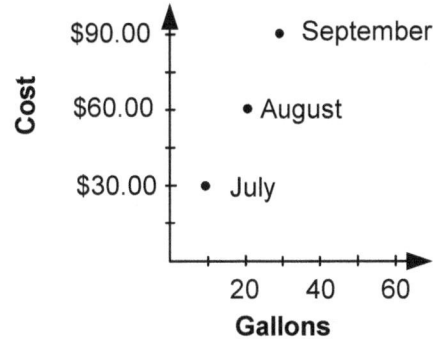

**a.** $0.33

**b.** $3.00

**c.** $5.00

**d.** $7.50

**6.** The graph below shows Kayla's movie rental bill for three different months. What is the price per movie?

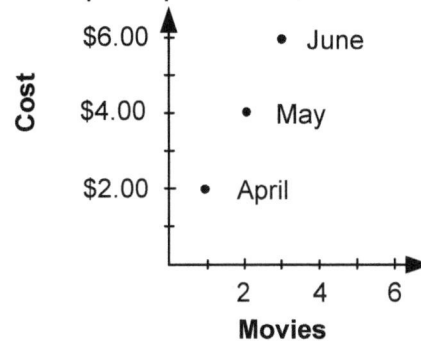

**a.** $0.10

**b.** $0.20

**c.** $2.00

**d.** $5.00

**7.** The graph below shows Marquisha's phone bill for three different months. What is the price per minute for Marquisha's phone?

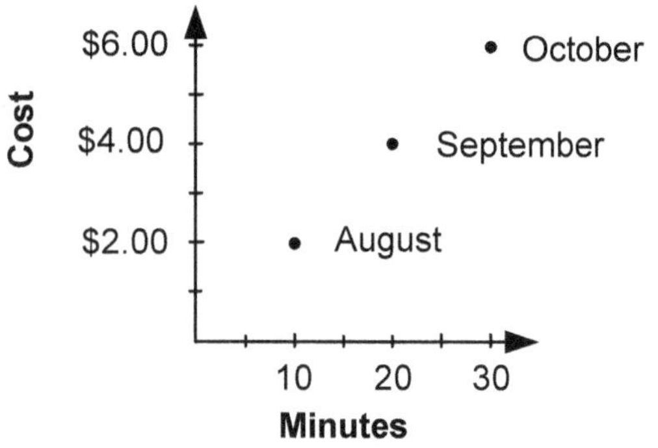

**a.** $0.10     **b.** $0.20

**c.** $2.50     **d.** $5.00

**8.** The graph below shows the cost of three bags of candy. What is the price per pound of the candy?

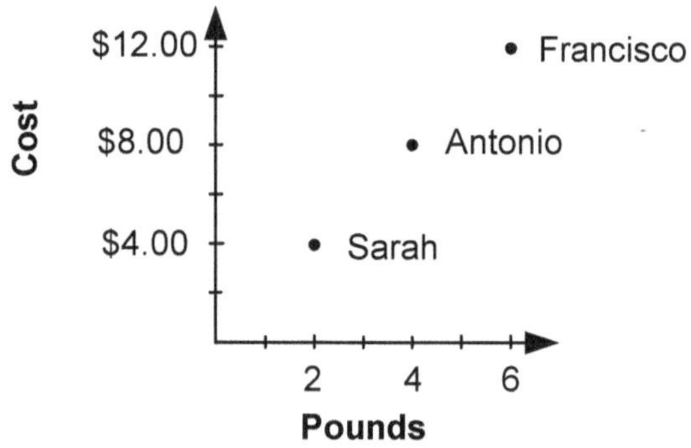

**a.** $0.25     **b.** $0.50

**c.** $2.00     **d.** $3.50

**9.** Three friends go to a carnival. The graph below shows the cost of tickets for the rides. What is the price per ticket?

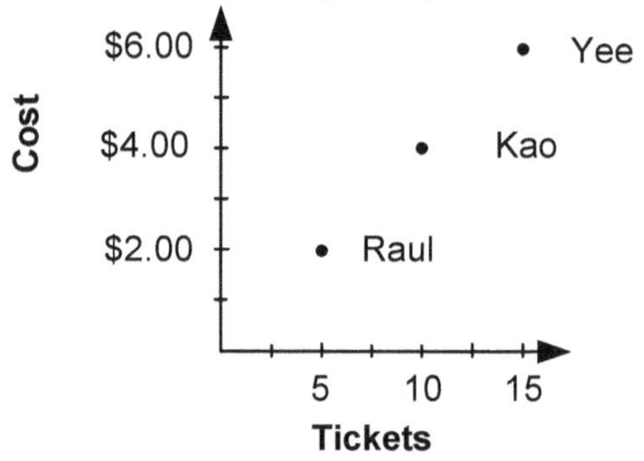

**a.** $0.10     **b.** $0.20

**c.** $0.40     **d.** $2.50

**10.** The graph below shows the cost to rent 3 different limousines for senior ball. What is the price per hour to rent a limousine?

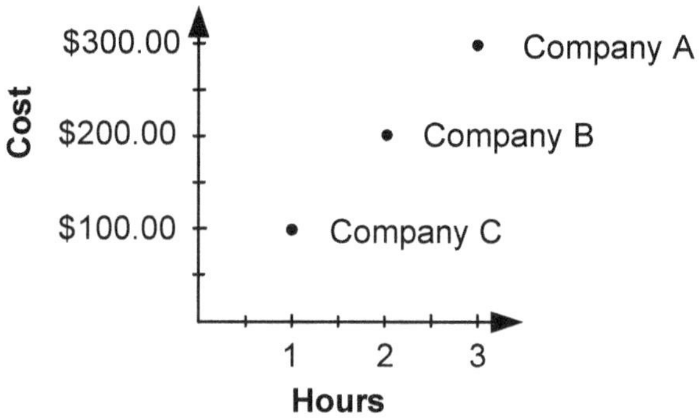

**a.** $0.50     **b.** $25.00

**c.** $50.00     **d.** $100.00

**11.** The graph below shows Tyrone's gasoline bill for three different months. What is the price per gallon for gasoline?

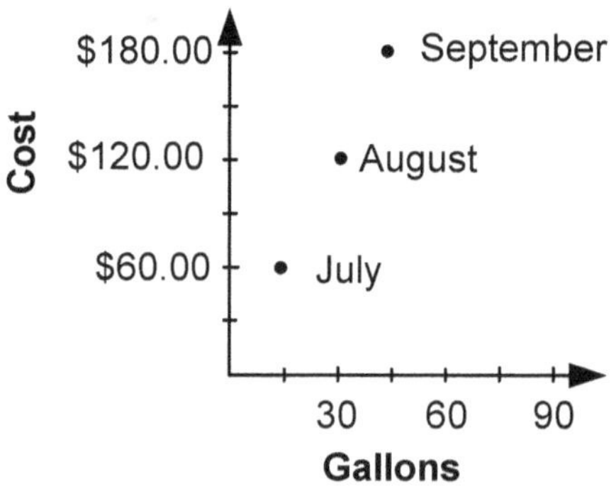

**a.** $0.25     **b.** $3.00

**c.** $4.00     **d.** $7.50

**12.** The graph below shows Matt's movie rental bill for three different months. What is the price per movie?

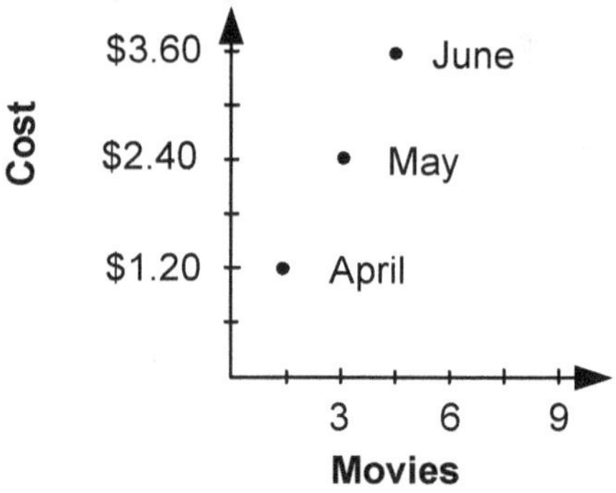

**a.** $0.10     **b.** $0.80

**c.** $2.00     **d.** $5.00

**13.** The graph below shows Mai Lia's phone bill for three different months. What is the price per minute for Mai Lia's phone?

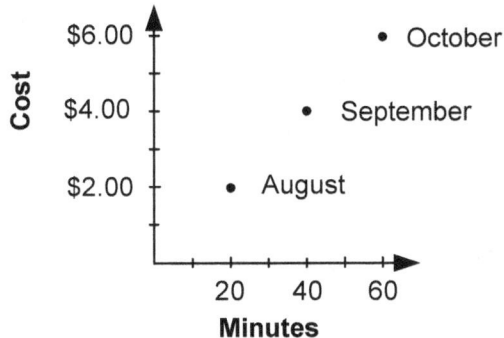

a. $0.10        b. $0.20

c. $2.50        d. $5.00

**14.** The graph below shows the cost of three bags of candy. What is the price per pound of the candy?

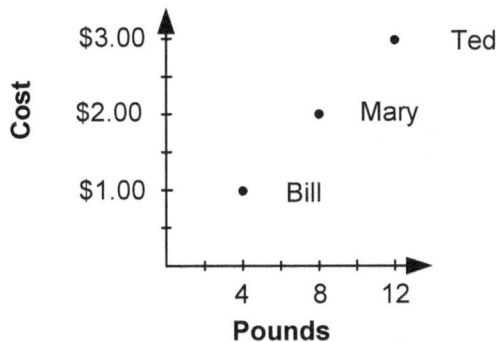

a. $0.25        b. $0.50

c. $2.00        d. $3.50

**15.** Three friends go to a carnival. The graph below shows the cost of tickets for the rides. What is the price per ticket?

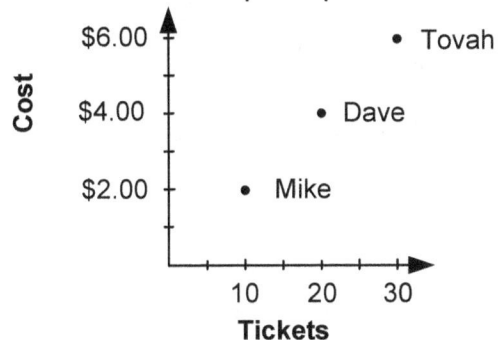

a. $0.10        b. $0.20

c. $5.00        d. $2.50

**16.** The graph below shows the cost to rent 3 different limousines for senior ball. What is the price per hour to rent a limousine?

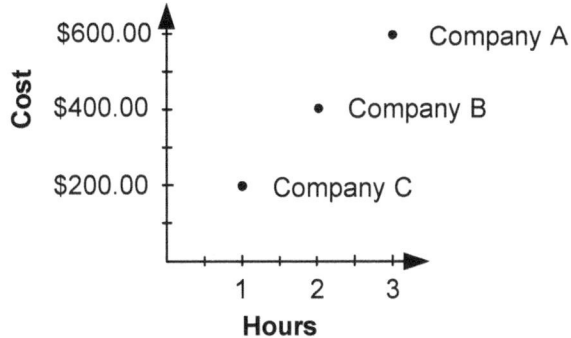

a. $200.00      b. $25.00

c. $100.00      d. $150.00

**17.** The graph below shows Rosalyn's gasoline bill for three different months. What is the price per gallon for gasoline?

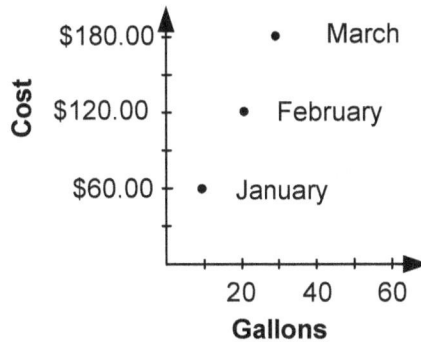

a. $0.33        b. $6.00

c. $6.50        d. $7.50

**18.** The graph below shows Barbara's movie rental bill for three different months. What is the price per movie?

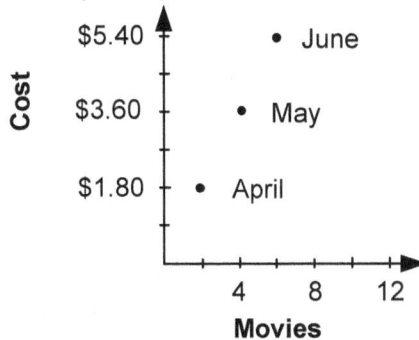

a. $0.90        b. $1.75

c. $2.00        d. $5.00

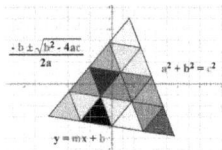

# CAHSEE Bench Mark 36
Students will successfully solve two-step equations and inequalities.

**CA Standard:** Grade 7, Algebra and Functions 4.1
**CAHSEE Strand:** Algebra and Functions

*Simplified Solutions For Math Inc.*

| Vocabulary: | | |
|---|---|---|
| | **equation** | a mathematical sentence that states that two expressions represent the same number |
| | **inequality** | a mathematical sentence containing <, >, $\leq$ or $\geq$; **not** the same in amount, size, or number |
| | **variable** | a letter used to represent an unknown number |
| | **solve** | find out what number the variable represents |

Solving an equation or inequality is a matter of using arithmetic and number properties to isolate the variable on one side of the equal or inequality sign.

For example, **6x - 7 = 41**     Our plan is to remove the -7 and 6 from the left side of the equation. We will accomplish this by doing the 'opposite'.

*Multiplication and division are opposites and addition and subtraction are opposites.*

We need to do the order of operations in reverse. We will add or subtract before multiplying or dividing.

$$6x - 7 = 41 \quad \text{add 7 to both sides}$$
$$6x = 48 \quad \text{divide both sides by 6}$$
$$x = 8 \quad \text{the solution is 8}$$

Inequalities solve in much the same fashion as equations with one big exception. **Whenever we multiply or divide by a negative number, we reverse the inequality.**

For example, **- 1 < 4 - 5x**

| $-1 < 4 - 5x$ | Subtract 4 from both sides |
|---|---|
| $-5 < -5x$ | Divide both sides by - 5 |
| | ***Reverse the inequality*** |
| $1 > x$ | The solution is any number less than 1 |

| EXAMPLE: | In the inequality 3x + $20,000 > $50,000, x represents the salary of part time employees in a music store. Which phrase most accurately describes the employee's salary? |
|---|---|

**a.** At least $10,000     **b.** At most $10,000

**c.** Less than $10,000     **d.** More than $10,000

$$3x + \$20,000 > \$50,000 \quad \text{subtract 20,000 from both sides}$$
$$3x > \$30,000 \quad \text{divide both sides by 3}$$
$$x > \$10,000$$

Since x represents the salary and x is greater than 10,000, we can see that the salaries are more than $10,000.

The correct answer is **d.**

1. In the inequality 3x + $20,000 > $50,000, x represents the salary of part time employees in a music store. Which phrase most accurately describes the employee's salary?

   a. At least $10,000     b. At most $10,000

   c. Less than $10,000    d. More than $10,000

2. Solve for x.     4x - 6 = 18

   a. -6                   b. -4

   c. 4                    d. 6

3. Solve for w.     6w + 2 < 38

   a. w < 6                b. w < 7

   c. w < 8                d. w < 9

4. The owner of a pear orchard ships pears in boxes that weigh 5 pounds when empty. The average pear weighs 0.25 pounds, and the total weight of a box filled with pears is 10 pounds. How many pears are packed in each box?

   a. 10                   b. 15

   c. 20                   d. 25

5. Solve for x.     -2x - 1 = 15

   a. -7                   b. -8

   c. 7                    d. 8

6. The owner of a candy store ships candy in containers that weigh 1 pound when empty. The average piece of candy weighs 0.1 pounds, and the total weight of a box filled with candy is 3 pounds. How many pieces of candy are packed in each box?

   a. 25                   b. 30

   c. 35                   d. 20

7. Solve for x.     -5x - 8 ≤ 22

   a. x ≤ 6                b. x ≤ -6

   c. x ≥ 6                d. x ≥ -6

8. In the inequality 2x + $10,000 > $50,000, x represents the salary of employees in a restaurant. Which phrase most accurately describes the employee's salary?

   a. At most $20,000      b. At least $20,000

   c. More than $20,000    d. Less than $20,000

9. Solve for x.     7x - 11 = 24

   a. 4                    b. 5

   c. 6                    d. 7

10. Solve for h.     2h + 5 > 35

    a. h > 15              b. h < 20

    c. h > 20              d. h < 15

**11.** In the inequality 4x + $10,000 ≥ $90,000, x represents the salary of part time employees at a school district office. Which phrase most accurately describes the employee's salary?

    **a.** At most $20,000    **b.** More than $20,000

    **c.** Less than $20,000    **d.** At least $20,000

**12.** Solve for x.    3x - 10 = 20

    **a.** 10    **b.** 13

    **c.** -10    **d.** -13

**13.** Solve for w.    4w + 3 < 31

    **a.** w < 6    **b.** w < 7

    **c.** w < 8    **d.** w < 9

**14.** The owner of a pear orchard ships pears in boxes that weigh 4 pounds when empty. The average pear weighs 0.20 pounds, and the total weight of a box filled with pears is 12 pounds. How many pears are packed in each box?

    **a.** 30    **b.** 35

    **c.** 40    **d.** 45

**15.** Solve for x.    -5x + 6 = 41

    **a.** -7    **b.** -8

    **c.** 7    **d.** 8

**16.** The owner of a candy store ships candy in containers that weigh 1 pound when empty. The average piece of candy weighs 0.2 pounds, and the total weight of a box filled with candy is 4 pounds. How many pieces of candy are packed in each box?

    **a.** 10    **b.** 15

    **c.** 20    **d.** 25

**17.** Solve for x.    -3x - 10 ≤ 23

    **a.** x ≤ -11    **b.** x ≤ 11

    **c.** x ≥ 11    **d.** x ≥ -11

**18.** In the inequality 2x + $10,000 ≤ $70,000, x represents the salary of employees in a book store. Which phrase most accurately describes the employee's salary?

    **a.** At most $30,000    **b.** At least $30,000

    **c.** More than $30,000    **d.** Less than $30,000

**19.** Solve for x.    3x - 14 = 10

    **a.** 8    **b.** 9

    **c.** 6    **d.** 7

**20.** Solve for h.    2h - 5 > 35

    **a.** h > 15    **b.** h < 20

    **c.** h > 20    **d.** h < 15

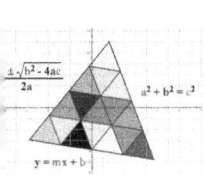

# CAHSEE Bench Mark 37

Students will successfully solve multi-step problems.

**CA Standard:** Grade 7, Algebra and Functions 4.2
**CAHSEE Strand:** Algebra and Functions

| Vocabulary: | ratio | a comparison of two quantities using division |
| | proportion | an equality of two ratios |
| | rate | a ratio that compares two quantities in different units |

Solving a proportion is a simple matter of cross multiplication and solving for the unknown. The real challenge lies in setting up the proportion.

**EXAMPLE:** Angelica is writing a 364 page paper. During the past 3 weeks she has written 156 pages. If she continues writing at the same rate, how many more weeks will it take her to complete the paper?
  **a.** 2    **b.** 3    **c.** 4    **d.** 5

We will set up the ratios as weeks over pages.
We are told that she has written 156 pages in 3 weeks.

$$\frac{3 \text{ weeks}}{156 \text{ pages}}$$

We can subtract and find that she has 208 pages remaining.
We are looking for the amount of time it will take her to write 208 pages.

$$\frac{3 \text{ weeks}}{156 \text{ pages}} = \frac{x \text{ weeks}}{208 \text{ pages}}$$   Cross multiply and solve for x.

$$156x = 3(208)$$
$$156x = 624$$
$$x = 4$$

The correct answer is **c.**

**EXAMPLE:** Mary is reading a 744-page book. During the past 5 days she has read 186 pages. If she continues reading at the same rate, how many more days will it take her to complete the book?

  **a.** 8    **b.** 12    **c.** 15    **d.** 17

Set up a proportion.

$$\frac{5 \text{ days}}{186 \text{ pages}} = \frac{x \text{ days}}{558 \text{ pages}}$$ ◄——— total pages less the pages read

Cross multiply and solve for x.

$$186x = 5(558)$$
$$186x = 2790$$
$$x = 15$$

The correct answer is **c.**

1. Mary is reading a 744-page book. During the past 5 days she has read 186 pages. If she continues reading at the same rate, how many more days will it take her to complete the book?

   **a.** 8              **b.** 12

   **c.** 15             **d.** 17

2. Pat's tractor travels at 15 miles per hour (mph) at high speed and 5 mph at low speed. If the tractor travels for 0.5 hours at high speed and 0.5 hours at low speed, what distance would the tractor have traveled?

   **a.** 10 miles       **b.** 12 miles

   **c.** 16 miles       **d.** 20 miles

3. Jim can paddle his kayak 2 miles in 30 minutes. At this rate, how many miles can he paddle in 45 minutes?

   **a.** 2.5            **b.** 2.75

   **c.** 3              **d.** 3.25

4. Teresa is writing a 384 page paper. During the past 3 weeks she has written 128 pages. If she continues writing at the same rate, how many more weeks will it take her to complete the paper?

   **a.** 5              **b.** 6

   **c.** 9              **d.** 11

5. Tovah can swim 4 miles in 2 hours. At this rate, how many miles can she swim in 5 hours?

   **a.** 10             **b.** 11

   **c.** 12             **d.** 13

6. Randy's toy truck travels at 20 inches per second (in/sec) at high speed and 12 in/sec at low speed. If the truck travels for 10 seconds at high speed and 20 seconds at low speed, what distance would the toy truck have traveled?

   **a.** 260 inches     **b.** 300 inches

   **c.** 400 inches     **d.** 440 inches

7. Tim can solve 7 math problems in 45 minutes. At this rate, how many problems can he solve in 180 minutes?

   **a.** 32             **b.** 24

   **c.** 30             **d.** 28

8. Robbie is reading a 306 page book. During the past 8 days she has read 204 pages. If she continues reading at the same rate, how many more days will it take her to complete the book?

   **a.** 2              **b.** 4

   **c.** 6              **d.** 7

9. Barbara can bake 12 cookies in 20 minutes. At this rate, how many cookies can she bake in 70 minutes?

   **a.** 42             **b.** 45

   **c.** 48             **d.** 51

10. Janie is writing a 360 page paper. During the past 2 weeks she has written 144 pages. If she continues writing at the same rate, how many more weeks will it take her to complete the paper?

    **a.** 2             **b.** 3

    **c.** 4             **d.** 5

**11.** Terry is reading a 108-page book. During the past 2 hours he has read 72 pages. If he continues reading at the same rate, how many more hours will it take him to complete the book?

a. 0.5

b. 1

c. 1.5

d. 1.75

**12.** Charlie's toy jeep travels at 100 feet per minute (ft/min) at high speed and 25 ft/min at low speed. If the jeep travels for 20 minutes at high speed and 40 minutes at low speed, what distance would the jeep have traveled?

a. 1,000 feet

b. 2,000 feet

c. 3,000 feet

d. 4,000 feet

**13.** Lauren can run 3 miles in 20 minutes. At this rate, how many miles can she run in 50 minutes?

a. 6

b. 7.5

c. 9

d. 10.25

**14.** Makita is writing a 28 page paper. During the past 3 weeks she has written 14 pages. If she continues writing at the same rate, how many more weeks will it take her to complete the paper?

a. 3

b. 4

c. 5

d. 6

**15.** Scott can drive 82 miles in 2 hours. At this rate, how many miles can he drive in 5 hours?

a. 150

b. 185

c. 195

d. 205

**16.** Randy's toy truck travels at 30 inches per second (in/sec) at high speed and 16 in/sec at low speed. If the tractor travels for 15 seconds at high speed and 35 seconds at low speed, what distance would the toy truck have traveled?

a. 1,110 inches

b. 910 inches

c. 1,010 inches

d. 1,210 inches

**17.** Amber can read 12 pages in 15 minutes. At this rate, how many pages can she read in 105 minutes?

a. 58

b. 62

c. 76

d. 84

**18.** Christy is riding her motorcycle 3,600 miles. During the past 5 days she has ridden 1,200 miles. If she continues riding at the same rate, how many more days will it take her to complete her trip?

a. 10

b. 15

c. 18

d. 21

**19.** Daisy can bake 6 muffins in 12 minutes. At this rate, how many muffins can she bake in 40 minutes?

a. 20

b. 24

c. 28

d. 32

**20.** Lynne is reading a 420 page book. During the past 3 days she has read 210 pages. If she continues reading at the same rate, how many more days will it take her to complete the book?

a. 3

b. 4

c. 5

d. 6

# CAHSEE Unit 7 Exam
## Bench Marks 1 - 37

**BM 1.** Mercury is $3.6 \times 10^7$ miles from the sun. What is this number in standard notation?

a. 360,000,000    b. 3,600,000

c. 36,000,000    d. 360,000

**BM 2.** 9 + 4 + (-8) - 7 =

a. 14    b. -2

c. -1    d. 15

**BM 3.** If one of the twenty rose bushes in Wanda's garden produce white flowers, what percentage of rose bushes produce flowers that are not white?

a. 95%    b. 5%

c. 85%    d. 15%

**BM 4.** The price of trash collection has increased from $8.00 a month to $11.00 a month. What is the percent of increase?

a. 62.5%    b. 37.5%

c. 87.5%    d. 12.5%

**BM 5.** A jar of pickles regularly sells for $3.00. It is on sale for 25% off. What is the sale price of the jar of pickles?

a. $4.50    b. $1.50

c. $2.00    d. $2.25

**BM 6.** Multiply. $13^{-8} \cdot 13^{-5}$

a. $\dfrac{1}{13^{13}}$    b. $13^{-3}$

c. $13^3$    d. $13^{40}$

**BM 7.** Which fraction is equivalent to $\dfrac{2}{4} + \dfrac{1}{8}$ ?

a. $\dfrac{3}{12}$    b. $\dfrac{4}{8}$

c. $\dfrac{3}{8}$    d. $\dfrac{5}{8}$

**BM 8.** $2^7 \cdot 2^3 =$

a. $2^4$    b. $2^{10}$

c. $2^{21}$    d. $4^{10}$

**BM 9.** The square of a <u>whole</u> number is between 700 and 800. The number must be between

a. 25 and 30    b. 30 and 35

c. 35 and 40    d. 40 and 45

**BM 10.** What is the absolute value of 6?

a. -6    b. $\dfrac{-1}{6}$

c. $\dfrac{1}{6}$    d. 6

**BM 11.** The football team auctioned off nine pies. Use the data in the box below to find the mode.

> $27.00, $33.00, $30.00, $34.00, $33.00, $32.00, $29.00, $33.00, $27.00

a. $27.00    b. $32.00

c. $33.00    d. $34.00

**BM 12.** The bar chart below represents the grades for one class.

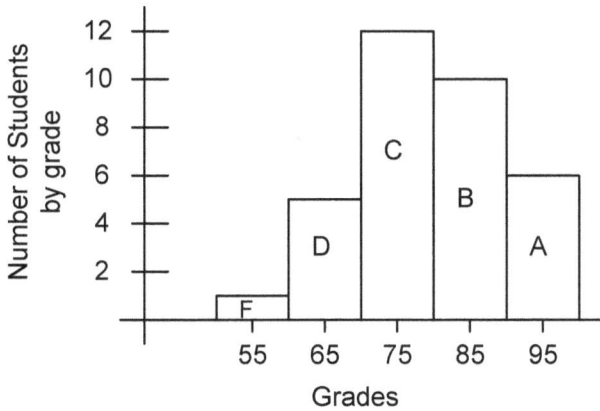

How many students are in the class?

a. 375      b. 78

c. 18      d. 34

**BM 13.** A bag contains 5 green marbles, 4 orange marbles, and 3 yellow marbles. If you cannot see the marbles and they are all the same size, what is the probability that you will be able to reach into the bag and pick an orange marble?

a. $\dfrac{1}{12}$      b. $\dfrac{1}{4}$

c. $\dfrac{1}{3}$      d. $\dfrac{2}{3}$

**BM 14.** A bag contains 5 green marbles, 4 orange marbles, and 3 yellow marbles. If you cannot see the marbles and they are all the same size, what is the probability that you will be able to reach into the bag and not pick an orange marble?

a. $\dfrac{1}{12}$      b. $\dfrac{5}{12}$

c. $\dfrac{3}{4}$      d. $\dfrac{2}{3}$

**BM 15.** Each letter of MATH IS FUN is on its own note card, lying face down on a desk. Lucky wants to pick two cards without replacement. What is the probability that he will pick the I and the N?

a. $\dfrac{1}{72}$      b. $\dfrac{1}{8}$

c. $\dfrac{1}{9}$      d. $\dfrac{2}{9}$

**BM 16.** The following pie chart represents the grades of fifty students in two math classes.

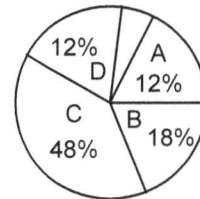

The information for the grade of F is missing. Determine which statement best describes the missing data.

a. Six students, which is ten percent of all the students, received a grade of F.

b. Five students, which is twelve percent of all the students, received a grade of F.

c. Five students, which is ten percent of all the students, received a grade of F.

d. Six students, which is twelve percent of all the students, received a grade of F.

**BM 17.** The below scatter plot appears to be what type of correlation?

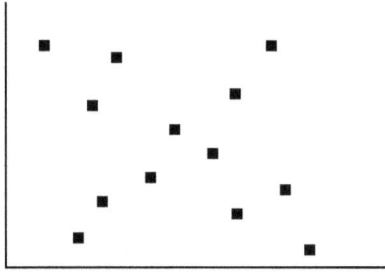

a.    Strong Positive Correlation

b.    Strong Negative Correlation

c.    Zero Correlation

d.    Weak Negative Correlation

**BM 18.** One millimeter is-

a. $\dfrac{1}{1000}$ of a kilometer    b. $\dfrac{1}{100}$ of a kilometer

c. $\dfrac{1}{10}$ of a centimeter    d. 100 centimeters

**BM 19.** The actual width ($w$) of a rectangle is 36 inches (in.). Use the scale drawing of the rectangle to find the actual length ($l$).

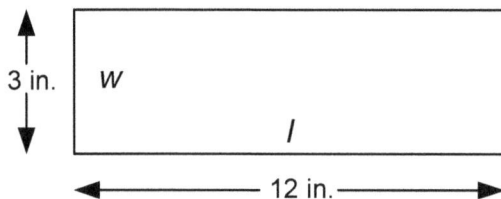

a. 100 in.        b. 121 in.

c. 144 in.        d. 169 in.

**BM 20.** Forty five miles per hour is the same as which of the following?

a. 0.75 miles per minute

b. 2 miles per minute

c. 4.5 miles per minute

d. 6 miles per minute

**BM 21.**

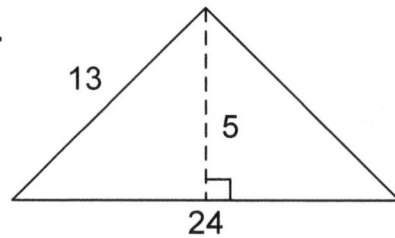

What is the area of the triangle shown above?

a. 42 square units        b. 60 square units

c. 312 square units       d. 120 square units

**BM 22.** A right triangle is removed from a rectangle as shown in the figure below. Find the area of the remaining part of the rectangle.

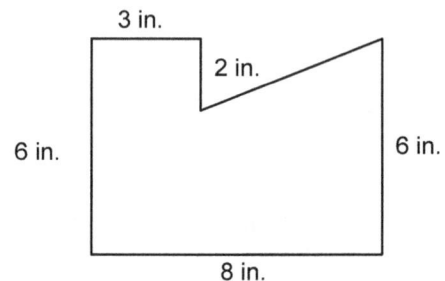

a. 61 in.²                b. 52 in.²

c. 47 in.²                d. 43 in.²

**BM 23.** Find the surface area.

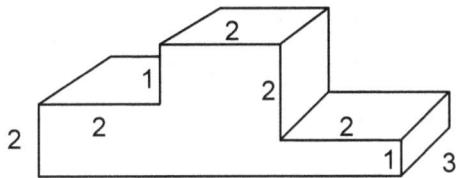

a. 78 units$^2$     b. 54 units$^2$

c. 45 units$^2$     d. 36 units$^2$

**BM 24.** Find the Perimeter (in centimeters) of the triangle below. {1 inch = 2.54 cm}

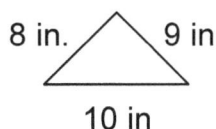

8 in.   9 in

10 in

a. 27 in.     b. 68.6 cm

c. 54 cm     d. 68.6 in.

**BM 25.** What is the length, in units, of $\overline{AB}$?

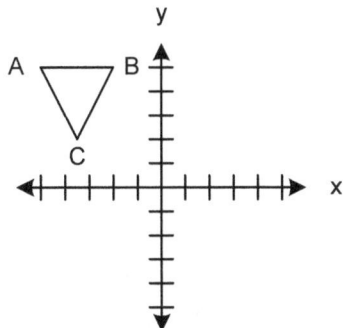

a. 5     b. 4

c. 3     d. 7

**BM 26.** Find the value of x in the right triangle below.

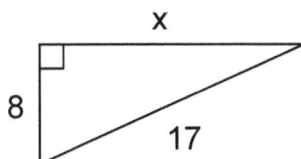

x

8

17

a. 6     b. 15

c. 24     d. 25

**BM 27.** The pentagon JACKS is congruent to pentagon NOVEL. Which side of pentagon NOVEL is the same length as $\overline{CK}$?

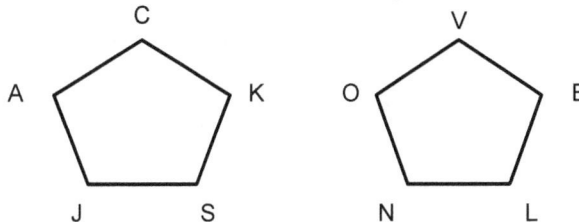

a. $\overline{OV}$     b. $\overline{AJ}$

c. $\overline{KS}$     d. $\overline{VE}$

**BM 28.** A gold miner finds gold that weighs x ounces. He sells 10 ounces and then sells another 12 ounces. Which expression represents the amount of gold the miner has now ?

a. x - 10 - 12     b. 12 - x + 10

c. x - 10 + 12     d. x - 12 + 10

**BM 29.** If a = 3 and b = 5, then $\dfrac{ab + 5}{4}$ - 2 =

a. 12     b. 1

c. 3     d. 20

**BM 30.** The cost of two internet providers, company A and company B, is shown on the graph below.

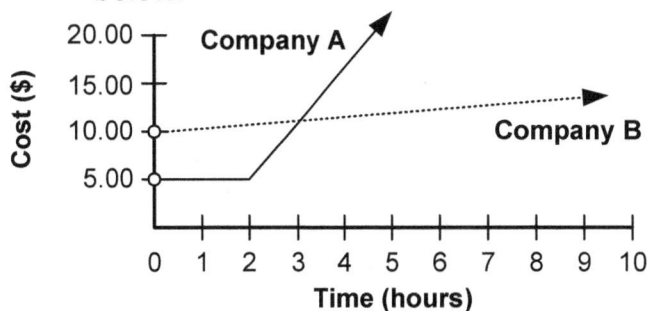

Company A is cheaper than company B for

a. more than 3 hours     b. 3 hours only

c. any amount of time     d. less than 3 hours

**BM 31.** Simplify the expression shown below.

$$(10ab^5c)(3a^4bc)$$

   **a.** $13a^5b^6c^2$       **b.** $30a^4b^5c$

   **c.** $30a^5b^6c^2$      **d.** $13a^2b^3c^6$

**BM 32.** $\sqrt{169h^2} =$

   **a.** $14h$          **b.** $13h^2$

   **c.** $12h$          **d.** $13h$

**BM 33.** Which of the following is the graph of $y = \frac{1}{2}|x|$ ?

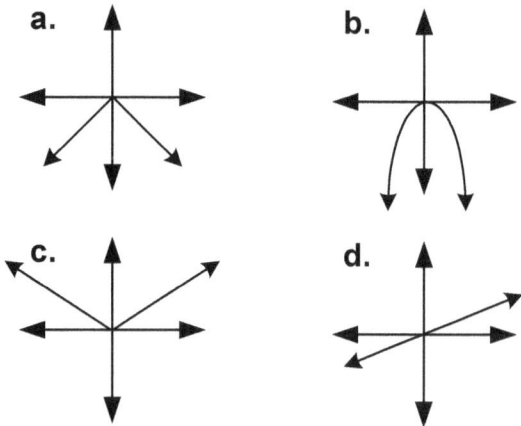

  **a.**               **b.**

  **c.**               **d.**

**BM 34.**

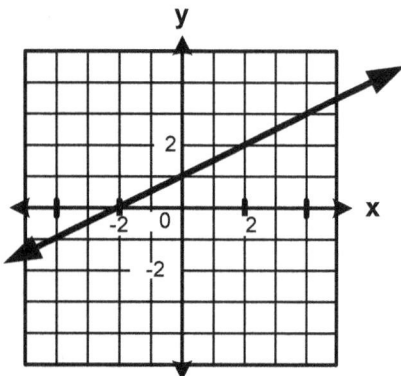

What is the slope of the line shown in the graph above?

   **a.** $\frac{-1}{2}$          **b.** 2

   **c.** -2            **d.** $\frac{1}{2}$

**BM 35.** The graph below shows Rosalyn's gasoline bill for three different months. What is the price per gallon for gasoline?

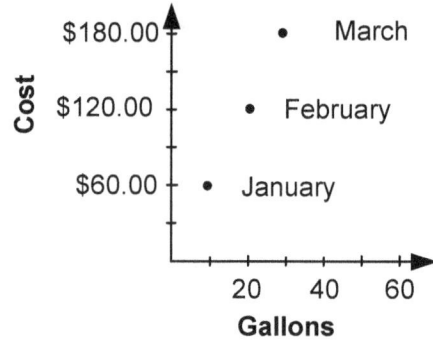

   **a.** $0.33         **b.** $6.00

   **c.** $6.50         **d.** $7.50

**BM 36.** Solve for x.    $-3x - 10 \leq 23$

   **a.** $x \leq -11$      **b.** $x \leq 11$

   **c.** $x \geq 11$       **d.** $x \geq -11$

**BM 37.** Christy is riding her motorcycle 3,600 miles. During the past 5 days she has ridden 1,200 miles. If she continues riding at the same rate, how many more days will it take her to complete her trip?

   **a.** 10          **b.** 15

   **c.** 18          **d.** 21

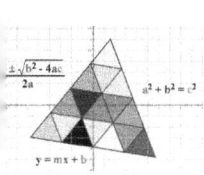

Students will successfully analyze word problems.

**CA Standard:** Grade 7, Mathematical Reasoning, 1.1
**CAHSEE Strand:** Mathematical Reasoning

---

Analyzing word problems can be tedious but if the following steps are followed, the process can be simplified.

### 1. Read the question
You cannot understand the problem if you do not read it.

### 2. Plan a strategy
You need to determine whether you can guess and check the answers or actually have to work out the problem.

### 3. Draw a picture, chart or diagram to model the problem
A picture is worth a thousand words.
A picture may help you understand the problem.

### 4. List any relevant formulas
A formula may help you sort the information.

### 5. Set-up and solve equations
Sometimes equations are easier to solve than word problems.

### 6. Answer the question
You may need to do a lot of calculations. Do not get lost in the numbers. Remember to answer the question.

---

**EXAMPLE:** Fou traveled for 3 hours to visit his grandmother who lived 120 miles away. Which computation below will provide Fou's average speed in miles per hour?

a. Multiply 120 by 3.      b. Multiply 3 by 120.

c. Divide 120 by 3.        d. Divide 3 by 120.

**1. Read the question**

**2. Plan a strategy**  It appears that we will have to work-out the problem

**3. Draw a picture, chart or diagram to model the problem**

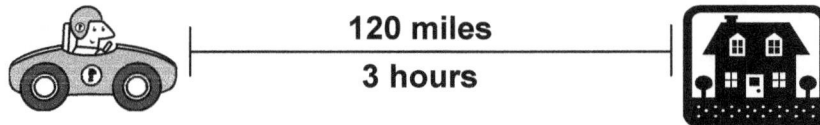

120 miles
3 hours

**4. List any relevant formulas**      $rt = d$

**5. Set-up and solve equations**      $3r = 120$
$r = 40$

**6. Answer the question**      To solve for r, we divided 120 by 3.

The correct answer is **c**.

1. Fou traveled for 3 hours to visit his grandmother who lived 120 miles away. Which computation below will provide Fou's average speed in miles per hour?

   a. Multiply 120 by 3.

   b. Multiply 3 by 120.

   c. Divide 120 by 3.

   d. Divide 3 by 120.

2. Maria's average speed was 45 miles per hour. If she traveled for 2 hours and 15 minutes, which computation below would be used to compute her total miles traveled?

   a. Multiply 45 by 2.25.

   b. Multiply 45 by 2.15.

   c. Divide 45 by 2.25.

   d. Divide 2.15 by 45.

3. 
   > Truong's Limo Service rents limousines by the hour. A customers bill for a rental is $350.00. How much did the limo cost per hour?

   Which piece of information would you need in order to solve the problem?

   a. The limo driver's name.

   b. The distance the limo traveled.

   c. The number of people in the limo.

   d. The number of hours the limo was rented.

4. It takes Thao two hours to finish a race. If she runs at a rate of 1 mile every 10 minutes, how far did she run?

   a. 20 miles

   b. 12 miles

   c. 60 miles

   d. 6 miles

5. 
   > Lilian went to the football game. Her ticket cost $2.00. Her two drinks cost $1.25 each and the hot-dog was $1.50.

   Based upon the story in the box above, which information is irrelevant if you had to answer the following question "How much did Lilian spend on drinks?"

   a. Ticket and hot-dog cost.

   b. Ticket cost and the fact that she had two drinks.

   c. Hot-dog cost and the fact that she had two drinks.

   d. All the information is required to answer the question.

6. Christina used 120 feet of fence to enclose her rectangular garden. If the length is three times the width, find the length of her garden.

   a. The width is 15 feet.

   b. The length is 21 feet.

   c. The length is 45 feet.

   d. The length is 30 feet.

**7.**

> Alexander bought some clothes for school. He spent $325.00 for some shirts, ties, and pants. If he bought four times as many shirts as pants, and twice as many ties as pants, then how many pairs of pants did he buy?

What other information would you need in order to solve the problem?

a. The cost of the ties.

b. The cost of the pants.

c. The cost of the shirts.

d. The number of items purchased.

**8.** If you divide a number by 3, add 4, multiply by 2, and subtract 5, the result is the number you started with. What is the number?

a. 3

b. 9

c. 6

d. 12

**9.** If you add 5 to a number, multiply by 3, subtract 6, and divide by 5, the result is one less than the number you started with. What is the number?

a. 7

b. 8

c. 9

d. 10

**10.** The mean exam score for one math class at a high school is 82. What additional information is needed if you must answer the question "How many students took the exam?"

a. The median score.

b. The mode.

c. The sum of all the scores.

d. Not enough information given in the problem to determine what additional information is needed.

**11.** Determine which information is irrelevant for the problem. Janise purchased four new tires and one used tire (the spare) for her truck. If the cost of the new tires was $132.00 and the cost for the spare was $15.00, then determine the cost of each new tire.

a. The cost of the new tires.

b. The cost of the spare tire.

c. The number of new tires purchased.

d. All the information is required to answer the question.

**12.** Marco missed class 41% of the time. How many days per semester was Marco absent? What additional information is needed to solve the problem?

a. The number of students in the class.

b. Information on why Marco was absent.

c. The number of days in a semester.

d. Adequate information is provided to solve the problem.

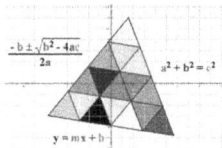

| Vocabulary: | **conjecture** | an inferring, theorizing, or predicting from incomplete or uncertain evidence; guesswork |
|---|---|---|
| | **counter example** | an example that proves a statement false |

Often, success in mathematics is based on recognizing a pattern and assuming that the pattern will continue. A conclusion based on this reasoning is a **conjecture**.
Often this is true, but sometimes it is not. Proving a conjecture is true can become complicated, however one **counterexample** can prove a conjecture false.

---

**EXAMPLE:** Select the shape that continues the pattern.

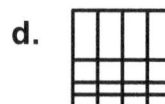

a.    b.    c.    d.

---

Numerically, the pattern is 1, 2, 4, 8...

We can conclude that the next shape will have 16 pieces. However, all answer choices have 16 pieces so we need to be more specific.

In the given pattern, the "odd numbered shapes" contain squares.
Choice **b** is the only answer that contains squares.

The correct answer is **b.**

---

**EXAMPLE:**

If x is any integer, find a counterexample to the conjecture x < 3x.

    **a.**    - 2     **b.** $\dfrac{1}{4}$     **c.** $\dfrac{1}{3}$     **d.**    2

We are looking for the answer choice that makes x < 3x false.

We can eliminate choices **b** and **c** because they are not integers.

**a.** - 2     -2 < 3(-2)     -2 < -6     This is a false statement

The correct answer is **a.**

---

156

1. If x is any integer, find a counterexample to the conjecture x < 3x.

   a.  - 2

   b.  $\frac{1}{4}$

   c.  $\frac{1}{3}$

   d.  2

2. If x is any real number, find a counterexample to the conjecture $x < x^2$.

   a.  $\frac{-1}{4}$

   b.  $\frac{4}{3}$

   c.  1

   d.  $\frac{-2}{3}$

3. If n is an even number, then which statement is true for n + 1?

   a.  n + 1 is less than n.

   b.  n + 1 is an odd number.

   c.  n + 1 is an even number.

   d.  None of the statements above are true.

4. If a and b are both positive numbers, which expression may be negative?

   a.  $\frac{a}{b}$

   b.  a + b

   c.  a(b)

   d.  a - b

5. The conjecture $x^2 + x + 17$ is prime for all numbers, when x is from the set {1, 2, 3, 4, ...}. This statement is false, find a counterexample.

   a.  3

   b.  7

   c.  17

   d.  11

6. The sum of an even number and an odd number is an odd number. Which statement supports the conjecture?

   a.  3(5) = 15

   b.  4 + 2 = 6

   c.  8(7) = 56

   d.  12 + 9 = 21

7. Given the sequence of numbers: 1, 4, 7, 10, ... , which conjecture best describes the sequence?

   a.  Beginning with the number 1, we multiply by four.

   b.  Beginning with the number 1, we add three.

   c.  Beginning with the number 1, we multiply by two and then add 1.

   d.  Beginning with the number 1, we square the number and then add three.

8. The Goldbach Conjecture claims that it is possible to write any even number greater than 2 as the sum of two primes. Which statement supports this conjecture?

    a. 8 = 3 + 5

    b. 12 = 3 + 9

    c. 6 = 2 + 4

    d. 4 = 1 + 3

9. Meuy claims that "if a number is evenly divisible by 4, then it is evenly divisible by 8." Which of the following is a counterexample to Meuy's conjecture?

    a. 8          b. 16

    c. 12         d. 24

10. The Twin Primes Conjecture states that an infinite number of primes differing by two can be found. Which example below supports this conjecture?

    a. 23 and 25

    b. 29 and 31

    c. 33 and 35

    d. 49 and 51

11. A Perfect Number is equal to the sum of its divisors, not including the number itself. Example: 6 = 1 + 2 + 3. Vanpou claims that there exists another Perfect Number. Which example below supports his conjecture?

    a. 12         b. 18

    c. 20         d. 28

12. Euclid claims that their are an infinite number of primes. If his partial list consists of the following primes 2, 3, 5, 7, 11, 13, 17, 19, ... , then which example below supports Euclid's conjecture?

    a. 23, 29, 31, ...

    b. 23, 25, 27, ...

    c. 23, 27, 29, ...

    d. 23, 29, 39, ...

13. Lor claims that if a number n divides the quantity of x times y, then the number divides both x and y. Which example below is a counterexample to Lor's conjecture?

    a. n = 3, x = 6, and y = 9

    b. n = 3, x = 4, and y = 6

    c. n = 3, x = 6, and y = 12

    d. n = 3, x = 9, and y = 12

14. A certain airline offers flights from Sacramento, CA to Miami, FL. The table below shows four flight times.

| Take Off Time in Sacramento | Arrival Time in Miami |
|---|---|
| 7:30 a.m. | 4:10 p.m. |
| 8:40 a.m. | 5:25 p.m. |
| 9:35 a.m. | 6:25 p.m. |
| 11:55 a.m. | 8:25 p.m. |

Which flight takes the least amount of time?

a. The flight arriving at 4:10 p.m.

b. The flight arriving at 5:25 p.m.

c. The flight arriving at 6:25 p.m.

d. The flight arriving at 8:25 p.m.

15. Each student claims to have found a Pythagorean triple with satisfies the Pythagorean Theorem. Which student's conjecture is false?

| Steven | a = 3, b = 4, c = 5 |
|---|---|
| Laura | a = 5, b = 12, c = 13 |
| Tatiana | a = 6, b = 9, c = 10 |
| Jose | a = 7, b = 24, c = 25 |

a. Steven

b. Laura

c. Tatiana

d. Jose

16. A certain railroad company offers train rides from Durango, CO to Silverton, CO. The tables below show four possible ride times.

| Leaves Durango | Arrives in Silverton |
|---|---|
| 7:05 a.m. | 10:30 a.m. |
| 2:40 p.m. | 6:10 p.m. |

| Leaves Silverton | Arrives in Durango |
|---|---|
| 10:50 a.m. | 2:25 p.m. |
| 6:30 p.m. | 10:10 p.m. |

If you wanted the longest "one way" train ride possible, determine which town and time would you board the train.

a. Durango at 7:05 a.m.

b. Silverton at 10:50 a.m.

c. Durango at 2:40 p.m.

d. Silverton at 6:30 p.m.

# CAHSEE Bench Mark 40

Students will successfully estimate to verify the
reasonableness of a calculation.

**CA Standard:** Grade 7, Mathematical Reasoning, 2.1
**CAHSEE Strand:** Mathematical Reasoning

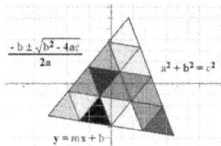

| **Vocabulary: rounding** | to increase or decrease one number to another number divisible by ten; or change to a whole number in the case of fractions and decimals |
|---|---|
| **estimating** | to make an approximate computation or general calculation |

We round numbers to make mental calculations easier. Below are the conventional rounding guidelines for whole numbers, decimals and fractions.

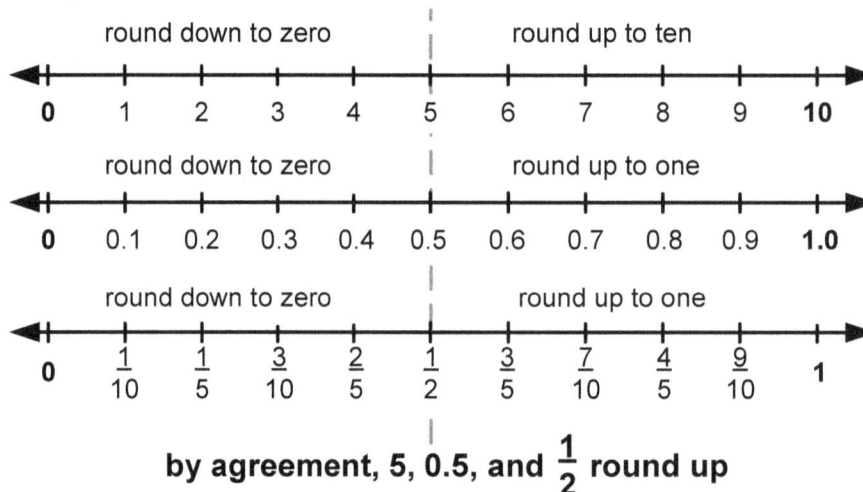

round down to zero   |   round up to ten

```
 0   1   2   3   4   5   6   7   8   9   10
```

round down to zero   |   round up to one

```
 0  0.1  0.2  0.3  0.4  0.5  0.6  0.7  0.8  0.9  1.0
```

round down to zero   |   round up to one

```
 0   1/10  1/5  3/10  2/5  1/2  3/5  7/10  4/5  9/10   1
```

by agreement, 5, 0.5, and $\frac{1}{2}$ **round up**

Rounding numbers is the first step of estimating. We want to round so we can do mental calculations. Estimations are not accurate but do give an idea as to the final answer. Estimating is also a good way to judge the reasonableness of calculations.

---

**EXAMPLE:** Mureed wants to approximate his bill before he gets to the cashier to pay. The items cost $5.12, $2.98, and $6.85. Which expression is the best estimate for Mureed's cost?

**a.** 4 + 3 + 7    **b.** 5 + 3 + 7    **c.** 5 + 2 + 7    **d.** 5 + 3 + 6

$5.12 will round down to 5.

$2.98 will round up to 3.

$6.85 will round up to 7.

Therefore, 5 + 3 + 7, will be a fairly accurate estimate for Mureed's cost.

The correct answer is **b.**

---

**EXAMPLE:**    Which is the best estimate of 28 times 102?

**a.** 30    **b.** 300    **c.** 3,000    **d.** 30,000

102 ——— round down ——→ 100
x 28 ——— round up ——→ x 30

This is 3(1) with 3 zeros or 3,000

The correct answer is **c.**

---

1. Which is the best estimate of 28 times 102?

   a. 30

   b. 300

   c. 3,000

   d. 30,000

2. Which is the best estimate of 382 times 227?

   a. 800

   b. 8,000

   c. 80,000

   d. 800,000

3. Chue wants to approximate his bill before he gets to the cashier to pay. The items are marked in dollars: 4.89 , 3.29 , 6.99 , 2.39, and 7.75. Determine which expression is the best estimate for Chue's cost.

   a. 4.00 + 3.00 + 7.00 + 2.00 + 8.00

   b. 4.00 + 3.00 + 7.00 + 2.00 + 7.00

   c. 5.00 + 3.00 + 7.00 + 2.00 + 7.00

   d. 5.00 + 3.00 + 7.00 + 2.00 + 8.00

4. Estimate the area of a square with a side length of 7.12 feet.

   a. 49 Square Feet

   b. 7 Square Feet

   c. 8 Square Feet

   d. 64 Square Feet

5. In a class of 39 students, what is the best estimate for the mean test score if the sum of the all tests is 3187?

   a. 75

   b. 80

   c. 85

   d. 90

6. What is the best estimate for the radius of a circle whose circumference is 41.6 meters?

   a. 7 meters

   b. 8 meters

   c. 9 meters

   d. 10 meters

7. If a fair number cube with six sides is rolled twenty times, what is the best estimate for the number of times that a four would appear?

   a. 0

   b. 1

   c. 2

   d. 3

8. If a fair coin was flipped 148 times, what is the best estimate for the number of times that a head would appear?

   a. 65

   b. 75

   c. 85

   d. 95

9. Three decimal numbers need to be multiplied. What is the best estimate if the numbers are 6.875, 5.125, and 1.9375?

    a. 30

    b. 60

    c. 70

    d. 84

10. What is the best estimate for the square root of 80.7?

    a. 8

    b. 9

    c. 10

    d. 11

11. The table below shows the number of tickets sold for a school raffle.

| Ticket Cost | # of Tickets Sold |
|---|---|
| $10.00 | 186 |
| $7.00 | 208 |
| $4.00 | 792 |

Which is the best estimate for the amount of money collected?

    a. $6,600

    b. $4,800

    c. $7,300

    d. $8,100

12. On a certain birthday, Van's living grandmother will be three times older than Van. Which age for Van seems most unlikely based upon the information?

    a. 25

    b. 30

    c. 35

    d. 40

13. In a class of 21 students, what is the best estimate for the mean test score if the sum of the all tests is 1514?

    a. 65

    b. 70

    c. 75

    d. 80

14. What is the best estimate for the radius of a circle whose area is 74.8 inches?

    a. 4 inches

    b. 5 inches

    c. 6 inches

    d. 12 inches

15. If one rod is 16.5 feet, then which is the best estimate for 19 rods?

    a. 240 feet

    b. 340 feet

    c. 440 feet

    d. 540 feet

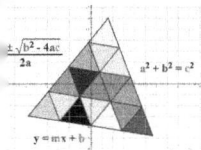

Students will successfully estimate unknown
quantities graphically.

**CA Standard:** Grade 7, Mathematical Reasoning, 2.3
**CAHSEE Strand:** Mathematical Reasoning

Estimating from graphs is a simple process of observation and rounding. By definition, estimating is not tremendously exact, but being as precise as possible will help the accuracy of the answers.

**EXAMPLE:** Estimate the area of the figure.

a. 10 square units

b. 12 square units

c. 14 square units

d. 16 square units

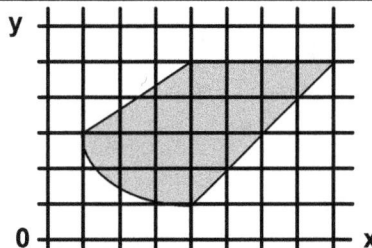

First, we count the full squares. In this example, there are 10.

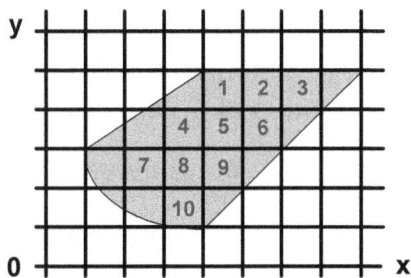

Next, we count those squares that are more than half full. In this example, there are 4.

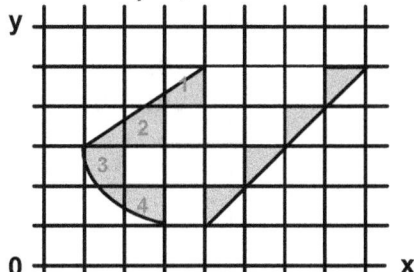

Next, we count the half full squares. In this example, there are four for a total of 2 whole squares.

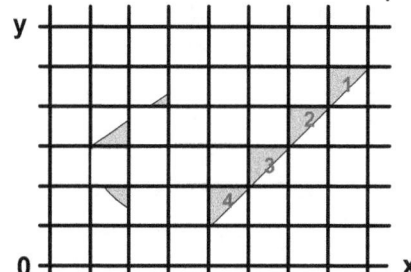

*Note: we are not concerned with those pieces less than half full. They will make up the difference for the missing parts of the second step.*

We add the results. **10 + 4 + 2 = 16** The correct answer is **d.**

**EXAMPLE:**

Use the line of best fit in the scatter plot below to estimate the number of pet food types that a store carried at two and one-half years in business.

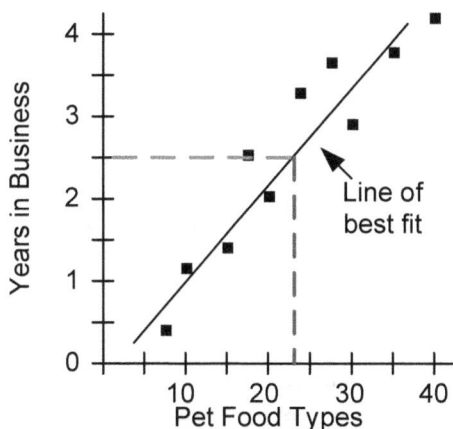

a. Between 10 and 20 types.

b. Between 20 and 30 types.

c. Between 30 and 40 types.

d. More than 40 types.

For this problem, the line of best fit has been provided. In similar problems, it is not.

Again, estimating from a graph is a simple process of observation and estimation.

We first find two and a half years on the vertical axis, draw a horizontal line to the line of best fit, then estimate where a vertical line will intersect the horizontal axis.

At two and a half years, it appears that the store carried between 20 and 30 food types.

The correct answer is **b.**

1. Use the line of best fit in the scatter plot below to estimate the number of pet food types that a store carried at two and one-half years in business.

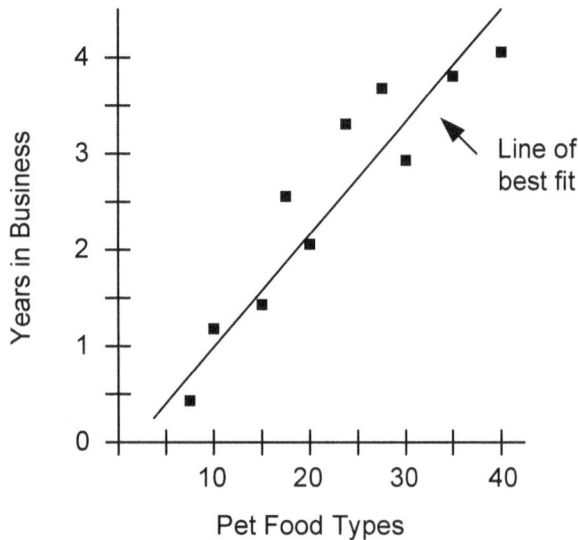

a. Between 10 and 20 types.

b. Between 20 and 30 types.

c. Between 30 and 40 types.

d. More than 40 types.

2. Estimate the area of the figure.

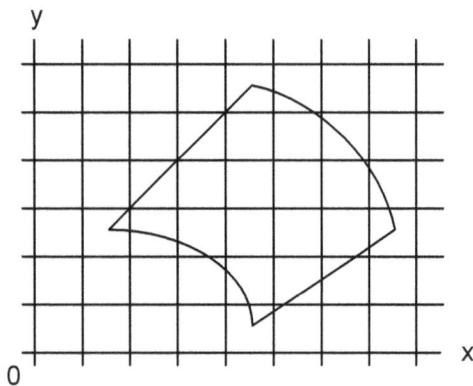

a. 8 square units

b. 10 square units

c. 12 square units

d. 14 square units

3. A chemist is using the Henderson-Hasselbalch equation to measure the the pH balance of the acid alanine as a base is slowly added. The scatter plot below is the result of the data collected.

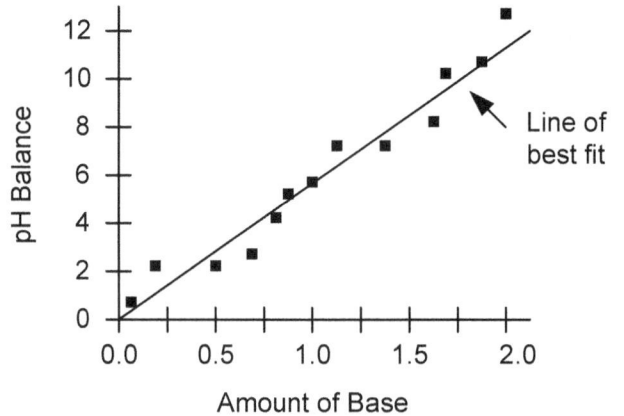

Using the line of best fit, estimate the pH Balance when the amount of base is at 1.25 units.

a. Between 0 and 2.   b. Between 2 and 4.

c. Between 4 and 6.   d. Between 6 and 8.

4. The graph below shows the relationship between the number of weekly hours worked and the amount of money earned by a high school student.

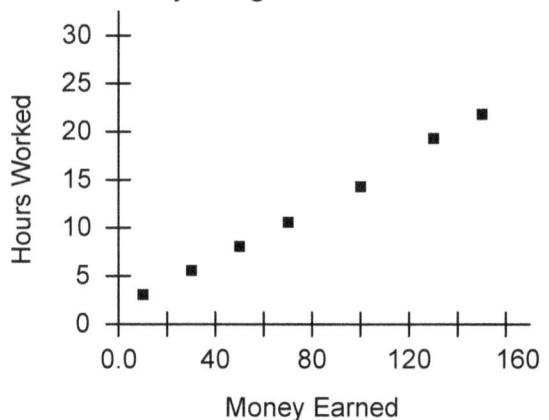

Using the data for 15 hours worked, estimate the amount of money a student would make if she worked 30 hours per week.

a.   90               b.   160

c.   200              d.   240

**5.** The graph below shows the relationship between the number of weekly hours worked and the grade point average of students at the local university.

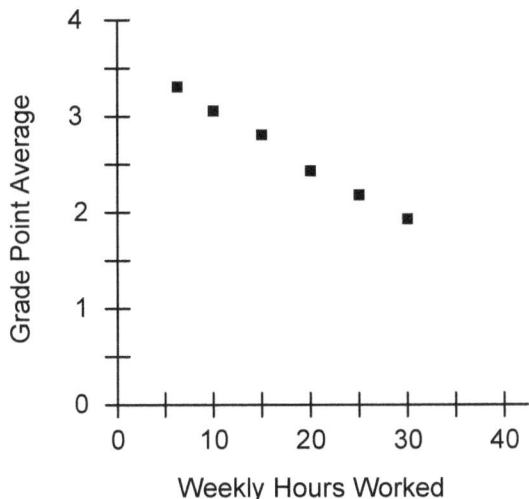

From the graph, which grade point average listed below is the most probable for students that do not work?

|  |  |  |  |
|---|---|---|---|
| **a.** | 3.8 | **b.** | 3.5 |
| **c.** | 3.3 | **d.** | 3.0 |

**6.** Estimate the area of the figure.

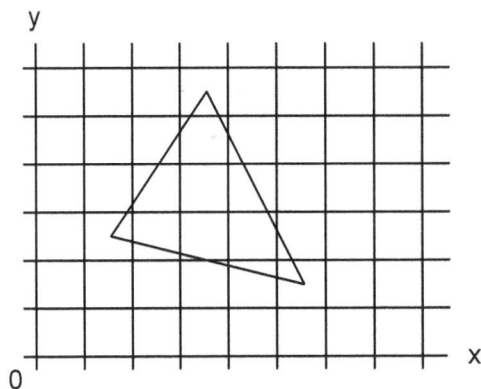

- **a.** 5 square units
- **b.** 7 square units
- **c.** 9 square units
- **d.** 11 square units

**7.** A company ships three different boxes of materials, where the weights of the boxes are not equal. See the graph below.

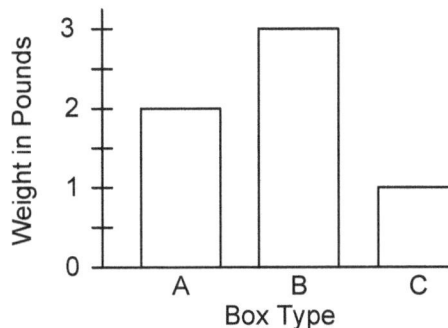

The company can ship at most 20 pounds. If the number of boxes must be 10, determine which combination of boxes will be at most 20 pounds.

- **a.** 5 of A; 2 of B; and 3 of C.
- **b.** 6 of A; 1 of B; and 3 of C.
- **c.** 4 of A; 3 of B; and 3 of C.
- **d.** 4 of A; 4 of B; and 2 of C.

**8.** A certain college has produced a scatter plot of their students income at age 25 as compared to the number of years that the student attended the college.

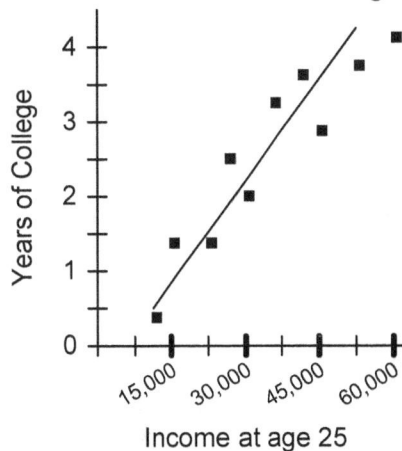

Use the line of best fit to estimate the amount of money a student could expect to earn if they completed three years of college.

|  |  |  |  |
|---|---|---|---|
| **a.** | 35,000 | **b.** | 37,500 |
| **c.** | 45,000 | **d.** | 50,000 |

**9.** Estimate the area of the figure.

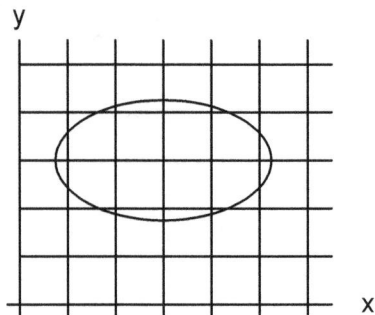

a. 2 square units

b. 4 square units

c. 6 square units

d. 8 square units

**10.** A nutritionist has produced a scatter plot of the number of calories as carbohydrates in foods.

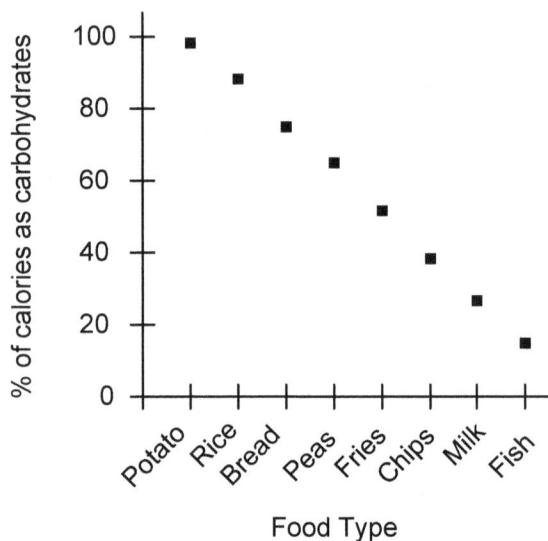

If you wanted to ensure that you had at least 60% of your calories as carbohydrates, which of the following foods should you eat?

a. Peas

b. Fries

c. Chips

d. Milk

**11.** The number of horses at four ranches is shown in the below graph. Estimate the total number of horses.

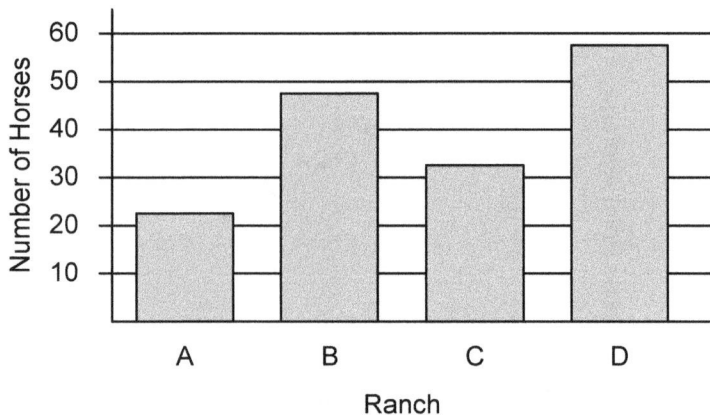

a. 120

b. 140

c. 160

d. 180

**12.** The number of different breads carried by four stores is shown in the below graph. Estimate the total number of breads.

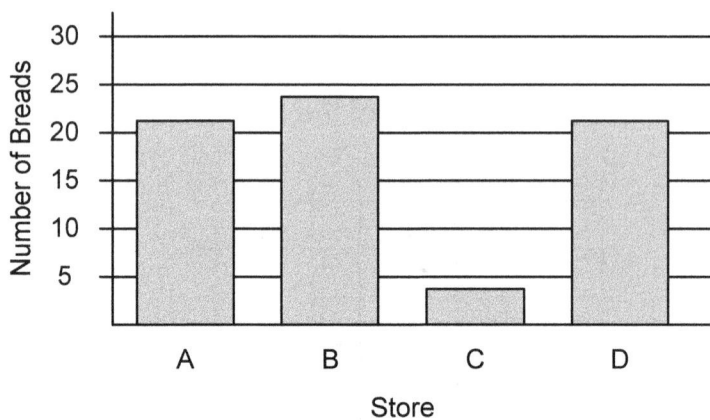

a. 65

b. 70

c. 75

d. 80

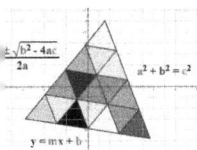

Students will successfully use inductive and
deductive reasoning.

**CA Standard:** Grade 7, Mathematical Reasoning, 2.4
**CAHSEE Strand:** Mathematical Reasoning

| | | |
|---|---|---|
| **Vocabulary:** | **reasoning** | the drawing of inferences or conclusions from known or assumed facts |
| | **deductive reasoning** | the process of reasoning logically from given facts to a conclusion |
| | **inductive reasoning** | the process of making conclusions based on patterns you observe |
| | **conjecture** | an inferring, theorizing, or predicting from incomplete or uncertain evidence; guesswork |
| | **conditional statement** | an 'if...then' statement, in which there is usually a cause and effect relationship; typically in the form *"If p, then q"* |
| | **contrapositive statement** | is a statement that means the same as the given conditional statement; typically in the form *"If not q, then not p"* |

The advantage of **inductive reasoning** is that a relationship can be readily discovered. One disadvantage is that an inductive conclusion is only a conjecture. **Deductive reasoning** is based upon previously proven facts and acceptable assumptions so it not only shows what the relationship is, but also why the relationship exists.

Simply stated, **inductive reasoning** usually moves from the specific to the general while **deductive reasoning** moves from the general to the specific.

---

**EXAMPLE:** If it is a rabbit, then it has long ears. What can you conclude in the statements below?

**a.** If it is not a rabbit, then it does not have long ears.

**b.** If it does have long ears, then it is a rabbit.

**c.** If it does not have long ears, then it is a rabbit.

**d.** If it does not have long ears, then it is not a rabbit.

---

By definition, a contrapositive statement means the same as the given conditional statement. Therefore, the solution is the answer choice that has the form *"If not q, then not p."*

The correct answer is **d.**

---

**EXAMPLE:** Given the sequence 1, 2, 4, ..., determine which of the following would be the next three terms.

**a.** 6, 8, 10     **b.** 8, 12, 16     **c.** 3, 2, 1     **d.** 8, 16, 32

One possible pattern to observe might be begin at one and to get from one term to the next, add one more than the previous term;

**1**

1 + 1   **2**

2 + 2 = **4**

So we would consider 4 + 3 = 7 to be the next term.

None of the answer choices begin with 7, so this is incorrect.

Another possible pattern to observe might be to begin with one and to get from one term to the next multiply by two;

**1**

1(2) = **2**

2(2) = **4**

So we would consider 4(2) = **8**, 8(2) = **16**, and 16(2) = **32** to be the next three terms.

The correct answer is **d.**

1. Given the sequence 1, 2, 4, ...,
   determine which of the following
   would be the next three terms.

   a. 6, 8, 10     b. 8, 12, 16

   c. 3, 2, 1      d. 8, 16, 32

2. Given the sequence 1, 2, 4, ...,
   determine which of the following
   would be the next three terms.

   a. 6, 9, 12     b. 7, 11, 16

   c. 8, 10, 12    d. 5, 8, 11

3. Given the sequence 2, 5, 10, 17, ...,
   determine which of the following
   would be the next three terms.

   a. 26, 37, 50   b. 18, 20, 22

   c. 19, 25, 29   d. 24, 32, 41

4. The table below shows the input
   values and the corresponding output
   values. Determine the missing input
   value.

   | Input | Output |
   |-------|--------|
   | 2     | 6      |
   | 5     | 15     |
   | 8     | 24     |
   | ?     | 33     |

   a. 9           b. 10

   c. 11          d. 12

5. Determine a number that is less than
   40, with factors 2, 3, and 5.

   a. 20          b. 30

   c. 15          d. 10

6. The table below shows input values (x)
   and the corresponding output values (y).

   | x  | y  |
   |----|----|
   | 27 | 18 |
   | 15 | 10 |
   | 9  | 6  |
   | 6  | 4  |

   Which of the following represents the
   relationship between x and y?

   a. $y = x - 9$     b. $y = x - 5$

   c. $y = \frac{3}{2} x$     d. $y = \frac{2}{3} x$

7. The table below shows the Domain (x)
   and the Range (y).

   | x  | y  |
   |----|----|
   | 8  | 4  |
   | 16 | 12 |
   | 28 | 24 |
   | 36 | 32 |

   Which of the following represents the
   relationship between x and y?

   a. $y = x - 4$     b. $y = x + 4$

   c. $y = \frac{1}{2} x$     d. $y = \frac{1}{4} x$

8. A certain number is a multiple of 4, 5,
   and 10. If the number is less than 50,
   what is the number?

   a. 10          b. 30

   c. 20          d. No solution.

168

9. If it is raining, then you use an umbrella. What can you conclude in the statements below?

   a. If it is not raining, then you do not use an umbrella.

   b. If you do not use an umbrella, then it is not raining.

   c. If you use an umbrella, then it is raining.

   d. If you do not use an umbrella, then it is raining.

10. If the figure is not a rectangle, then it is not a square. Which conclusion can you claim below?

    a. If the figure is a rectangle, then it is not a square.

    b. If it is not a square, then the figure is not a rectangle.

    c. If the figure is a rectangle, then it is a square.

    d. If it is a square, then the figure is a rectangle.

11. If x equals the square root of 9, then x does not equal negative 3. What can you conclude based upon the given information?

    a. If x equals negative 3, then x does not equal the square root of 9.

    b. If x does not equal negative 3, then x equals the square root of 9.

    c. If x does not equal the square root of 9, then x equals negative 3.

    d. If x does not equal the square root of 9, then x does not equal negative 3.

12. If today is not Wednesday, then yesterday was not Tuesday. What can you conclude if yesterday was Tuesday?

    a. Today is not Wednesday.

    b. Today is Thursday.

    c. Today is Wednesday.

    d. The day cannot be determined.

13. During a semester of high school, the first student progress report was sent out at week 5; the second student progress report was sent out at week 10; and the third student progress report was sent out at week 15. Based upon the data, what conclusion may be drawn?

    a. Students should expect one progress report during the semester.

    b. The progress reports will arrive at student's home on Saturday.

    c. The school sends out weekly student progress reports.

    d. Student progress reports are sent out every five weeks during the semester.

14. If the animal is a German Shepherd, then it is a dog. Which conclusion can you claim below?

    a. If the animal is not a German Shepherd, then it is not a dog.

    b. If the animal is not a German Shepherd, then it is a dog.

    c. If the animal is not a dog, then it is a German Shepherd.

    d. If the animal is not a dog, then it is not a German Shepherd.

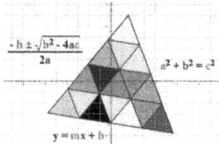

# CAHSEE Bench Mark 43

Students will successfully develop generalizations
based on mathematical results.

**CA Standard:** Grade 7, Mathematical Reasoning, 3.3
**CAHSEE Strand:** Mathematical Reasoning

*Simplified Solutions For Math Inc.*

---

| **Vocabulary:** | **generalize** | to formulate general principles or inferences from particulars |
| --- | --- | --- |
| | **reasoning** | the drawing of inferences or conclusions from known or assumed facts |

The method of reasoning in mathematics is quite similar to that used by people who reason about non-mathematical situations. People, especially math students, should be able to develop generalizations based upon given facts or results.

**EXAMPLE:** Given the quadratic function $f(x) = 3x^2 + 5x + 6$, the discriminant is $5^2 - 4(3)(6)$. Mai notices that the quadratic function is in the general form of $f(x) = ax^2 + bx + c$. Given the quadratic function $f(x) = ax^2 + bx + c$, find the discriminant.

   **a.** $b^2 + ac$    **b.** $b^2 + 4ac$    **c.** $b^2 - 4ac$    **d.** $b - 4ac$

Given the quadratic function $f(x) = 3x^2 + 5x + 6$ and the disciminant $5^2 - 4(3)(6)$, we can find the discriminant using $f(x) = ax^2 + bx + c$ by substituting a, b, and c for 3, 5, and 6 respectively.

$5^2 - 4(3)(6)$
$b^2 - 4(a)(c)$

Therefore, the descriminant is $b^2 - 4ac$.

The correct answer is **c.**

**EXAMPLE:** Seng solved the following linear equation in standard form for y:

$Ax + By = C$ , where A, B, and C are integers.

| Step 1: Subtract "Ax" from both sides. | $By = -Ax + C$ |
| --- | --- |
| Step 2: Divide each side by "B". | $y = \dfrac{-A}{B}x + \dfrac{C}{B}$ |

Seng noticed that if he solved a linear equation in standard form for y, then the new equation was in the slope-intercept form: $y = mx + b$, where m is the slope and b is the y-intercept. Which of the following would be the correct substitution for Seng's equation in Step 2?

**a.** Let $m = \dfrac{C}{B}$ and $b = \dfrac{-A}{B}$     **b.** Let $m = \dfrac{-C}{B}$ and $b = \dfrac{A}{B}$

**c.** Let $m = \dfrac{-A}{B}$ and $b = \dfrac{C}{B}$     **d.** Let $m = \dfrac{A}{B}$ and $b = \dfrac{-C}{B}$

Looking at the two formulas, $y = mx + b$ and $y = \dfrac{-A}{B}x + \dfrac{C}{B}$ it is a simple matter of substitution to see that

$m = \dfrac{-A}{B}$ and $b = \dfrac{C}{B}$

The correct answer is **c.**

# CAHSEE Bench Mark Practice 43

1. Seng solved the following linear equation in standard form for y:
$Ax + By = C$, where A, B, and C are integers.

| Step 1: Subtract Ax from both sides. | $By = -Ax + C$ |
| Step 2: Divide each side by B. | $y = \dfrac{-A}{B}x + \dfrac{C}{B}$ |

Seng noticed that if he solved a linear equation in standard form for y, then the new equation was in the slope-intercept form: $y = mx + b$, where m is the slope and b is the y-intercept. Which of the following would be the correct substitution for Seng's equation in Step 2?

   a. Let $m = \dfrac{C}{B}$ and $b = \dfrac{-A}{B}$

   b. Let $m = \dfrac{-C}{B}$ and $b = \dfrac{A}{B}$

   c. Let $m = \dfrac{-A}{B}$ and $b = \dfrac{C}{B}$

   d. Let $m = \dfrac{A}{B}$ and $b = \dfrac{-C}{B}$

2. Newton's law states that Force (F) is equal to mass (m) times acceleration (a). Which of the following formulas is not like Newton's law?

   a. Hook's Law: $d = kF$

   b. Einstein's equation: $E = mc^2$

   c. Ohm's Law: $E = IR$

   d. Work: $W = Fd$

3. Sandy solved the following linear equation in point-slope form for y: $y - y_1 = m(x - x_1)$, where m is the slope and $x_1$ and $y_1$ is the point.

| Step 1: Distribute m. | $y - y_1 = mx - mx_1$ |
| Step 2: Add $y_1$ to both sides. | $y = mx - mx_1 + y_1$ |

Sandy noticed that if she solved a linear equation in point-slope form for y, then the new equation was in the slope-intercept form: $y = mx + b$, where m is the slope and b is the y-intercept. Which of the following would be the correct substitution for Sandy's equation in Step 2?

   a. Let $m = y_1$

   b. Let $b = y_1$

   c. Let $m = -mx_1 + y_1$

   d. Let $b = -mx_1 + y_1$

4. Factorial (!) is just multiplication of every integer, including the number in question, down to one. For example, three factorial is written as: $3! = 3 * 2 * 1$.

Which of the following would represent five factorial?

   a. $5! = 5 * 4 * 3 * 2 * 1$

   b. $5! = 4 * 3 * 2 * 1$

   c. $5! = 5 * 3 * 2 * 1$

   d. $5! = 5 * 4 * 2 * 1$

5. In Geometry, we know that a circle is an ellipses with a congruent major and minor axes. Determine which figures below are most alike.

   a. A Triangle is a Pentagon.

   b. A Square is a Triangle.

   c. A Square is a Trapezoid.

   d. A Square is a Rectangle.

6. In Trigonometry, if we know that the sine of some angle is 3 over 5, then the cosecant of the same angle is the reciprocal of the sine. Determine which ratio is the cosecant of the angle in question.

   a. $\frac{5}{3}$

   b. $\frac{-5}{3}$

   c. $\frac{-3}{5}$

   d. $\frac{3}{5}$

7. Douglas converted 23,000 into scientific notation. Which number below is most like the answer that Douglas found, once he converted 23,000 into scientific notation?

   a. $6.7 \times 10^{-4}$

   b. $6.7 \times 10^{4}$

   c. $6.7 \times 10^{-3}$

   d. $67 \times 10^{4}$

8. A six sided number cube is rolled once, where success is rolling a 3. Which of the following experiments below would be most like this one in probability?

   a. Flipping a fair coin, where success is the coin landing tails up.

   b. Picking a card from a deck of cards, where success is drawing an Ace.

   c. The letters of MATH on individual note cards, where success is drawing the M.

   d. In a bag of 24 marbles, success is drawing one of the four red marbles.

9. Jameshia received a 5000 dollar scholarship for college. If she wants the money to last for the school year, which is 10 months long, how much can Jameshia spend every month?

Which of the problems below can be solved by the same arithmetic operations that are used to solve the problem of Jameshia's scholarship?

   a. Cindy reads one page every two minutes. How long would it take Cindy to read seventy-six pages?

   b. If a school bus seat holds two students, then how many students can ride a bus that has nineteen seats?

   c. A plane can fly 300 miles in two and one-half hours. How fast is the plane flying?

   d. If one piece of firewood weighs one and one-half pounds, then how much would seven pieces of firewood weigh?

10. Kimberly was converting from decimal to fractions, when she noticed the following: 0.777... became seven over nine and 0.1313... became thirteen over ninety-nine. Which of the following decimals would not work with Kimberly's observation?

   a. 0.44444444...

   b. 0.151551555...

   c. 0.123123123...

   d. 0.131113111311...

**BM 1.** The tallest building in the world is Taipei 101 in Taiwan. It is 1,670 feet tall. What is this number in scientific notation?

    **a.** $1.67 \times 10^5$       **b.** $1.67 \times 10^3$

    **c.** $16.7 \times 10^8$       **d.** $1.67 \times 10^4$

**BM 2.** $4 - 3 - (-5) + (-6) =$

    **a.** 1           **b.** 0

    **c.** 2           **d.** 3

**BM 3.** If 15 out of 25 families on the block own cats, what is the percentage of families that own cats?

    **a.** 85%       **b.** 80%

    **c.** 50%       **d.** 60%

**BM 4.** The price of a cup of coffee has decreased from $4.00 to $2.20. What is the percent of decrease?

    **a.** 55%       **b.** 50%

    **c.** 45%       **d.** 25%

**BM 5.** A sales person at a music store earns a 3% commission on all sales. How much commission does the sales person earn on a $400.00 sale?

    **a.** $10.00       **b.** $12.00

    **c.** $18.50       **d.** $17.50

**BM 6.** Which of the following inequalities represents the statement, "A number, x, decreased by 4 is less than or equal to 7?"

    **a.** $x - 4 \leq 7$       **b.** $x - 7 < 4$

    **c.** $x - 4 > 7$       **d.** $4 - x \leq 7$

**BM 7.** What is $\dfrac{3}{8} - \dfrac{1}{6}$ ?

    **a.** $\dfrac{2}{2}$       **b.** $\dfrac{4}{14}$

    **c.** $\dfrac{5}{24}$       **d.** $\dfrac{2}{48}$

**BM 8.** $(5^4)^6 =$

    **a.** $5^{24}$       **b.** $5^{10}$

    **c.** $20^6$       **d.** $25^6$

**BM 9.** The square root of 154 is between

    **a.** 11 and 12       **b.** 12 and 13

    **c.** 13 and 14       **d.** 14 and 15

**BM 10.** If $|x| = 13$, what is the value of x?

    **a.** 6 or 7       **b.** -13 or 13

    **c.** 13 or 0       **d.** -13 or 1

**BM 11.** Amondo's first seven homework scores are 3, 5, 4, 5, 3, 4, and 5. What is the median of Amondo's scores?

    **a.** 4       **b.** 3

    **c.** 9       **d.** 5

**BM 12.** The following two pie charts represent the same set of data.

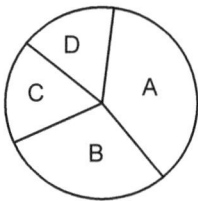
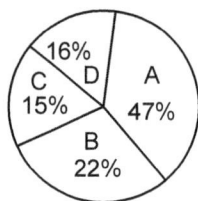

Figure 1                    Figure 2

If Figure 1 was the only circle graph given, why would it be misleading?

**a.** Group B appears much bigger than it should.

**b.** The pie chart in figure 1 is divided into four equal parts.

**c.** Group C appears to be smaller than Group D.

**d.** Group C appears to be bigger than Group A.

**BM 13.** If you pick a card at random from a complete deck of cards, what is the probability that it will be black?

a. $\frac{1}{4}$          b. $\frac{1}{2}$

c. $\frac{1}{12}$          d. $\frac{2}{13}$

**BM 14.** If a fair number cube is rolled once, what is the probability of not getting a two?

a. $\frac{1}{6}$          b. $\frac{1}{2}$

c. $\frac{5}{6}$          d. $\frac{1}{3}$

**BM 15.** Each letter of the word MATH is on its own note card, lying face down on a desk. Jacob will pick up two note cards without replacement. On the first card, Jacob picks up the M, what is the probability that the next card will be the letter A?

a. $\frac{1}{4}$          b. $\frac{1}{12}$

c. $\frac{1}{3}$          d. $\frac{1}{2}$

**BM 16.** The line graph below represents the change of the daily cost of fresh lobster during one week in December.

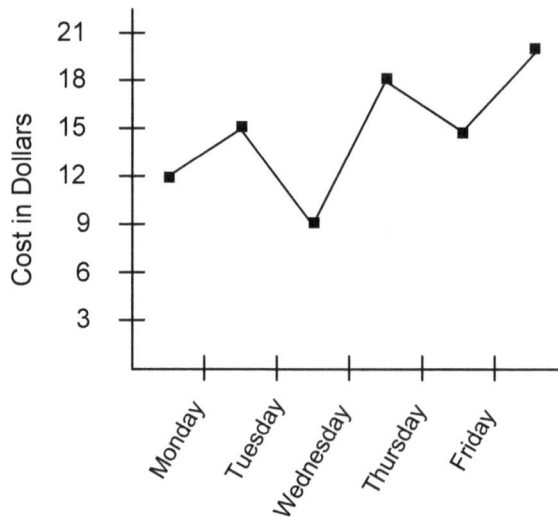

Determine which day experienced the greatest change in Lobster daily cost.

a. Monday

b. Tuesday

c. Wednesday

d. Friday

174

**BM 17.** The below scatter plot appears to be what type of correlation?

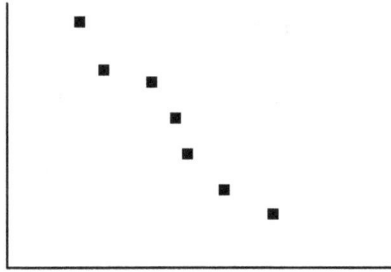

a.  Strong Positive Correlation

b.  Strong Negative Correlation

c.  Zero Correlation

d.  Weak Negative Correlation

**BM 18.** Juan is driving at 60 miles per hour, what is his approximate speed in kilometers per hour? (1 mile ≈ 1.6 kilometers)

**a.** 64  **b.** 72

**c.** 84  **d.** 96

**BM 19.** The scale drawing of the hockey rink shown below is drawn using a scale of 1 inch (in.) = 50 feet (ft).

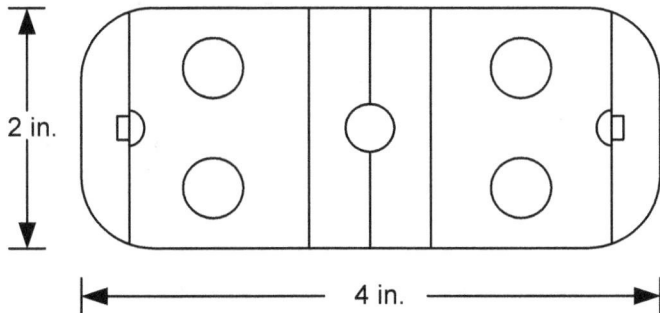

What is the length of the rink in feet?

**a.** 200 ft  **b.** 180 ft

**c.** 160 ft  **d.** 140 ft

**BM 20.** Maurice can read about 35 words per minute. If he reads at this rate for 40 minutes without stopping, about how many words will he read?

**a.** 1,400  **b.** 1,200

**c.** 2,100  **d.** 1,700

**BM 21.**

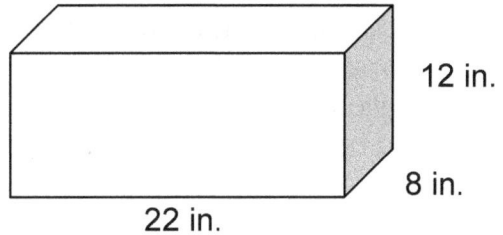

What is the volume of the box shown above in cubic inches (in.$^3$)?

**a.** 25  **b.** 2,112

**c.** 564  **d.** 1,056

**BM 22.** One-inch square cubes are stacked as shown in the drawing below.

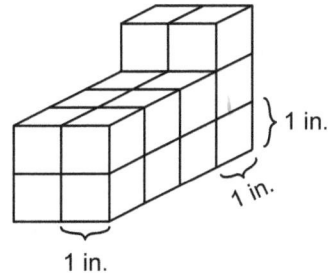

What is the <u>total</u> surface area?

**a.** 46 in.$^2$  **b.** 52 in.$^2$

**c.** 64 in.$^2$  **d.** 78 in.$^2$

**BM 23.** Emily has a rectangular box with square ends. If the square ends have a side length of 7 inches and the box is 15 inches long, then what is the surface area of the box?

    **a.** 518 in²      **b.** 468 in²

    **c.** 336 in²      **d.** 434 in²

**BM 24.** Gasoline is made from oil which is sold in barrels. If one barrel of oil is equal to 42 gallons, then how many barrels would be needed to hold 882 gallons of oil?

    **a.** 21 barrels      **b.** 37002 barrels

    **c.** 882 barrels      **d.** 42 barrels

**BM 25.** Suppose that point R(-2, 0) will reflect about the y-axis. Which of the following are the coordinates of R'?

    **a.** R'(0, 0)      **b.** R'(2, 0)

    **c.** R'(-2, 0)      **d.** R'(0, -2)

**BM 26.** In a right triangle, if a = 9 and b = 12, then c = ?

    **a.** 12      **b.** 13

    **c.** 14      **d.** 15

**BM 27.** If quadrilateral ABCD is congruent to quadrilateral PQRS, then which of the following is false?

    **a.** Angle C is congruent to angle R.

    **b.** Side $\overline{AB}$ is congruent to side $\overline{PQ}$.

    **c.** Angle D is congruent to angle S.

    **d.** Side $\overline{PR}$ is congruent to side $\overline{AC}$.

**BM 28.** At a certain car lot, the number of cars, c, is equal to 3 times the number of trucks, t. Which equation matches the information?

    **a.** c = 3t      **b.** 3c = t

    **c.** ct = 3      **d.** 3c = 3t

**BM 29.** If f = 12 and g = 8, then g(f - 2)=

    **a.** 72      **b.** 96

    **c.** 108      **d.** 80

**BM 30.** The graph below shows the relationship between the number of people at the park with the number of hot dogs sold at a certain stand.

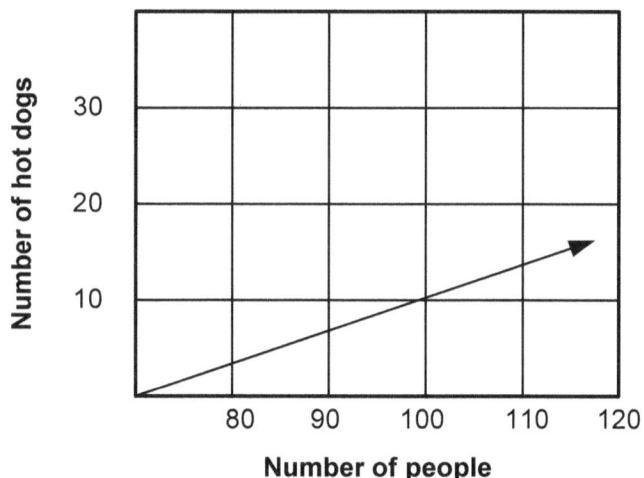

What is the approximate number of hot dogs sold when 100 people are at the park?

    **a.** 40      **b.** 10

    **c.** 20      **d.** 30

**BM 31.** Which expression is equivalent to $12x^2y \cdot 4xz^5$ ?

    **a.** $48x^3yz^5$         **b.** $16x^3y^5z$

    **c.** $16x^3yz^5$         **d.** $48x^5yz^3$

**BM 32.** $\sqrt{64x^2y^6}$ =

    **a.** $8xy$         **b.** $8xy^3$

    **c.** $64xy$         **d.** $8x^3y$

**BM 33.** Which of the following is the graph of $y = -x^3$?

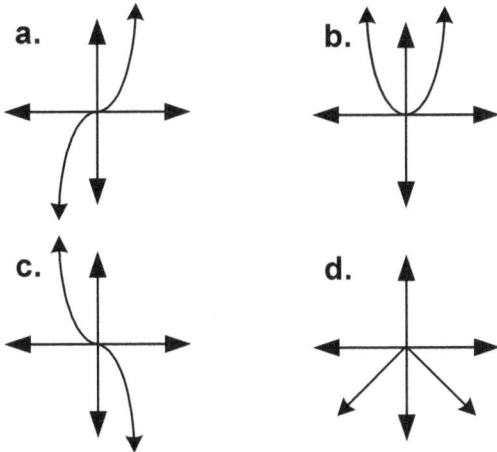

    **a.**

    **b.**

    **c.**

    **d.**

**BM 34.** What is the slope of the line below?

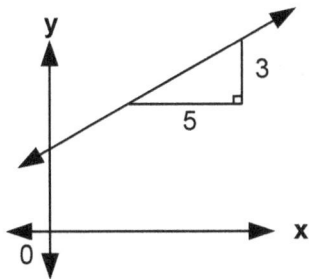

    **a.** $\dfrac{3}{5}$         **b.** $\dfrac{-3}{5}$

    **c.** $\dfrac{-5}{3}$         **d.** $\dfrac{5}{3}$

**BM 35.** Three friends go to a carnival. The graph below shows the cost of tickets for the rides. What is the price per ticket?

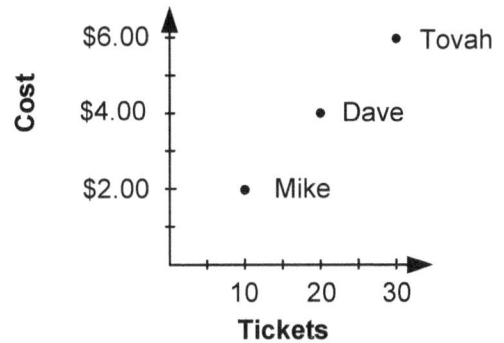

    **a.** $0.10         **b.** $0.20

    **c.** $5.00         **d.** $2.50

**BM 36.** The owner of a pear orchard ships pears in boxes that weigh 4 pounds when empty. The average pear weighs 0.20 pounds, and the total weight of a box filled with pears is 12 pounds. How many pears are packed in each box?

    **a.** 30         **b.** 35

    **c.** 40         **d.** 45

**BM 37.** Scott can drive 82 miles in 2 hours. At this rate, how many miles can he drive in 5 hours?

    **a.** 150         **b.** 185

    **c.** 195         **d.** 205

**BM 38.** Christina used 120 feet of fence to enclose her rectangular garden. If the length is three times the width, find the length of her garden?

    **a.**   The width is 15 feet.

    **b.**   The length is 21 feet.

    **c.**   The length is 45 feet.

    **d.**   The length is 30 feet.

**BM 39.** Lor claims that if a number n divides the quantity of x times y, then the number divides both x and y. Which example below is a counterexample to Lor's conjecture?

    **a.**   n = 3, x = 6, and y = 9

    **b.**   n = 3, x = 4, and y = 6

    **c.**   n = 3, x = 6, and y = 12

    **d.**   n = 3, x = 9, and y = 12

**BM 40.** If one rod is 16.5 feet, then which is the best estimate for 19 rods?

    **a.**   240 feet

    **b.**   340 feet

    **c.**   440 feet

    **d.**   540 feet

**BM 41.** Estimate the area of the figure.

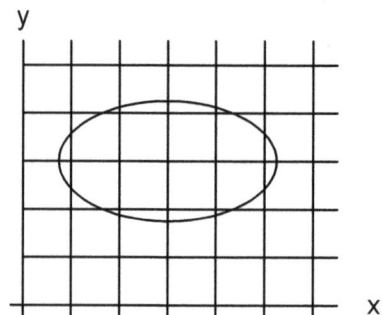

    **a.**   2 square units

    **b.**   4 square units

    **c.**   6 square units

    **d.**   8 square units

**BM 42.** If today is not Wednesday, then yesterday was not Tuesday. What can you conclude if yesterday was Tuesday?

    **a.**   Today is not Wednesday.

    **b.**   Today is Thursday.

    **c.**   Today is Wednesday.

    **d.**   The day cannot be determined.

**BM 43.** In Trigonometry, if we know that the sine of some angle is 3 over 5, then the cosecant of the same angle is the reciprocal of the sine. Determine which ratio is the cosecant of the angle in question.

    **a.**   $\dfrac{5}{3}$       **b.**   $\dfrac{-5}{3}$

    **c.**   $\dfrac{-3}{5}$       **d.**   $\dfrac{3}{5}$

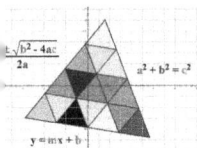

Students will successfully understand and use
reciprocals, roots, and rules of exponents.

**CA Standard:** Algebra 1, 2.0
**CAHSEE Strand:** Algebra I

---

| **Vocabulary:** | **reciprocals** | two rational numbers whose product is one |
| | **opposites** | two numbers the same distance from zero but on opposite sides of zero (i.e. 5 and -5) |
| | **additive inverses** | two rational numbers whose sum is zero |

Roots, reciprocals and inverses are mathematically easy and very important conceptually. On the CAHSEE, students will have to answer very straightforward questions involving these concepts.

*Students should be cautioned not to confuse inverses with reciprocals.*

---

**EXAMPLE:** If m = -3 then -m =

    **a.** -3      **b.** 3      **c.** $\dfrac{1}{3}$      **d.** $\dfrac{-1}{3}$

---

-m implies that we are looking for the opposite of -3 or more simply, what do we add to -3 to make 0?

3 + (-3) = 0, therefore, the correct answer is **b.**

---

**EXAMPLE:** What is the reciprocal of $\dfrac{w}{x}$ ?

    **a.** $\dfrac{x}{w}$      **b.** $\dfrac{-w}{x}$      **c.** $\dfrac{w}{x}$      **d.** $\dfrac{-x}{w}$

---

The reciprocal of $\dfrac{w}{x}$ is $\dfrac{x}{w}$ because $\dfrac{w}{x} \cdot \dfrac{x}{w} = 1$

The correct answer is **a.**

---

**EXAMPLE:** The perimeter, P, of a square may be found by using the formula $\frac{1}{4}P = \sqrt{A}$, where A is the area of the square. What is the perimeter of the square with an area of 64 square inches?

    **a.** 8 inches      **b.** 24 inches      **c.** 32 inches      **d.** 48 inches

We begin by substituting 64 for A in the given formula.

$$\frac{1}{4} P = \sqrt{64}$$

Next, we solve for P.      $\frac{1}{4} P = 8$    Multiply by the reciprocal.

$$\frac{4}{1} \cdot \frac{1}{4} P = 8(4)$$

$$P = 32$$      The correct answer is **c.**

---

**1.** The perimeter, P, of a square may be found by using the formula $\frac{1}{4}P = \sqrt{A}$, where A is the area of the square. What is the perimeter of the square with an area of 64 square inches?

    **a.** 8 inches      **b.** 24 inches

    **c.** 32 inches      **d.** 48 inches

**2.** If x = -8, then -x =

    **a.** -8            **b.** $\frac{-1}{8}$

    **c.** 8             **d.** $\frac{1}{8}$

**3.** What is the reciprocal of $\frac{ab^2}{c}$ ?

    **a.** $\frac{-ab^2}{c}$      **b.** $\frac{a}{cb^2}$

    **c.** $\frac{-c}{ab^2}$      **d.** $\frac{c}{ab^2}$

**4.** If x =10, then -x =

    **a.** -10         **b.** $\frac{-1}{10}$

    **c.** $\frac{1}{10}$       **d.** -10

**5.** What is the reciprocal of $\frac{c^2d}{e}$ ?

    **a.** $\frac{-c^2d}{e}$      **b.** $\frac{c}{ed^2}$

    **c.** $\frac{e}{c^2d}$      **d.** $\frac{c}{ab^2}$

**6.** The perimeter, P, of a square may be found by using the formula $\frac{1}{4}P = \sqrt{A}$, where A is the area of the square. What is the perimeter of the square with an area of 81 square inches?

    **a.** 48 inches      **b.** 36 inches

    **c.** 24 inches      **d.** 12 inches

**7.** If x = -5, then -x =

    **a.** $\frac{1}{5}$          **b.** $\frac{-1}{5}$

    **c.** 5             **d.** -5

**8.** What is the reciprocal of $\frac{wx}{z}$ ?

    **a.** $\frac{z}{wx}$      **b.** $\frac{-z}{wx}$

    **c.** $\frac{-wx}{z}$      **d.** $\frac{x}{wz}$

**9.** If x = 20, then -x =

    **a.** $\frac{-1}{20}$      **b.** -20

    **c.** 20         **d.** $\frac{1}{20}$

**10.** The perimeter, P, of a square may be found by using the formula $\frac{1}{4}P = \sqrt{A}$, where A is the area of the square. What is the perimeter of the square with an area of 25 square inches?

    **a.** 5 inches      **b.** 24 inches

    **c.** 22 inches      **d.** 20 inches

**11.** If x = -2, then -x =

    **a.** -2         **b.** $\frac{-1}{2}$

    **c.** $\frac{1}{2}$        **d.** 2

**12.** What is the reciprocal of $\frac{xy^2}{z}$ ?

    **a.** $\frac{xy^2}{z}$       **b.** $\frac{z}{yx^2}$

    **c.** $\frac{z}{xy^2}$       **d.** $\frac{x}{yz^2}$

**13.** The perimeter, P, of a square may be found by using the formula $\frac{1}{4}$ P = $\sqrt{A}$, where A is the area of the square. What is the perimeter of the square with an area of 100 square inches?

    **a.** 40 inches     **b.** 10 inches

    **c.** 36 inches     **d.** 48 inches

**14.** If x = -15, then -x =

    **a.** $\frac{1}{15}$       **b.** $\frac{-1}{15}$

    **c.** $\frac{1}{-15}$      **d.** 15

**15.** What is the reciprocal of $\frac{u^2v}{w}$ ?

    **a.** $\frac{-u^2v}{w}$     **b.** $\frac{w}{uv^2}$

    **c.** $\frac{w}{v^2u}$     **d.** $\frac{w}{u^2v}$

**16.** The perimeter, P, of a square may be found by using the formula $\frac{1}{4}$ P = $\sqrt{A}$, where A is the area of the square. What is the perimeter of the square with an area of 16 square inches?

    **a.** 16 inches     **b.** 24 inches

    **c.** 4 inches      **d.** 12 inches

**17.** If x = 25, then -x =

    **a.** $\frac{1}{25}$       **b.** -25

    **c.** 25        **d.** 5

**18.** What is the reciprocal of $\frac{f^5g}{h}$ ?

    **a.** $\frac{h}{fg}$       **b.** $\frac{h}{f^5g}$

    **c.** $\frac{-fg}{h}$      **d.** $\frac{h}{fg^5}$

**19.** If x = - $\frac{1}{2}$ , then -x =

    **a.** $\frac{-1}{2}$       **b.** 2

    **c.** -2        **d.** $\frac{1}{2}$

**20.** The perimeter, P, of a square may be found by using the formula $\frac{1}{4}$ P = $\sqrt{A}$, where A is the area of the square. What is the perimeter of the square with an area of 144 square inches?

    **a.** 12 inches     **b.** 48 inches

    **c.** 22 inches     **d.** 54 inches

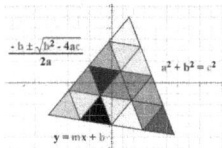

# CAHSEE Bench Mark 45
Students will successfully solve equations
and inequalities with absolute value.
**CA Standard:** Algebra 1, 3.0
**CAHSEE Strand:** Algebra I

*S*implified *S*olutions
**For Math Inc.**

Absolute value is asking the question,
"how far is a number from zero on the number line?"

---

**EXAMPLE:** Assume that x is an integer and solve for x.  $|x - 1| = 3$

    **a.** {-4}      **b.** {4}      **c.** {-4, 2}      **d.** {-2, 4}

---

This equation is telling us that the absolute value of x - 1 is three away from zero on the number line.

Graphically, we observe that if the absolute value of x - 1 is three away from zero, then x - 1 is equal to 3 and x - 1 is equal to -3.

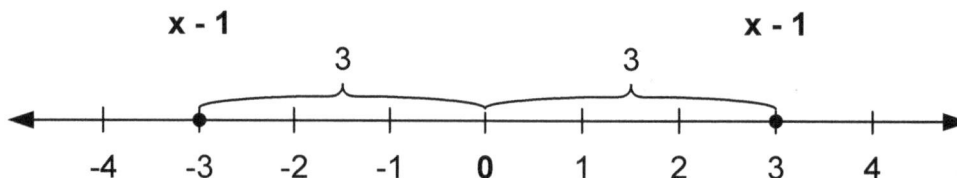

Mathematically,

$$x - 1 = 3 \text{ and } x - 1 = -3 \qquad \text{Add 1 to both sides of each equation.}$$

$$x = 4 \text{ and } x = -2$$

The correct answer is **d.**

---

**EXAMPLE:** If x is an integer, what is the solution to $|x + 3| < 2$?

    **a.** {-4, -3, -2}   **b.** {2}   **c.** {-3}   **d.** {-5, -4, -3, -2, -1}

This inequality is telling us that the absolute value of x + 3 is less than two away from zero on the number line.

Mathematically,

$$x + 3 < 2 \text{ and } x + 3 > -2 \qquad \text{Subtract 3 from both sides of each}$$
$$x < -1 \text{ and } x > -5 \qquad\qquad\qquad \text{inequality}$$

The only integers less than -1 and greater than -5 are -4, -3, and -2.

The correct answer is **a.**

---

1. If x is an integer, what is the solution to $|x + 3| < 2$?

   **a.** {-4, -3, -2}    **b.** {2}

   **c.** {-3}    **d.** {-5, -4, -3, -2, -1}

2. Assume that y is an integer and solve for y.
   $$|y + 5| = 8$$

   **a.** {-3, 13}    **b.** {-3, 3}

   **c.** {-13, 3}    **d.** {-13, 13}

3. If x is an integer, which of the following is the solution set for $2|x| = 14$?

   **a.** {0, 7}    **b.** {-7, 0}

   **c.** {0, 28}    **d.** {-7, 7}

4. If x is an integer, what is the solution to $|x - 1| < 2$?

   **a.** {-2}    **b.** {-1}

   **c.** {0, 1, 2}    **d.** {-1, 0, 1, 2, 3}

5. Assume that y is an integer and solve for y.
   $$|y + 2| = 7$$

   **a.** {-5, 9}    **b.** {-9, 5}

   **c.** {-5, 5}    **d.** {-9, 9}

6. If x is an integer, which of the following is the solution set for $4|x| = 16$?

   **a.** {-4, 4}    **b.** {-4, 0}

   **c.** {0, 64}    **d.** {0, 4}

7. If x is an integer, what is the solution to $|x - 2| < 2$?

   **a.** {1, 2, 3}    **b.** {0, 1, 2, 3, 4}

   **c.** {0}    **d.** {4}

8. Assume that y is an integer and solve for y.
   $$|y + 1| = 12$$

   **a.** {-13, 13}    **b.** {-13, 11}

   **c.** {-11, 11}    **d.** {-11, 13}

9. If x is an integer, which of the following is the solution set for $2|x| = 18$?

   **a.** {0, 9}    **b.** {-9, 0}

   **c.** {-9, 9}    **d.** {36}

10. If x is an integer, what is the solution to $|x - 1| < 3$?

    **a.** {-3}    **b.** {1}

    **c.** {-1, 0, 1, 2, 3}    **d.** {-2, -1, 0, 1, 2, 3, 4}

**11.** If x is an integer, what is the solution to $|x + 1| < 2$?

    **a.** { -3, -2}      **b.** {-2, -1, 0}

    **c.** {-3}      **d.** { -3, -2, -1, 0, 1}

**12.** Assume that y is an integer and solve for y.
$$|y + 7| = 2$$

    **a.** {-5}      **b.** {-9}

    **c.** {-5, -9}      **d.** {-5, 5}

**13.** If x is an integer, which of the following is the solution set for $3|x| = 18$?

    **a.** {-6, 6}      **b.** {0, 54}

    **c.** {0, 6}      **d.** {-6, 0}

**14.** If x is an integer, what is the solution to $|x - 1| < 4$?

    **a.** {-2, -1, 0, 1, 2, 3, 4}      **b.** {-5}

    **c.** {-1, 0, 1, 2, 3}      **d.** {5}

**15.** Assume that y is an integer and solve for y.
$$|y + 9| = 1$$

    **a.** {-10, 0}      **b.** {-10, -8}

    **c.** {-8, 8}      **d.** {-8, 0}

**16.** If x is an integer, which of the following is the solution set for $5|x| = 15$?

    **a.** {-3, 3}      **b.** {-3, 0}

    **c.** {0, 45}      **d.** {0, 3}

**17.** If x is an integer, what is the solution to $|x - 2| < 3$?

    **a.** {1, 2, 3}      **b.** {-1, 0, 1, 2, 3, 4, 5}

    **c.** {0, 1, 2, 3, 4}      **d.** {5}

**18.** Assume that y is an integer and solve for y.
$$|y + 8| = 17$$

    **a.** {-9, 25}      **b.** {-25, 9}

    **c.** {-25, 25}      **d.** {-9, 9}

**19.** If x is an integer, which of the following is the solution set for $2|x| = 18$?

    **a.** {-25, 9}      **b.** {-9, 25}

    **c.** {-9, 9}      **d.** {36}

**20.** If x is an integer, what is the solution to $|x + 1| < 1$?

    **a.** {0}      **b.** {-1}

    **c.** {-2, -1, 0, 1}      **d.** {2}

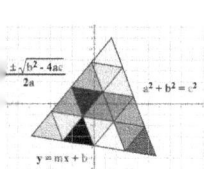

Students will successfully simplify equations and inequalities.

**CA Standard:** Algebra 1, 4.0
**CAHSEE Strand:** Algebra I

For this lesson we will be simplifying equations and inequalities.

The first concept to be examined is the **distributive property of multiplication over addition.**

Consider -2(x + 1)

-2(x + 1)      Distribute (multiply) the -2 to each term in parenthesis (x + 1)

-2 (x) + -2 (1) = -2x - 2

Next we examine the topic of **collecting like terms**

What we are effectively discussing is adding terms that are alike.

A **term** is that part of a math sentence separated by a + or - sign.

**Like terms** are those terms with <u>identical variables</u>.

**Collecting like terms** means add those like terms together.

Consider   -5x + 3y - x

There are three terms in this expression; -5x, 3y and − x.
-5x and -x are like terms so we add them together   -5x - x = - 6x.
List the terms in alphabetical order according to the variables;
**-6x + 3y**

Simplifying inequalities is very similar to simplifying equations.

---

**EXAMPLE:**      Which of the following is equivalent to  6 + 2x > 3(x + 5)?

  **a.** -9 > x      **b.** -x > -9      **c.** x < 9      **d.** x > -9

---

6 + 2x > 3(x + 5)      distribute the 3

6 + 2x > 3x + 15      subtract 2x and 15 from both sides of the inequality

  -9 > x                                        The correct answer is **a.**

**NOTE:** *Remember to reverse the inequality when you multiply or divide by a negative number.*

---

**EXAMPLE:**      Which of the following is equivalent to 4(x + 5) - 6(x - 2) = 16?

  **a.** 4x + 5 - 6x + 12 = 16          **b.** 4x + 20 - 6x - 12 = 16

  **c.** 4x + 20 - 6x + 12 = 16          **d.** 4x + 20 - 6x - 2 = 16

The answer selections indicate that we need to use the distributive property.

4(x + 5) - 6(x - 2) = 16

4(x) + 4(5) - 6(x) - 6(-2) = 16

4x + 20 - 6x + 12 = 16                    The correct answer is **c.**

---

1. Which of the following is equivalent to 4(x + 5) - 6(x - 2) = 16?

   **a.** 4x + 5 - 6x + 12 = 16

   **b.** 4x + 20 - 6x - 12 = 16

   **c.** 4x + 20 - 6x + 12 = 16

   **d.** 4x + 20 - 6x - 2 = 16

2. Which of the following is equivalent to  8 + 2x > 3(x - 5)?

   **a.** x < 23          **b.** -x > 23

   **c.** -x < 23          **d.** x > -23

3. $\dfrac{25}{x} = \dfrac{3}{x - 6}$

   Which of the following is equivalent to  the equation shown above?

   **a.** 25x = 3x(x - 6)      **b.** 3x = 25(x - 6)

   **c.** 25 + x = 3x - 6      **d.** 3(x - 6) = 25 + x

4. Which of the following is equivalent to 4 - 3x > 2(x + 2)?

   **a.** 4 - 3x < 2x + 2

   **b.** 4 - 3x < 2x + 4

   **c.** 4 - 3x > 2x + 4

   **d.** 4 - 3x > 2x + 2

5. Which of the following is equivalent to  6 - 3x ≤ 2(x - 1)?

   **a.** 8 ≤ 5x          **b.** 8 ≥ 5x

   **c.** -5x < -8          **d.** -5x > -8

6. $\dfrac{12}{x} = \dfrac{2}{x + 4}$

   Which of the following is equivalent to  the equation shown above?

   **a.** 12x = 2(x + 4)      **b.** x + 12 = 2(x + 4)

   **c.** 2x = 12(x + 4)      **d.** 2(x + 4) = 12 + x

7. Which of the following is equivalent to 2x + 1 < 3(x + 5)?

   **a.** 2x + 1 < 3x + 15

   **b.** 2x + 1 < 3x + 5

   **c.** 2x + 1 > 3x + 15

   **d.** 2x + 1 > 3x + 5

8. Which of the following is equivalent to  2x + 7 ≥ 3(x - 7)?

   **a.** x > 28          **b.** x ≥ 28

   **c.** -x > -28          **d.** 28 ≥ x

9. Which of the following is equivalent to 2(x - 1) - 3(x - 5) = 31?

   **a.** 2x + 2 - 3x - 5 = 31

   **b.** 2x - 2 + 3x - 15 = 31

   **c.** 2x + 2 - 3x + 15 = 31

   **d.** 2x - 2 - 3x + 15 = 31

10. Which of the following is equivalent to  4 + x > 5(x + 8)?

    **a.** 36 < 4x          **b.** 4x < 36

    **c.** -36 > 4x          **d.** -4x ≥ -36

11. Which of the following is equivalent to $2(x - 5) - 4(x + 2) = 12$?

    **a.** $2x - 10 + 4x - 8 = 12$

    **b.** $2x - 10 - 4x - 8 = 12$

    **c.** $2x - 5 - 4x - 8 = 12$

    **d.** $2x - 10 - 4x + 8 = 12$

12. Which of the following is equivalent to $3 + 2x > 3(x + 2)$?

    **a.** $x < -3$      **b.** $-x < -3$

    **c.** $-x < 3$      **d.** $-x > -3$

13. $\dfrac{5}{x} = \dfrac{9}{x + 4}$

    Which of the following is equivalent to the equation shown above?

    **a.** $5x = 9x(x + 4)$      **b.** $5x = 9(x + 4)$

    **c.** $5 + x = 9x + 4$      **d.** $9x = 5(x + 4)$

14. Which of the following is equivalent to $5 + 2x > 4(x - 1)$?

    **a.** $5 + 2x < 4x - 1$

    **b.** $5 + 2x < 4x - 4$

    **c.** $5 + 2x > 4x - 4$

    **d.** $5 + 2x > 4x + 4$

15. Which of the following is equivalent to $7 - 2x \le 3(x + 8)$?

    **a.** $17 \le 5x$      **b.** $17 \ge 5x$

    **c.** $5x \ge -17$      **d.** $-5x > -17$

16. $\dfrac{9}{x} = \dfrac{7}{x + 2}$

    Which of the following is equivalent to the equation shown above?

    **a.** $9x = 7(x + 2)$      **b.** $7x = 9(x + 2)$

    **c.** $9 + x = 7(x + 2)$      **d.** $7(x + 2) = 9 + x$

17. Which of the following is equivalent to $3x - 12 < 4(x - 3)$?

    **a.** $3x - 12 < 4x - 3$

    **b.** $3x - 12 < 4x - 12$

    **c.** $3x - 12 > 4x - 3$

    **d.** $3x - 12 > 4x - 12$

18. Which of the following is equivalent to $4x + 1 < 3(x - 8)$?

    **a.** $x < -25$      **b.** $x \ge 25$

    **c.** $-x > -25$      **d.** $-25 \ge x$

19. Which of the following is equivalent to $5(x - 1) - 4(x - 5) = -8$?

    **a.** $5x - 5 + 4x + 20 = -8$

    **b.** $5x - 5 - 4x - 20 = -8$

    **c.** $5x - 1 - 4x - 20 = -8$

    **d.** $5x - 5 - 4x + 20 = -8$

20. Which of the following is equivalent to $9 - 6x > 6(x + 1)$?

    **a.** $3 > 12x$      **b.** $3x < 12$

    **c.** $-3 > 12x$      **d.** $-3x \ge -12$

Students will successfully solve multi-step equations and inequalities.

**CA Standard:** Algebra 1, 5.0
**CAHSEE Strand:** Algebra I

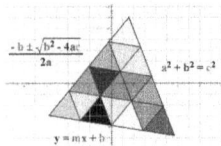

---

To solve some equations and inequalities, you may need to employ several different strategies.

These strategies include:
1. Distributive property
2. Collect like terms
3. Addition, subtraction, multiplication, and division

For example, consider the equation $3(2x - 5) + 5x = -4$

| | |
|---|---|
| $3(2x - 5) + 5x = -4$ | Use the distributive property. |
| $6x - 15 + 5x = -4$ | Collect like terms. |
| $11x - 15 = -4$ | Add 15 to both sides of the equation. |
| $11x = 11$ | Divide both sides of the equation by 11. |
| $x = 1$ | Solution |

For another example, consider the inequality $6 - 8x \geq -18$

| | |
|---|---|
| $6 - 8x \geq -18$ | We will need to move the six from one side of the inequality to the other by subtraction. |
| $-8x \geq -24$ | Next, we will divide both sides of the inequality by -8. *Remember to **reverse the inequality*** |
| $x \leq 3$ | The solution is any number less than or equal to 3 |

---

**EXAMPLE:**

Reggie solved the equation $2(x + 6) = 10$ using the following steps.

| | | |
|---|---|---|
| **Given :** | $2(x + 6) = 10$ | To get from Step 1 to Step 2, Reggie- |
| **Step 1:** | $2x + 12 = 10$ | **a.** added 12 to both sides. |
| **Step 2:** | $2x = -2$ | **b.** multiplied both sides by 2. |
| **Step 3:** | $x = -1$ | **c.** subtracted 12 from both sides. |
| | | **d.** divided both sides by 2. |

First, isolate steps 1 and 2.

| | |
|---|---|
| **Step 1:** | $2x + 12 = 10$ |
| **Step 2:** | $2x = -2$ |

By observation, we can see that the 12 was moved to the right side of the equation by subtraction.

The correct answer is **c.**

1. Reggie solved the equation $2(x + 6) = 10$ using the following steps.

   | | |
   |---|---|
   | **Given :** | $2(x + 6) = 10$ |
   | **Step 1:** | $2x + 12 = 10$ |
   | **Step 2:** | $2x = -2$ |
   | **Step 3:** | $x = -1$ |

   To get from Step 1 to Step 2, Reggie-

   **a.** added 12 to both sides.

   **b.** multiplied both sides by 2.

   **c.** subtracted 12 from both sides.

   **d.** divided both sides by 2.

2. Solve for x.   $2(3x - 1) - 5x > 1$

   **a.** $x > 3$          **b.** $x > 1.25$

   **c.** $x < -3$          **d.** $x > 11$

3. Anna solved the equation $4(2x + 1) = 28$ using the following steps.

   | | |
   |---|---|
   | **Given :** | $4(2x + 1) = 28$ |
   | **Step 1:** | $8x + 4 = 28$ |
   | **Step 2:** | $8x = 24$ |
   | **Step 3:** | $x = 3$ |

   To get from Step 2 to Step 3, Anna-

   **a.** added 4 to both sides.

   **b.** multiplied both sides by 8.

   **c.** subtracted 4 from both sides.

   **d.** divided both sides by 8.

4. Solve for x.   $2(2x + 1) - 5x = 7$

   **a.** $x = 5$          **b.** $x = 6$

   **c.** $x = -5$          **d.** $x = -3$

5. Solve for x.   $2(x - 3) - x > 4$

   **a.** $x > -2$          **b.** $x > 10$

   **c.** $x > 2$          **d.** $x < -10$

6. Kia solved the equation $5(2x + 9) = 25$ using the following steps.

   | | |
   |---|---|
   | **Given :** | $5(2x + 9) = 25$ |
   | **Step 1:** | $10x + 45 = 25$ |
   | **Step 2:** | $10x = -20$ |
   | **Step 3:** | $x = -2$ |

   To get from Step 2 to Step 3, Kia-

   **a.** multiplied both sides by 10.

   **b.** added 45 to both sides.

   **c.** divided both sides by 10.

   **d.** subtracted 45 from both sides.

7. Solve for x.   $3(5x + 9) - 14x = 11$

   **a.** $x = -16$          **b.** $x = 16$

   **c.** $x = -11$          **d.** $x = -7$

8. Solve for x.   $2(5x - 7) - 9x > 6$

   **a.** $x > -20$          **b.** $-x > -20$

   **c.** $x \geq 20$          **d.** $20 < x$

9. Solve for x.   $7(x - 3) - 5x > 17$

   **a.** $x > 19$          **b.** $x > 17$

   **c.** $x > -19$          **d.** $x < -17$

10. Solve for x.   $2(4x + 1) - 7x = 46$

    **a.** $x = 45$          **b.** $x = 32$

    **c.** $x = -7$          **d.** $x = 44$

**11.** Kayla solved the equation $5(x + 6) = 20$ using the following steps.

**Given :**      $5(x + 6) = 20$

**Step 1:**     $5x + 30 = 20$

**Step 2:**     $5x = -10$

**Step 3:**     $x = -2$

To get from Step 1 to Step 2, Kayla-

a. added 30 to both sides.

b. multiplied both sides by 5.

c. divided both sides by 5.

d. subtracted 30 from both sides.

**12.** Solve for x.   $3(3x - 1) - 8x \leq 14$

a. $x \geq 11$          b. $x \geq -17$

c. $x \leq -11$        d. $x \leq 17$

**13.** Shyla solved the equation $2(3x + 7) = 50$ using the following steps.

**Given :**      $2(3x + 7) = 50$

**Step 1:**     $6x + 14 = 50$

**Step 2:**     $6x = 36$

**Step 3:**     $x = 6$

To get from Step 2 to Step 3, Shyla-

a. added 14 to both sides.

b. subtracted 14 from both sides.

c. divided both sides by 6.

d. multiplied both sides by 6.

**14.** Solve for x.   $2(2x + 8) - 5x = 32$

a. $x = -48$       b. $x = 16$

c. $x = 48$        d. $x = -16$

**15.** Solve for x.   $8(x + 1) - 7x \geq 19$

a. $x < 11$        b. $x \geq -11$

c. $x \geq 11$        d. $x < -11$

**16.** Carlos solved the equation $6(2x - 7) = 6$ using the following steps.

**Given :**      $6(2x - 7) = 6$

**Step 1:**     $12x - 42 = 6$

**Step 2:**     $12x = 48$

**Step 3:**     $x = 4$

To get from Step 2 to Step 3, Carlos-

a. subtracted 42 from both sides.

b. added 42 to both sides.

c. divided both sides by 12.

d. multiplied both sides by 12.

**17.** Solve for x.   $3(2x + 1) - 7x = 7$

a. $x = -1$        b. $x = -4$

c. $x = 4$         d. $x = -2$

**18.** Solve for x.   $2(2x - 1) - x \geq 7$

a. $x > -3$        b. $x \geq -4$

c. $x \geq 3$         d. $-4 < x$

**19.** Solve for x.   $2(3x - 1) - 5x < 1$

a. $x > 3$        b. $x \geq 3$

c. $x > -3$      d. $x < 3$

**20.** Solve for x.   $4(4x + 1) - 10x = 22$

a. $x = 4$        b. $x = 3$

c. $x = -2$      d. $x = 1$

In order to graph a two variable linear equation in slope-intercept form we need two pieces of information. One is the **slope** of the line and the other is the **y-intercept**. The **slope** of the line is the steepness of the line and the **y-intercept** is the location where the graph of the line crosses the y-axis.
The slope-intercept form of a linear equation is **y = mx + b**, where **m** is the **slope** and **b** is the **y-intercept**.

---

**EXAMPLE:**
Which of the following is the equation of the graph?

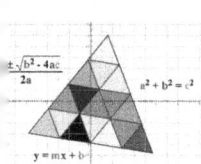

**a.** $y = -2x + 1$   **b.** $y = 2x + 1$

**c.** $y = -\frac{1}{2}x + 1$   **d.** $y = \frac{1}{2}x + 1$

---

The answer to this can be determined without knowing the exact values of the **slope** or **y-intercept**. By observation, we know that the **slope** and **y-intercept** are both positive. We can now examine our answer choices and eliminate those that have negative values.

All answers have the same **y-intercept** but answers **a** and **c** have negative **slopes** so they **cannot** be the correct answers.
We need to look at the slope values of answers **b** and **d**.
Answer **b** has a **slope** of **2** and answer **d** has a **slope** of $\frac{1}{2}$.

By observation we can see that the slope is steeper than 1, so **b** is the correct answer.

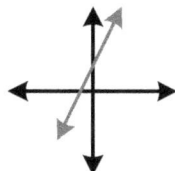

lines steeper than 1 will have a slope greater than 1
m = 1
lines shallower than 1 will have a fractional slope less than 1

---

**EXAMPLE:** Which of the following is the graph of $y = -3x + 2$ ?

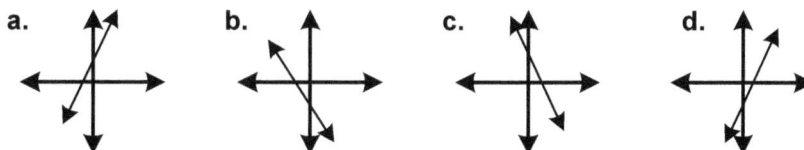

**a.**   **b.**   **c.**   **d.**

The answer to this can be determined with the same line of thinking as before. By observation, we know that the **slope** is negative and the **y-intercept** is positive. The only answer that meets this criteria is answer **c**.

---

**EXAMPLE:**   Which of the following is the graph of $y = \frac{1}{3}x + 1$ ?

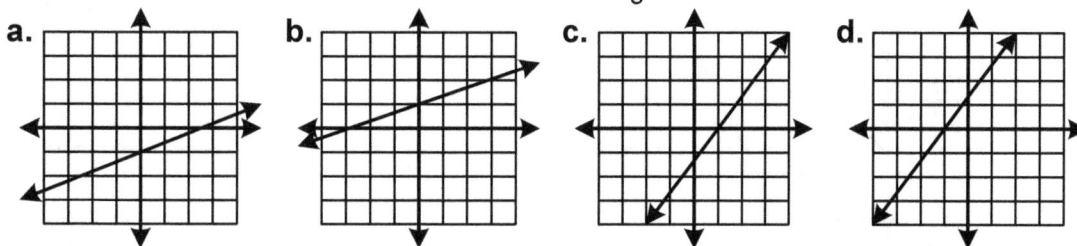

**a.**   **b.**   **c.**   **d.**

By observation, we know that the **slope** and **y-intercept** are positive.

The slope is $\frac{1}{3}$, so the graph will not be too steep.

The only answer that meets our criteria is answer **b**.

**1.** Which of the following is the graph of $y = \frac{1}{3}x + 1$ ?

**a.**

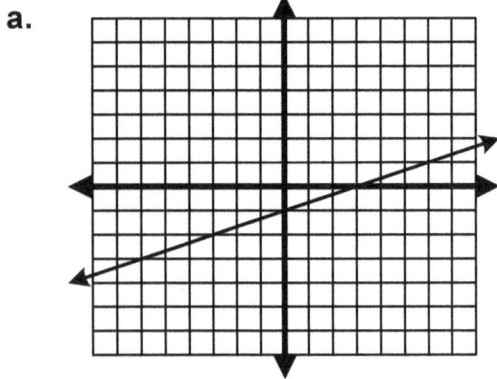

**b.**

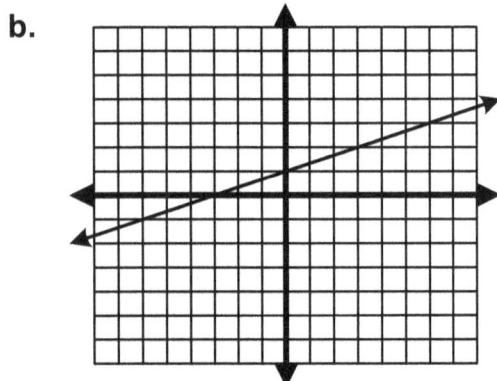

**c.**

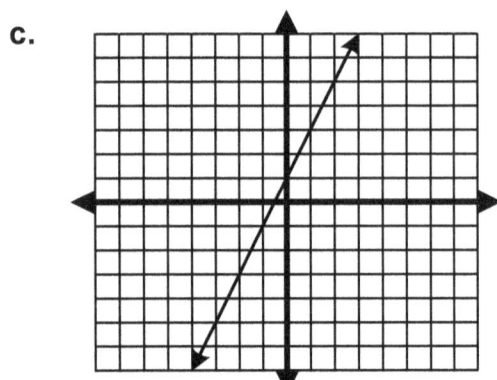

**d.**

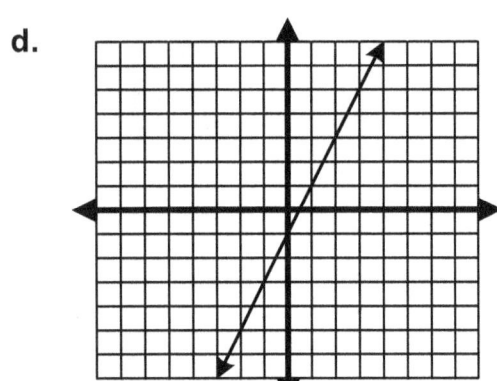

**2.** Which of the following is the equation of

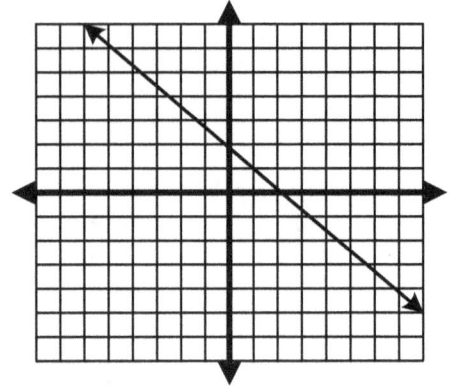

**a.** $y = -x + 2$    **b.** $y = x + 2$

**c.** $y = -x + 1$    **d.** $y = x + 1$

**3.** Which of the following is the equation of

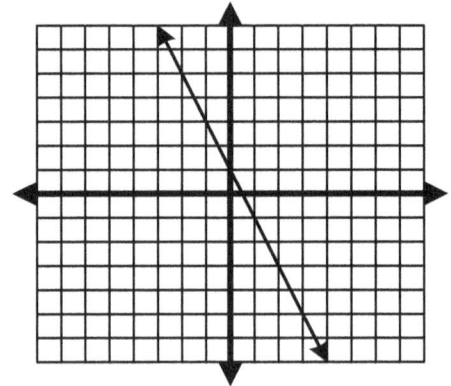

**a.** $y = -2x + 1$    **b.** $y = -\frac{1}{3}x + 1$

**c.** $y = 2x - 1$    **d.** $y = \frac{1}{3}x - 1$

**4.** Which of the following is the equation of

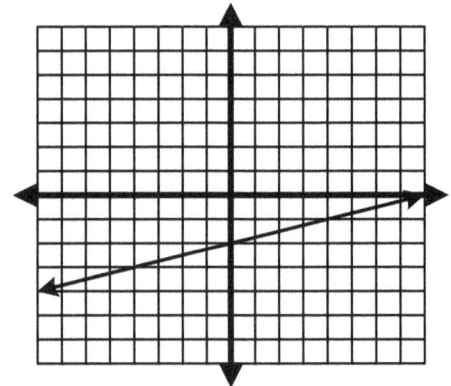

**a.** $y = -4x - 2$    **b.** $y = \frac{1}{4}x + 2$

**c.** $y = 4x - 2$    **d.** $y = \frac{1}{4}x - 2$

**5.** Which of the following is the graph of
y = -3x + 1 ?

a.

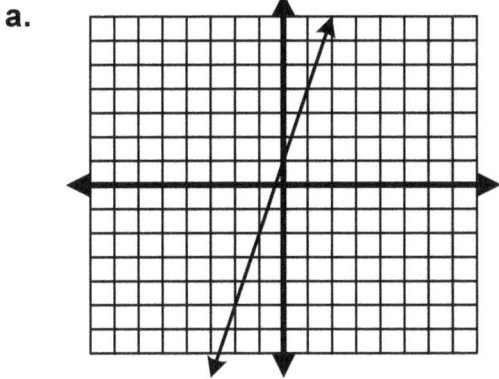

b.

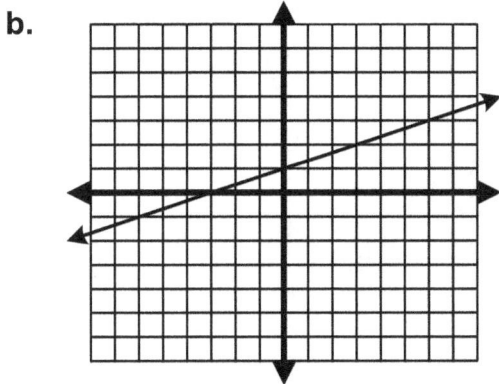

c.

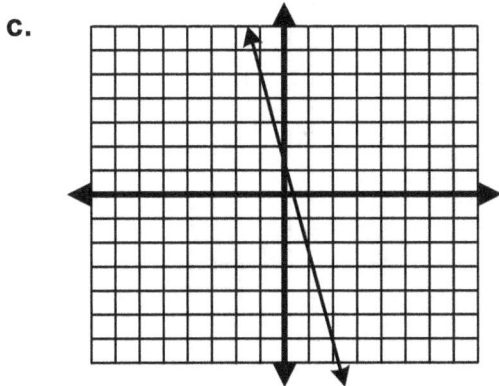

d.

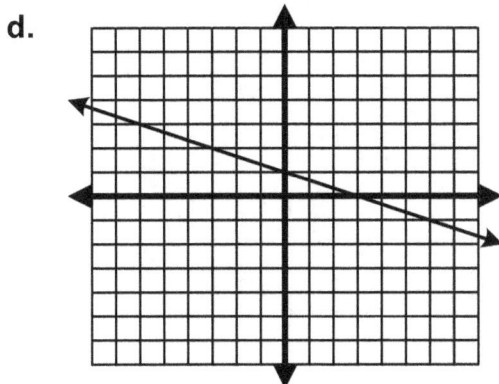

**6.** Which of the following is the graph of
y = 2x - 1 ?

a.

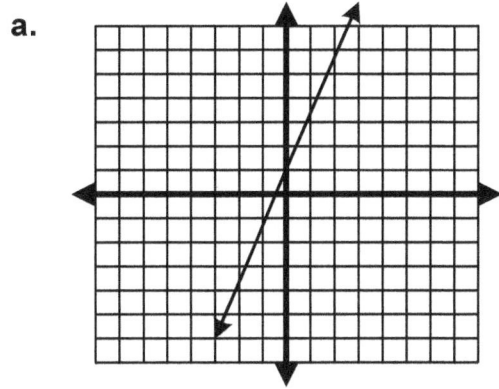

b.

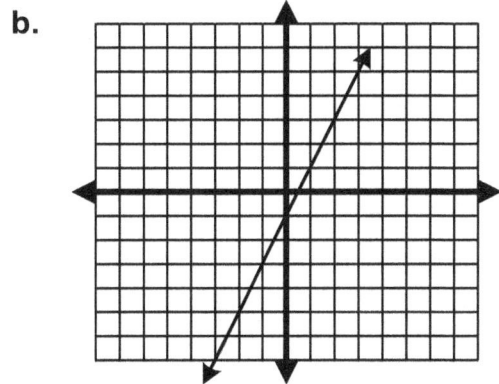

c.

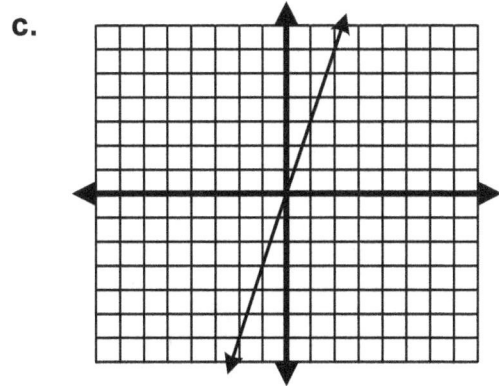

d.

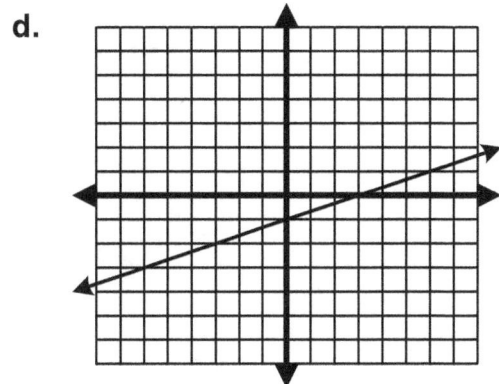

**7.** Which of the following is the graph of $y = -\frac{1}{2}x + 3$ ?

a.

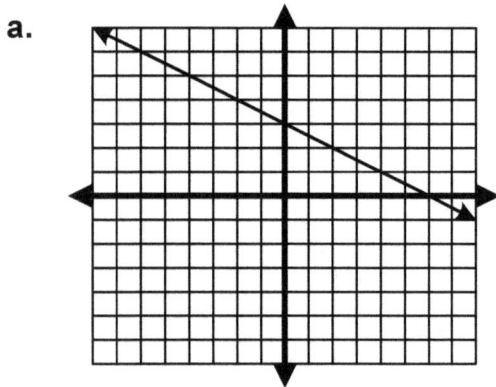

b.

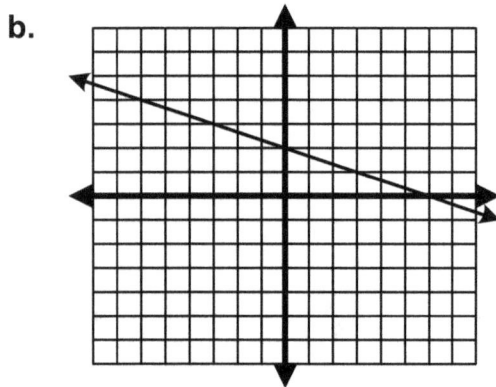

c.

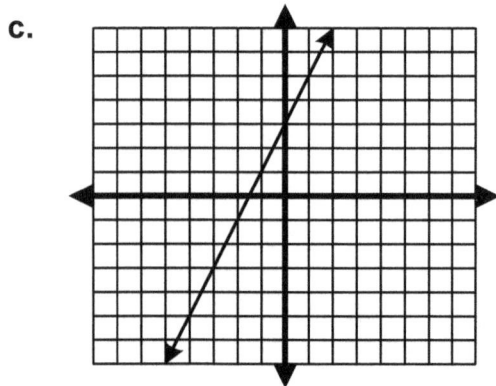

d.

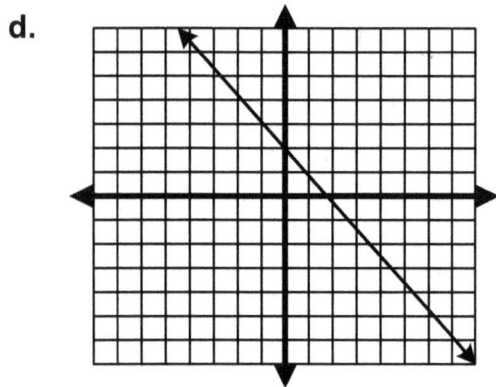

**8.** Which of the following is the graph of $y = 5x - 4$ ?

a.

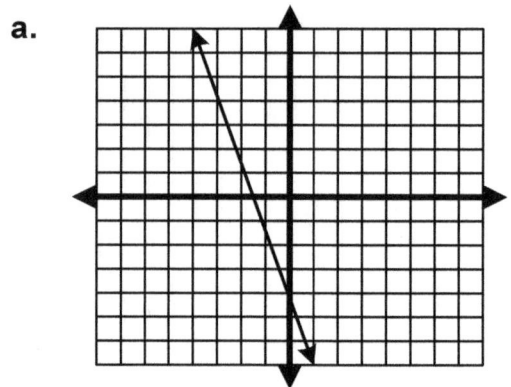

b.

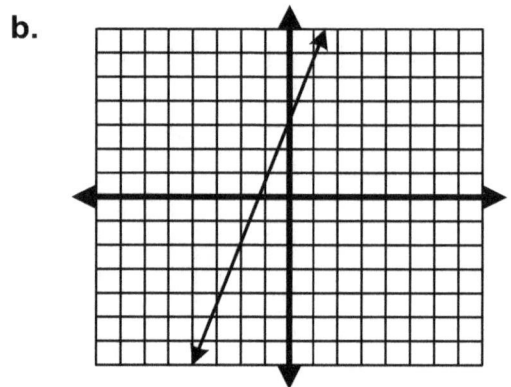

c.

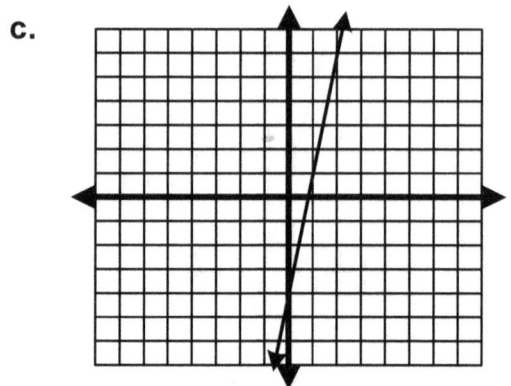

d.

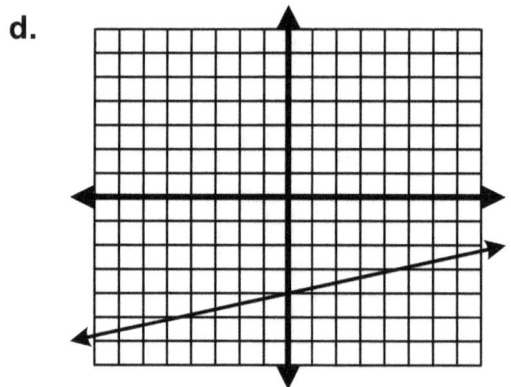

**9.** Which of the following is the graph of $y = \frac{3}{4}x - 2$ ?

**a.**

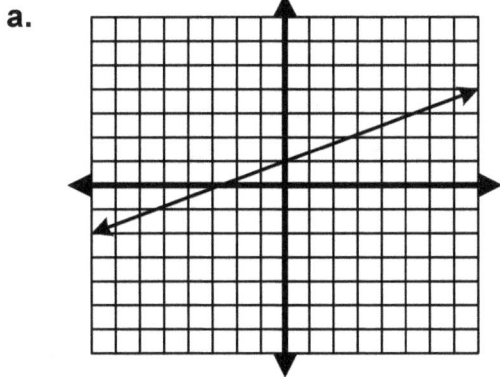

**b.**

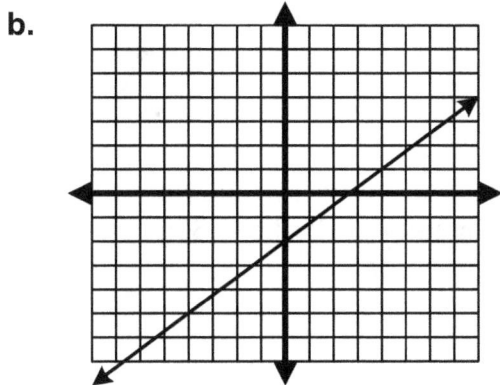

**c.**

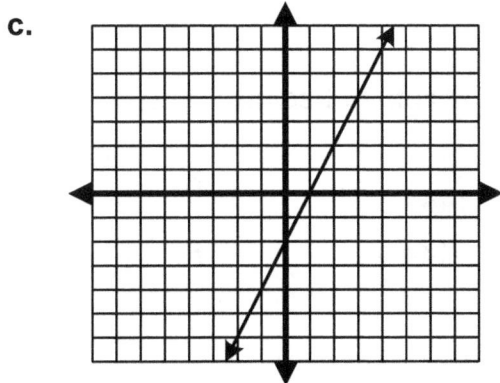

**d.**

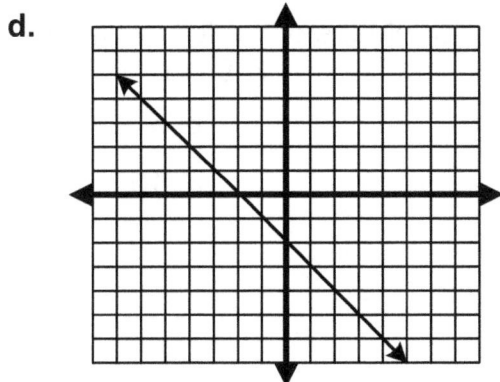

**10.** Which of the following is the equation of

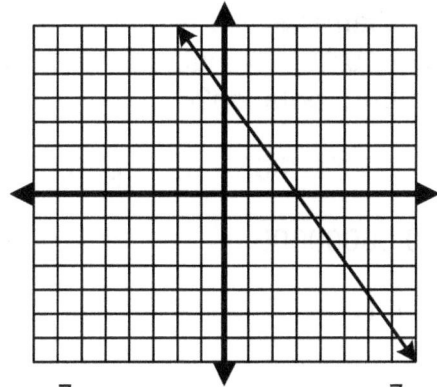

**a.** $y = -\frac{7}{5}x + 4$     **b.** $y = -\frac{7}{5}x + 2$

**c.** $y = -4x + 3$     **d.** $y = -4x - 4$

**11.** Which of the following is the equation of

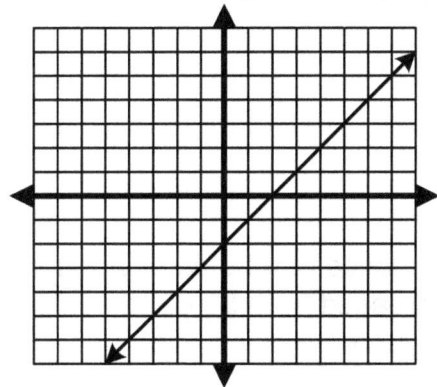

**a.** $y = x + 1$     **b.** $y = \frac{9}{2}x - 2$

**c.** $y = x + 2$     **d.** $y = x - 2$

**12.** Which of the following is the equation of

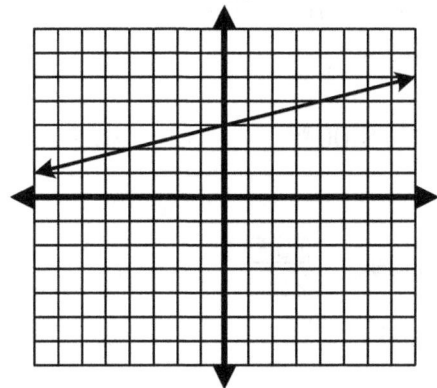

**a.** $y = -4x - 3$     **b.** $y = \frac{1}{4}x + 3$

**c.** $y = 4x + 3$     **d.** $y = -\frac{1}{4}x - 3$

**BM 1.** The diameter of a hydrogen atom is $5.0 \times 10^{-8}$ cm. What is this number in standard notation?

    **a.** 0.000000005      **b.** 0.0000005

    **c.** 0.00000005      **d.** 0.000005

**BM 2.** $9 + (-1) =$

    **a.** -8      **b.** 10

    **c.** 8      **d.** -10

**BM 3.** If Charlie has missed 9 out of 50 days of school, what is the percentage of school days he has missed?

    **a.** 27%      **b.** 30%

    **c.** 10%      **d.** 18%

**BM 4.** The price of a bottle of water has increased from $3.00 to $4.50. What is the percent of increase?

    **a.** 10%      **b.** 25%

    **c.** 50%      **d.** 35%

**BM 5.** Lauren bought a bicycle for $50.00 and later sold it for a 20% profit. How much did Lauren sell the bicycle for?

    **a.** $40.00      **b.** $55.00

    **c.** $70.00      **d.** $60.00

**BM 6.** Divide. $\dfrac{25^{-8}}{25^{-2}}$

    **a.** $25^{-10}$      **b.** $25^{10}$

    **c.** $\dfrac{1}{25^{-6}}$      **d.** $\dfrac{1}{25^{6}}$

**BM 7.** Which of the following is the prime factored form of the lowest common denominator of $\dfrac{5}{7} + \dfrac{2}{3}$ ?

    **a.** $21 \cdot 1$      **b.** $5 \cdot 2$

    **c.** $2 \cdot 3 \cdot 7$      **d.** $3 \cdot 7$

**BM 8.** $\left(\dfrac{8}{9}\right)^{5} =$

    **a.** $\dfrac{40}{9}$      **b.** $\dfrac{8^{5}}{9^{5}}$

    **c.** $\dfrac{8}{45}$      **d.** $\dfrac{40}{45}$

**BM 9.** The square of a <u>whole</u> number is between 4,500 and 4,600. The number must be between

    **a.** 60 and 65      **b.** 65 and 70

    **c.** 70 and 75      **d.** 75 and 80

**BM 10.** What is the absolute value of -144?

    **a.** $\dfrac{-1}{144}$      **b.** 12

    **c.** -144      **d.** 144

**BM 11.** Find the Mode of the following six numbers: 2, 5, 7, 7, 9, 12.

    **a.** 7      **b.** 5

    **c.** 9      **d.** 10

**BM 12.** The bar chart below represents the grades for one class.

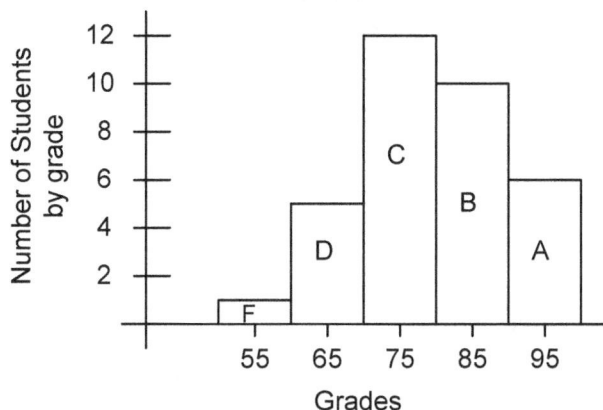

Which of the following statements is true?

**a.** Eighteen students had a grade below C.

**b.** Ten students scored between 60 and 70.

**c.** Only one student failed the class.

**d.** Twice the number of students received an A as compared to the number of students who received a D.

**BM 13.** If you pick a card at random from a complete suit of clubs, what is the probability that it will be an 8?

**a.** $\frac{1}{2}$   **b.** $\frac{8}{13}$

**c.** $\frac{1}{12}$   **d.** $\frac{1}{13}$

**BM 14.** If the probability of an event happening is 37%, then what is the probability that the event will not happen?

**a.** 0.63   **b.** 37%

**c.** $\frac{2}{3}$   **d.** $\frac{3}{5}$

**BM 15.** Each letter of MATH IS FUN is on its own note card, lying face down on a desk. Sou wants to pick a card and then roll a six sided number cube. If Sou picks the letter I, what is the probability that he will roll a five?

**a.** $\frac{1}{9}$   **b.** $\frac{5}{54}$

**c.** $\frac{1}{54}$   **d.** $\frac{1}{6}$

**BM 16.** The histogram below represents the grades for one class.

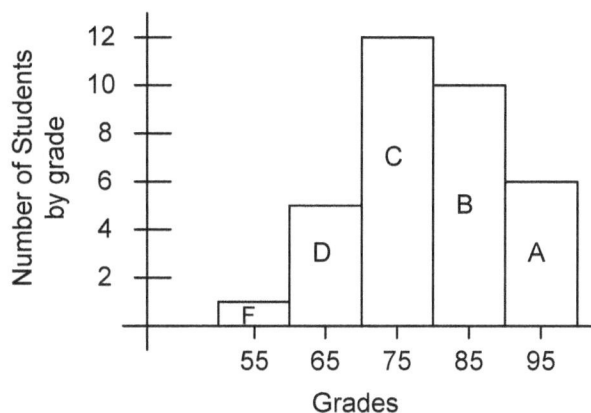

Which of the following statements best describes the data?

**a.** About 32% of the students had a grade of C.

**b.** About 5% of the students had a grade of F.

**c.** About 29% of the students had a grade of B.

**d.** About 21% of the students had a grade of A.

**BM 17.** The below scatter plot appears to be what type of correlation?

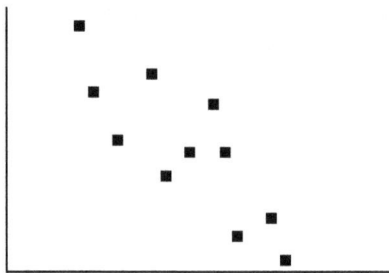

a. Zero Correlation

b. Strong Negative Correlation

c. Weak Positive Correlation

d. Weak Negative Correlation

**BM 18.** A ladder is 4 meters tall. About how tall is the ladder in feet (ft) and inches (in.)? (1 meter ≈ 39 inches)

a. 13 ft 0 in.　　　b. 13 ft 6 in.

c. 14 ft 0 in.　　　d. 14 ft 6 in.

**BM 19.** The actual width (*w*) of a rectangle is 22 inches (in.). Use the scale drawing of the rectangle to find the actual length (*l*).

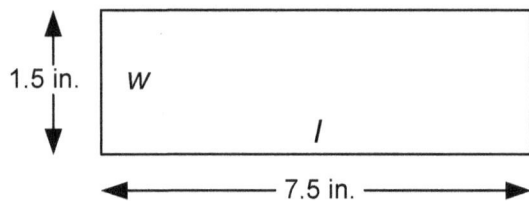

a. 84 in.　　　b. 92 in.

c. 104 in.　　　d. 110 in.

**BM 20.** Amber ran 8 miles at the speed of five miles per hour. How long did it take her to run that distance?

a. $\frac{4}{5}$ hr

b. $1\frac{1}{5}$ hrs

c. $1\frac{3}{5}$ hrs

d. 2 hrs

**BM 21.**

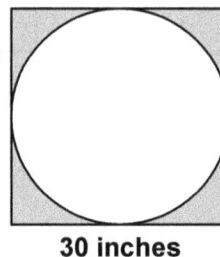

**30 inches**

The largest possible circle is to be cut from a 30-inch square board. What will be the approximate area, in square inches, of the remaining board (shaded region)?

$(A = \pi r^2$ and $\pi \approx 3.14)$

a. 190　　　b. 210

c. 230　　　d. 250

**BM 22.** In the figure shown below, all the corners form right angles.

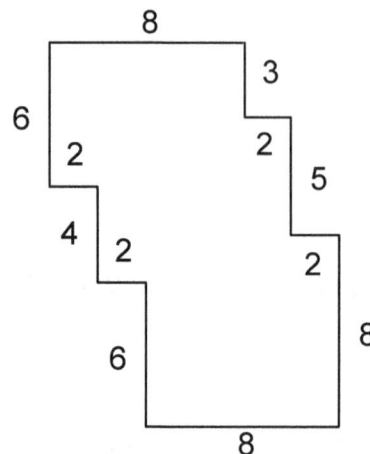

What is the area of the figure in square units?

a. 114　　b. 138　　c. 156　　d. 164

**BM 23.** Alexander has two similar rectangular boxes. The dimensions of box A are three times bigger then box B. How many times greater is the surface area of box A?

  **a.** 1           **b.** 3

  **c.** 6           **d.** 9

**BM 24.** If one mile per hour is equal to 88 feet per minute, then how many miles per hour is a car traveling when it is going 5984 feet per minute?

  **a.** 65 mph       **b.** 70 mph

  **c.** 68 mph       **d.** 680 mph

**BM 25.** Point B has translated to point B'. Use the graph below to describe the translation.

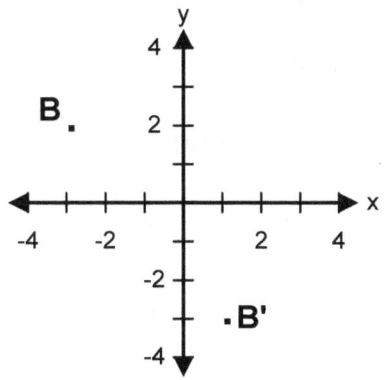

  **a.** left 4, down 3       **b.** right 4, down 3

  **c.** right 4, up 5        **d.** right 4, down 5

**BM 26.** In a right triangle, if the length of one leg equals 12 and the length of the hypotenuse equals 13, what is the length of the other leg?

  **a.** 12           **b.** 4

  **c.** 13           **d.** 5

**BM 27.** The two triangles are congruent. Find the value of x.

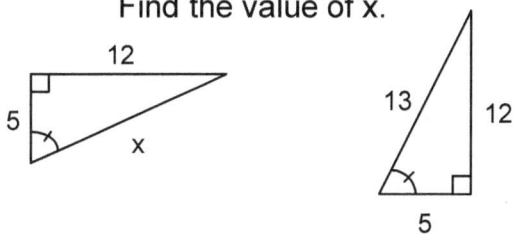

  **a.** 24           **b.** 13

  **c.** 17           **d.** 25

**BM 28.** Multiply a number by 2 and subtract 12 from the result. The answer is 36. Which of the following equations matches these statements?

  **a.** $2x - 12 = 36$     **b.** $36 = 12 - 2x$

  **c.** $2x + 12 = 36$     **d.** $36 - 2x = 12$

**BM 29.** If $h = 4$ and $k = \frac{1}{2}$, then $h(k + 2)=$

  **a.** 10           **b.** 3

  **c.** 16           **d.** 8

**BM 30.**

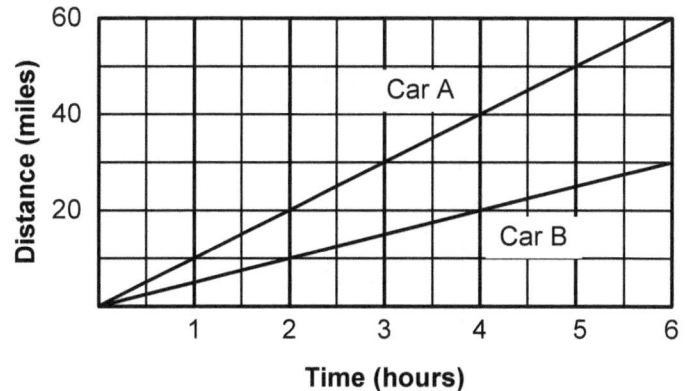

After six hours of travel, Car A is about how many miles ahead of Car B?

  **a.** 30           **b.** 35

  **c.** 20           **d.** 25

# CAHSEE Unit 9 Exam
## Bench Marks 1 - 48

**BM 31.** If m = -2 and n = 4, then 2mn² =

a. 64

b. -32

c. -64

d. $\frac{-1}{32}$

**BM 32.** $\sqrt{9m^2 n^{18}}$ =

a. $9mn^9$

b. $9mn$

c. $3mn^9$

d. $3mn$

**BM 33.** Which of the following is the graph of y = -x²?

a.

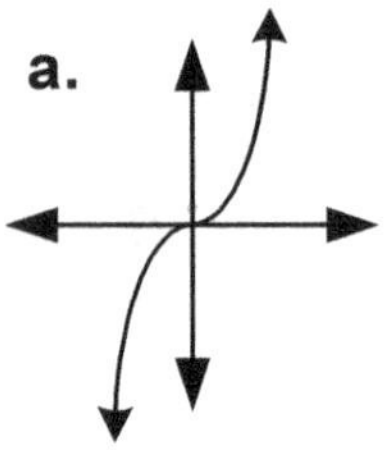

b.

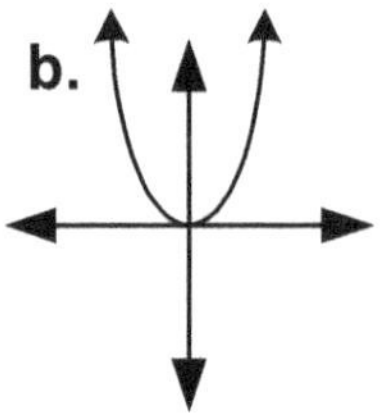

c.

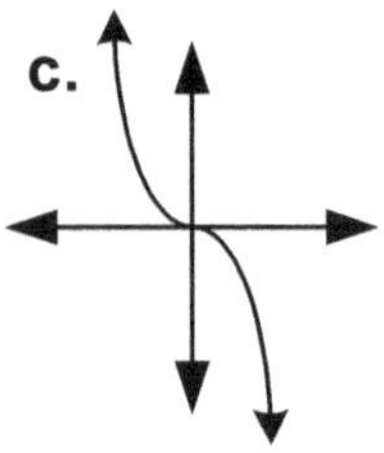

d.

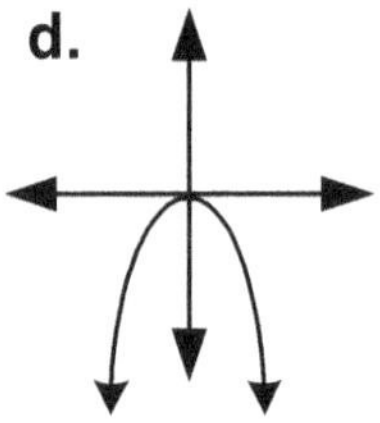

**BM 34.** The slope of the line shown below is $\frac{-3}{4}$.

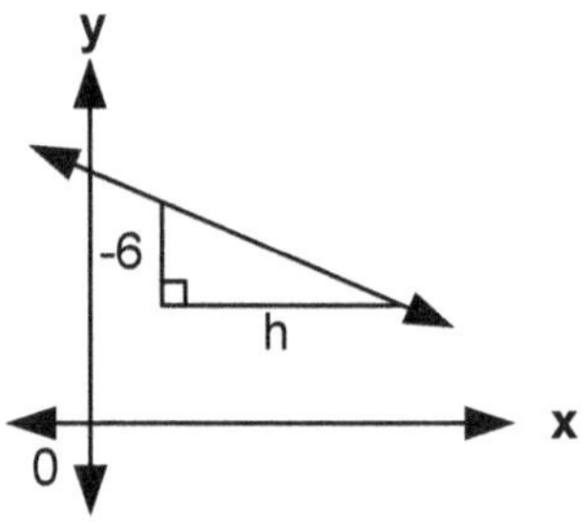

What is the value of h?

a. 3

b. 7

c. 8

d. 4

**BM 35.** The graph below shows the cost to rent 3 different limousines for senior ball. What is the price per hour to rent a limousine?

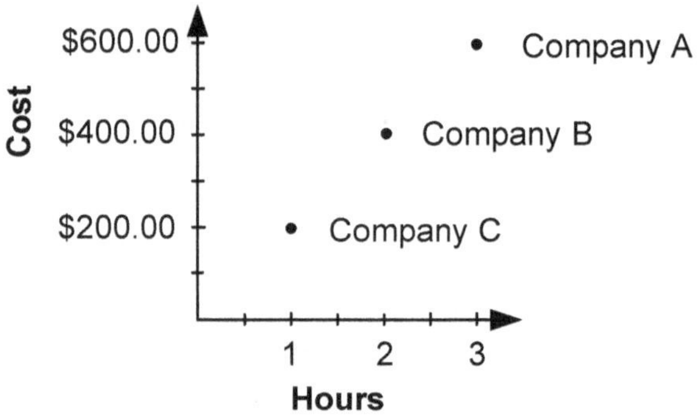

a. $200.00

b. $25.00

c. $100.00

d. $150.00

**BM 36.** In the inequality 2x + $10,000 ≤ $70,000, x represents the salary of employees in a book store. Which phrase most accurately describes the employee's salary?

a. More than $30,000

b. At least $30,000

c. At most $30,000

d. Less than $30,000

**BM 37.** Tovah can swim 4 miles in 2 hours. At this rate, how many miles can she swim in 5 hours?

a. 10

b. 11

c. 12

d. 13

**BM 38.** It takes Thao two hours to finish a race. If she runs at a rate of 1 mile every 10 minutes, how far did she run?

    **a.**  20 miles

    **b.**  12 miles

    **c.**  60 miles

    **d.**  6 miles

**BM 39.** The Twin Primes Conjecture states that an infinite number of primes differing by two can be found. Which example below supports this conjecture?

    **a.**  49 and 51

    **b.**  33 and 35

    **c.**  29 and 31

    **d.**  23 and 25

**BM 40.** In a class of 21 students, what is the best estimate for the mean test score if the sum of the all tests is 1514?

    **a.**  65

    **b.**  70

    **c.**  75

    **d.**  80

**BM 41.** The graph below shows the relationship between the number of weekly hours worked and the grade point average of students at the local university.

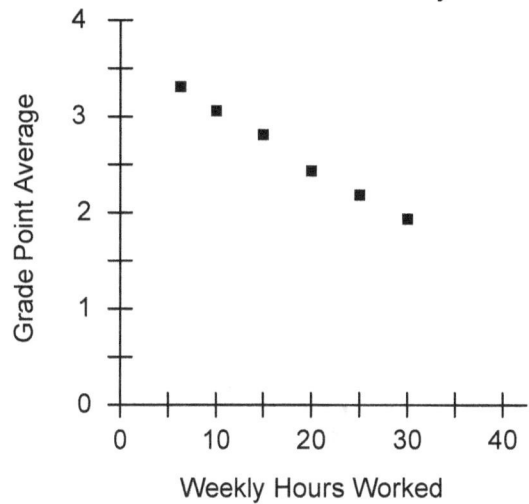

From the graph, which grade point average listed below is the most probable for students that do not work?

    **a.**  3.8        **b.**  3.0

    **c.**  3.3        **d.**  3.5

**BM 42.** Given the sequence 1, 2, 4, ..., determine which of the following would be the next three terms.

    **a.**  7, 11, 16      **b.**  6, 9, 12

    **c.**  8, 10, 12      **d.**  5, 8, 11

**BM 43.** Douglas converted 23,000 into scientific notation. Which number below is most like the answer that Douglas found, once he converted 23,000 into scientific notation?

    **a.**  $6.7 \times 10^{-4}$    **b.**  $6.7 \times 10^{-3}$

    **c.**  $6.7 \times 10^{4}$    **d.**  $67 \times 10^{4}$

**BM 44.** What is the reciprocal of $\dfrac{f^5 g}{h}$ ?

    **a.** $\dfrac{h}{fg}$      **b.** $\dfrac{h}{f^5 g}$

    **c.** $\dfrac{-fg}{h}$      **d.** $\dfrac{h}{fg^5}$

**BM 45.** Assume that y is an integer and solve for y.

$$|y + 8| = 17$$

    **a.** {-9, 25}      **b.** {-25, 9}

    **c.** {-25, 25}      **d.** {-9, 9}

**BM 46.** Which of the following is equivalent to $5 + 2x > 4(x - 1)$?

    **a.** $5 + 2x < 4x - 1$

    **b.** $5 + 2x < 4x - 4$

    **c.** $5 + 2x > 4x - 4$

    **d.** $5 + 2x > 4x + 4$

**BM 47.** Anna solved the equation $4(2x + 1) = 28$ using the following steps.

    **Given :**      $4(2x + 1) = 28$
    **Step 1:**      $8x + 4 = 28$
    **Step 2:**      $8x = 24$
    **Step 3:**      $x = 3$

To get from Step 2 to Step 3, Anna-
    **a.** added 4 to both sides.
    **b.** multiplied both sides by 8.
    **c.** subtracted 4 from both sides.
    **d.** divided both sides by 8.

**BM 48.** Which of the following is the graph of $y = 5x - 4$ ?

**a.**

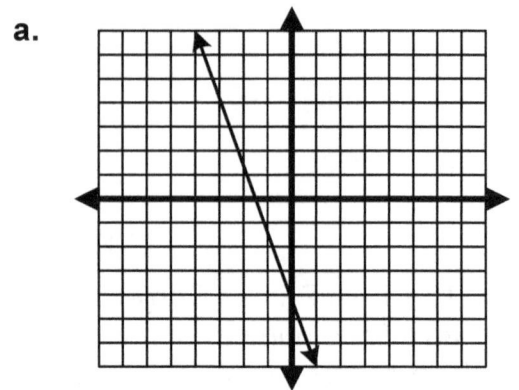

**b.**

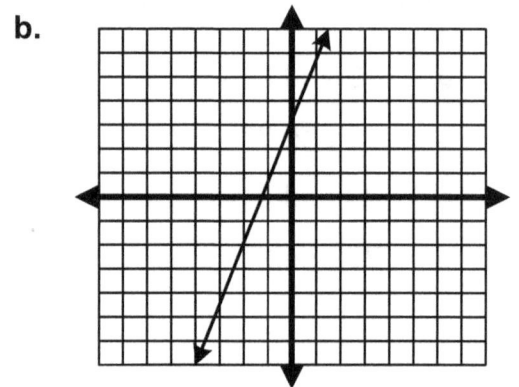

**c.**

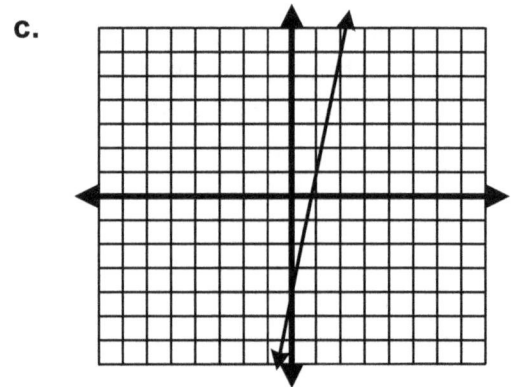

**d.**

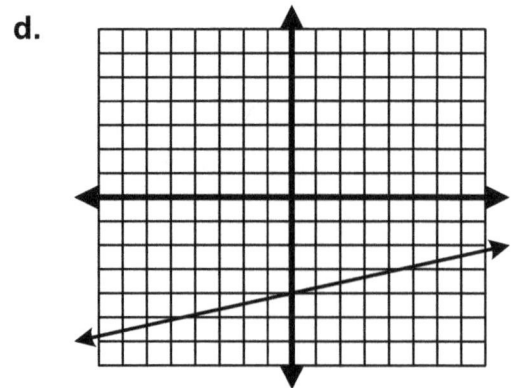

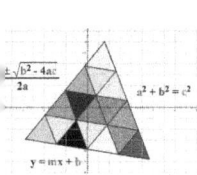

Students will successfully verify if a point lies on
a line and calculate intercepts.

**CA Standard:** Algebra I, 6.0 and 7.0
**CAHSEE Strand:** Algebra I

| Vocabulary: | coordinate | the numbers in an ordered pair that give the position of a point relative to the x and y axis |
| --- | --- | --- |
| | x-intercept | point where a graph crosses the x-axis |
| | y-intercept | point where a graph crosses the y-axis |

On the drawing to the right, we can see that the point P is on the line y = x + 2.
Mathematically, we can make the same determination by substituting 2 for x and 4 for y, then check for a true statement.

$$y = x + 2 \longrightarrow \mathbf{4 = 2 + 2}$$
$$4 = 4$$

This is a true statement and therefore shows that the point (2, 4) lies on the line y = x + 2.

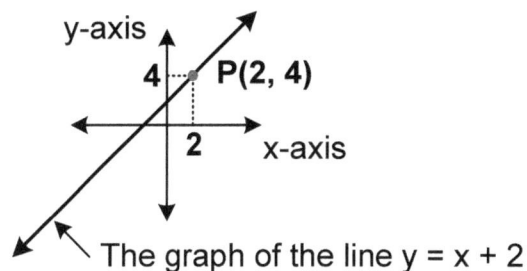

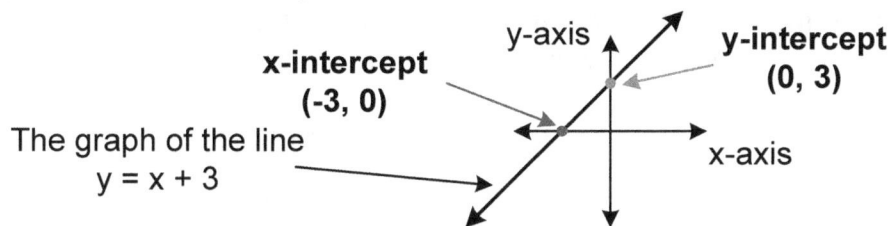

The graph of the line y = x + 2

**x-intercept (-3, 0)**

**y-intercept (0, 3)**

The graph of the line
y = x + 3

On the drawing to the left, we can see that there are two special points on the line y = x + 3. These are the x and y intercepts.

Mathematically, we can find the **x-intercept** by substituting 0 for y and solving for x

$$y = x + 3 \longrightarrow 0 = x + 3$$
$$-3 = x$$

Therefore, the **x-intercept** is
(-3, 0)

Mathematically, we can find the **y-intercept** by substituting 0 for x and solving for y

$$y = x + 3 \longrightarrow y = 0 + 3$$
$$y = 3$$

Therefore, the **y-intercept** is
(0, 3)

---

**EXAMPLE:** Which of the following points lies on the line y = 2x?

**a.** (0, 2)   **b.** (2, 1)   **c.** (1, 0)   **d.** (1, 2)

The most straightforward way to answer this question is to check each answer by substituting and evaluating.

**a.** (0, 2)  2 = 2(0)?  False  2 ≠ 0

**b.** (2, 1)  1 = 2(2)?  False  1 ≠ 4

**c.** (1, 0)  0 = 2(1)?  False  0 ≠ 2

**d.** (1, 2)  2 = 2(1)?  **True**  2 = 2

The correct answer is **d.**

1. Which of the following points lies on the line y = 2x?

   **a.** (0, 2)          **b.** (2, 1)

   **c.** (1, 0)          **d.** (1, 2)

2. What are the coordinates of the the x-intercept of the line 2x + 5y = 10?

   **a.** (5, 0)          **b.** (2, 0)

   **c.** (0, 5)          **d.** (0, 2)

3. Which of the following points lies on the line 3x + 2y = 6?

   **a.** (0, 2)          **b.** (2, 3)

   **c.** (2, 0)          **d.** (3, 0)

4. What are the coordinates of the the y-intercept of the line 3x + 4y = 12?

   **a.** (4, 0)          **b.** (3, 0)

   **c.** (0, 4)          **d.** (0, 3)

5. Which of the following points lies on the line 3x + 5y = 15?

   **a.** (3, 0)          **b.** (3, 5)

   **c.** (0, 3)          **d.** (5, 3)

6. What are the coordinates of the the x-intercept of the line 2x + 6y = 12?

   **a.** (2, 6)          **b.** (2, 0)

   **c.** (6, 2)          **d.** (6, 0)

7. Which of the following points lies on the line 3x + 6y = 18?

   **a.** (0, 6)          **b.** (6, 3)

   **c.** (6, 0)          **d.** (3, 6)

8. What are the coordinates of the the y-intercept of the line 3x + 4y = 24?

   **a.** (0, 8)          **b.** (0, 6)

   **c.** (8, 0)          **d.** (6, 0)

9. Which of the following points lies on the line 4x + 5y = 20?

   **a.** (5, 0)          **b.** (5, 4)

   **c.** (0, 5)          **d.** (4, 5)

10. What are the coordinates of the the x-intercept of the line 6x + 5y = 30?

   **a.** (5, 0)          **b.** (6, 0)

   **c.** (0, 5)          **d.** (0, 6)

204

11. Which of the following points lies on the line y = 3x?

   **a.** (3, 0)       **b.** (1, 3)

   **c.** (0, 1)       **d.** (3, 1)

16. What are the coordinates of the the x-intercept of the line 7x + 6y = 42?

   **a.** (6, 0)       **b.** (7, 6)

   **c.** (6, 7)       **d.** (0, 7)

12. What are the coordinates of the the x-intercept of the line 4x + 5y = 40?

   **a.** (10, 0)      **b.** (8, 0)

   **c.** (0, 10)      **d.** (0, 8)

17. Which of the following points lies on the line 3x + y = 6?

   **a.** (2, 6)       **b.** (6, 2)

   **c.** (6, 0)       **d.** (0, 6)

13. Which of the following points lies on the line 7x + 2y = 14?

   **a.** (7, 2)       **b.** (0, 7)

   **c.** (2, 7)       **d.** (7, 0)

18. What are the coordinates of the the y-intercept of the line x + 4y = 4?

   **a.** (0, 4)       **b.** (0, 1)

   **c.** (4, 0)       **d.** (1, 0)

14. What are the coordinates of the the y-intercept of the line 2x + 8y = 16?

   **a.** (8, 0)       **b.** (2, 0)

   **c.** (8, 2)       **d.** (0, 2)

19. Which of the following points lies on the line x + y = 7?

   **a.** (3, 3)       **b.** (7, 7)

   **c.** (0, 7)       **d.** (4, 2)

15. Which of the following points lies on the line 7x + 5y = 35?

   **a.** (7, 5)       **b.** (0, 5)

   **c.** (5, 7)       **d.** (5, 0)

20. What are the coordinates of the the x-intercept of the line x + 5y = 10?

   **a.** (2, 0)       **b.** (2, 10)

   **c.** (10, 0)      **d.** (10, 2)

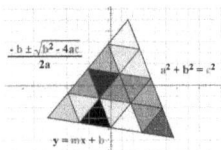

# CAHSEE Bench Mark 50

Students will successfully understand
parallel and perpendicular lines.

**CA Standard:** Algebra I, 8.0
**CAHSEE Strand:** Algebra I

*Simplified Solutions*
For Math Inc.

---

| **Vocabulary:** | **parallel lines** | coplanar lines that never intersect; lines with the same slope and different y-intercepts |
| --- | --- | --- |
| | **perpendicular lines** | lines than intersect to form 90° angles; lines where the slope of one is the negative reciprocal of the other |

We can observe the definition of parallel lines graphically. The lines will never intersect, they have the same slope, and different y-intercepts.

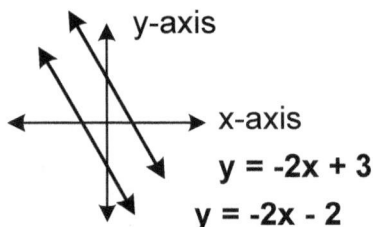

y-axis
x-axis
$y = -2x + 3$
$y = -2x - 2$

We can observe the definition of perpendicular lines graphically. The lines intersect to form 90° angles, and the slope of one is the negative reciprocal of the other.

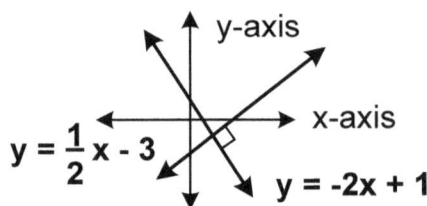

y-axis
x-axis
$y = \frac{1}{2}x - 3$
$y = -2x + 1$

---

**EXAMPLE:** What is the slope of the line perpendicular to the line below?

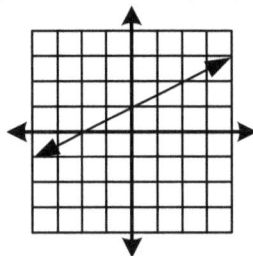

**a.** 0.5    **b.** -2

**c.** -0.5    **d.** 2

---

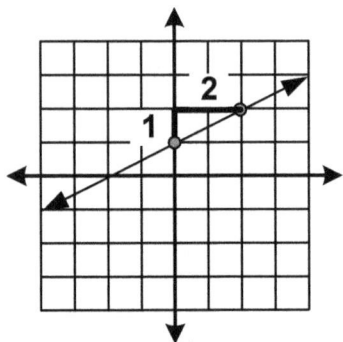

To find the slope of the line perpendicular to the given line, we must first find the slope of the given line.

By counting and determining the rise over the run,

we see that the slope is $\frac{1}{2}$.

The negative reciprocal of $\frac{1}{2}$ is -2.

The correct answer is **b.**

---

**EXAMPLE:** What is the slope of the line parallel to the line $y = 2x + 3$?

**a.** 3    **b.** 2    **c.** $\frac{1}{2}$    **d.** -2

The slope of the given line is 2 because $y = mx + b$ where m is the slope.

Parallel lines have the same slope, so the slope of the parallel line is also 2.

The correct answer is **b.**

---

**1.** What is the slope of the line parallel to the line $y = 2x + 3$?

    **a.** 3         **b.** 2

    **c.** $\dfrac{1}{2}$         **d.** -2

**2.** Which of the following statements describes parallel lines?

    **a.** same slopes, different y-intercepts

    **b.** opposite slopes, same y-intercepts

    **c.** opposite x-intercepts, same y-intercepts

    **d.** different slopes, same y-intercepts

**3.** Which of the following could be the equation of a line perpendicular to the line $y = 3x - 5$?

    **a.** $y = 3x - 2$     **b.** $y = -5x + 3$

    **c.** $y = \dfrac{-1}{3}x + 2$     **d.** $y = \dfrac{1}{3}x - 5$

**4.** What is the slope of the line parallel to the line below?

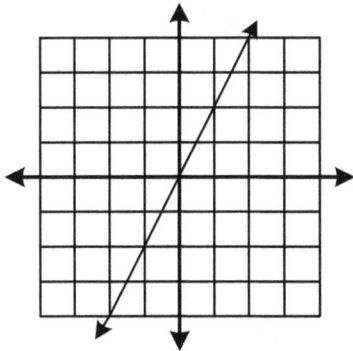

    **a.** 1
    **b.** -2
    **c.** 0
    **d.** 2

**5.** What is the slope of the line perpendicular to the line $y = \dfrac{2}{3}x + 3$?

    **a.** -3         **b.** -2

    **c.** $\dfrac{-2}{3}$         **d.** $\dfrac{-3}{2}$

**6.** Which of the following could be the equation of a line perpendicular to the line $y = -2x + 3$?

    **a.** $y = -2x - 2$     **b.** $y = -3x + 2$

    **c.** $y = \dfrac{-1}{2}x + 2$     **d.** $y = \dfrac{1}{2}x - 5$

**7.** What is the slope of the line parallel to the line below?

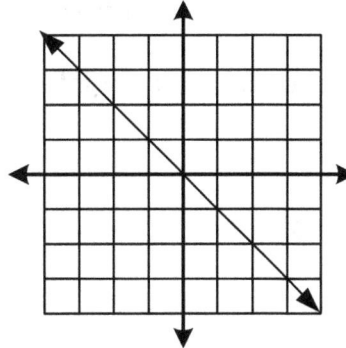

    **a.** -1
    **b.** -2
    **c.** 0
    **d.** 2

**8.** What is the slope of the line perpendicular to the line $y = \dfrac{-5}{4}x + 3$?

    **a.** $\dfrac{4}{5}$         **b.** -3

    **c.** $\dfrac{5}{4}$         **d.** $\dfrac{-4}{5}$

**9.** What is the slope of the line parallel to the line $y = -8x$?

    **a.** 0         **b.** 8

    **c.** $\dfrac{1}{8}$         **d.** -8

**10.** Which of the following statements describes perpendicular lines?

    **a.** same slopes, different y-intercepts

    **b.** slopes are negative reciprocals

    **c.** opposite x-intercepts, same y-intercepts

    **d.** different slopes, same x-intercepts

11. What is the slope of the line parallel to the line $y = 0.5x + 4$?

    a. 3          b. 2

    c. $\dfrac{1}{2}$    d. -2

12. Which of the following statements describes parallel lines?

    a. opposite slopes, same y-intercepts

    b. opposite x-intercepts, same y-intercepts

    c. never intersect

    d. same x-intercepts, different slopes

13. Which of the following could be the equation of a line perpendicular to the line $y = 0.5x + 12$?

    a. $y = -2x - 3$          b. $y = -12x + 3$

    c. $y = \dfrac{-1}{5}x + 2$    d. $y = \dfrac{1}{5}x - 5$

14. What is the slope of the line perpendicular to the line below?

    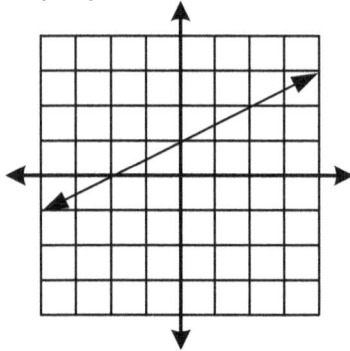

    a. 1

    b. 2

    c. 0.5

    d. -2

15. What is the slope of the line perpendicular to the line $y = \dfrac{7}{2}x + 3$?

    a. -5          b. $\dfrac{-2}{7}$

    c. $\dfrac{-7}{2}$    d. $\dfrac{7}{2}$

16. Which of the following could be the equation of a line perpendicular to the line $y = -x + 3$?

    a. $y = -3x - 7$          b. $y = x + 2$

    c. $y = \dfrac{-1}{2}x + 5$    d. $y = \dfrac{1}{3}x - 5$

17. What is the slope of the line parallel to the line below?

    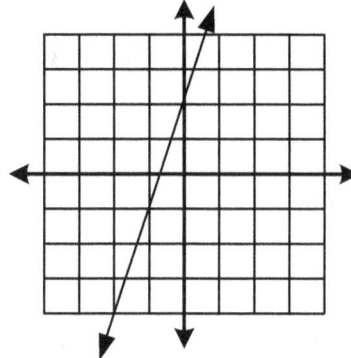

    a. 3

    b. -3

    c. $\dfrac{1}{3}$

    d. $\dfrac{-1}{3}$

18. What is the slope of the line perpendicular to the line $y = \dfrac{-8}{3}x + 2$?

    a. $\dfrac{8}{3}$          b. -2

    c. $\dfrac{3}{8}$          d. $\dfrac{-3}{8}$

19. What is the slope of the line parallel to the line $y = x$?

    a. 0          b. 1

    c. $\dfrac{1}{2}$    d. -1

20. Which of the following statements describes perpendicular lines?

    a. same slopes, different x-intercepts

    b. never intersect

    c. same x-intercepts, same y-intercepts

    d. intersect at right angles

208

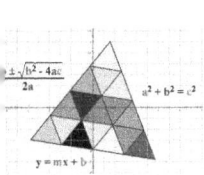

Students will successfully solve a system of linear
equations in two variables.

**CA Standard:** Algebra I, 9.0
**CAHSEE Strand:** Algebra I

A **system of equations** is more than one line on the same graph. In this lesson, we will be working with two linear equations.

When we plot two lines
on the same graph,
three different situations
can arise.

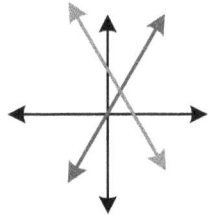

the lines cross

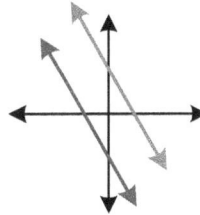

the lines are parallel
and never cross

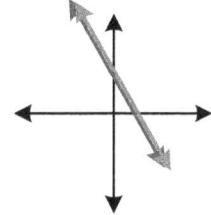

the lines are on top of one
another and always cross

When we **solve a system of linear equations**, we are looking for the point where the lines cross.

Mathematically, the point where the lines cross can be substituted into each equation and make a true statement.

**EXAMPLE:** What is the solution to the following system of equations?
$$\begin{cases} x + y = 6 \\ x - 2y = 0 \end{cases}$$
**a.** (2, 4)   **b.** (3, 3)   **c.** (4, 2)   **d.** (5, 1)

The most straightforward way to find the correct answer is to substitute the given points into each equation and find the point that makes **both** equations true.

**a.** (2, 4)  $\begin{cases} x + y = 6 \\ x - 2y = 0 \end{cases}$  → $\begin{matrix} 2 + 4 = 6 & \textbf{True} \\ 2 - 8 = 0 & \textbf{False} \end{matrix}$  incorrect

**b.** (3, 3)  $\begin{cases} x + y = 6 \\ x - 2y = 0 \end{cases}$  → $\begin{matrix} 3 + 3 = 6 & \textbf{True} \\ 3 - 6 = 0 & \textbf{False} \end{matrix}$  incorrect

**c.** (4, 2)  $\begin{cases} x + y = 6 \\ x - 2y = 0 \end{cases}$  → $\begin{matrix} 4 + 2 = 6 & \textbf{True} \\ 4 - 4 = 0 & \textbf{True} \end{matrix}$  CORRECT

The correct answer is **c.**

**EXAMPLE:** Which graph represents the system of equations?
$$\begin{cases} y = x + 2 \\ y = -x + 2 \end{cases}$$

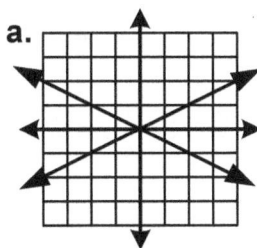

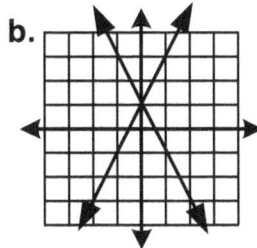

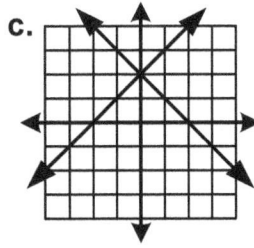

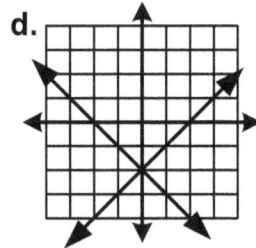

**a.**   **b.**   **c.**   **d.**

We can examine the answer choices and eliminate those that are incorrect.

Choices **a** and **b** show lines whose slopes are **not** 1 and -1 and are therefore incorrect.

Choices **c** and **d** show lines whose slopes are 1 and -1, however, choice **c** shows lines which have y-intercepts of 2.

The correct answer is **c.**

**1.** Which graph represents the system of equations shown below?

$$\begin{cases} y = x + 2 \\ y = -x + 2 \end{cases}$$

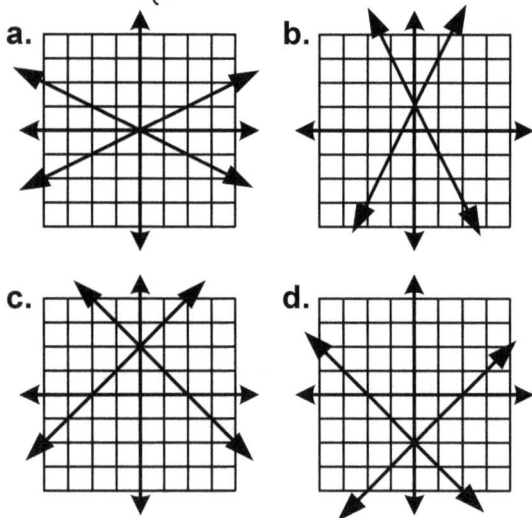

**a.**

**b.**

**c.**

**d.**

**2.**
$$\begin{cases} 2x - y = 4 \\ x + y = 5 \end{cases}$$

What is the solution to the system of equations shown above?

**a.** (4, 5)          **b.** (3, 2)

**c.** (5, 4)          **d.** (2, 3)

**3.**
$$\begin{cases} y = 2x + 1 \\ y = -x + 4 \end{cases}$$

What is the solution to the system of equations shown above?

**a.** (1, 3)          **b.** (3, 1)

**c.** (1, 4)          **d.** (4, 3)

**4.**
$$\begin{cases} 4x + 2y = 2 \\ x - 2y = 8 \end{cases}$$

What is the solution to the system of equations shown above?

**a.** (-3, 2)          **b.** (3, 2)

**c.** (2, -3)          **d.** (2, 3)

**5.** Which graph represents the system of equations shown below?

$$\begin{cases} y = x \\ y = 2x - 1 \end{cases}$$

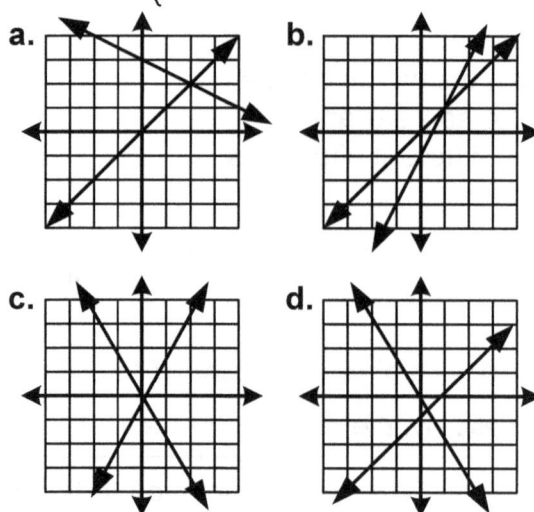

**a.**

**b.**

**c.**

**d.**

**6.** Which graph represents the system of equations shown below?

$$\begin{cases} y = x + 3 \\ y = -x + 1 \end{cases}$$

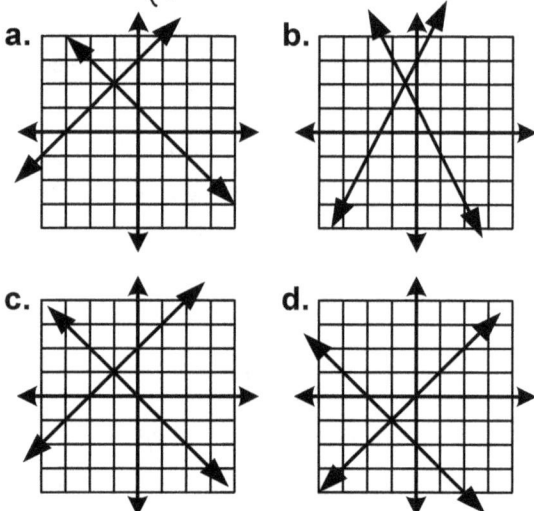

**a.**

**b.**

**c.**

**d.**

**7.**
$$\begin{cases} x + y = 5 \\ x - y = 1 \end{cases}$$

What is the solution to the system of equations shown above?

**a.** (2, 3)          **b.** (3, 4)

**c.** (3, 2)          **d.** (3, 5)

**8.** Which graph represents the system of equations shown below?

$$\begin{cases} y = x + 3 \\ y = -x - 1 \end{cases}$$

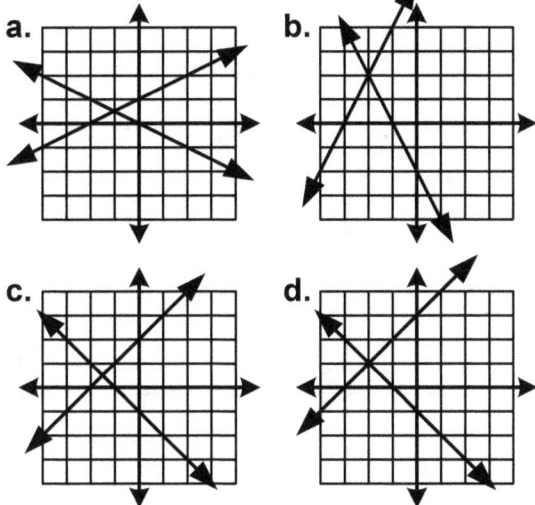

a.

b.

c.

d.

**9.**
$$\begin{cases} y = x - 1 \\ y = 2x - 5 \end{cases}$$

What is the solution to the system of equations shown above?

a. (4, 3)          b. (3, 4)

c. (-1, -5)        d. (-5, -1)

**10.**
$$\begin{cases} x + y = 5 \\ x - y = 3 \end{cases}$$

What is the solution to the system of equations shown above?

a. (5, 3)          b. (3, 5)

c. (1, 4)          d. (4, 1)

**11.**
$$\begin{cases} 2x + y = 1 \\ x - y = -4 \end{cases}$$

What is the solution to the system of equations shown above?

a. (-4, 1)         b. (-1, 3)

c. (1, -4)         d. (3, -1)

**12.** Which graph represents the system of equations shown below?

$$\begin{cases} y = x \\ y = -x - 2 \end{cases}$$

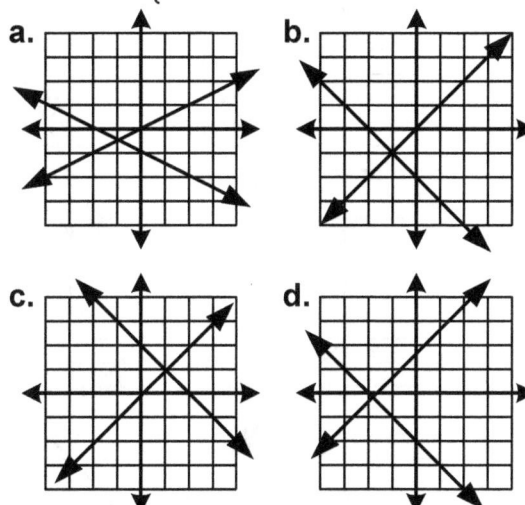

a.

b.

c.

d.

**13.** Which graph represents the system of equations shown below?

$$\begin{cases} y = -x + 1 \\ y = -2x + 4 \end{cases}$$

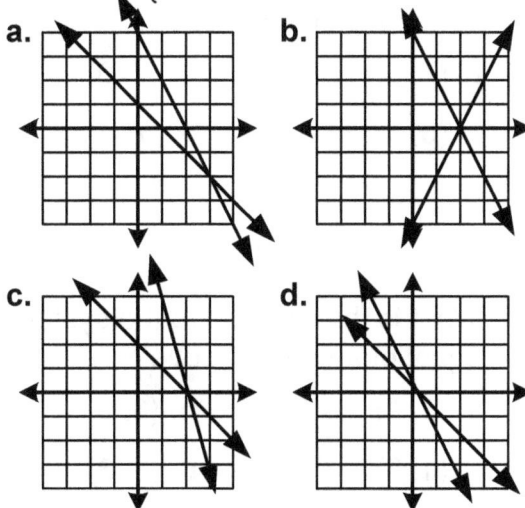

a.

b.

c.

d.

**14.**
$$\begin{cases} x - y = 1 \\ 2x + y = 5 \end{cases}$$

What is the solution to the system of equations shown above?

a. (2, 0)          b. (1, 0)

c. (2, 1)          d. (1, 3)

**15.** Which graph represents the system of equations shown below?

$$\begin{cases} y = x - 3 \\ y = -x - 1 \end{cases}$$

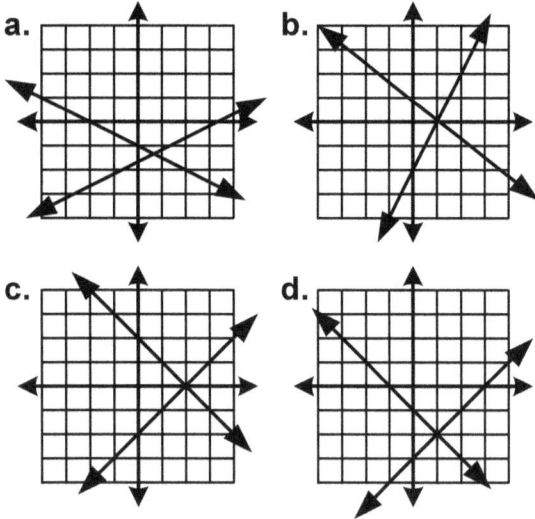

a.

b.

c.

d.

**16.**

$$\begin{cases} x - 2y = -1 \\ -x + y = -3 \end{cases}$$

What is the solution to the system of equations shown above?

**a.** (7, -4)   **b.** (7, 0)

**c.** (0, 4)    **d.** (7, 4)

**17.**

$$\begin{cases} x + y = 4 \\ x - y = 2 \end{cases}$$

What is the solution to the system of equations shown above?

**a.** (3, 1)   **b.** (3, 0)

**c.** (1, 3)   **d.** (3, 3)

**18.**

$$\begin{cases} 2x - y = 2 \\ x + y = 13 \end{cases}$$

What is the solution to the system of equations shown above?

**a.** (5, 0)   **b.** (5, -2)

**c.** (5, 8)   **d.** (0, 8)

**19.** Which graph represents the system of equations shown below?

$$\begin{cases} y = x \\ y = -x + 4 \end{cases}$$

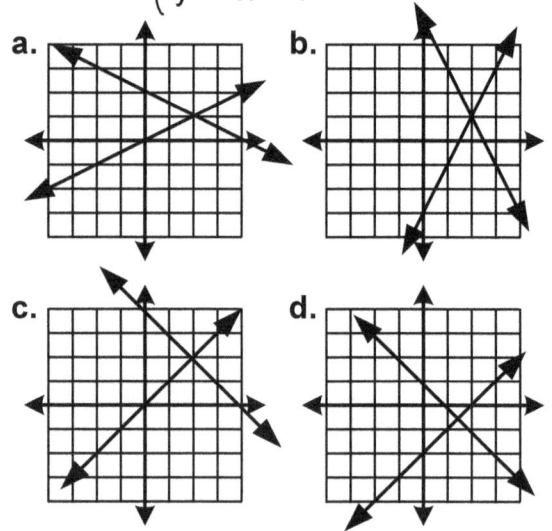

a.

b.

c.

d.

**20.** Which graph represents the system of equations shown below?

$$\begin{cases} y = x - 4 \\ y = -x + 2 \end{cases}$$

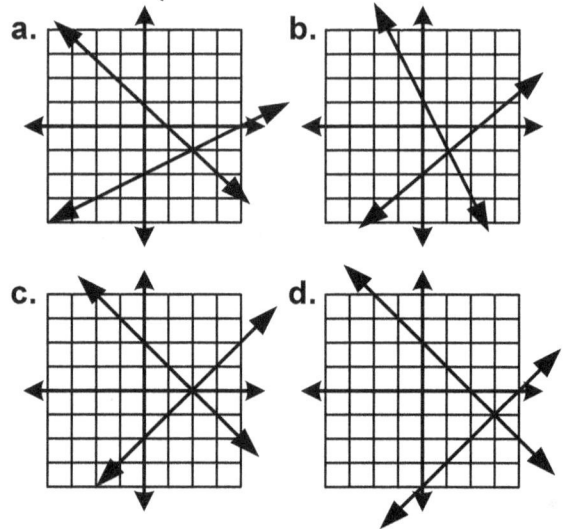

a.

b.

c.

d.

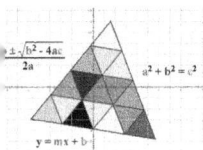

# CAHSEE Bench Mark 52

Students will successfully add, subtract, multiply and divide polynomials.

**CA Standard:** Algebra I, 10.0
**CAHSEE Strand:** Algebra I

| Vocabulary: | **term** | part of an expression separated by a plus or minus sign |
|---|---|---|
| | **polynomial** | an expression consisting of one or more terms |
| | **coefficient** | the numerical factor of a term |

**To add or subtract polynomials**, we simply collect like terms (i.e. add). When subtracting, it is beneficial to distribute the negative sign, then add.

**EXAMPLE:** Simplify. $(x^2 - 3x + 1) - (x^2 - x - 6)$     **a.** $-4x - 5$   **b.** $-3x + 7$   **c.** $2x^2 - 4x - 5$   **d.** $-2x + 7$

$(x^2 - 3x + 1) - (x^2 - x - 6)$     distribute the negative sign
$= x^2 - 3x + 1 - x^2 + x + 6$     collect like terms
$= -2x + 7$

The correct answer is **d.**

**To multiply polynomials**, we use the distributive property, then collect like terms.

**EXAMPLE:** Simplify. $(x + 2)(x - 4)$     **a.** $2x - 1$   **b.** $x^2 - 2x - 8$   **c.** $2x^2 - 4x - 6$   **d.** $x^2 + 2x - 8$

$(x + 2)(x - 4)$     first distribute the x, then distribute the 2 over (x - 4)
$x(x) + x(-4) + 2(x) + 2(-4)$     simplify
$x^2 - 4x + 2x - 8$     collect like terms
$x^2 - 2x - 8$

The correct answer is **b.**

**To divide polynomials**, with a monomial denominator, we separate the expression into individual fractions, then simplify.

**EXAMPLE:** Simplify. $\dfrac{16x^3 - 8x^2 + 12x}{4x}$

**a.** $4x^2 - 2x + 3$   **b.** $2x^2 - 2x + 3$   **c.** $4x^2 + 2x - 3$   **d.** $2x^2 - x - 3$

$\dfrac{16x^3 - 8x^2 + 12x}{4x} = \dfrac{16x^3}{4x} - \dfrac{8x^2}{4x} + \dfrac{12x}{4x}$

$= 4x^2 - 2x + 3$

The correct answer is **a.**

**EXAMPLE:** Simplify. $(x^2 - 4x + 5) - (x^2 + x - 4)$

**a.** $-3x + 1$   **b.** $-3x + 9$   **c.** $2x^2 - 3x + 1$   **d.** $-5x + 9$

$(x^2 - 4x + 5) - (x^2 + x - 4)$     distribute the negative sign
$x^2 - 4x + 5 - x^2 - x + 4$     collect like terms
$= -5x + 9$

The correct answer is **d.**

© 2007 Simplified Solutions for Math, Inc.

213

1. Simplify. $(x^2 - 4x + 5) - (x^2 + x - 4)$

   **a.** $-3x + 1$  **b.** $-3x + 9$

   **c.** $2x^2 - 3x + 1$  **d.** $-5x + 9$

2.

**x + 4**

   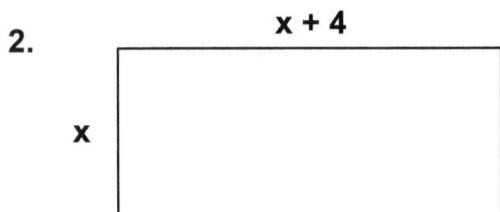

   **x**

   The length of the rectangle above is 4 units longer than the width. Which expression could be used to represent the area of the rectangle?

   **a.** $x^2 + 4x$  **b.** $2x + 4$

   **c.** $x^2 - 4x$  **d.** $6x$

3. Simplify. $(2x^2 - 3x + 1) + (x^2 + x - 4)$

   **a.** $3x^2 - 2x + 3$  **b.** $2x^2 - 3x - 3$

   **c.** $3x^2 - 3x - 3$  **d.** $3x^2 - 2x - 3$

4. Simplify. $\dfrac{10x^3 - 5x^2 + 15x}{5x}$

   **a.** $2x^2 - x - 3$  **b.** $2x^2 - x + 3$

   **c.** $2x^2 - 5x - 3$  **d.** $3x^2 - x - 3$

5. Simplify. $(x^2 - 3x + 1) - (x^2 - x - 6)$

   **a.** $-4x - 5$  **b.** $-3x + 7$

   **c.** $2x^2 - 4x - 5$  **d.** $-2x + 7$

6.

**x + 2**

   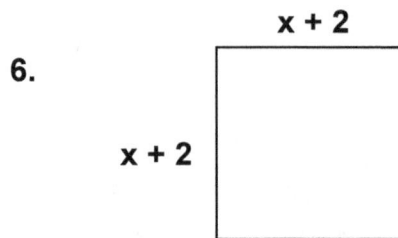

   **x + 2**

   The length of the square above is equal to the width. Which expression could be used to represent the area of the square?

   **a.** $2x + 4$  **b.** $x^2 + 4x + 4$

   **c.** $x^2 - 4x + 4$  **d.** $2x^2 + 4x + 4$

7. Simplify. $(2x^2 + 5x + 1) + (3x^2 - x + 1)$

   **a.** $5x^2 - 4x - 2$  **b.** $5x^2 + 4x$

   **c.** $5x^2 + 4x + 2$  **d.** $5x^2 + 6x + 2$

8. Simplify. $\dfrac{12x^3 + 8x^2 + 16x}{4x}$

   **a.** $3x^2 - 2x - 4$  **b.** $3x^2 + 4x$

   **c.** $3x^2 + 4x + 2$  **d.** $3x^2 + 2x + 4$

9. Simplify. $(x^2 + 7x - 9) - (x^2 + 6x - 8)$

   **a.** $x - 1$  **b.** $2x^2 + 13x - 17$

   **c.** $13x + 1$  **d.** $x + 1$

10. Simplify. $(x + 2)(x - 3)$

    **a.** $2x - 1$  **b.** $x^2 - x - 6$

    **c.** $2x^2 - x - 6$  **d.** $x^2 + x - 6$

**11.** Simplify. $(3x^2 - 2x + 1) - (3x^2 + 2x - 7)$

    **a.** $-4x + 8$         **b.** $8$

    **c.** $6x^2 - 4x + 8$     **d.** $4x + 8$

**12.**

x + 6

x

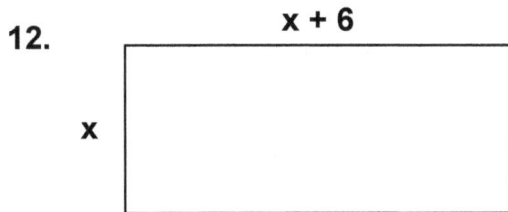

The length of the rectangle above is 6 units longer than the width. Which expression could be used to represent the area of the rectangle?

    **a.** $2x + 6$         **b.** $x^2 - 6x$

    **c.** $8x$            **d.** $x^2 + 6x$

**13.** Simplify. $(2x^2 + x + 2) + (4x^2 - x - 2)$

    **a.** $6x^2 - 2x + 4$     **b.** $6x^2 - 2x - 4$

    **c.** $8x^2$            **d.** $6x^2$

**14.** Simplify. $\dfrac{12x^3 + 3x^2 + 15x}{3x}$

    **a.** $4x^2 - x + 5$     **b.** $4x^2 + x + 5$

    **c.** $4x^2 - 3x + 5$     **d.** $4x^2 + x - 5$

**15.** Simplify. $(2x^2 + 6x + 21) - (x^2 + 5x + 20)$

    **a.** $x^2 + x + 1$     **b.** $3x^2 + x + 1$

    **c.** $x^2 - x + 1$     **d.** $x^2 + x - 1$

**16.**

x + 5

x + 5

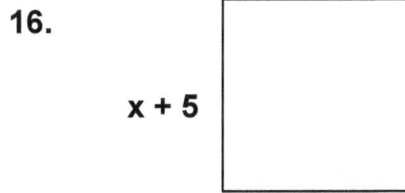

The length of the square above is equal to the width. Which expression could be used to represent the area of the square?

    **a.** $2x^2 + 10x + 25$     **b.** $x^2 + 10x + 5$

    **c.** $x^2 + 10x + 25$     **d.** $2x + 10$

**17.** Simplify. $(x + 4)(x - 3)$

    **a.** $2x + 1$         **b.** $x^2 - x - 12$

    **c.** $2x^2 + x - 12$     **d.** $x^2 + x - 12$

**18.** Simplify. $\dfrac{5x^3 + 2x^2 + x}{x}$

    **a.** $5x^2 + 2x + 1$     **b.** $5x^2 + 2x - 1$

    **c.** $5x^2 - 2x + 1$     **d.** $5x^2 + 2x$

**19.** Simplify. $(x^2 + 5x - 7) - (2x^2 + 6x - 8)$

    **a.** $-x^2 - x + 1$     **b.** $-x^2 + x - 1$

    **c.** $3x^2 - x + 1$     **d.** $-x^2 - x$

**20.** Simplify. $(x - 2)(x + 5)$

    **a.** $x^2 + 3x + 10$     **b.** $x^2 + 3x - 10$

    **c.** $2x + 3$         **d.** $x^2 - 3x + 10$

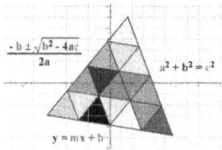

Solving word problems can be difficult.
However, there are many different ways to simplify the procedure.

1. **Read the problem.**  You can only understand the problem if you read it.

2. **Draw a picture, chart, diagram, etc.**  This will help catalogue your information and help you to understand the problem.

3. **Answer the question.**  Some problems may take a lot of calculating to solve. Do not get lost in the numbers. Answer the question.

---

**EXAMPLE:** A car traveling at 30 miles per hour (mph) leaves a restaurant along a dirt road. Two hours later, another car traveling at 50 mph leaves the same restaurant along the same road. How far from the restaurant will they meet?

    **a.** 120 miles     **b.** 130 miles     **c.** 140 miles    **d.** 150 miles

---

We will need to use the formula $d = rt$ (distance equals rate multiplied by time).

A chart can sometimes be beneficial to understand what is being asked.

|        | rate   | time  | distance |
|--------|--------|-------|----------|
| Car 1  | 30 mph | t     | d        |
| Car 2  | 50 mph | t - 2 | d        |

         Two hours
         later

Set up the equations.

**d = rt**     $d = 30t$ and $d = 50(t - 2)$     Both equations equal d, so we can substitute one equation into the other for d.

        $30t = 50(t - 2)$         Distribute the 50.

        $30t = 50t - 100$       Subtract 50t from both sides.

        $-20t = -100$          Divide by -20

          $t = 5$

We have solved for the time but we are asked for the distance. We need to substitute 5 for t into either of the original equations.

        $d = 30t$ so, $d = 30(5) = 150$

The correct answer is **d.**

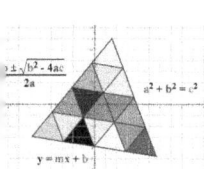

**EXAMPLE:** Eric can mow all of the lawns on his block in 30 hours. Deshaun can mow the same lawns in 15 hours. How long will it take them to mow the lawns if they work together?

**a.** 8 hours    **b.** 9 hours    **c.** 10 hours    **d.** 11 hours

The job will be completed faster if both are working together.

As a rule, if a certain job can be done in x hours, then $\frac{1}{x}$ of the job can be done in one hour.

We need the fractional part of the job that each can complete in one hour. We will add these fractions together, because they will be working together, and set the sum equal to the amount of work that can be done in an hour.

$\frac{1}{30}$  The amount of the job Eric can do in an hour

$\frac{1}{15}$  The amount of the job Deshaun can do in an hour

$\frac{1}{x}$  The amount of the job that can be done in an hour

**Set-up the equation**

$$\frac{1}{30} + \frac{1}{15} = \frac{1}{x}$$    Find a common denominator

$$\frac{x + 2x = 30}{30x}$$    Solve the numerator

$$x + 2x = 30$$    Collect like terms

$$3x = 30$$    Divide by 3

$$x = 10$$

The correct answer is **c.**

**EXAMPLE:** How much soft candy that sells for $0.75 per pound must be added to 8 pounds of hard candy that sells for $2.00 per pound to make a mixture worth $1.75 per pound?

**a.** 1 pound    **b.** 2 pounds    **c.** 3 pounds    **d.** 4 pounds

A chart can sometimes be beneficial to understand what is being asked.

| Type of candy | Amount | Price | Total |
|---|---|---|---|
| Soft | x | $0.75 | 0.75x |
| Hard | 8 | $2.00 | 2(8) |
| Mix | x + 8 | $1.75 | 1.75(x + 8) |

We know that we will be adding hard candy to soft candy in order to get our mixture. So mathematically we will add the totals for the hard and soft and set it equal to the total of the mix.

$$0.75x + 2(8) = 1.75(x + 8)$$

$$0.75x + 16 = 1.75x + 14$$

$$2 = 1.00x$$

$$2 = x$$

Therefore, we know that we need to add 2 pound of soft candy to the 8 pounds of hard candy to make a mix worth $1.75 per pound.

The correct answer is **b.**

**EXAMPLE:** It takes Scott 10 hours to paint a house and it takes Ted 15 hours to paint the same size house. How long will it take them to paint the house if they worked together?

**a.** 5 hours    **b.** 6 hours    **c.** 7 hours    **d.** 8 hours

The job will be completed faster if both are working together.
We need the fractional part of the job that each can complete in one hour. We will add these fractions together, because they will be working together, and set the sum equal to the amount of work that can be done in an hour.

$\frac{1}{10}$  The amount of the job Scott can do in an hour

$\frac{1}{15}$  The amount of the job Ted can do in an hour

$\frac{1}{x}$  The amount of the job that can be done in an hour

$$\frac{1}{10} + \frac{1}{15} = \frac{1}{x}$$

$$\frac{3x + 2x = 30}{30x}$$

$$5x = 30$$

$$x = 6$$    The correct answer is **b.**

1. It takes Scott 10 hours to paint a house and it takes Ted 15 hours to paint the same size house. How long will it take them to paint the house if they worked together?

   **a.** 5 hours     **b.** 6 hours

   **c.** 7 hours     **d.** 8 hours

2. How much 20% paint thinner solution should be added to a gallon of 5% paint thinner solution to make a solution that is 15% paint thinner.

   **a.** 0.5 gallons     **b.** 1 gallon

   **c.** 2 gallons     **d.** 3 gallons

3. A car traveling at 20 miles per hour (mph) leaves a restaurant along a dirt road. One hour later, another car traveling at 30 mph leaves the same restaurant along the same road. How far from the restaurant will they meet?

   **a.** 60 miles     **b.** 70 miles

   **c.** 80 miles     **d.** 90 miles

4. A plumber finds that Amos can complete a certain job in 30 hours and Bradley can complete the same job in 20 hours. How long would it take them to complete the job if they worked together?

   **a.** 9 hours     **b.** 10 hours

   **c.** 11 hours     **d.** 12 hours

5. A restaurant supply manager wants to offer a special on two types of lettuce. If the butter leaf sells for $3 per head and the ice berg sells for $1 per head, how many heads of ice berg should be added to 13 heads of butter leaf given that the special price is $2?

   **a.** 11 heads     **b.** 12 heads

   **c.** 13 heads     **d.** 14 heads

6. Loquisha runs 6 miles every Sunday. If she doubles her usual pace, she can complete the 6 miles an hour sooner. What is her normal pace?

   **a.** 3 mph     **b.** 4 mph

   **c.** 5 mph     **d.** 6 mph

7. Carl can set up the chairs in the gym in 50 minutes and Dave can set them up in 75 minutes. How long will it take them to set up the chairs if they worked together?

   **a.** 20 minutes     **b.** 30 minutes

   **c.** 40 minutes     **d.** 50 minutes

8. A candy maker has two types of candy to mix together. The hard candy sells for $3 per pound and the soft candy sells for $6 per pound. How much hard candy should be added to three pounds of soft candy, if the mixed price is going to be $4 per pound?

   **a.** 3 pounds     **b.** 4 pounds

   **c.** 5 pounds     **d.** 6 pounds

**9.** Kao can unload a truck in 40 minutes and Yee can unload the same truck in 60 minutes. How long would it take them to unload the truck if they worked together?

    **a.** 15 minutes      **b.** 24 minutes

    **c.** 30 minutes      **d.** 48 minutes

**10.** How much 85% hydrochloric acid should a chemist add to 3 liters of 25% hydrochloric acid to obtain a new mixture of 45% hydrochloric acid?

    **a.** 0.5 liters      **b.** 1 liters

    **c.** 1.5 liters      **d.** 2 liters

**11.** A car traveling at 40 miles per hour (mph) leaves a store along a highway. Two hours later, another car traveling at 50 mph leaves the same store along the same road. How long after the first car leaves will they meet?

    **a.** 4 hours      **b.** 6 hours

    **c.** 8 hours      **d.** 10 hours

**12.** An experienced tailor can create a suit in 30 hours. A less experienced tailor can create the same suit in 45 hours. How long would it take to create the suit if they worked together?

    **a.** 18 hours      **b.** 20 hours

    **c.** 22 hours      **d.** 24 hours

**13.** A candlestick maker mixes pure bees wax and regular wax in order to get the candles to burn longer. If the desired mixture contains 34% bee's wax, then how much bee's wax should be added to 33 pints of regular wax?

    **a.** 15 pints      **b.** 16 pints

    **c.** 17 pints      **d.** 18 pints

**14.** Javier drives his car 120 miles in one direction. He returns along the same route at double the speed in 2 hours less time. How fast was he going on the way out?

    **a.** 40 mph      **b.** 30 mph

    **c.** 60 mph      **d.** 50 mph

**15.** A contractor has two tractors. He knows that tractor A can dig a ditch in 30 minutes and tractor B can dig the same ditch in 70 minutes. How long would it take them to dig the ditch if they worked together?

    **a.** 15 minutes      **b.** 18 minutes

    **c.** 21 minutes      **d.** 25 minutes

**16.** A florist wants a flower arrangement to sell for $11. If the florist has 15 bunches of daisies, which sell for $7, then how many bunches of tulips should be added, if the tulips sell for $16.

    **a.** 10 bunches      **b.** 12 bunches

    **c.** 14 bunches      **d.** 16 bunches

**BM 1.** Venus is $6.724 \times 10^7$ miles from the sun. What is this number in standard notation?

a. 67,240,000      b. 6,724,000

c. 672,400,000      d. 6,724,000,000

**BM 2.** Which of the following expressions has a zero value?

a. 2 - 3 + 1      b. 1 + 2 + 3

c. 3 - 2 + 1      d. 1 - 3 - 2

**BM 3.** Teressa has worked on her degree 7 out of the last 10 years. What is the percentage of years she has worked on her degree?

a. 80%      b. 75%

c. 70%      d. 50%

**BM 4.** The price of a printer has decreased from $80.00 to $66.00. What is the percent of decrease?

a. 82.5%      b. 80%

c. 17.5%      d. 20%

**BM 5.** Joe bought a tractor for $380.00 and later sold it for a 20% profit. How much did Joe sell the tractor for?

a. $660.00      b. $456.00

c. $470.00      d. $387.60

**BM 6.** Multiply. $2^{-3} \cdot 2^{-4}$

a. $2^{-7}$      b. $4^{-7}$

c. $8^{-7}$      d. 2

**BM 7.** What is $\dfrac{3}{4} + \dfrac{2}{3}$ ?

a. $\dfrac{5}{12}$      b. $\dfrac{17}{12}$

c. $\dfrac{17}{7}$      d. $\dfrac{5}{7}$

**BM 8.** $(7^2 \cdot 9^8)^3 =$

a. $7^6 \cdot 9^{24}$      b. $7^5 \cdot 9^{11}$

c. $7^6 \cdot 9^{11}$      d. $7^5 \cdot 9^{24}$

**BM 9.** The square root of 246 is between

a. 14 and 15      b. 15 and 16

c. 16 and 17      d. 17 and 18

**BM 10.** What is the absolute value of 100?

a. 10      b. -100

c. 100      d. $\dfrac{-1}{10}$

**BM 11.** Find the Mean of the following four numbers: 3, 4, 5, and 8.

a. 4      b. 4.5

c. 20      d. 5

**BM 12.** The table below shows the quiz scores for four students. Which student had the third lowest quiz score?

|       | Q1 | Q2 | Q3 | Q4 | Q5 | Q6 |
|-------|----|----|----|----|----|----|
| Hien  | 7  | 6  | 5  | 5  | 6  | 1  |
| Myles | 8  | 9  | 0  | 6  | 8  | 9  |
| Ida   | 9  | 5  | 7  | 8  | 4  | 8  |
| Jaime | 8  | 10 | 9  | 7  | 10 | 9  |

a. Hien   b. Myles

c. Ida    d. Jaime

**BM 13.** Each letter of the word ALGEBRA is on its own note card, lying face down on a desk. If you pick up one note card, what is the probability it will be the letter A?

a. $\dfrac{1}{2}$   b. $\dfrac{3}{4}$

c. $\dfrac{2}{7}$   d. $\dfrac{1}{3}$

**BM 14.** A classroom raffle contains the names of 20 students. If there are 12 females and 8 males in the class, what is the probability that the name selected will not be a male?

a. $\dfrac{1}{2}$   b. $\dfrac{2}{5}$

c. $\dfrac{2}{3}$   d. $\dfrac{3}{5}$

**BM 15.** Philip's **event** will list the **outcomes** of drawing two cards from a complete deck of 52 cards. Philip will draw the first card and then, without putting the first card back in the deck, he will draw the second card. Which of the following best describes Philip's event?

a. Independent

b. Dependent

c. Need more information to determine independence or dependence.

d. If Philip draws two hearts in a row, he should get a different deck of cards.

**BM 16.** A teacher drew the following circle graph to represent the number of siblings of his thirty-four students.

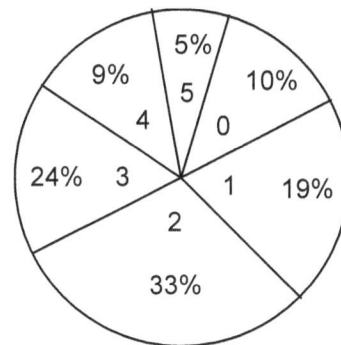

Use the pie chart above to determine which statement is true?

a. About five students have five siblings.

b. About eleven students have two siblings.

c. About ten students have three siblings.

d. About five students are only children.

**BM 17.** The below scatter plot appears to be what type of correlation?

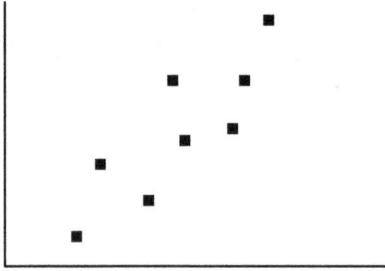

a.   Strong Positive Correlation

b.   Zero Correlation

c.   Weak Positive Correlation

d.   Weak Negative Correlation

**BM 18.** Rosa slept for 10,800 seconds. How many <u>hours</u> did Rosa sleep?

**a.** 2.5          **b.** 3.0

**c.** 3.5          **d.** 4.0

**BM 19.** The scale drawing of the football field shown below is drawn using a scale of 1 inch (in.) = 80 feet (ft).

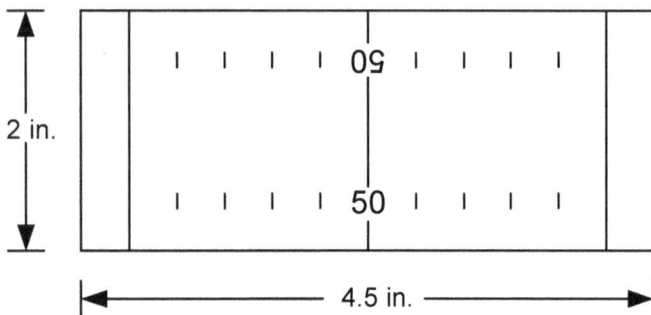

What is the width of the field in feet?

**a.** 132 ft          **b.** 144 ft

**c.** 152 ft          **d.** 160 ft

**BM 20.** An electrician estimates that a new job will take one person 60 hours to complete. If two people work on the job and they each work 6-hour days, how many days are needed to complete the job?

**a.** 2          **b.** 3

**c.** 4          **d.** 5

**BM 21.**

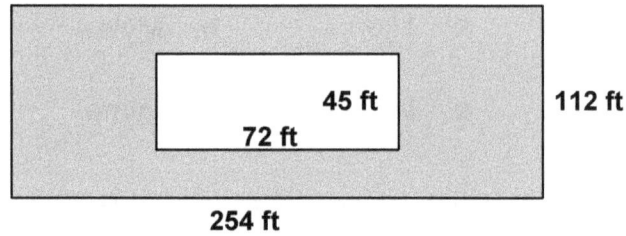

A rectangular pool 72 feet by 45 feet is on a rectangular lot 254 feet by 112 feet. The rest of the lot is grass. Approximately how many square feet is grass?

**a.** 2,300          **b.** 25,200

**c.** 2,500          **d.** 27,900

**BM 22.**

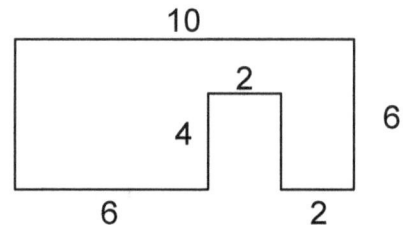

In the figure shown above, all the corners form right angles. What is the area of the figure in square units?

**a.** 78          **b.** 64

**c.** 52          **d.** 44

**BM 23.** The two circles below have a diameter as indicated. Find the scale factor of circle 1 to circle 2.

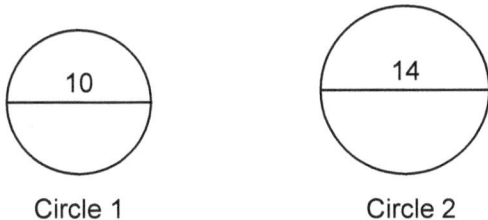

Circle 1          Circle 2

**a.** $\dfrac{5}{7}$          **b.** $\dfrac{2}{1}$

**c.** $\dfrac{7}{5}$          **d.** $\dfrac{1}{2}$

**BM 24.** One cubic foot is equal to approximately 7.5 gallons. How many gallons of milk can "the farmer in the dell" put in a tank that is 3 ft x 5 ft x 6 ft?

**a.** 90 gallons          **b.** 180 gallons

**c.** 12 gallons          **d.** 675 gallons

**BM 25.** Suppose that point A(1, -1) will be moved right two units and up three units. Which of the following are the coordinates of A'?

**a.** A'(3, 2)          **b.** A'(2, 3)

**c.** A'(-3, 2)          **d.** A'(3, 3)

**BM 26.** Which of the following does not satisfy the Pythagorean Theorem?

**a.** Let a = 16, b = 30, and c = 34

**b.** Let a = 24, b = 7, and c = 25

**c.** Let a = $\sqrt{6}$, b = $\sqrt{5}$, and c = $\sqrt{11}$

**d.** Let a = $\dfrac{1}{2}$, b = $\dfrac{1}{6}$, and c = $\dfrac{2}{3}$

**BM 27.** Right triangle ABC is congruent to right triangle PQR. If the length of the sides, in units, are p = 7, q = 24, and r = 25, then which statement below is false?

**a.** Side a = 7.

**b.** Side b = 25

**c.** The measure of angle R is equal to the measure of angle C.

**d.** The perimeter of triangle ABC is equal to the perimeter of triangle PQR.

**BM 28.** A store owner has x pounds of flour in stock. She receives 25 pounds and then sells a new shipment of 50 pounds. Which expression represents the weight of the flour she now has?

**a.** x - 25 - 50          **b.** x - 25 + 50

**c.** x - 50 - 25          **d.** x + 25 - 50

**BM 29.** If s = 11 and t = 5, then 2s(t - 4)=

**a.** 19          **b.** 18

**c.** 22          **d.** 26

**BM 30.**

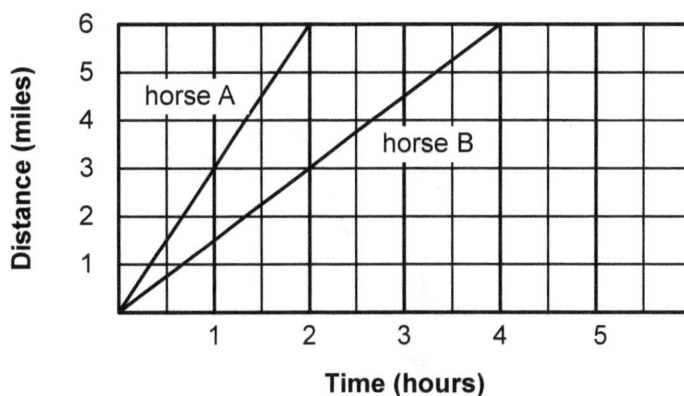

After two hours of racing, horse A is about how many miles ahead of horse B?

**a.** 2          **b.** 4

**c.** 3          **d.** 6

223

**BM 31.** $c^3d^6 =$

    **a.** cccdddddd          **b.** $(cd)^9$

    **c.** 9cd               **d.** ccccccddd

**BM 32.** $\sqrt{36x^2} =$

    **a.** 6x               **b.** 36x

    **c.** $6x^2$            **d.** $36x^2$

**BM 33.** Which of the following is the graph of $y = 3x^2$?

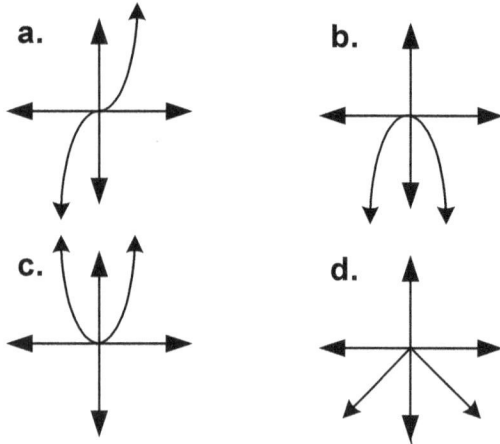

**BM 34.** What is the equation of the graph shown below?

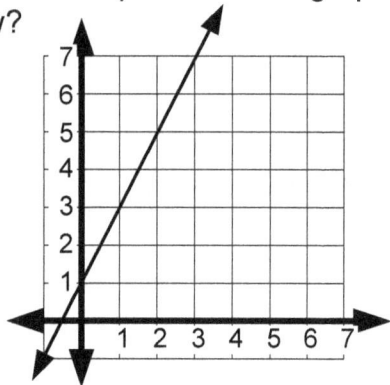

    **a.** y = 2x + 1          **b.** y = 2x - 1

    **c.** y = 2x - 2          **d.** y = 2x + 2

**BM 35.** The graph below shows Mai Lia's phone bill for three different months. What is the price per minute for Mai Lia's phone?

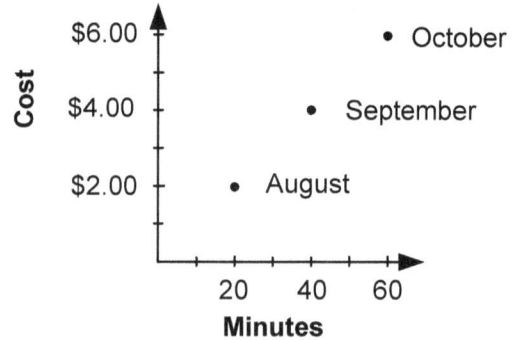

    **a.** $0.10          **b.** $0.20

    **c.** $2.50          **d.** $5.00

**BM 36.** Solve for w.      4w + 3 < 31

    **a.** w < 6          **b.** w < 7

    **c.** w < 8          **d.** w < 9

**BM 37.** Teresa is writing a 384 page paper. During the past 3 weeks she has written 128 pages. If she continues writing at the same rate, how many more weeks will it take her to complete the paper?

    **a.** 5              **b.** 6

    **c.** 9              **d.** 11

**BM 38.**

Lilian went to the football game. Her ticket cost $2.00. Her two drinks cost $1.25 each and the hot-dog was $1.50.

Based upon the story in the box above, which information is irrelevant if you had to answer the following question "How much did Lilian spend on drinks?"

a. Ticket and hot-dog cost.

b. Ticket cost and the fact that she had two drinks.

c. Hot-dog cost and the fact that she had two drinks.

d. All the information is required to answer the question.

**BM 39.** If n is an even number, then which statement is true for n + 1?

a. n + 1 is less than n.

b. n + 1 is an odd number.

c. n + 1 is an even number.

d. None of the statements above are true.

**BM 40.** Chue wants to approximate his bill before he gets to the cashier to pay. The items are marked in dollars: 4.89 , 3.29 , 6.99 , 2.39, and 7.75. Determine which expression is the best estimate for Chue's cost.

a. 4.00 + 3.00 + 7.00 + 2.00 + 8.00

b. 4.00 + 3.00 + 7.00 + 2.00 + 7.00

c. 5.00 + 3.00 + 7.00 + 2.00 + 7.00

d. 5.00 + 3.00 + 7.00 + 2.00 + 8.00

**BM 41.** The number of different breads carried by four stores is shown in the below graph. Estimate the total number of breads.

a. 65  b. 70

c. 75  d. 80

**BM 42.** If the figure is not a rectangle, then it is not a square. Which conclusion can you claim below?

a. If the figure is a rectangle, then it is not a square.

b. If it is not a square, then the figure is not a rectangle.

c. If the figure is a rectangle, then it is a square.

d. If it is a square, then the figure is a rectangle.

**BM 43.** A six sided number cube is rolled once, where success is rolling a 3. Which of the following experiments below would be most like this one in probability?

a. Flipping a fair coin, where success is the coin landing tails up.

b. Picking a card from a deck of cards, where success is drawing an Ace.

c. The letters of MATH on individual note cards, where success is drawing the M.

d. In a bag of 24 marbles, success is drawing one of the four red marbles.

**BM 44.** The perimeter, P, of a square may be found by using the formula $\frac{1}{4}P = \sqrt{A}$, where A is the area of the square. What is the perimeter of the square with an area of 144 square inches?

    **a.** 12 inches     **b.** 48 inches

    **c.** 22 inches     **d.** 54 inches

**BM 45.** If x is an integer, which of the following is the solution set for $2|x| = 18$?

    **a.** {-25, 9}     **b.** {-9, 25}

    **c.** {-9, 9}     **d.** {36}

**BM 46.** $\dfrac{5}{x} = \dfrac{9}{x + 4}$

Which of the following is equivalent to the equation shown above?

    **a.** $5x = 9x(x + 4)$     **b.** $5x = 9(x + 4)$

    **c.** $5 + x = 9x + 4$     **d.** $9x = 5(x + 4)$

**BM 47.** Solve for x.    $2(2x - 1) - x \geq 7$

    **a.** $x > -3$     **b.** $x \geq -4$

    **c.** $x \geq 3$     **d.** $-4 < x$

**BM 48.** Which of the following is the equation of

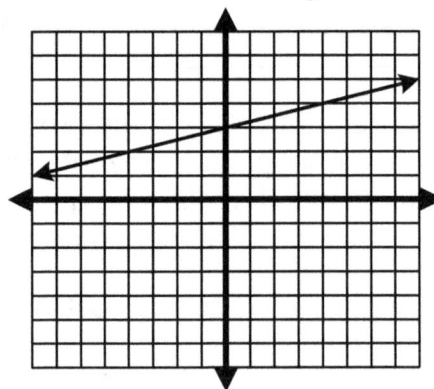

    **a.** $y = -4x - 3$     **b.** $y = \frac{1}{4}x + 3$

    **c.** $y = 4x + 3$     **d.** $y = -\frac{1}{4}x - 3$

**BM 49.** What are the coordinates of the the x-intercept of the line $2x + 6y = 12$?

    **a.** (2, 6)     **b.** (2, 0)

    **c.** (6, 2)     **d.** (6, 0)

**BM 50.** What is the slope of the line parallel to the line below?

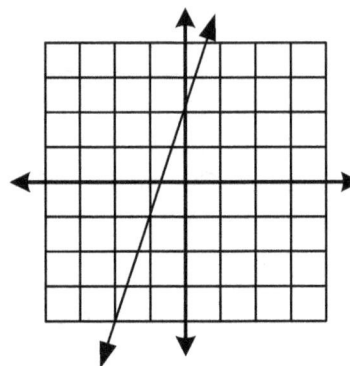

    **a.** 3     **b.** -3

    **c.** $\dfrac{1}{3}$     **d.** $\dfrac{-1}{3}$

**BM 51.** Which graph represents the system of equations shown below?

$$\begin{cases} y = x \\ y = -x + 4 \end{cases}$$

**a.**

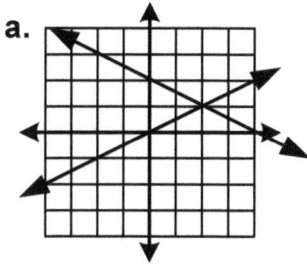

**b.**

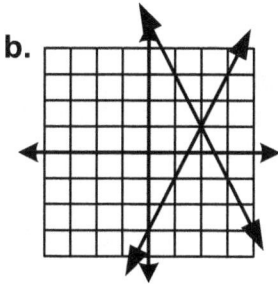

**c.**

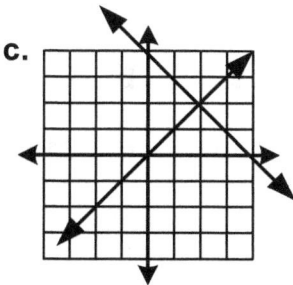

**d.**

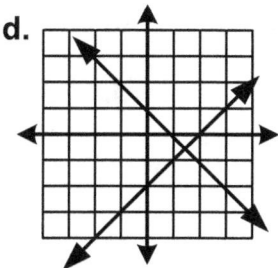

**BM 52.**

x + 4

x

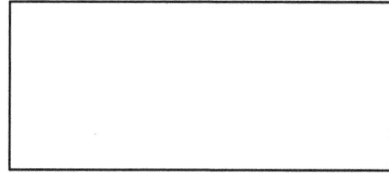

The length of the rectangle above is 4 units longer than the width. Which expression could be used to represent the area of the rectangle?

**a.** $x^2 + 4x$       **b.** $2x + 4$

**c.** $x^2 - 4x$       **d.** $6x$

**BM 53.** A plumber finds that Amos can complete a certain job in 30 hours and Bradley can complete the same job in 20 hours. How long would it take them to complete the job if they worked together?

**a.** 9 hours       **b.** 10 hours

**c.** 11 hours       **d.** 12 hours

**BM 1.** The diameter of an oxygen atom is $1.0 \times 10^{-8}$ mm. What is this number in standard notation?

a. 0.00000001          b. 0.0000001

c. 0.000001          d. 0.00000000001

**BM 2.** Which of the following expressions results in a positive number?

a. 1 + (-2)          b. -1 + 2

c. -1 - 2          d. -2 - 1

**BM 3.** If Lauren's dog Ginger has a cast on one of her four legs, what is the percentage of legs on which Ginger has a cast?

a. 90%          b. 25%

c. 75%          d. 65%

**BM 4.** The price of a hamburger has decreased from $1.00 to $0.50. What is the percent of decrease?

a. 10%          b. 50%

c. 30%          d. 25%

**BM 5.** A CD regularly sells for $22.00. It is on sale for 25% off. What is the sale price of the CD?

a. $11.00          b. $15.60

c. $17.00          d. $16.50

**BM 6.** Divide. $\dfrac{10^{-2}}{10^{-7}}$

a. $10^{-9}$          b. $10^5$

c. $10^{-5}$          d. $\dfrac{1}{10^5}$

**BM 7.** $\dfrac{8}{14} + \left( \dfrac{1}{2} - \dfrac{1}{7} \right) =$

a. $\dfrac{10}{14}$          b. $\dfrac{8}{23}$

c. $\dfrac{13}{14}$          d. $\dfrac{8}{9}$

**BM 8.** $(4^2)^3 =$

a. $4^5$          b. $16^6$

c. $8^3$          d. $4^6$

**BM 9.** The square of a <u>whole</u> number is between 1,400 and 1,500. The number must be between

a. 25 and 30          b. 30 and 35

c. 35 and 40          d. 40 and 45

**BM 10.** If $|x| = 9$, what is the value of x?

a. -9 or 9          b. -9 or 0

c. -9 or 1          d. -81 or 81

**BM 11.** At Jaimes's fund raiser, he collected checks for $12.00, $9.00, $13.00, $10.00, $8.00, and $12.00. What is the median value of the checks collected?

a. $12.00          b. $11.00

c. $5.00          d. $23.50

**BM 12.** Two-thirds of 24 students attended the field trip. Two of those who did not go on the field trip were female. Which of the following statements can be answered with the given information?

   **a.** How many males went on the field trip?

   **b.** How many males did not go on the field trip?

   **c.** How many females went on the field trip?

   **d.** How many females were suppose to go on the field trip?

**BM 13.** A classroom raffle contains the names of 20 students. If there are 12 females and 8 males in the class, what is the probability that the name selected will be a male?

   **a.** $\dfrac{1}{2}$      **b.** $\dfrac{3}{5}$

   **c.** $\dfrac{2}{3}$      **d.** $\dfrac{2}{5}$

**BM 14.**

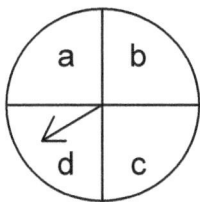

What is the probability that the spinner will not stop on c?

   **a.** $\dfrac{1}{2}$      **b.** $\dfrac{1}{4}$

   **c.** $\dfrac{3}{4}$      **d.** $\dfrac{2}{3}$

**BM 15.** Veronica's **event** will list the **outcomes** of flipping a fair coin five times. Which of the following best describes Veronica's event?

   **a.** Independent

   **b.** Dependent

   **c.** Need more information to determine independence or dependence.

   **d.** If Veronica's coin lands Tails up twice in a row, she should get a different coin.

**BM 16.** A certain drug company wants to market a new anti-depression drug. The bar graph below shows the results of testing.

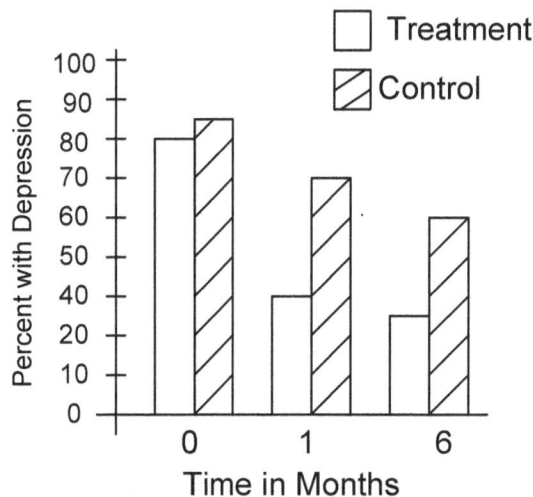

The Treatment group is the only group receiving the drug. Using the information displayed in the bar graph, determine which statement is true?

   **a.** At a certain point in time, all the participants had an 85% depression rate.

   **b.** The treatment group had an increase in depression over the six month study.

   **c.** At a certain point in time, the participants experienced similar rates of depression.

   **d.** Based upon the results of the six month study, the company should conclude that the drug is not working.

**BM 17.** A certain college has produced a scatter plot of their students income at age 25 as compared to the number of years that the student attended the college.

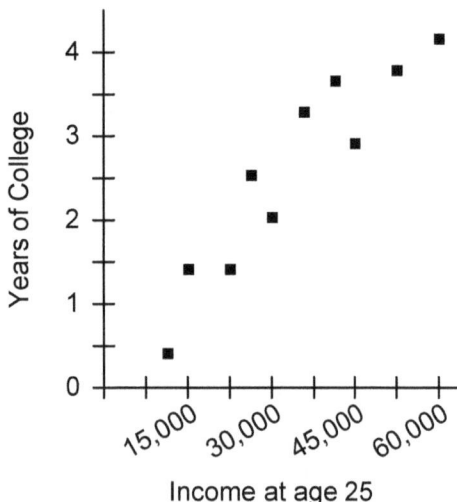

Income at age 25

Which statement best supports the data graphed on the scatter plot?

a. No correlation exists between years in college and income earned.

b. As the time in college increases, the future income earned decreases.

c. As the time in college decreases, the future income earned decreases.

d. As the time in college decreases, the future income earned increases.

**BM 18.** One meter is-

a. 100 centimeters      b. 100 millimeters

c. $\frac{1}{10}$ of a kilometer      d. 1,000 centimeters

**BM 19.** The actual width ($w$) of a rectangle is 20 inches (in.). Use the scale drawing of the rectangle to find the actual length ($l$).

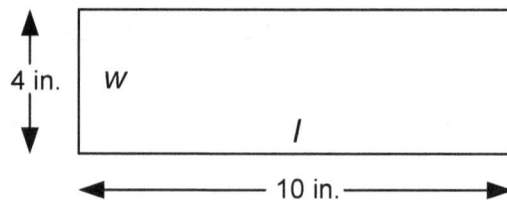

a. 30 in.      b. 40 in.

c. 50 in.      d. 60 in.

**BM 20.** One hundred and eighty miles per hour is the same as which of the following?

a. 3 miles per minute

b. 2 miles per minute

c. 6 miles per minute

d. 18 miles per minute

**BM 21.**

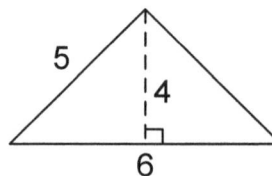

What is the area of the triangle shown above?

a. 10 square units      b. 12 square units

c. 8 square units      d. 6 square units

**BM 22.** What is the area of the shaded region in the figure shown below?

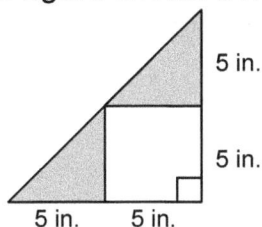

5 in.

5 in.

5 in.    5 in.

a. 10 in.²

b. 25 in.²

c. 50 in.²

d. 40 in.²

**BM 23.** Lor found the circumference of circle A to be $8\pi$ and the circumference of circle B to be $6\pi$. Which of the following is the scale factor of circle A to circle B?

a. $\dfrac{4}{3}$

b. $\dfrac{3}{4}$

c. $\dfrac{16}{9}$

d. $\dfrac{9}{16}$

**BM 24.** Tanisha knows that the area of her patio is 28 square yards. She needs to convert the area into square feet. If there are 9 square feet in one square yard, find the area of the patio in square feet.

a. 27 ft²

b. 81 ft²

c. 252 ft²

d. 9 ft²

**BM 25.** Suppose that point C(3, 2) will reflect about the y-axis. Which of the following are the coordinates of C'?

a. C'(6, 4)

b. C'(0, 0)

c. C'(-3, 2)

d. C'(-3, -2)

**BM 26.** In a right triangle, if a = 5 and b = 12, then c = ?

a. 11

b. 13

c. 15

d. 17

**BM 27.** Triangle LMN is congruent to triangle STU. If the measure of angle S = 36⁰, the measure of angle T = 70⁰ and the measure of angle U = 74⁰, then what is the measure of angle L?

a. 36⁰

b. 70⁰

c. 74⁰

d. 54⁰

**BM 28.** Which of the following inequalities represents the statement, "A number, x, decreased by 6 is less than or equal to 5?"

a. $6 - x > 5$

b. $x - 6 \le 5$

c. $x - 6 \ge 5$

d. $6 - x \le 5$

**BM 29.** If w = 2 and r = 3, then r(w + 5)=

a. 16

b. 9

c. 21

d. 27

**BM 30.** The cost of two internet providers, company A and company B, is shown on the graph below.

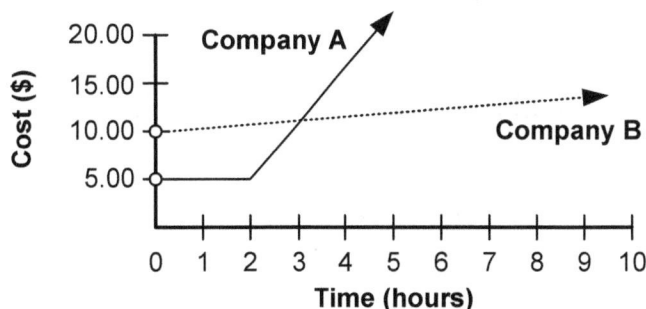

Company A is cheaper than company B for

a. more than 3 hours

b. 3 hours only

c. any amount of time

d. less than 3 hours

**BM 31.** What does $g^3$ equal when $g = -3$?

    **a.** $\dfrac{1}{9}$          **b.** -27

    **c.** -9          **d.** $\dfrac{1}{27}$

**BM 32.** $\sqrt{25x^6} =$

    **a.** $5x$          **b.** $5x^3$

    **c.** $25x$          **d.** $25x^6$

**BM 33.** Which of the following is the graph of $y = 5\,|x|$ ?

    **a.**          **b.**

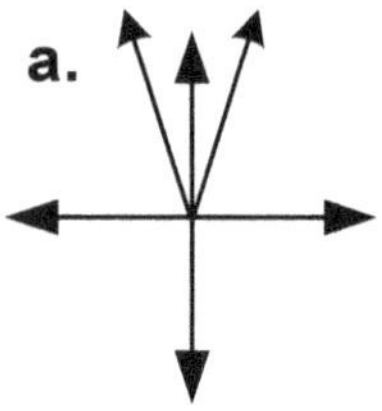

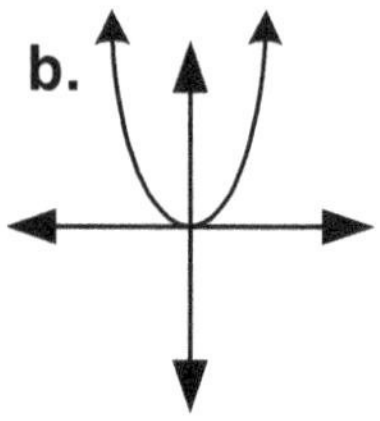

    **c.** 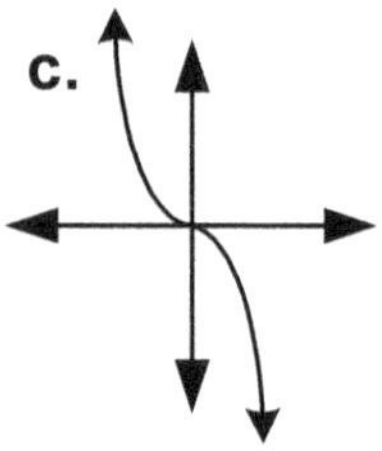          **d.**

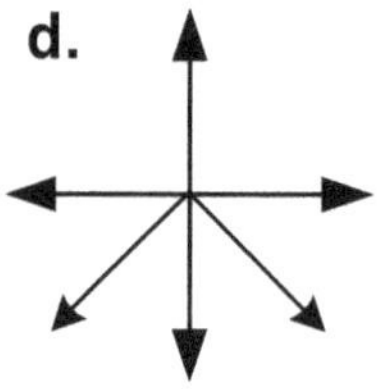

**BM 34.** What is the slope of the line below?

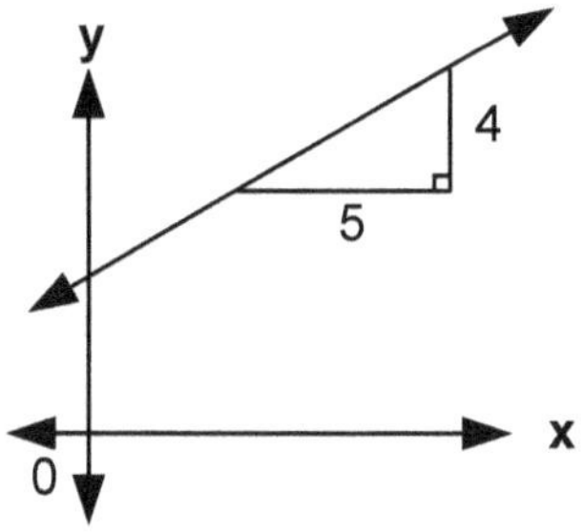

    **a.** $\dfrac{5}{4}$          **b.** $\dfrac{-4}{5}$

    **c.** $\dfrac{4}{5}$          **d.** $\dfrac{-5}{4}$

**BM 35.** The graph below shows Kayla's movie rental bill for three different months. What is the price per movie?

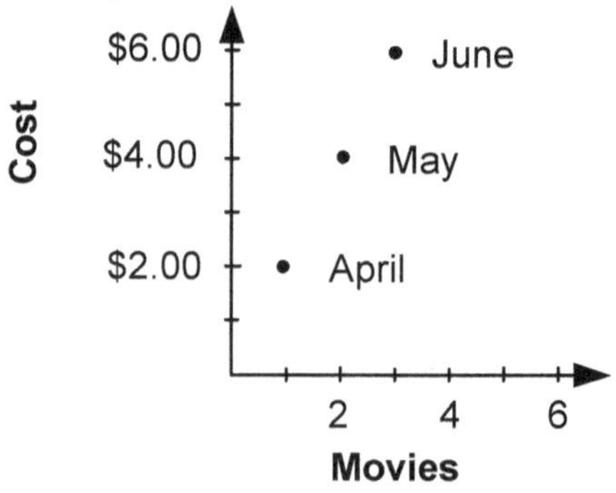

    **a.** $0.10          **b.** $0.20

    **c.** $2.00          **d.** $5.00

**BM 36.** In the inequality $3x + \$20{,}000 > \$50{,}000$, x represents the salary of part time employees in a music store. Which phrase most accurately describes the employee's salary?

    **a.** At least $10,000

    **b.** At most $10,000

    **c.** Less than $10,000

    **d.** More than $10,000

**BM 37.** Randy's toy truck travels at 20 inches per second (in/sec) at high speed and 12 in/sec at low speed. If the truck travels for 10 seconds at high speed and 20 seconds at low speed, what distance would the toy truck have traveled?

    **a.** 260 inches          **b.** 300 inches

    **c.** 400 inches          **d.** 440 inches

**BM 38.** Fou traveled for 3 hours to visit his grandmother who lived 120 miles away. Which computation below will provide Fou's average speed in miles per hour?

    **a.** Multiply 120 by 3.

    **b.** Multiply 3 by 120.

    **c.** Divide 120 by 3.

    **d.** Divide 3 by 120.

**BM 39.** If x is any real number, find a counterexample to the conjecture $x < x^2$.

    **a.** $\dfrac{-1}{4}$      **b.** $\dfrac{4}{3}$

    **c.** $1$      **d.** $\dfrac{-2}{3}$

**BM 40.** Which is the best estimate of 382 times 227?

    **a.** 800

    **b.** 8,000

    **c.** 80,000

    **d.** 800,000

**BM 41.** A company ships three different boxes of materials, where the weights of the boxes are not equal. See the graph below.

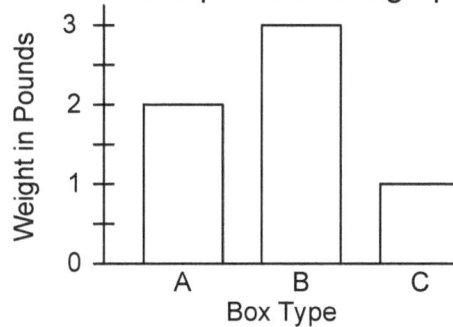

The company can ship at most 20 pounds. If the number of boxes must be 10, determine which combination of boxes will be at most 20 pounds.

    **a.** 5 of A; 2 of B; and 3 of C.

    **b.** 6 of A; 1 of B; and 3 of C.

    **c.** 4 of A; 3 of B; and 3 of C.

    **d.** 4 of A; 4 of B; and 2 of C.

**BM 42.** The table below shows the input values and the corresponding output values. Determine the missing input value.

| Input | Output |
|-------|--------|
| 2 | 6 |
| 5 | 15 |
| 8 | 24 |
| ? | 33 |

    **a.** 9

    **b.** 10

    **c.** 11

    **d.** 12

**BM 43.** In Geometry, we know that a circle is an ellipses with a congruent major and minor axes. Determine which figures below are most alike.

    **a.** A Triangle is a Pentagon.

    **b.** A Square is a Triangle.

    **c.** A Square is a Trapezoid.

    **d.** A Square is a Rectangle.

233

**BM 44.** If x = -15, then -x =

    **a.** $\frac{1}{15}$         **b.** $\frac{-1}{15}$

    **c.** $\frac{1}{-15}$         **d.** 15

**BM 45.** If x is an integer, what is the solution to |x + 1| < 1?

    **a.** {0}         **b.** {-1}

    **c.** {-2, -1, 0, 1}     **d.** {2}

**BM 46.** Which of the following is equivalent to 4(x + 5) - 6(x - 2) = 16?

    **a.** 4x + 5 - 6x + 12 = 16

    **b.** 4x + 20 - 6x - 12 = 16

    **c.** 4x + 20 - 6x + 12 = 16

    **d.** 4x + 20 - 6x - 2 = 16

**BM 47.** Kia solved the equation 5(2x + 9) = 25 using the following steps.

    **Given :**     5(2x + 9) = 25
    **Step 1:**     10x + 45 = 25
    **Step 2:**     10x = -20
    **Step 3:**     x = -2

    To get from Step 2 to Step 3, Kia-

    **a.** multiplied both sides by 10.
    **b.** added 45 to both sides.
    **c.** divided both sides by 10.
    **d.** subtracted 45 from both sides.

**BM 48.** Which of the following is the graph of y = -3x + 1 ?

**a.**

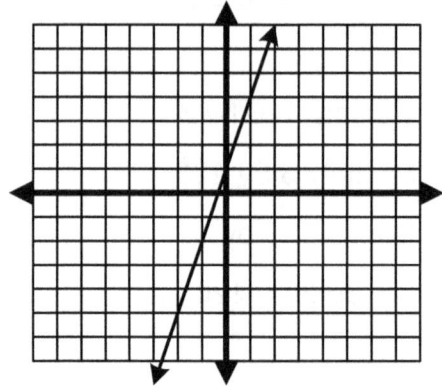

**b.**

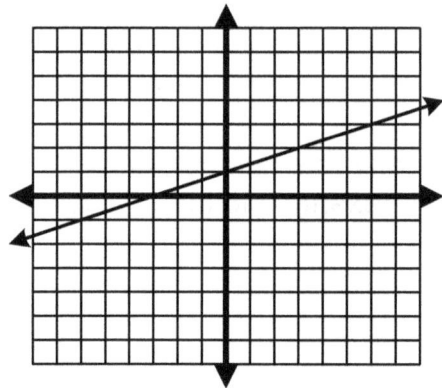

**c.**

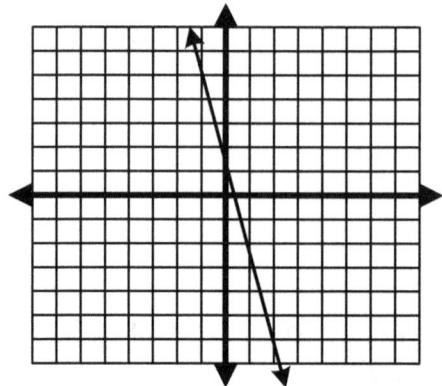

**d.**

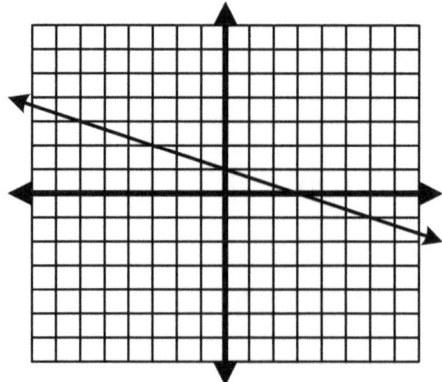

**BM 49.** Which of the following points lies on the line 3x + 2y = 6?

    **a.** (0, 2)

    **b.** (2, 3)

    **c.** (2, 0)

    **d.** (3, 0)

**BM 50.** What is the slope of the line perpendicular to the line $y = \frac{-8}{3}x + 2$?

    **a.** $\frac{8}{3}$

    **b.** -2

    **c.** $\frac{3}{8}$

    **d.** $\frac{-3}{8}$

**BM 51.**
$$\begin{cases} x - 2y = -1 \\ -x + y = -3 \end{cases}$$

What is the solution to the system of equations shown above?

    **a.** (7, -4)

    **b.** (7, 0)

    **c.** (0, 4)

    **d.** (7, 4)

**BM 52.** Simplify. $\dfrac{10x^3 - 5x^2 + 15x}{5x}$

    **a.** $2x^2 - x - 3$

    **b.** $2x^2 - x + 3$

    **c.** $2x^2 - 5x - 3$

    **d.** $3x^2 - x - 3$

**BM 53.** How much 85% hydrochloric acid should a chemist add to 3 liters of 25% hydrochloric acid to obtain a new mixture of 45% hydrochloric acid?

    **a.** 0.5 liters

    **b.** 1 liters

    **c.** 1.5 liters

    **d.** 2 liters

**BM 1.** The estimated population of China is 1,370,000,000. What is this number in scientific notation?

    **a.** $1.37 \times 10^7$      **b.** $1.4 \times 10^9$

    **c.** $1.37 \times 10^8$      **d.** $1.37 \times 10^9$

**BM 2.** Which of the following expressions results in a negative number?

    **a.** 5 - 4 + 3      **b.** -5 - (-4) + 3

    **c.** 3 - 4 + 5      **d.** 5 - 4 - 3

**BM 3.** Senator Haddeman won 6 out of his 8 districts in the last election. What percentage of districts did he win?

    **a.** 75%      **b.** 90%

    **c.** 50%      **d.** 85%

**BM 4.** The price of a plane ticket has increased from $50.00 to $57.50. What is the percent of increase?

    **a.** 15%      **b.** 25%

    **c.** 7.5%      **d.** 35%

**BM 5.** A sales person at a clothing store earns a 5% commission on all sales. How much commission does the sales person earn on a $200.00 sale?

    **a.** $12.00      **b.** $10.00

    **c.** $18.50      **d.** $17.50

**BM 6.** Which number equals $5^{-2}$?

    **a.** $\dfrac{1}{25}$      **b.** $\dfrac{1}{10}$

    **c.** -10      **d.** $\dfrac{-1}{25}$

**BM 7.** Which of the following is the prime factored form of the lowest common denominator of $\dfrac{2}{5} - \dfrac{3}{8}$ ?

    **a.** $2 \cdot 2 \cdot 2 \cdot 5$      **b.** $2 \cdot 2 \cdot 3 \cdot 5$

    **c.** $5 \cdot 1$      **d.** $4 \cdot 2$

**BM 8.** $\left(\dfrac{3^4}{5^6}\right)^2 =$

    **a.** $\dfrac{3^6}{5^8}$      **b.** $\left(\dfrac{12}{30}\right)^2$

    **c.** $\dfrac{3^8}{5^{12}}$      **d.** $5^2$

**BM 9.** The square of a <u>whole</u> number is between 1,600 and 1,700. The number must be between

    **a.** 25 and 30      **b.** 30 and 35

    **c.** 35 and 40      **d.** 40 and 45

**BM 10.** What is the absolute value of -7?

    **a.** $\dfrac{1}{7}$      **b.** $\dfrac{-1}{7}$

    **c.** -7      **d.** 7

**BM 11.** Davion compared the prices for a certain birthday gift. See the box below.

| $11.00, $8.00, $10.00, $13.00, $15.00, $10.00 |
|---|

What is the mode of the data?

    **a.** $10.00      **b.** $7.00

    **c.** $10.50      **d.** $11.00

**BM 12.** A family wanted to look at their expenses for a year.

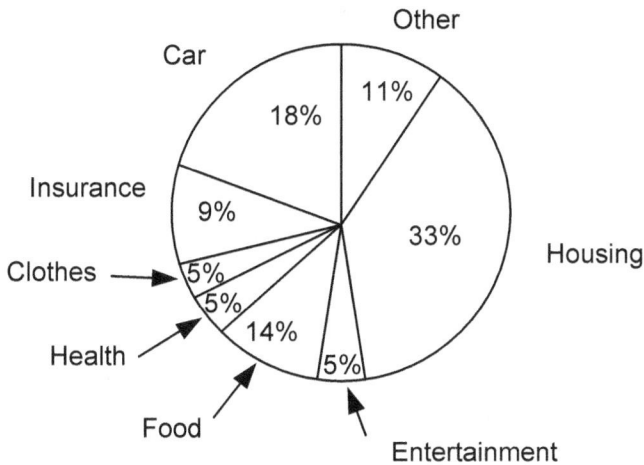

According to the circle graph shown -

a. Food and Car expenses combined are the greatest expenses.

b. Housing is approximately one-third of the total budget.

c. More than one-half of the expenses are Insurance, Other, Entertainment, Health, and Car combined.

d. Health and Car expenses combined are more than Food and Other combined.

**BM 13.** What is the probability of flipping a quarter and it lands heads up?

a. $\frac{1}{2}$          b. $\frac{1}{4}$

c. $\frac{1}{3}$          d. $\frac{2}{3}$

**BM 14.** If a fair number cube is rolled once, what is the probability of not getting a one?

a. $\frac{1}{6}$          b. $\frac{1}{2}$

c. $\frac{5}{6}$          d. $\frac{1}{3}$

**BM 15.** A bag contains 5 green marbles, 4 orange marbles, and 2 yellow marbles. What is the theoretical probability that two orange marbles will be drawn at the same time?

a. $\frac{1}{5}$          b. $\frac{6}{55}$

c. $\frac{4}{11}$          d. $\frac{3}{10}$

**BM 16.** The table below represents the enrollment cost and monthly cost of a cell phone for four companies. If the number of minutes is the same for each plan, which company would cost the least for one year?

| Company | Enrollment Cost | Monthly Cost |
|---------|-----------------|--------------|
| 1 | 110 | 65 |
| 2 | 140 | 60 |
| 3 | 130 | 55 |
| 4 | 150 | 50 |

a. 1          b. 2

c. 3          d. 4

**BM 17.** A doctor has ordered a glucose tolerance test to check the patient for diabetes. After an initial blood test, the patient drinks 75 grams of a glucose solution and the blood is drawn at regular intervals. The scatter plot below is the result of the data collected.

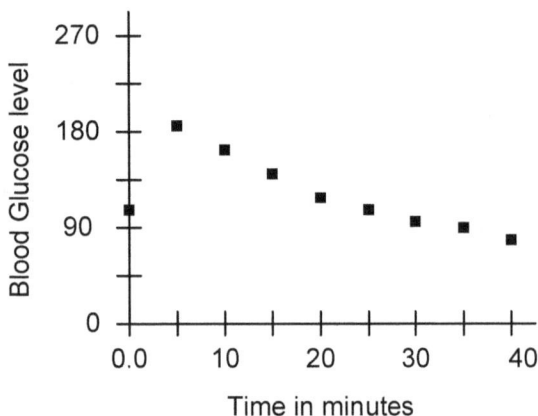

Which statement best supports the data graphed on the scatter plot?

a. Not counting the initial test, as the time increases, the blood glucose increases.

b. Not counting the initial test, as the time increases, the blood glucose decreases.

c. Not counting the initial test, there does not appear to be any correlation between the data.

d. Not counting the initial test, the blood glucose remains constant as the time increases.

**BM 18.** Chandra ran for one hour and 30 minutes. How many <u>seconds</u> did Chandra run?

a. 4,500          b. 5,400

c. 6,300          d. 7,200

**BM 19.** The scale drawing of the soccer field shown below is drawn using a scale of 1 inch (in.) = 30 yards (yd).

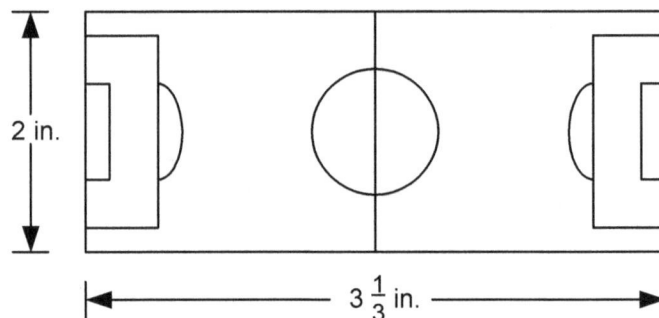

What is the length of the field in yards?

a. 100 yd          b. 120 yd

c. 140 yd          d. 160 yd

**BM 20.** Matt can read about 25 words per minute. If he reads at this rate for 35 minutes without stopping, about how many words will he read?

a. 825          b. 850

c. 875          d. 900

**BM 21.**

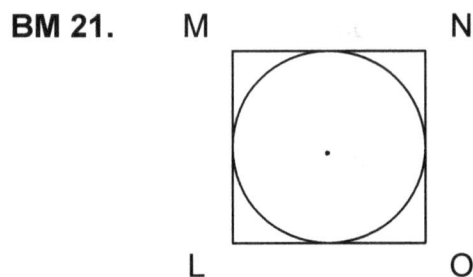

In the figure above, the radius of the inscribed circle is 10 inches (in.). What is the perimeter of the square LMNO?

a. $100\pi$ in.          b. $80\pi$ in.

c. 100 in.          d. 80 in.

**BM 22.** A right triangle is removed from a rectangle as shown in the figure below. Find the area of the remaining part of the rectangle.

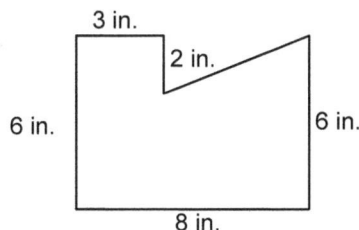

3 in.

2 in.

6 in.          6 in.

8 in.

**a.** 61 in.$^2$          **b.** 52 in.$^2$

**c.** 47 in.$^2$          **d.** 43 in.$^2$

**BM 23.** Thao has computed the scale factor between two similar figures to be two-thirds. She wants to convert the scale factor to find Surface Area and Volume respectively. Which of the following are the correct conversions for the scale factor?

**a.** $\frac{2}{3}$ and $\frac{4}{9}$          **b.** $\frac{4}{9}$ and $\frac{8}{27}$

**c.** $\frac{2}{3}$ and $\frac{8}{27}$          **d.** $\frac{2}{9}$ and $\frac{8}{9}$

**BM 24.** The height of a horse is measured in hands. If one hand equals 4 inches, find the height of a horse (in feet) that is 18 hands tall.

**a.** 72 in.          **b.** 5.5 ft

**c.** 6 ft          **d.** 6.5 ft

**BM 25.**

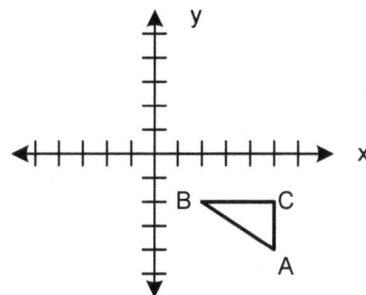

Which of the following triangles A'B'C' is the image of triangle ABC that results from reflecting triangle ABC across the x-axis?

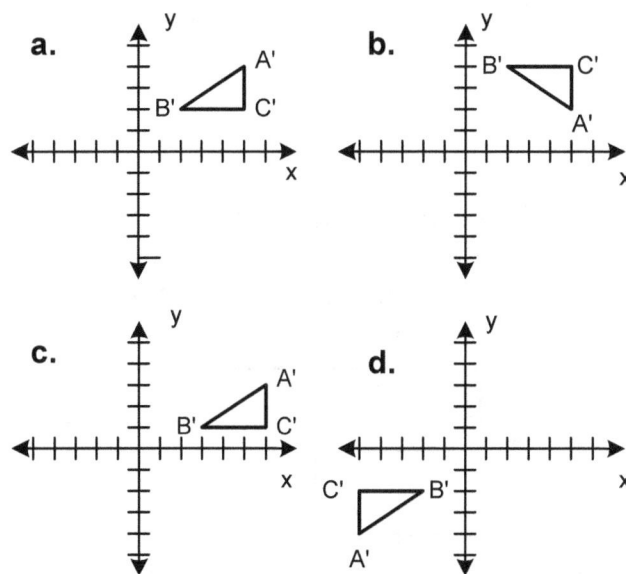

**a.**

**b.**

**c.**

**d.**

**BM 26.** In a right triangle, if the length of one leg equals 8 and and the length of the other leg equals 15, what is the length of the hypotenuse?

**a.** 15          **b.** 16

**c.** 17          **d.** 18

**BM 27.** If triangle ABC is congruent to triangle PQR, then which of the following is false?

**a.** Angle B is congruent to angle Q.

**b.** Side $\overline{AB}$ is congruent to side $\overline{PQ}$.

**c.** Angle C is congruent to angle P.

**d.** Side $\overline{PR}$ is congruent to side $\overline{AC}$.

239

**BM 28.** Multiply a number by 2 and subtract 10 from the result. The answer is 24. Which of the following equations matches these statements?

    **a.** $2x - 24 = 10$      **b.** $2x - 10 = 24$

    **c.** $2x + 10 = 24$      **d.** $2x + 24 = 10$

**BM 29.** If $w = 10$ and $x = 4$, then $\dfrac{4wx}{80} - 1 =$

    **a.** 8            **b.** 5

    **c.** 21          **d.** 1

**BM 30.** The graph below shows the relationship between the number of people at the park with the number of hot dogs sold at a certain stand.

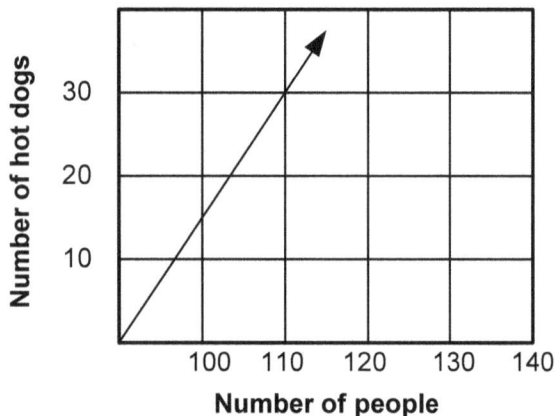

What is the approximate number of hot dogs sold when 110 people are at the park?

    **a.** 50          **b.** 20

    **c.** 40          **d.** 30

**BM 31.** Simplify the expression shown below.

$$(7ab^2c)(2a^3bc)$$

    **a.** $14a^2b^3c^4$      **b.** $49a^4b^3c^2$

    **c.** $49a^2b^3c^4$      **d.** $14a^4b^3c^2$

**BM 32.** $\sqrt{196w^{14}} =$

    **a.** $196w^7$       **b.** $14w$

    **c.** $14w^7$        **d.** $14w^{14}$

**BM 33.** Which of the following is the graph of $y = -|x|$ ?

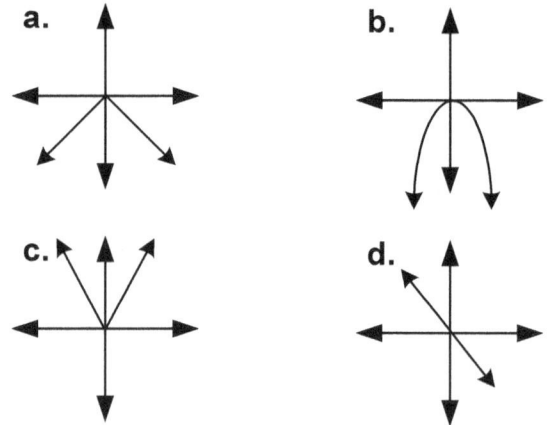

**BM 34.** The slope of the line shown below is $\dfrac{3}{5}$.

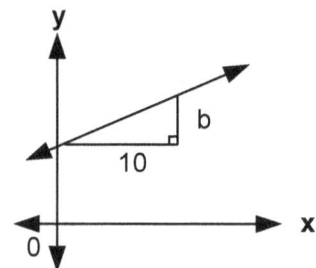

What is the value of b?

    **a.** 6           **b.** 3

    **c.** 8           **d.** 5

**BM 35.** The graph below shows Marquette's gasoline bill for three different months. What is the price per gallon for gasoline?

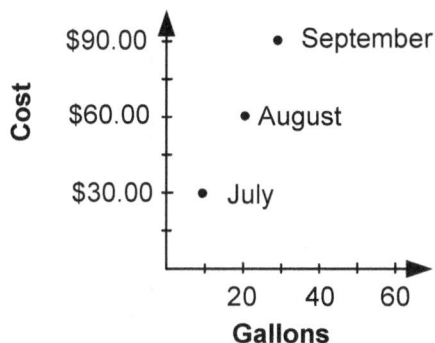

   **a.** $0.33        **b.** $3.00

   **c.** $5.00        **d.** $7.50

**BM 36.** Solve for x.     $3x - 10 = 20$

   **a.** 10        **b.** 13

   **c.** -10        **d.** -13

**BM 37.** Jim can paddle his kayak 2 miles in 30 minutes. At this rate, how many miles can he paddle in 45 minutes?

   **a.** 2.5        **b.** 2.75

   **c.** 3        **d.** 3.25

**BM 38.** If you divide a number by 3, add 4, multiply by 2, and subtract 5, the result is the number you started with. What is the number?

   **a.** 3        **b.** 9

   **c.** 6        **d.** 12

**BM 39.** A Perfect Number is equal to the sum of its divisors, not including the number itself. Example: $6 = 1 + 2 + 3$. Vanpou claims that there exists another Perfect Number. Which example below supports his conjecture?

   **a.** 12        **b.** 18

   **c.** 20        **d.** 28

**BM 40.** What is the best estimate for the square root of 80.7?

   **a.** 8        **b.** 9

   **c.** 10        **d.** 11

**BM 41.** Estimate the area of the figure.

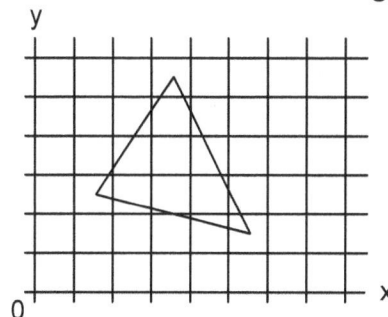

   **a.** 5 square units   **b.** 7 square units

   **c.** 9 square units   **d.** 11 square units

**BM 42.** Determine a number that is less than 40, with factors 2, 3, and 5.

   **a.** 20        **b.** 30

   **c.** 15        **d.** 10

**BM 43.** Factorial (!) is just multiplication of every integer, including the number in question, down to one. For example, three factorial is written as:
$$3! = 3 * 2 * 1.$$

Which of the following would represent five factorial?

   **a.** $5! = 5 * 4 * 3 * 2 * 1$

   **b.** $5! = 4 * 3 * 2 * 1$

   **c.** $5! = 5 * 3 * 2 * 1$

   **d.** $5! = 5 * 4 * 2 * 1$

**BM 44.** What is the reciprocal of $\dfrac{wx}{z}$ ?

    **a.** $\dfrac{z}{wx}$         **b.** $\dfrac{-z}{wx}$

    **c.** $\dfrac{-wx}{z}$         **d.** $\dfrac{x}{wz}$

**BM 45.** If x is an integer, what is the solution to $|x - 1| < 4$?

    **a.** {-2, -1, 0, 1, 2, 3, 4}     **b.** {-5}

    **c.** {-1, 0, 1, 2, 3}         **d.** {5}

**BM 46.** Which of the following is equivalent to $9 - 6x > 6(x + 1)$?

    **a.** $3 > 12x$         **b.** $3x < 12$

    **c.** $-3 > 12x$        **d.** $-3x \geq -12$

**BM 47.** Solve for x.   $3(5x + 9) - 14x = 11$

    **a.** $x = -16$        **b.** $x = 16$

    **c.** $x = -11$        **d.** $x = -7$

**BM 48.** Which of the following is the graph of $y = 2x - 1$ ?

**a.**

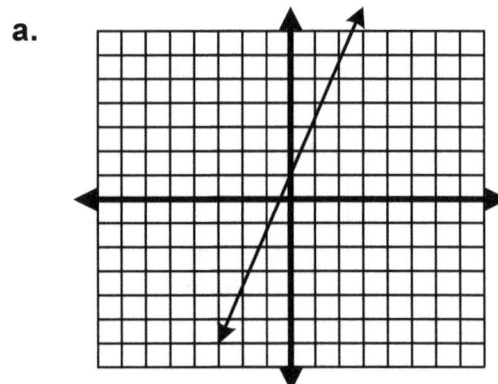

**b.**

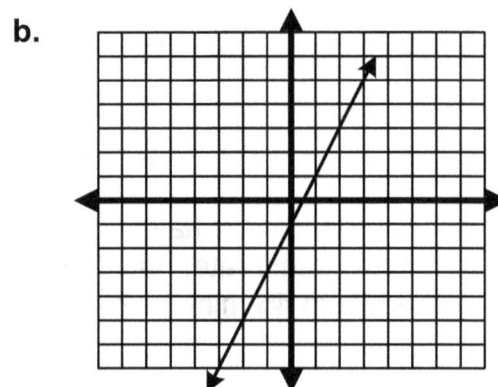

**c.**

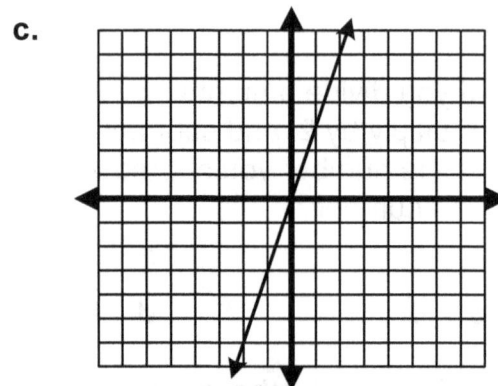

**d.**

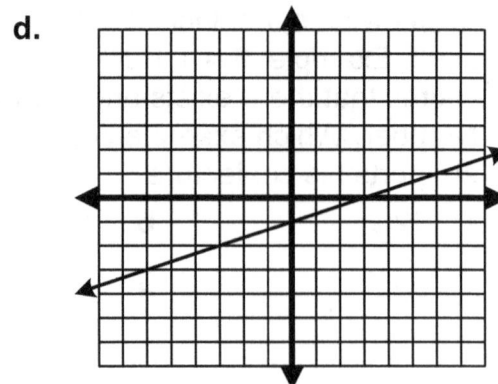

**BM 49.** What are the coordinates of the the y-intercept of the line x + 4y = 4?

   **a.** (0, 4)

   **b.** (0, 1)

   **c.** (4, 0)

   **d.** (1, 0)

**BM 50.** Which of the following statements describes parallel lines?

   **a.** opposite slopes, same y-intercepts

   **b.** opposite x-intercepts, same y-intercepts

   **c.** never intersect

   **d.** same x-intercepts, different slopes

**BM 51.** Which graph represents the system of equations shown below?

$$\begin{cases} y = -x + 1 \\ y = -2x + 4 \end{cases}$$

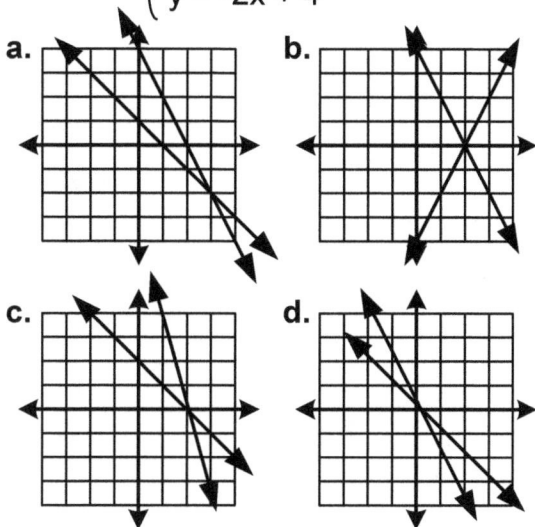

**BM 52.** Simplify. $(x^2 - 3x + 1) - (x^2 - x - 6)$

   **a.** -4x - 5

   **b.** -3x + 7

   **c.** $2x^2 - 4x - 5$

   **d.** -2x + 7

**BM 53.** Javier drives his car 120 miles in one direction. He returns along the same route at double the speed in 2 hours less time. How fast was he going on the way out?

   **a.** 40 mph

   **b.** 30 mph

   **c.** 60 mph

   **d.** 50 mph

# CAHSEE Bench Mark Unit 1 Answers
## (Bench Mark Practice 1-5 and Unit 1 Exam)

## CAHSEE Bench Mark Practice 1 Answers

| | | | |
|---|---|---|---|
| 1. b | 6. a | 11. b | 16. b |
| 2. a | 7. b | 12. d | 17. a |
| 3. d | 8. a | 13. c | 18. c |
| 4. c | 9. d | 14. d | 19. b |
| 5. d | 10. c | 15. a | 20. a |

## CAHSEE Bench Mark Practice 2 Answers

| | | | |
|---|---|---|---|
| 1. a | 6. d | 11. a | 16. d |
| 2. d | 7. c | 12. d | 17. d |
| 3. b | 8. b | 13. d | 18. c |
| 4. b | 9. b | 14. c | 19. a |
| 5. b | 10. d | 15. c | 20. a |

## CAHSEE Bench Mark Practice 3 Answers

| | | | |
|---|---|---|---|
| 1. d | 6. a | 11. a | 16. a |
| 2. a | 7. b | 12. b | 17. c |
| 3. a | 8. d | 13. d | 18. b |
| 4. c | 9. c | 14. a | 19. a |
| 5. d | 10. d | 15. c | 20. a |

## CAHSEE Bench Mark Practice 4 Answers

| | | | |
|---|---|---|---|
| 1. b | 6. b | 11. c | 16. c |
| 2. d | 7. a | 12. c | 17. b |
| 3. a | 8. c | 13. b | 18. a |
| 4. c | 9. d | 14. a | 19. a |
| 5. d | 10. a | 15. b | 20. c |

## CAHSEE Bench Mark Practice 5 Answers

| | | | |
|---|---|---|---|
| 1. b | 6. b | 11. a | 16. b |
| 2. a | 7. c | 12. d | 17. c |
| 3. d | 8. b | 13. b | 18. d |
| 4. b | 9. a | 14. b | 19. a |
| 5. c | 10. d | 15. c | 20. d |

## CAHSEE Unit 1 Exam Key
### Bench Marks 1 - 5

1. a
2. c
3. b
4. b
5. d

# CAHSEE Bench Mark Unit 2 Answers
## (Bench Mark Practice 6-10 and Unit 2 Exam)

### CAHSEE Bench Mark Practice 6 Answers

| | | | |
|---|---|---|---|
| 1. c | 6. c | 11. a | 16. b |
| 2. b | 7. a | 12. d | 17. a |
| 3. a | 8. a | 13. c | 18. c |
| 4. d | 9. b | 14. b | 19. d |
| 5. b | 10. b | 15. a | 20. a |

### CAHSEE Bench Mark Practice 7 Answers

| | | | |
|---|---|---|---|
| 1. a | 6. d | 11. b | 16. a |
| 2. d | 7. b | 12. c | 17. d |
| 3. c | 8. c | 13. c | 18. b |
| 4. b | 9. d | 14. b | 19. a |
| 5. a | 10. c | 15. c | 20. c |

### CAHSEE Bench Mark Practice 8 Answers

| | | | |
|---|---|---|---|
| 1. d | 6. b | 11. a | 16. d |
| 2. c | 7. d | 12. b | 17. a |
| 3. b | 8. b | 13. c | 18. c |
| 4. a | 9. a | 14. a | 19. b |
| 5. c | 10. d | 15. b | 20. a |

### CAHSEE Bench Mark Practice 9 Answers

| | | | |
|---|---|---|---|
| 1. c | 6. a | 11. a | 16. a |
| 2. b | 7. d | 12. c | 17. a |
| 3. d | 8. c | 13. b | 18. d |
| 4. a | 9. d | 14. b | 19. b |
| 5. d | 10. c | 15. b | 20. c |

### CAHSEE Bench Mark Practice 10 Answers

| | | | |
|---|---|---|---|
| 1. a | 6. b | 11. b | 16. d |
| 2. d | 7. a | 12. d | 17. b |
| 3. c | 8. c | 13. a | 18. d |
| 4. d | 9. c | 14. b | 19. d |
| 5. b | 10. b | 15. d | 20. c |

### CAHSEE Unit 2 Exam Key
### Bench Marks 1 - 10

| | |
|---|---|
| 1. d | 6. b |
| 2. c | 7. a |
| 3. a | 8. c |
| 4. c | 9. d |
| 5. b | 10. d |

# CAHSEE Bench Mark Unit 3 Answers
## (Bench Mark Practice 11-17 and Unit 3 Exam)

### CAHSEE Bench Mark Practice 11 Answers

| | | | |
|---|---|---|---|
| 1. d | 6. a | 11. c | 16. a |
| 2. c | 7. d | 12. a | 17. b |
| 3. a | 8. b | 13. d | 18. d |
| 4. b | 9. d | 14. b | 19. a |
| 5. c | 10. a | 15. c | 20. c |

### CAHSEE Bench Mark Practice 12 Answers

| | | |
|---|---|---|
| 1. b | 6. c | 11. d |
| 2. a | 7. a | 12. c |
| 3. d | 8. d | 13. b |
| 4. c | 9. a | |
| 5. b | 10. b | |

### CAHSEE Bench Mark Practice 13 Answers

| | | | | | |
|---|---|---|---|---|---|
| 1. a | 4. a | 7. c | 12. d | 15. d | 19. c |
| 2. b | 5. d | 8. a | 13. c | 16. a | 20. c |
| 3. c | 6. b | 9. b | 14. c | 17. b | 21. d |
| | | 10. d | | 18. d | |
| | | 11. b | | | |

### CAHSEE Bench Mark Practice 14 Answers

| | | | |
|---|---|---|---|
| 1. c | 6. d | 11. d | 16. d |
| 2. d | 7. b | 12. b | 17. a |
| 3. c | 8. c | 13. a | 18. b |
| 4. d | 9. c | 14. c | |
| 5. a | 10. a | 15. b | |

### CAHSEE Bench Mark Practice 15 Answers

| | | | | | | | |
|---|---|---|---|---|---|---|---|
| 1. a | 4. a | 6. c | 8. a | 10. b | 13. a | 16. d | 19. b |
| 2. c | 5. b | 7. d | 9. d | 11. c | 14. c | 17. c | 20. d |
| 3. b | | | | 12. b | 15. b | 18. a | |

### CAHSEE Bench Mark Practice 16 Answers

| | | | |
|---|---|---|---|
| 1. b | 4. d | 7. c | 10. c |
| 2. a | 5. a | 8. b | 11. a |
| 3. c | 6. b | 9. a | |

### CAHSEE Bench Mark Practice 17 Answers

| | | | |
|---|---|---|---|
| 1. a | 4. c | 7. a | 10. c |
| 2. b | 5. c | 8. b | 11. b |
| 3. d | 6. d | 9. d | |

### CAHSEE Unit 3 Exam Key
### Bench Marks 1 - 17

| | | | |
|---|---|---|---|
| 1. c | 7. c | 12. c | 15. b |
| 2. b | 8. a | 13. c | 16. d |
| 3. d | 9. b | 14. d | 17. c |
| 4. a | 10. d | | |
| 5. d | 11. b | | |
| 6. c | | | |

# CAHSEE Bench Mark Unit 4 Answers
## (Bench Mark Practice 18-22 and Unit 4 Exam)

### CAHSEE Bench Mark Practice 18 Answers

| | | | |
|---|---|---|---|
| 1. b | 6. c | 11. a | 16. c |
| 2. d | 7. a | 12. a | 17. c |
| 3. b | 8. d | 13. c | 18. b |
| 4. a | 9. a | 14. d | 19. c |
| 5. b | 10. b | 15. a | 20. a |

### CAHSEE Bench Mark Practice 19 Answers

| | | | |
|---|---|---|---|
| 1. c | 4. a | 7. c | 10. d |
| 2. d | 5. c | 8. a | 11. c |
| 3. a | 6. b | 9. b | 12. d |

### CAHSEE Bench Mark Practice 20 Answers

| | | | |
|---|---|---|---|
| 1. d | 6. d | 11. a | 16. d |
| 2. c | 7. c | 12. d | 17. a |
| 3. a | 8. c | 13. c | 18. b |
| 4. a | 9. b | 14. b | 19. a |
| 5. c | 10. c | 15. d | 20. b |

### CAHSEE Bench Mark Practice 21 Answers

| | | | | | |
|---|---|---|---|---|---|
| 1. b | 4. b | 7. c | 10. d | 13. d | 16. a |
| 2. a | 5. d | 8. a | 11. d | 14. a | 17. b |
| 3. b | 6. a | 9. b | 12. a | 15. c | 18. a |

### CAHSEE Bench Mark Practice 22 Answers

| | | |
|---|---|---|
| 1. a | 6. b | 11. a |
| 2. d | 7. b | 12. c |
| 3. d | 8. a | 13. b |
| 4. d | 9. c | 14. d |
| 5. b | 10. b | 15. c |

### CAHSEE Unit 4 Exam Key
### Bench Marks 1 - 22

| | | | | | |
|---|---|---|---|---|---|
| 1. d | 7. c | 12. b | 16. a | 18. a | 21. a |
| 2. b | 8. a | 13. c | 17. b | 19. d | 22. b |
| 3. a | 9. b | 14. a | | 20. b | |
| 4. c | 10. b | 15. c | | | |
| 5. a | 11. c | | | | |
| 6. d | | | | | |

# CAHSEE Bench Mark Unit 5 Answers
## (Bench Mark Practice 23-27 and Unit 5 Exam)

### CAHSEE Bench Mark Practice 23 Answers

| | | | |
|---|---|---|---|
| 1. b | 5. b | 9. a | 13. c |
| 2. a | 6. d | 10. c | 14. d |
| 3. c | 7. a | 11. b | 15. a |
| 4. d | 8. d | 12. d | 16. b |

### CAHSEE Bench Mark Practice 24 Answers

| | | | |
|---|---|---|---|
| 1. c | 5. d | 10. b | 14. b |
| 2. b | 6. b | 11. c | 15. c |
| 3. a | 7. c | 12. a | 16. a |
| 4. c | 8. a | 13. d | 17. d |
| | 9. d | | |

### CAHSEE Bench Mark Practice 25 Answers

| | | | | | |
|---|---|---|---|---|---|
| 1. a | 5. c | 8. b | 12. d | 15. c | 18. c |
| 2. c | 6. a | 9. d | 13. c | 16. b | 19. a |
| 3. d | 7. b | 10. a | 14. d | 17. c | 20. c |
| 4. b | | 11. d | | | |

### CAHSEE Bench Mark Practice 26 Answers

| | | | |
|---|---|---|---|
| 1. d | 8. c | 13. c | 17. b |
| 2. b | 9. b | 14. b | 18. c |
| 3. a | 10. d | 15. a | 19. c |
| 4. c | 11. a | 16. d | 20. c |
| 5. b | 12. b | | |
| 6. d | | | |
| 7. a | | | |

### CAHSEE Bench Mark Practice 27 Answers

| | | | |
|---|---|---|---|
| 1. c | 5. c | 7. d | 10. c |
| 2. d | 6. b | 8. a | 11. a |
| 3. b | | 9. d | 12. b |
| 4. a | | | |

### CAHSEE Unit 5 Exam Key
### Bench Marks 1 - 27

| | | | | | | | |
|---|---|---|---|---|---|---|---|
| 1. b | 7. d | 12. a | 15. c | 18. c | 21. b | 24. b | 26. d |
| 2. d | 8. a | 13. b | 16. d | 19. d | 22. c | 25. d | 27. c |
| 3. c | 9. b | 14. d | 17. c | 20. a | 23. d | | |
| 4. a | 10. b | | | | | | |
| 5. d | 11. a | | | | | | |
| 6. b | | | | | | | |

# CAHSEE Bench Mark Unit 6 Answers
## (Bench Mark Practice 28-32 and Unit 6 Exam)

### CAHSEE Bench Mark Practice 28 Answers

| | | | |
|---|---|---|---|
| 1. b | 6. c | 11. a | 16. a |
| 2. a | 7. a | 12. d | 17. b |
| 3. d | 8. c | 13. d | 18. c |
| 4. a | 9. c | 14. a | 19. d |
| 5. c | 10. a | 15. a | 20. a |

### CAHSEE Bench Mark Practice 29 Answers

| | | | |
|---|---|---|---|
| 1. c | 6. c | 11. d | 16. c |
| 2. d | 7. b | 12. d | 17. a |
| 3. a | 8. d | 13. c | 18. c |
| 4. b | 9. d | 14. b | 19. a |
| 5. b | 10. c | 15. c | 20. b |

### CAHSEE Bench Mark Practice 30 Answers

| | | | | |
|---|---|---|---|---|
| 1. c | 5. a | 9. c | 13. c | 17. a |
| 2. b | 6. a | 10. d | 14. c | 18. d |
| 3. c | 7. c | 11. d | 15. b | 19. b |
| 4. b | 8. b | 12. b | 16. d | 20. c |

### CAHSEE Bench Mark Practice 31 Answers

| | | | |
|---|---|---|---|
| 1. c | 6. c | 11. a | 16. b |
| 2. b | 7. c | 12. c | 17. a |
| 3. d | 8. d | 13. d | 18. c |
| 4. c | 9. a | 14. c | 19. b |
| 5. a | 10. a | 15. b | 20. c |

### CAHSEE Bench Mark Practice 32 Answers

| | | | |
|---|---|---|---|
| 1. b | 6. c | 11. b | 16. c |
| 2. a | 7. a | 12. b | 17. d |
| 3. d | 8. d | 13. b | 18. c |
| 4. a | 9. d | 14. a | 19. b |
| 5. d | 10. c | 15. a | 20. c |

### CAHSEE Unit 6 Exam Key
### Bench Marks 1 - 32

| | | | | |
|---|---|---|---|---|
| 1. a | 7. d | 12. a | 15. b | 17. c |
| 2. c | 8. b | 13. a | 16. a | |
| 3. b | 9. b | 14. d | | |
| 4. a | 10. a | | | |
| 5. c | 11. a | | | |
| 6. b | | | | |

| | | | | |
|---|---|---|---|---|
| 18. a | 21. d | 24. c | 28. b | 31. b |
| 19. d | 22. d | 25. d | 29. b | 32. c |
| 20. d | 23. a | 26. b | 30. c | |
| | | 27. d | | |

# CAHSEE Bench Mark Unit 7 Answers
## (Bench Mark Practice 33-37 and Unit 7 Exam)

### CAHSEE Bench Mark Practice 33 Answers

| | | |
|---|---|---|
| 1. a | 7. a | 13. b |
| 2. b | 8. c | 14. c |
| 3. c | 9. a | 15. d |
| 4. d | 10. b | 16. c |
| 5. c | 11. a | 17. c |
| 6. a | 12. c | 18. d |

### CAHSEE Bench Mark Practice 34 Answers

| | | | | | |
|---|---|---|---|---|---|
| 1. b | 4. a | 7. a | 10. c | 13. b | 16. a |
| 2. c | 5. a | 8. d | 11. d | 14. a | 17. c |
| 3. a | 6. c | 9. c | 12. c | 15. b | 18. d |

### CAHSEE Bench Mark Practice 35 Answers

| | | | | | |
|---|---|---|---|---|---|
| 1. b | 4. c | 7. b | 10. d | 13. a | 16. a |
| 2. c | 5. b | 8. c | 11. c | 14. a | 17. b |
| 3. b | 6. c | 9. c | 12. b | 15. b | 18. a |

### CAHSEE Bench Mark Practice 36 Answers

| | | | |
|---|---|---|---|
| 1. d | 6. d | 11. d | 16. b |
| 2. d | 7. d | 12. a | 17. d |
| 3. a | 8. c | 13. b | 18. a |
| 4. c | 9. b | 14. c | 19. a |
| 5. b | 10. a | 15. a | 20. c |

### CAHSEE Bench Mark Practice 37 Answers

| | | | |
|---|---|---|---|
| 1. c | 6. d | 11. b | 16. c |
| 2. a | 7. d | 12. c | 17. d |
| 3. c | 8. b | 13. b | 18. a |
| 4. b | 9. a | 14. a | 19. a |
| 5. a | 10. b | 15. d | 20. a |

### CAHSEE Unit 7 Exam Key
### Bench Marks 1 - 37

| | | | | |
|---|---|---|---|---|
| 1. c | 7. d | 12. d | 15. a | 17. c |
| 2. b | 8. b | 13. c | 16. c | 18. c |
| 3. a | 9. a | 14. d | | 19. c |
| 4. b | 10. d | | | |
| 5. d | 11. c | | | |
| 6. a | | | | |

| | | | | |
|---|---|---|---|---|
| 20. a | 23. a | 27. d | 31. c | 35. b |
| 21. b | 24. b | 28. a | 32. d | 36. d |
| 22. d | 25. c | 29. c | 33. c | 37. a |
| | 26. b | 30. d | 34. d | |

# CAHSEE Bench Mark Unit 8 Answers
## (Bench Mark Practice 38-43 and Unit 8 Exam)

### CAHSEE Bench Mark Practice 38 Answers

| | | | |
|---|---|---|---|
| 1. c | 4. b | 7. d | 10. c |
| 2. a | 5. a | 8. b | 11, b |
| 3. d | 6. c | 9. a | 12. c |

### CAHSEE Bench Mark Practice 39 Answers

| | | | | | |
|---|---|---|---|---|---|
| 1. a | 5. c | 8. a | 11. d | 14. d | 16. d |
| 2. c | 6. d | 9. c | 12. a | 15. c | |
| 3. b | 7. b | 10. b | 13. b | | |
| 4. d | | | | | |

### CAHSEE Bench Mark Practice 40 Answers

| | | | |
|---|---|---|---|
| 1. c | 5. b | 9. c | 12. d |
| 2. c | 6. a | 10. b | 13. c |
| 3. d | 7. d | 11. a | 14. b |
| 4. a | 8. b | | 15. b |

### CAHSEE Bench Mark Practice 41 Answers

| | | | | | |
|---|---|---|---|---|---|
| 1. b | 3. d | 5. a | 7. c | 9. d | 11. c |
| 2. d | 4. c | 6. b | 8. b | 10. a | 12. b |

### CAHSEE Bench Mark Practice 42 Answers

| | | | |
|---|---|---|---|
| 1. d | 6. d | 9. b | 12. c |
| 2. b | 7. a | 10. d | 13. d |
| 3. a | 8. c | 11. a | 14. d |
| 4. c | | | |
| 5. b | | | |

### CAHSEE Bench Mark Practice 43 Answers

| | | | |
|---|---|---|---|
| 1. c | 3. d | 5. d | 9. c |
| 2. b | 4. a | 6. a | 10. b |
| | | 7. b | |
| | | 8. d | |

### CAHSEE Unit 8 Exam Key
### Bench Marks 1 - 43

| | | | | | | | | | | | |
|---|---|---|---|---|---|---|---|---|---|---|---|
| 1. b | 7. c | 12. a | 15. c | 17. b | 20. a | 23. a | 28. a | 31. a | 35. b | 38. c | 41. d |
| 2. b | 8. a | 13. b | 16. c | 18. d | 21. b | 24. a | 29. d | 32. b | 36. c | 39. b | 42. c |
| 3. d | 9. b | 14. c | | 19. a | 22. a | 25. b | 30. b | 33. c | 37. d | 40. b | 43. a |
| 4. c | 10. b | | | | | 26. d | | 34. a | | | |
| 5. b | 11. a | | | | | 27. d | | | | | |
| 6. a | | | | | | | | | | | |

# CAHSEE Bench Mark Unit 9 Answers
## (Bench Mark Practice 44-48 and Unit 9 Exam)

### CAHSEE Bench Mark Practice 44 Answers

| | | | |
|---|---|---|---|
| 1. c | 6. b | 11. d | 16. a |
| 2. c | 7. c | 12. c | 17. b |
| 3. d | 8. a | 13. a | 18. b |
| 4. a | 9. b | 14. d | 19. d |
| 5. c | 10. d | 15. d | 20. b |

### CAHSEE Bench Mark Practice 45 Answers

| | | | |
|---|---|---|---|
| 1. a | 6. a | 11. b | 16. a |
| 2. c | 7. a | 12. c | 17. c |
| 3. d | 8. b | 13. a | 18. b |
| 4. c | 9. c | 14. a | 19. c |
| 5. b | 10. c | 15. b | 20. b |

### CAHSEE Bench Mark Practice 46 Answers

| | | | |
|---|---|---|---|
| 1. c | 6. c | 11. b | 16. b |
| 2. a | 7. a | 12. a | 17. b |
| 3. b | 8. d | 13. d | 18. a |
| 4. c | 9. d | 14. c | 19. d |
| 5. a | 10. c | 15. c | 20. a |

### CAHSEE Bench Mark Practice 47 Answers

| | | | |
|---|---|---|---|
| 1. c | 6. c | 11. d | 16. c |
| 2. a | 7. a | 12. d | 17. b |
| 3. d | 8. d | 13. c | 18. c |
| 4. c | 9. a | 14. d | 19. d |
| 5. b | 10. d | 15. c | 20. b |

### CAHSEE Bench Mark Practice 48 Answers

| | | | | | | | | |
|---|---|---|---|---|---|---|---|---|
| 1. b | 2. a | 5. c | 6. b | 7. a | 8. c | 9. b | 10. a | |
| | | 3. a | | | | | 11. d | |
| | | 4. d | | | | | 12. b | |

### CAHSEE Unit 9 Exam Key
### Bench Marks 1 - 48

| | | | | | | |
|---|---|---|---|---|---|---|
| 1. c | 7. d | 12. c | 15. d | 17. d | 20. c | 23. d |
| 2. c | 8. b | 13. d | 16. c | 18. a | 21. a | 24. c |
| 3. d | 9. b | 14. a | | 19. d | 22. b | 25. d |
| 4. c | 10. d | | | | | 26. d |
| 5. d | 11. a | | | | | |
| 6. d | | | | | | |

| | | | | | | |
|---|---|---|---|---|---|---|
| 27. b | 31. c | 35. a | 38. b | 41. a | 44. b | 48. c |
| 28. a | 32. c | 36. c | 39. c | 42. a | 45. b | |
| 29. a | 33. d | 37. a | 40. c | 43. c | 46. c | |
| 30. a | 34. c | | | | 47. d | |

# CAHSEE Bench Mark Unit 10 Answers
## (Bench Mark Practice 49-53)

| CAHSEE Bench Mark Practice 49 Answers | | | |
|---|---|---|---|
| 1. d | 6. d | 11. b | 16. a |
| 2. a | 7. c | 12. a | 17. d |
| 3. c | 8. b | 13. b | 18. b |
| 4. d | 9. a | 14. d | 19. c |
| 5. c | 10. a | 15. d | 20. c |

| CAHSEE Bench Mark Practice 50 Answers | | | |
|---|---|---|---|
| 1. b | 6. d | 11. c | 16. b |
| 2. a | 7. a | 12. c | 17. a |
| 3. c | 8. a | 13. a | 18. c |
| 4. d | 9. d | 14. d | 19. b |
| 5. d | 10. b | 15. b | 20. d |

| CAHSEE Bench Mark Practice 51 Answers | | | | | |
|---|---|---|---|---|---|
| 1. c | 5. b | 8. d | 12. b | 15. d | 19. c |
| 2. b | 6. a | 9. a | 13. a | 16. d | 20. d |
| 3. a | 7. c | 10. d | 14. c | 17. a | |
| 4. c | | 11. b | | 18. c | |

| CAHSEE Bench Mark Practice 52 Answers | | | |
|---|---|---|---|
| 1. d | 6. b | 11. a | 16. c |
| 2. a | 7. c | 12. d | 17. d |
| 3. d | 8. d | 13. d | 18. a |
| 4. b | 9. a | 14. b | 19. a |
| 5. d | 10. b | 15. a | 20. b |

| CAHSEE Bench Mark Practice 53 Answers | | | |
|---|---|---|---|
| 1. b | 5. c | 9. b | 13. c |
| 2. c | 6. a | 10. c | 14. b |
| 3. a | 7. b | 11. d | 15. c |
| 4. d | 8. d | 12. a | 16. b |

# CAHSEE Bench Mark Unit 10 Answers
## (Unit 10 Exams)

### CAHSEE Unit 10 Exam A Key
#### Bench Marks 1 - 53

| | | | | | | | | | | | | | | | | |
|---|---|---|---|---|---|---|---|---|---|---|---|---|---|---|---|---|
| 1. a | 7. b | 12. c | 15. b | 17. c | 20. d | 23. a | 27. b | 31. a | 35. a | 38. a | 41. b | 44. b | 48. b | 51. c | 52. a |
| 2. a | 8. a | 13. c | 16. b | 18. b | 21. b | 24. d | 28. d | 32. a | 36. b | 39. b | 42. d | 45. c | 49. d | | 53. d |
| 3. c | 9. b | 14. d | | 19. d | 22. c | 25. a | 29. c | 33. c | 37. b | 40. d | 43. d | 46. d | 50. a | | |
| 4. c | 10. c | | | | | 26. d | 30. c | 34. a | | | | 47. c | | | |
| 5. b | 11. d | | | | | | | | | | | | | | |
| 6. a | | | | | | | | | | | | | | | |

### CAHSEE Unit 10 Exam B Key
#### Bench Marks 1 - 53

| | | | | | | | | | | | | | | | | |
|---|---|---|---|---|---|---|---|---|---|---|---|---|---|---|---|---|
| 1. a | 7. c | 12. b | 15. a | 17. c | 19. c | 22. b | 27. a | 31. b | 35. c | 38. c | 41. c | 44. d | 48. c | 49. c | 52. b |
| 2. b | 8. d | 13. d | 16. c | 18. a | 20. a | 23. a | 28. b | 32. b | 36. d | 39. c | 42. c | 45. b | | 50. c | 53. c |
| 3. b | 9. c | 14. c | | | 21. b | 24. c | 29. c | 33. a | 37. d | 40. c | 43. d | 46. c | | 51. d | |
| 4. b | 10. a | | | | | 25. c | 30. d | 34. c | | | | 47. c | | | |
| 5. d | 11. b | | | | | 26. b | | | | | | | | | |
| 6. b | | | | | | | | | | | | | | | |

### CAHSEE Unit 10 Exam C Key
#### Bench Marks 1 - 53

| | | | | | | | | | | | | | | | | |
|---|---|---|---|---|---|---|---|---|---|---|---|---|---|---|---|---|
| 1. d | 7. a | 12. b | 14. c | 17. b | 19. a | 22. d | 25. a | 28. b | 31. d | 35. b | 40. b | 44. a | 48. b | 49. b | 52. d |
| 2. d | 8. c | 13. a | 15. b | 18. b | 20. c | 23. b | 26. c | 29. d | 32. c | 36. a | 41. b | 45. a | | 50. c | 53. b |
| 3. a | 9. d | | 16. d | | 21. d | 24. c | 27. c | 30. d | 33. a | 37. c | 42. b | 46. a | | 51. a | |
| 4. a | 10. d | | | | | | | | 34. a | 38. b | 43. a | 47. a | | | |
| 5. b | 11. a | | | | | | | | | 39. d | | | | | |
| 6. a | | | | | | | | | | | | | | | |

www.ingramcontent.com/pod-product-compliance
Lightning Source LLC
Chambersburg PA
CBHW080513090426
42734CB00015B/3039